Energy, Environment and Development

Energy, Environment and Development

José Goldemberg and Oswaldo Lucon

publishing for a sustainable future

London • Sterling, VA

First published by Earthscan in the UK and USA in 2010

Copyright © Professor José Goldemberg and Oswaldo Lucon, 2010
First edition published in 1996

ISBN: HB 978-1-84407-748-9
     PB 978-1-84407-749-6

Typeset by 4word Ltd, Bristol, UK
Cover design by Andrew Corbett

For a full list of publications, please contact:

Earthscan
Dunstan House
14a St Cross Street
London EC1N 8XA, UK
Tel: +44 (0)20 7841 1930
Fax: +44 (0)20 7242 1474
Email: earthinfo@earthscan.co.uk
Web: **www.earthscan.co.uk**

1006695967

22883 Quicksilver Drive, Sterling, VA 20166-2012, USA

Earthscan publishes in association with the International Institute for Environment
and Development

A catalogue record for this book is available from the British Library

Library of Congress Cataloging-in-Publication Data
Goldemberg, José, 1928-
  Energy, environment and development / José Goldemberg and Oswaldo Lucon.
    p. cm.
  Includes bibliographical references and index.
  ISBN 978-1-84407-748-9 (hardback) - ISBN 978-1-84407-749-6 (pbk.) 1. Energy
development-Environmental aspects. 2. Energy consumption. I. Lucon, Oswaldo. II. Title.
  TD195.E49G85 2009
  333.79'14-dc22
                         2009006512

At Earthscan we strive to minimize our environmental impacts and carbon footprint
through reducing waste, recycling and offsetting our CO_2 emissions, including those
created through publication of this book. For more details of our environmental policy,
see www.earthscan.co.uk

This book was printed in the UK by Cromwell Press Group
The paper used is FSC certified and the inks are vegetable based.

Mixed Sources
Product group from well-managed
forests and other controlled sources
www.fsc.org Cert no. TT-COC-2082
© 1996 Forest Stewardship Council

Contents

List of Figures, Tables and Boxes

Figures

Tables

Boxes

Foreword to the Second Edition

Thirty-seven years after the Stockholm Conference and 17 years after Rio-92, issues related to pollution, global climate change, exhaustion of natural resources and geopolitical instability are present daily in the media.

Experience shows that many have strong perceptions of the main topics related to energy, environment and sustainable development. These subjects are part of school and academic syllabuses, in different courses and research.

Currently, people with backgrounds outside the technological area are becoming interested in understanding energy problems, and are providing contributions to topics such as policies, governance and management related to it. The dissemination of information through the internet has significantly contributed to the systematic expansion of knowledge boundaries.

Nevertheless, as information spreads, it becomes increasingly necessary for there to be some control of its quality and of the most commonly used analytical tools that allow the understanding and assessment of the problems involved. It is also necessary to reduce and, if possible, eliminate the barriers to full understanding of these problems. It is not unusual to be confronted with experts in a certain area – such as technology or regulation – without even the minimum capacity necessary to connect pieces of information, fundamental to eliminating the gap between theory and practice, and thus making the best of their potential.

This book aims to present and discuss these relations, guiding the reader to face the present challenges in the energy, environment and sustainable development areas – themes that cannot be approached in a disconnected way.

The awareness of global problems gained momentum in 2002, at the World Summit for Sustainable Development held in Johannesburg, South Africa. At the Conference, sponsored by the United Nations, multilateral discussions began on the changes in the world energy matrix, including goals and deadlines to increase the parcel of renewable energy. Another important theme discussed was the eradication of social exclusion, which intrinsically depends on the supply of the minimum adequate energy services.

Without analytical tools, gathering information on energy, environment and development is like trying to dry ice with a piece of cloth. Discussing these themes without connecting them is walking in the dark.

Method is thus one of the main aims in this book, a result of years of study, experience and observation.

José Goldemberg and Oswaldo Lucon
Sao Paulo, March 2009

Foreword by Achim Steiner

José Goldemberg and Oswaldo Lucon's book *Energy, Environment and Development* comes at a significant moment in the affairs of humanity as it faces multiple challenges, but also inordinate opportunities, for a sustainable future.

More creative and transformational options towards developing sustainable energy systems will be among the central challenges on a planet of six billion people, rising to over nine billion by 2050.

Climate change, concerns over peak oil and the urgent needs of two billion people without access to energy – set aside the impacts on human health and economically important ecosystems such as forests and croplands from other pollutants linked to the burning of fossil fuels – demand a dramatic, global response.

There are signs that the green shoots of a low carbon, more resource efficient Green Economy are indeed emerging, driven in part by the existing emission reduction targets of the United Nation's Kyoto Protocol and its various markets and mechanisms, and the anticipation of even deeper reductions over the coming years and decades.

The number of projects under the Protocol's Clean Development Mechanism – many of which are renewable energy schemes alongside the energy efficiency ones now emerging – totals over 4000 either approved or in the pipeline.

And while the lion's share have been secured by the rapidly developing economies such as China, India, Brazil and Mexico, many smaller countries on continents like Africa are starting to realize CDM projects and the range of technologies involved is also broadening – geothermal in Indonesia being one example.

Falls in the cost of generating renewable energy have also occurred, allied to decisions by some governments to introduce smart market mechanisms such as feed-in tariffs.

In Kenya, a private consortium is now commencing development of a 300MW wind farm in Turkana, one of the poorest and most energy deprived parts of the country, following a change in the Kenyan law.

Another consortium is rapidly evolving a vast solar project called Desertec, with plans to link the project via interconnectors from North Africa to Europe.

These developments come against a backdrop of new investment in renewable energies outstripping new investments in fossil fuel generation for the first time.

UNEP, through its Sustainable Energy Finance Initiative, reported that investments in new renewables, and excluding large-scale hydro, hit $155 billion in 2008 versus $110 billion in fossil fuels.

There is also the question of employment which some countries, including the United States and the Republic of Korea, have recognized as part of recent stimulus packages – so called Green New Deals.

Currently 1.3 billion people are unemployed or under-employed, with half a billion young people set to join the workforce over the next decade. Studies indicate that renewable energy employs three to four times more people than the same investment in fossil fuels.

It is time to accelerate these transformations. One way is to phase-out or phase-down fossil fuel subsidies – an estimated $300 billion a year is spent, the majority of the funds used to subsidize fuels such as oil and coal.

Governments often do this to assist the poor – but the reality is that most subsidies benefit the better off in an economy along with the fuel producers and equipment makers.

Meanwhile, there are a wealth of mechanisms that can assist in unleashing the market towards a low carbon future.

It was once said that the rural poor of India could not afford solar power. A UN project, in collaboration with Indian banks, has bought down the cost of solar loans and within a year or two 100,000 people there had solar.

If a cave man somehow was brought to life in the first decade of the 21st century, he might marvel at telecommunications and the unravelling of the human genome. But our time traveller would be all too familiar with the way we power our society via the burning of biomass and fossilized fuels.

I would urge everyone who believes in a different future to one rooted in the past to read Goldemberg and Lucon's new book as an aid, a guide and an inspiration to delivering tomorrow's energy economy today.

Achim Steiner,
UNEP Executive Director
UN Under-Secretary General
Director-General of the UN Office at Nairobi

List of Acronyms and Abbreviations

a	acceleration
ACCS	Assured Combinable Crops Scheme
ALCC	life cycle cost annualized
BIG	biomass integrated gasifier
BOE	barrels of oil equivalent
BTU	British thermal unit
C	carbon
C	celsius
CAFÉ	corporate average fuel economy
CARB	California Air Resources Board
CDM	clean development mechanism
CER	certified emission reduction
CFC	chlorofluorocarbon
CH_4	methane
CNG	compressed natural gas
CO_2	carbon dioxide
E	energy
ESCO	energy service company
F	fahrenheit
FAO	Food and Agricultural Organization
FFV	flex-fuel vehicle
GDP	gross domestic product
GHG	greenhouse gas effect
GW	gigawatt
GWP	Global Warming Potential
H	enthalpy
HDI	Human Development Index
HHV	gross calorific value
HP	horsepower
I	ampere
IBEP	International Bioenergy Platform
IEO	International Energy Outlook
IGCC	integrated combined cycle plant
IPCC	Intergovernmental Panel on Climate Change

IRR	internal rate of return
J	joule
kcal	kilocalorie
kW	kilowatt
LCC	life cycle cost
LHV	lower heating value or net calorific value
LPG	liquefied natural gas
lt	long ton
LULUCF	land use, land-use change and forestry
m	mass
MEA	Multilateral Environmental Agreement
MW	megawatt
mW	milliwatt
NGO	non-governmental organization
NNI	net national income
NNP	net national product
nW	nanowatt
OPEC	Organization of Petroleum Exporting Countries
P	power
P	pressure
POP	persistent organic pollutants
PPP	purchasing power parity
Proalcool	Brazilian Ethanol Programme
PW	petawatt
pW	picowatt
Q	heat
RPS	renewable portfolio standards
RRSO	Roundtable on Responsible Soy Oil
RSPO	Round Table on Sustainable Palm Oil
SBS	sick building syndrome
st	short ton
T	temperature
TCE	tons of coal equivalent
TFR	total fertility rate
toe	tons of oil equivalent
TW	terawatt
U	internal energy
UNCCO	UN Convention on Combating Desertification
UNFCCC	United Nations Framework Convention on Climate Change
V	volts
V	volume

VER	verified emission reduction
W	watt
W	work
WEO	World Energy Outlook
WU	wage unit
μW	microwatt

Chapter 1

Connections

The connection between energy and the environment has been the subject of many studies, and it is sometimes possible to establish a 'cause and effect' relationship between energy use and environmental damage. In 400BC, for example, Plato mourned the lost forests, described by Homer centuries before, which had once covered the barren hills of Greece. In this particular case, it was the use of wood, mainly for shipbuilding and in forges to produce weapons, which led to the destruction of the ancient Greek forests. A more recent example is the soil degradation and desertification observed in some areas of Africa, due to the use of fuelwood as a source of energy. For a more detailed timeline, see Annex 1.

The energy–development connection has also been studied, albeit in a very simplified way: development has been considered as the capacity of an economy to support an increase in its gross domestic product (GDP) – an indicator widely employed by economists as a gross measure of the general welfare of a population. However, GDP fails to consider the issue of social inequalities. The poor not only consume less energy than the rich, but also different types of energy. As a consequence, the environmental impact of the energy consumed by the different groups in society is different.

We propose to study the *energy–development–environment* connection, initially classifying the population by income levels and identifying the environmental impacts caused by each level. This is especially relevant in developing countries, characterized by wide disparities in income and quality of life within society, which make the per capita income a less meaningful indicator. By identifying how the many social groups consume energy (and from which respective source), it is possible to better understand the differences between local, regional and global impacts and so determine who is responsible for them. Thus, policies can be formulated aiming to reduce environmental degradation at different levels.

The issue of the limits to natural resources and their distribution among the social strata, countries and generations is discussed in relation to these topics.

To pave the way for such a discussion, the physical concept of energy will be reviewed (Chapter 2), then its relationship with human activities (Chapter 3) and their main sources (Chapter 4).

Next, what economists understand by the term 'development' (Chapter 5) will be discussed, followed by a factual description of the environmental degradation problems related to energy (Chapter 6) and their causes (Chapter 7).

In Chapter 8, technical solutions that have been proposed for solving the environmental problems are presented and a discussion is conducted on the policies to promote development that minimizes the environmental impacts of energy use (Chapter 9).

Chapters 10 and 11, respectively, present the future trends of energy consumption and issues related to different lifestyles and their preferences.

Finally, in Chapter 12, suggestions from the scientific community to achieve energy sustainability in the long run are reported.

Chapter 2

Energy

Forces

We live on the surface of a planet that exerts a gravitational pull on all objects, attracting them towards its centre. In order for us to move or to move objects, this attraction has to be overcome. This is what our muscles do, originating *forces* that are the cause of movement. If the body is still, a force applied to it makes it move. If the movement occurs horizontally, it is necessary to maintain the force applied to overcome friction, otherwise the body stops moving.

In nature there are three types of forces considered *fundamental*:

1 *Gravitational forces* that exist between bodies due to their mass. Universal gravitational law teaches us that the force between two point masses is always attractive, being proportional to the product of the masses and inversely proportional to the square of the distance between them.
2 *Electromagnetic* (electric and magnetic) *forces* that exist due to electric charges. Electric forces (between electric charges) are attractive when they have different signals (positive and negative) or repulsive when having the same signal. Electric forces follow a law similar to that of universal gravitation. Magnetic forces are derived from charges in movement.
3 *Nuclear forces* that exist between the particles constituting the nuclei of atoms (protons and neutrons) when they are separated by distances smaller than 10^{-13} cm.

There are also *derivative* forces. These are contact forces (friction, osmosis, capillarity, surface tension, chemical forces) that represent the total sum of a huge number of electromagnetic interactions between very close molecules, in which there are moving positive and negative charges. For example, two very clean glass plates, once put into contact, even in a void, will hardly separate. It is as if there were 'tentacles' emanating from one surface and holding on to the other, making it necessary to break them to separate them. After the movement is started, however, the force necessary to maintain the movement becomes smaller, but not null.

Concept of energy

In order to live and move, a human being needs to overcome the attraction exerted by the Earth on all objects. Moreover, there are other obstacles to movement, as is the case with friction. With muscular effort, human beings manage to overcome such obstacles, and thus lift bodies or

Box 2.1 The evolution of the concept of energy

The existence of energy in itself may lead to profound philosophical discussions.[1] Its definition is operational, allowing measurement and calculation procedures, without answering its real nature. The idea of energy has existed since antiquity; but the current concept of energy, however, took many years to develop. Isaac Newton (1642–1727) formulated the laws of movement and defined the potential and kinetic energy. Later, Fahrenheit (F) and Celsius (C) established the temperature scales. These scales helped to measure the heat content, but no clear connection with mechanical energy was established. While manufacturing cannons, Thompson (1753–1814) clearly established the concept of converting mechanical work into heat. Thomas Young (1773–1829) adopted the word Energy in 1807, from the Greek *energeia* (at work or in activity), to unify the aspects observed on heat and work. James P. Joule (1818–89) determined the energy equivalence between heat, work and electric power (1 calorie = 4184 joules). Max Planck (1858–1947) clarified the energy characteristics of light. Finally, Albert Einstein developed the theory of relativity, unifying all the forms of energy and providing them with an equivalence in mass, in the form $E = mc^2$ (mass of an electron at rest = 511 ketoelectron volts (keV)).

Thus *Energy* may be defined as the capacity to produce work. Work, in turn, is the result of the action of a force on the displacement of a body. The energy may be *kinetic* (from the force deriving from waves and winds), *gravitational* (from waterfalls), *electric* (from turbines and batteries), *chemical* (obtained from exothermic reactions, such as diesel and gasoline combustion), *thermal* (from burning charcoal or wood), *radiant* (from sunlight) and *nuclear* (obtained from the fission of uranium atoms or the fusion of hydrogen nuclei). Some forms are more useful than others; several can be transformed. The energy obtained from a nuclear reaction may be used to heat water and produce high pressure steam which, in turn, can produce work to move a turbine to produce electricity. We need energy to live and our needs are better supplied with more energy.

set them into movement. In order to move a piano, a human being needs to make a lot of effort, whereas to move an ashtray on a table requires little effort.

The concept of energy has evolved over time (Box 2.1).

Isaac Newton (1642–1727) named *force* as any agent capable of causing bodies to move and went further to establish a relationship that says which force is necessary to cause a certain movement[2]:

$$\text{force } (F) = \text{mass } (m) \times \text{acceleration } (a).$$

Frequently, it is not enough to apply a force to a body to make it move. It is necessary to keep it there while it moves. A wagon needs horses to pull it, overcoming the obstacles and the friction provided by the road. Hence the need to define work, which is the product of force by the distance over which the displacement took place:

$$\text{work } (W) = \text{force } (F) \times \text{distance } (d).$$

The unit commonly used for both work and mechanical energy is the joule (J), which is the energy needed to lift a small 102-gram apple one metre against the Earth's gravity (approximately 9.8 newtons).[3]

Since the total variation of potential energy or of kinetic energy is the work done (Box 2.2), the sum of these two energies is named *mechanical energy*, which is the capacity to produce work.

Box 2.2 Energy conservation in the gravitational field

Let us consider a body with mass m, dropped from a height h above ground. Due to the gravity attraction, its speed increases until it reaches the ground at velocity v. When it is at a height y_2 (point A), its velocity is v_2. At a height y_1 (point B), its velocity is v_1 (Figure 2.1).

Physics books demonstrate that the work performed by the force of gravity mg between A and B is:

$$W = mgh = mg\,(y_2 - y_1) = \tfrac{1}{2}\,mv_1{}^2 - \tfrac{1}{2}\,mv_2{}^2$$

that is

$$mgy_2 + \tfrac{1}{2}\,mv_2{}^2 = mgy_1 + \tfrac{1}{2}\,mv_1{}^2.$$

During the fall, the sum of the two quantities [mgy] and [$\tfrac{1}{2}\,mv^2$] remains constant; [mgy] is the potential energy and [$\tfrac{1}{2}\,mv^2$] is the kinetic

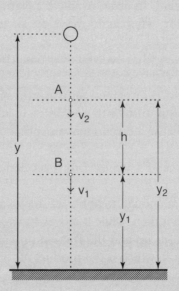

Figure 2.1 Potential and kinetic energy

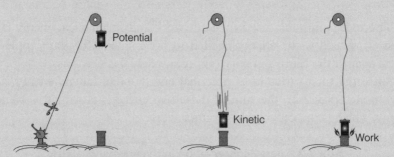

Figure 2.2 Relationship between potential and kinetic energies and work

energy. Therefore, in the gravitational field, the sum of the potential and kinetic energies of the falling body is constant at all times (Figure 2.2).

At the point from which the body is dropped, velocity v is zero and all the energy is potential:

$$W = [mgy].$$

At the point where the body hits the ground with velocity v, height h is zero and all the energy is kinetic:

$$W = [\tfrac{1}{2}\, mv^2].$$

Potential energy (*P*) is the system's energy due to a gravitational or electro-magnetic force exerted on a mass and taking a surface as reference. Considering the free fall of a body under the action of gravity, the work is given by the product of force by the distance, which corresponds to the intuitive idea of work we have.[4] A water reservoir at the top of a hill is a typical example of potential (hydraulic) energy. Another example of potential energy is a bent bow, ready to shoot an arrow.

Kinetic energy (*Ec* or *K*) is a 'scalar' (i.e. entirely described by its magnitude without a direction as a 'vector') energy the system possesses due to its velocity in relation to a reference system.

Work and heat are forms of *energy transfer* between a physical system and its surrounding without mass transfer.

Mechanical energy: work, kinetic energy and potential energy

Work is a term frequently used in everyday language ('let's go to work'); however, it has a special meaning in terms of energy systems. Work cannot be stored, since it represents an energy transfer between a system and its surroundings. This transfer may be positive (when the system receives more energy than it loses) or negative (when the opposite occurs). Work

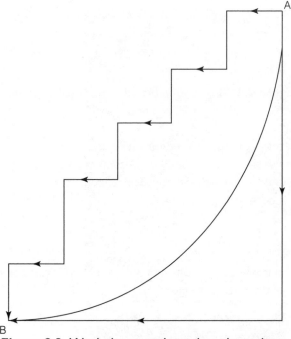

Figure 2.3 Work does not depend on the pathway

(*W*), is thus a *pathway function*. It can be demonstrated that for a body falling in the Earth's gravitational field, work only depends on the initial and final point of the falling mass, independently of the path followed in the fall (Figure 2.3).[5]

This fact excludes the possibility of building a 'perpetual motion of the first kind', that is, a device that, working in a cycle, produces work without the need of external agents; that is, without a source of energy external to the system (Box 2.3).

Box 2.3 Perpetual motion

In antiquity, slaves, animals, water and other natural sources provided all the energy needs of society. Before the establishment of the principle of energy conservation, people believed in the existence of perpetual motion, or *perpetuum mobile*, whereby a machine, once set into motion, would never stop (just as a pendulum or a clock) or whereby a machine produced external work, without receiving energy from any source. The idea of perpetual motion arose in the East. The first known description of the idea was made by the Indian mathematician and astronomer Brahmagupta in AD624, by means of a wooden wheel with uniform mercury containers, separated by regular intervals (Figures 2.4). Set into motion, it should never stop.

Figure 2.4
Perpetual motion:
left the symbol of a
wheel in Indian Sanchi
Stupa; *above* the
principle described by
Brahmagupta
(Strzygowski, 1930)

In 1630, Robert Fludd proposed several perpetual motion machines, one in which the force of gravity would move a waterwheel connected to an endless bolt which, in turn, moved all the water back to the original reservoir (Figure 2.5).

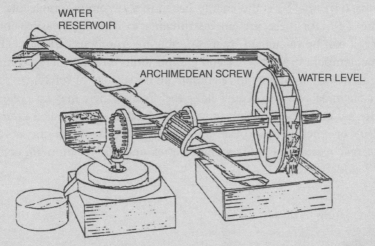

Figure 2.5 Robert Fludd's perpetual motion presented at 'De Simila Naturae' (*apud* Simanek, 2007)

The human spirit has always been fascinated by the idea of accomplishing 'perpetual motion', and the Paris Academy of Sciences, until the mid-18th century, offered a prize to the person who managed to construct a mechanism that would achieve this. No one ever succeeded in winning the prize.

Heat, internal energy and enthalpy

In the mid-19th century, Joule showed that mechanical work could be fully transformed into heat. Heat is a widely used term in everyday language, but it should be used more selectively when dealing with energy transfers.

Energy can be transformed from one form into another, but it cannot be created or destroyed. This law suggests that energy transfer, losses and gains can be accounted for precisely since, whenever energy is transformed, there are losses.

Heat (Q) is the form of energy that flows between two bodies due to their differences in temperature. It may also be defined as another path function which corresponds to the parcel of the energy flow across the boundaries of a system caused by the difference in temperatures between the system and its surroundings. Heat cannot be stored or created out of nothing, but it may be transferred by means of conduction (direct contact between a hot and a cold body), convection (mass flows with different temperatures, such as the movement of water heated inside a pan) or radiation (by electromagnetic waves, without mass transfer or direct contact between bodies, as is the case when sunlight hits a surface).[6]

Internal energy (U) is the energy stored in a system at a molecular level (Figure 2.6). As there are no instruments to directly measure internal energy, it can be calculated by measurable macroscopic variables, such as volume, temperature, pressure and composition. Internal energy cannot be absolutely calculated; only in relation to an initial state of reference.[7]

If a chemical reaction occurs along the process, there may be a release of the internal energy of the substances (involved in the so-called *exothermic reaction*) or energy absorption by the final product (in the so-called *endothermic reaction*). Good examples of exothermic reaction are combustion or oxidation (Box 2.4).

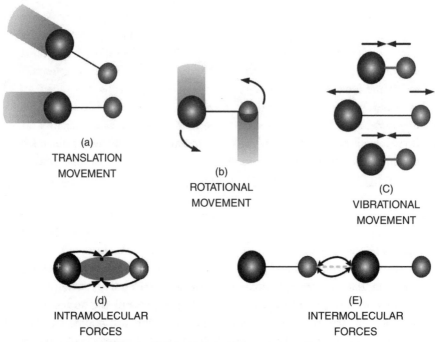

(a)
TRANSLATION
MOVEMENT

(b)
ROTATIONAL
MOVEMENT

(C)
VIBRATIONAL
MOVEMENT

(d)
INTRAMOLECULAR
FORCES

(E)
INTERMOLECULAR
FORCES

Figure 2.6 Internal energy components

Box 2.4 Conversion of chemical energy into combustion heat and of light into photosynthesis chemical energy

Combustion is a chemical exothermic reaction in which oxygen is combined with some other element, releasing heat. All the important fuels, such as coal, petroleum, gas or biomass, contain carbon. The 'oxidation' of carbon occurs through the reaction $C + O_2 \rightarrow CO_2 + 94.03$kcal. Since carbon has atomic weight 12, 7.8kcal carbon per gram are produced.

Most fuels and biomass (including foodstuff) also contain hydrogen, the 'oxidation' of which is given by equation $H_2 + O \rightarrow H_2O + 68.37$kcal; 34.2kcal of heat are produced per gram of H, that is, more than four times the heat produced in the combustion of 1g of C. Some fuels are already partially oxygenated (i.e. contain oxygen) and lose part of the energy they could produce when oxidized.

Fats, proteins, sugars and starches are contained in most of the food we eat. When they are ingested and 'burnt' in our body, they are converted into carbon dioxide (CO_2) and water, producing energy. About 2000kcal/day are necessary to keep an adult human being alive, and the approximate amount of food necessary for that is several hundred grams per day. Table 2.1 provides the combustion heat of the most common foods and fuels.

The lower heating value (LHV, also known as net calorific value) of a fuel is the amount of heat released by combusting a specified quantity (at a reference state) and returning the temperature of the combustion products to 150°C. The LHV assumes that the latent heat of vaporization of water in the fuel and the reaction products are not recovered. The higher heating value (HHV, or gross calorific value), in turn, includes the heat of condensation of water in the combustion products. Methane (CH_4), for example, has an LHV of 50.1MJ/kg and an HHV of 55.5MJ/kg.

The final production of CO_2 is an inevitable consequence of burning carbonated fuels, such as biomass (firewood, wastes) and fossil fuels (coal, oil, gas). In the case of biomass, the CO_2 emitted into the atmosphere may be reincorporated in new plants that grow through photosynthesis. In this endothermic reaction, chlorophyll acts as a catalyser, allowing plants (biomass) to produce sugars from the CO_2 in the air. The energy necessary for the reaction comes from the Sun. Biomass is thus considered a *renewable* form of energy.

The chemical reaction involved in photosynthesis is basically $6CO_2 + 6H_2O$ (+ 120kcal of sunlight) $\rightarrow C_6H_{12}O_6 + 6O_2 + 112$kcal. In addition to being the source of energy that feeds us, photosynthesis also generates the oxygen we breathe. It is for this reason that deforestation is currently such a great concern.

Fossil fuels once were biomass and were formed below ground at great depths over millions of years. As its extraction for human use has increased since the 19th century, these fuels are considered *non-renewable*.

Table 2.1 Combustion heat of the most common fuels

Component	Formula	Combustion heat (kcal/g)
Methane (natural gas)	CH_4	13.2
Oil	(variable)	10.0
Fat	$C_{57}H_{104}O_6$	9.1
Carbon (coal)	C	7.8
Ethyl alcohol	C_2H_6O	7.1
Protein	$C_{1864}H_{3012}O_{6576}N_{468}S_{21}$	5.7
Glucose (sugar)	$C_6H_{12}O_6$	4.1

Most chemical reactions are *exothermic*, that is, produce heat. In general, part of this heat warms the system and part of it flows out of its boundaries (Box 2.5).

Box 2.5 (Open and closed) systems and (exo- and endothermic) reactions

A *system* can be understood as any arbitrary specification of materials or a segment of a process that will be the object of a study, defined by boundaries. It can be, for example, a free-falling mass, a moving vehicle, an operating equipment room, a country or Planet Earth. The *system boundaries* do not necessarily have to coincide with physical boundaries as walls. A system is *closed* (or *without flows*) when no mass transfers cross its boundaries, as is the case with Planet Earth (Figure 2.7).[8] *Boundaries* can be understood as the system limits, which can be real, physical (such as walls) or imaginary, arbitrated (such as a country's borders). Conversely, the system is *open* when mass exchange is allowed (such as a piece of firewood burning in a fireplace) through the boundaries of its *control volume* (which may be, for example, an inflatable balloon, a gas cylinder or the city boundaries).

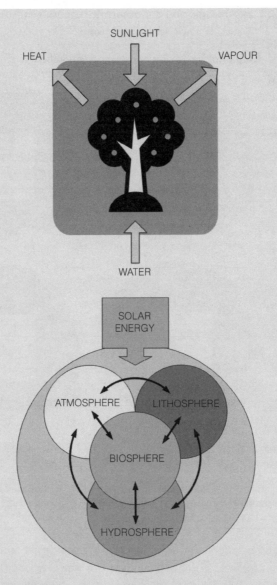

Figure 2.7 Examples of an open (tree) and a closed (Planet Earth) system

Let us consider a new heat source (e.g. chemical reaction) in a system. If the system is open, that is, non-isolated, and there is no change in internal temperature, an instantaneous heat flow occurs. If, conversely, the system is isolated (closed), there is no heat transfer to the surroundings and the system is heated. Table 2.2 presents exothermic and endothermic reactions in closed and open (i.e. non-isolated) systems with instantaneous heat flow, and the situations usually observed.

Table 2.2 Exothermic and endothermic reactions in isolated and non-isolated systems

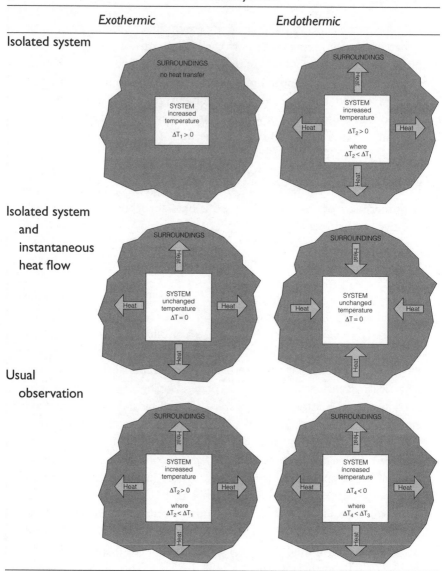

An important concept is that of enthalpy (H), or the calorific content of a system, a variable frequently used in energy balances (Box 2.6).

Box 2.6 Enthalpy

Enthalpy can be understood by imagining water vapour produced in a boiler. When the vapour mass goes through the piping, it carries energy to another place, for example, to a building that needs heating. There is no chemical reaction, but the transportation of a heated mass up to a heat exchanger.

In a closed system, enthalpy combines the internal energy and variations of pressure and of volume.[9] As with internal energy, it does not have an absolute value and only its variations (ΔH) can be calculated in relation to a state of reference.[10]

In exothermic reactions, the enthalpy is negative ($\Delta H < 0$). A practical example is the formation of water from hydrogen combustion.[11] In an endothermic reaction, in turn, there is heat absorption, and thus with positive enthalpy ($\Delta H > 0$). A practical example is that of water vaporization underneath a waterfall: the water in liquid state turns into a gas with heat absorption generated by the kinetic energy of the falling water.[12]

Energy consumed as heat during a chemical transformation under constant pressure may be defined as *reaction enthalpy* and may be measured by a device called a 'calorimeter', or calculated by the difference between the formation heats of products and of chemical reagents. However, understanding and interpreting the reaction heat (enthalpy) for a particular transformation requires understanding how chemical energy accumulates in matter. Molecules are formed because electrons from simple atoms may become more stable when associated with those of other atoms. In general, stabilization is associated with the interaction between the pairs of atoms, called chemical bonds. Different elements have different abilities to form bonds, different values of stabilization energy and associate different properties to the molecules formed. For example, molecule C_2H_6O has two isomers: ethanol (CH_3CH_2OH) and dimethyl ether (CH_3OCH_3). The bonds among molecules are different, providing them with different properties. The boiling point of ethanol is 352K (79°C) and that of ether is 248K (−25°C). The energy content is also different: −1328kJ/mol for ether and −1277kJ/mol for ethanol, both in gas phase (Brucat, 2000).

The expansion of gases and the evolution of steam engines

The expansive force of gases has been known since antiquity. Heron of Alexandria (AD10–AD70) developed an apparatus based on the expansive force of gas to perform mechanical work (Figure 2.8).[13]

Another well-known example of the use of the expansive force of gases is a device used to open temple doors, automatically, in Greece 2500 years ago (which must have caused an extraordinary impact on the credulous Athenians, seeming to be supernatural). Figure 2.9 shows how this was done: fire (A) heated a closed container (B) with air which, when expanded, forced water from another container (C) to go up tube (D), increasing the weight of container (E). As container (E) went down, a rope wound round a pole opened the doors of the temple. The operation could only be conducted once.

The ideal for producing work would be a machine operating in a cycle, that is, that could resume the initial situation and be repeated successively. By the early 18th century, the English blacksmith and mechanic Thomas Newcomen (1663–1729) managed to do it, with a huge low-power machine (approximately 4hp)[14] and high coal consumption (Figure 2.10). In Newcomen's engine, the heat of the fire heats the water in a boiler,

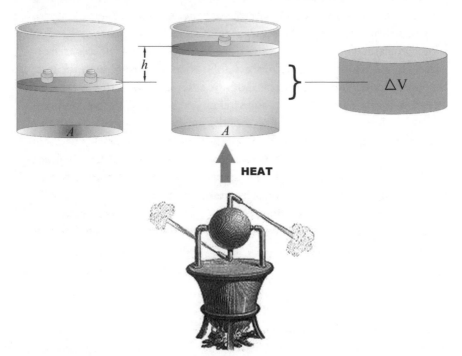

Figure 2.8 Expansion of gases and the experiment by Heron of Alexandria

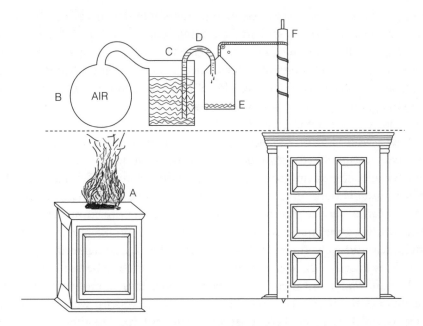

Figure 2.9 Mechanical work conducted by air expansion

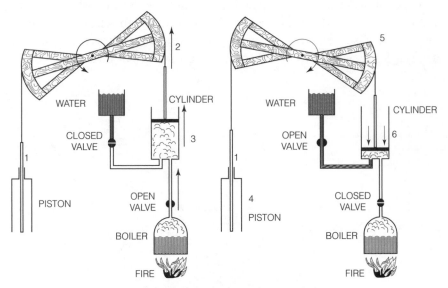

Figure 2.10 Newcomen's engine

generating steam that pushes the piston (cylinder) which, in turn, transmits the force through an axis, moving a lever. When the steam valve is closed and the water valve is opened, a gush reduces the cylinder temperature, condensing the steam and creating a void. The void 'pulls' the axis downwards, moving the lever and pulling the pump piston up. The efficiency of the system, or useful energy obtained in relation to the energy contained in the coal, was very low: less than 2 per cent. This, however, did not matter at the time, since the machine was originally used in coal mines to pump water, and coal was abundant. Newcomen's engine, besides being very big (the gas expansion cylinder lost a lot of heat through the walls), needed a man to operate the valves and to pour water to cool the cylinder. The cycles were spaced over time.[15]

James Watt (1736–1839) improved the system in the early 19th century, thermally insulating the cylinder and introducing an external condenser which cooled the steam, feeding it back into the cylinder. The machine efficiency rose to about 5 per cent, which made a huge difference. From then on, machines were improved and their efficiency increased, which allowed their use far from the coal mines. Smeaton and Woolf also built steam engines, as did Newcomen and Watt (Figure 2.11). Later, speed regulators were introduced in the steam engines and they started to be used on a large scale in the textile industry, then in railway engines (locomotives), marking the onset of the Industrial Revolution. Then other systems were developed, such as turbines, internal combustion engines (such as the Otto and Diesel cycle), jet turbines, reactors and jet rockets.

Original steam engines reached a maximum efficiency of 5 per cent. With a condenser, this value rises to 25 per cent. With reheating of steam by exhaust gases, 30 per cent is attained. In combined cycles (with heat recovery), efficiencies of 60 per cent can be achieved. Since the study on

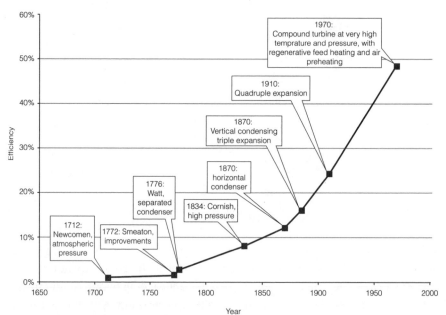

Figure 2.11 Evolution in steam engines' efficiency

gases developed independently of that on mechanical energy, the unit that measures thermal energy is the calorie, different from the one used to measure mechanical energy (joule).[16]

Power

The definition of work above does not provide any information on the time necessary to perform the task, which is very important in practice. For example, a man can lift 40 25-kg stones, one by one, from the ground and place them into a cart, but he is unable to do it by lifting 1000kg in a single operation, despite the total work done in the two cases being exactly the same.

Power (P) represents an energy flow per time unit or the rate at which work is conducted.[17] In the International System (IS) of units, power is measured in watts (W), which is defined as a joule per second (1W = 1J/s).

Power may also be measured in other units that represent a given amount of energy applied at a given period. The unit employed in many countries is the '*horse-power*' (or HP, equivalent to about 746W) which traditionally represented the 'power' of a horse, or 7.5 times the power of a man. The human being, on average, consumes energy at a power of about 100W (the power of an average incandescent light bulb), varying between 85W during sleep

Table 2.3 Power units

Unit	Notation	Magnitude
Picowatt	$pW = 10^{-12}W$	human cell
Nanowatt	$nW = 10^{-9}W$	microchip
Microwatt	$\mu W = 10^{-6}W$	quartz wrist watch
Milliwatt	$mW = 10^{-3}W$	laser beam in a CD player
Watt	W	lightbulb, house appliances in general
Kilowatt	$kW = 10^{3}W$	propelling engines in general
Megawatt	$MW = 10^{6}W$	power of train engines and power plants in general
Gigawatt	$GW = 10^{9}W$	large hydropower plants capacity, average power consumption in a country
Terawatt	$TW = 10^{12}W$	average world power consumption, global annual energy production by photosynthesis in the world
Petawatt	$PW = 10^{15}W$	solar power received by the Earth

and 800W or more during intense exercise. In an electric circuit, power P can be calculated by the product of the current intensity (I, 'amperes') and difference in 'electrical potential' (V, 'volts'). Sportspeople frequently use the term 'calories per hour' and menus sometimes list how many 'calories a day' should be ingested (in reality kilocalories – kcal – per hour or per day). Air-conditioning systems express energy in *British thermal units* (Btu) and power in Btu/hour; natural gas pipelines convey (powers of) millions of Btu per day.[18] Table 2.3 presents different orders of magnitude for power units, with their respective decimal prefixes.

It is not unusual to confuse concepts and units of power and energy; that is, the case of the installed capacity of a generator or a device (given in kW) with the power produced or consumed in a given period (in kWh). Table 2.4 provides some of the conversion factors for the energy and power units more commonly used. For units and factors, see also Annex 2.

Table 2.4 Work, energy and power units

Property	Unit	Equivalent to
Energy	1 joule (J)	$1N.m = 1kg . m/s^2$
		$0.2388cal = 2.388 \times 10^{-4}kcal$
		$9.4782 \times 10^{-4}Btu$
		$2.7778 \times 10^{-4}Wh$
		10^7 ergs
	1 calorie	4.1868J
	1 kilowatt-hour (kWh)	3.6×10^{13} ergs = 3600kJ
		860kcal
		8.6×10^{-5} toe
	1 ton of oil equivalent	10^{10} cal
	(toe)[19]	$41.8GJ = 4.18 . 10^{10}J$
		11.63MWh = 11,630kWh
		1.28 ton of coal equivalent
		39.68 million Btu of natural gas
	1 million of *British*	1.0551GJ
	Thermal Units	2.52×10^{-2} toe
	(1MBtu)	0.2931MWh
Power	1 watt (W)	1J/s
	1 *horse-power* (HP)	746W
	1GWh a year	86 toe/year

Table 2.5 gives roughly the chronological development of power in equipment available to the human being since prehistoric days.

Table 2.5 Chronological improvements of equipment power (Cook, 1976)

Equipment	Date	Developed power (HP)
Man using a lever	Before 3000 BC	0.05
Ox pulling load	Before 3000 BC	0.5
Water turbine	1000 BC	0.4
Vertical water wheel	350 BC	3
Windmill	1600 AD	14
Savery's steam engine	1697 AD	1
Newcomen's steam engine	1712 AD	5.5
Watt's steam engine (land)	1800 AD	40
Naval steam engine	1837 AD	750
Naval steam engine	1843 AD	1500
Water turbine	1854 AD	800
Naval steam engine	1900 AD	8000
Land steam engine	1900 AD	12,000
Steam turbine	1906 AD	17,500
Steam turbine	1921 AD	40,000
Steam turbine	1943 AD	288,000
Plant using steam power produced by coal burning	1973 AD	1,465,000
Nuclear reactor	1974 AD	1,520,000

The laws of thermodynamics

An essential characteristic of energy is the possibility of conversion between its different forms (radiation, chemical, nuclear, thermal, mechanical, electric and magnetic) being able to adapt to the desired end-use. Figure 2.12 shows the main energy conversion processes among the most common forms of energy.

A *thermodynamic property* is any measurable characteristic of a system, open or closed: pressure, temperature, mass, volume, density or energy. If the thermodynamic property depends on the amount of matter present (e.g. mass), it is called *extensive*; if not, it is *intensive* (e.g. temperature,

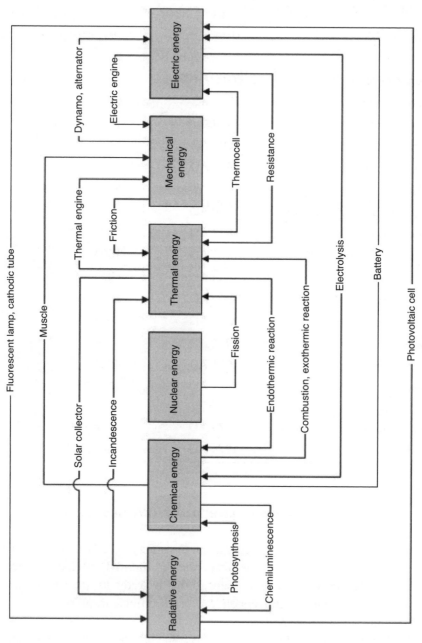

Figure 2.12 *Energy conversion processes*

pressure).[20] *Process* is a change of state in a system, which may be reversible (to the initial cition, as is the case of cyclic processes) or irreversible.

By definition, the work that leaves a system and the heat that enters it are positive; the heat that leaves a system and the work applied to it are negative (Figure 2.13).

The Zero Law of Thermodynamics

In an *equilibrium state,* the thermodynamic properties of an isolated system are not altered. The Zero Law of Thermodynamics establishes that if two systems are in a temperature equilibrium with a third one, they will be in equilibrium among themselves (Figure 2.14).

The First Law of Thermodynamics or Law of Energy Conservation

The First Law of Thermodynamics states that the total variation of energy contained in a closed system is equal to the (net) effect of the heat and work

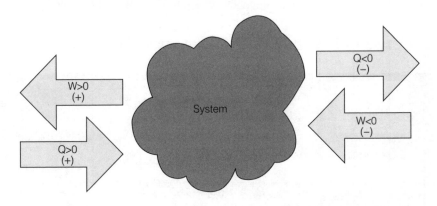

Figure 2.13 Signal convention for work (W) and heat (Q)

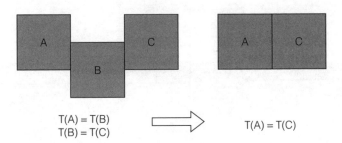

Figure 2.14 Law Zero of Thermodynamics: thermal equilibrium principle

interactions the system undergoes with the environment.[21] In other words, energy is conserved; it can neither be created nor destroyed.

The energy balance of a generic closed system is illustrated in Figure 2.15.

Figure 2.16 shows the energy balance of our planet, which is an isolated system in which there are no mass transfers.

In the case of open systems, mass conservation has to be verified before energy conservation (Figure 2.17).[22] In this case, the energy balance can be represented by the heat ($\dot{Q}$), work ($\dot{W}$) and enthalpy ($\dot{H}$) flows.[23]

In a practical example, one may imagine a turbine that receives 72 tons (i.e. 20kg/s) of steam (specific enthalpy of 2800kJ/kg) per hour and discharges the same mass of condensed and low-pressure steam (specific enthalpy of 2500kJ/kg), losing 10 per cent of its heat to the environment.

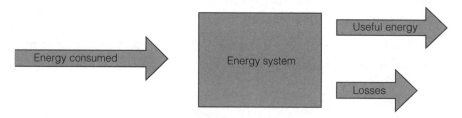

Figure 2.15 Energy balance in a closed system, without mass flows

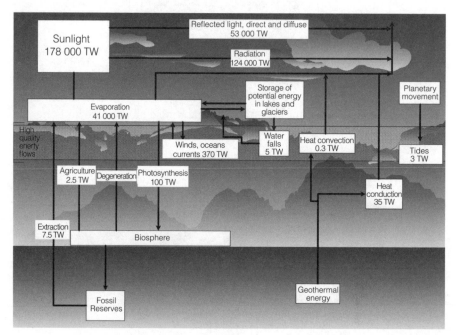

Figure 2.16 Energy balance of the Earth

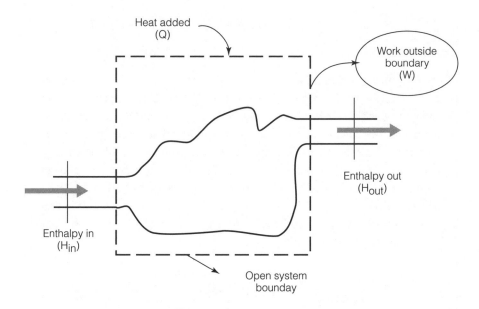

Figure 2.17 Energy balance in an open system

The power produced by the turbine will be $P = 20 \times (2800 - 2500) \times (100\% - 10\%) = 5400\text{kJ/s} = 5400\text{kW}$. This represents the useful power (i.e. $100\% - 10\%$ of losses). Therefore, the loss (of 10%) will be 600kW. Thus, per hour, $(5400 + 600)\text{kWh} = 6000\text{kWh}$ enter and leave the system. The system efficiency is $(100\% - 10\%) = 90\%$.

Entropy and the Second Law of Thermodynamics

Based on the concept of entropy (Box 2.7), the Second Law of Thermodynamics states that it is not possible to use all the forms of energy with the same efficiency. In other words, there are always losses in energy conversion and no process is 100 per cent reversible.

Box 2.7 Entropy

Arthur Eddington calls entropy *time arrow*, a name adopted by modern science (Angrist and Hepler, 1967). Entropy is the measure of chaos. A solid has less entropy than a liquid which, in turn, has less entropy than a gas. *Gibbs'* equation states that, in a closed system, the internal energy variations depend on volume and entropy. Mathematically:

$$dU = TdS - PdV.$$

Entropy (S) can be defined in a reversible process by the equation

$$dS = \delta Q / T.$$

As it never decreases in an isolated system, its rate of growth is always positive ($\Delta S > 0$). Entropy is an extensive thermodynamic property, the value of which never decreases to an isolated system. Microscopically, it measures the *randomness* of a system composed of many particles, as shown by the irreversible state (without external energy application) of a mixture of two different gases (Figure 2.18). It can be statistically proved (and not mathematically demonstrated) that the randomness of the particles always tend to increase. As there are always energy losses in real world processes, there are limits to energy conversion (and consequent thermodynamic efficiencies).

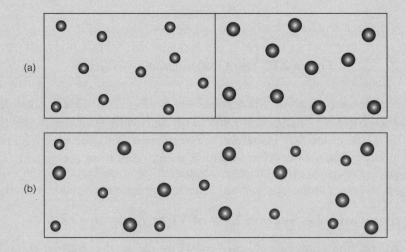

Figure 2.18 Entropy and mixture of two gases: (a) before and (b) after

The Second Law of Thermodynamics defines entropy as the measure of the unavailability of a system's energy to do work. The concept suggests that the universe tends to decelerate because it is expanding and, therefore, its need of support energy is growing. One of the results of this law is the inexistence of perpetual motion, as the energy is lost and cannot be fully recovered by a system.

Efficiency of heat engines and their limits

As already seen, the efficiency of an energy system is given by the ratio between the useful energy (or work done) and the total energy consumed by the system:

$$\eta = \frac{E_{useful}}{E_{consumed}} = \frac{E_{consumed} - Losses}{E_{consumed}} = 1 - \frac{Losses}{E_{consumed}}.$$

Mechanical equipment such as levers and pulleys usually have little friction and, therefore, high efficiencies of energy conversion.[24] The conversion of chemical energy into heat occurs efficiently by the combustion process. On the other hand, the conversion of heat into mechanical energy in general has low efficiency, with high level of losses to the external environment.

A thermal engine (Figure 2.19) is a device (also called 'working body') that performs work by means of the heat transfer from a body with high temperature to another body with low temperature.

Considering an isolated system in which a heat source sends an amount of Q_0 to a given device (thermal engine) to do some work W and discard an amount Q of heat, the First Law of Thermodynamics is applied: $Q_0 = Q + W$. Since Q represents the rejected heat, the thermal efficiency is $\varepsilon = W/Q_0 = (Q_0 - Q)/Q_0 = 1 - Q/Q_0$.

As an example, let us imagine a hypothetical cogeneration system that produces power and useful heat for industrial processes or ambient heating.

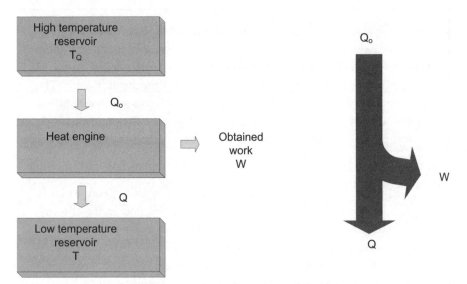

Figure 2.19 Efficiency of heat engines

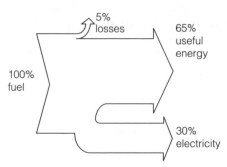

Figure 2.20 Sankey Diagram: energy flows and efficiency

Even recovering some of the heat, part of it is eventually lost. Let us consider that the system has 0.3 efficiency for power generation and 0.65 for producing useful heat. The global efficiency is 95 per cent and 5 per cent of the energy applied is 'lost', dissipated without being used. Figure 2.20 represents the situation for a cogeneration plant by means of the so-called *Sankey Diagram*.

The successive mechanical improvements developed over time in the first steam engines allowed improvements in efficiency, achieving a greater amount of work with the same amount of fuel.

The efficiency gains in heat engines led to questioning whether there was a theoretical limit to it. In 1824, Sadi Carnot determined this theoretical limit by calculating the efficiency of an ideal cycle (Box 2.8).

Box 2.8 The Carnot Cycle

A thermodynamic cycle occurs when a given system goes through a series of different states, and returns to its original state. In this process, there will always be losses. A heat engine transfers heat from a hotter region to a colder one, converting part of this energy into mechanical work. This cycle can also be reverted by applying external energy: this is how a refrigerator works. The Carnot Cycle is the most thermodynamically efficient possible. It can be represented by a temperature-entropy diagram, in four stages (Figures 2.21 and 2.22).

1. A–B: a force is applied onto a piston (e.g. in an air compressor), producing expansion work on the gas it contains (increasing entropy) without altering the temperature (i.e. in an *isothermal* process);
2. B–C: assuming the piston to be thermally isolated (without heat gains or losses), the gas expands (e.g. in a condenser) without altering the entropy (i.e. in an *adiabatic* process), cooling to temperature T_{cold}.

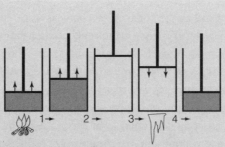

Figure 2.21 Examples of stages of the Carnot Cycle

3. C–D: The surrounding heat conducts the work on the gas (isothermal compression), which 'rejects' the heat and makes it flow to a low-temperature chamber (e.g. a radiator or the inside of a refrigerator).
4. D–A: the gas is again compressed by an external force without altering the entropy (adiabatically), again increasing the temperature to T_H and resuming its initial state (Kroemer and Kittel, 1980).

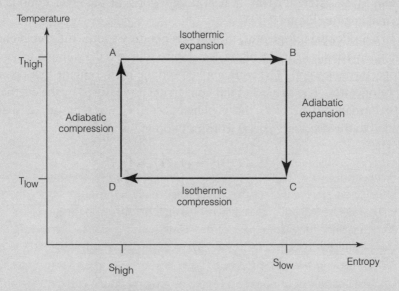

Figure 2.22 Demonstration of the Carnot Cycle, diagram *T-S*

The work done (ΔW) corresponds to the area of the rectangle ABCD and the heat applied to the process (ΔQ) is the area below the rectangle (i.e. $DCS_{high}S_{low}$). The total energy, therefore, is the sum of the work and the heat applied. Efficiency η is defined by ($\Delta W / \Delta Q$) = $1 - (T_{high}/T_{low})$ being the temperatures absolute (in Kelvin). For a heat engine, it can be said that the efficiency is the fraction of the heat extracted from the 'hot' thermal chamber and converted into mechanical work. In the specific case of a refrigeration cycle, efficiency is the ratio of the heat removed from the cold chamber on the total energy applied to the system. Carnot enunciated the following theorem: *no heat engine operating between two heat chambers can be more efficient than the ideal cycle.* That is, the maximum efficiency is obtained if and only if no additional entropy is created during the cycle. Since entropy is a function of the state of the system, the loss of heat into the environment (to release entropy excess) leads to a reduction in efficiency. Carnot realized that it is not possible to build such an ideal engine. In a real engine, entropy changes with temperature and there are irreversible losses due to, for example, friction.

The heat pump

A refrigerator or heat pump is a device that transfers energy such as heat from a cold source to a hot one; this is possible because work is done on the system by an external agent. A heat pump works as the reverse mode of a thermal engine (Figure 2.23).

In a residential refrigerator, the low-temperature source is the cold chamber, where food is kept; the high temperature source is the room in which the refrigerator is located. The work applied is done by the engine that operates the refrigerator. The success of this conversion is measured by the coefficient of performance (CoP or k), the 'cooling effect' (i.e. heat removal), desired in relation to the necessary energy consumption of the appliance:

$$k = Q_C/W = Q_C/(Q_H - Q_C).$$

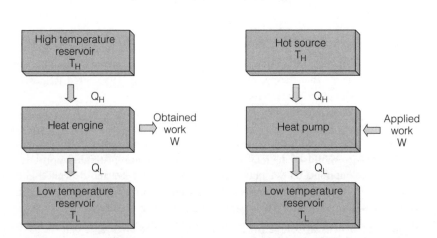

Figure 2.23 Thermal engine and heat pump

Table 2.6 Some examples of efficiency measures (η) in terms of work (W), work flow per time ($\dot{W}$), outflow or mass flow ($\dot{m}$), lower heating value of a substance (LHV) and enthalpy (h)

Application	Efficiency (η)	Units (example)
Engines	$\eta = \dfrac{W_{useful}}{\dot{m}_{comb} \cdot LHV}$	[kW]/[(kg/s) × (kJ/kg)]
Compressors and pumps	$\eta = \dfrac{W_{compression/pressure}}{W_{applied}}$	[kg.m^2/s^2]/[kWh]
Turbines	$\eta = \dfrac{W_{mechanical}}{W_{ideal\_foreseen}}$	[kg.m^2/s^2]/[kg.m^2/s^2]
Steam generators	$\eta = \dfrac{\dot{m}_{steam}\left(h_{steam} - h_{condensed}\right)}{\dot{m}_{comb} \cdot LHV}$	[(kg/s).(kJ/kg)]/[(kg/s).(kJ/kg)]
Heat recovery boiler	$\eta = \dfrac{\dot{m}_{steam}\left(h_{steam} - h_{condensed}\right)}{\dot{m}_{heating\_fluid}\left(h_{in} - h_{out}\right)}$	[(kg/s).(kJ/kg)]/[(kg/s).(kJ/kg)]

Efficiency measurement

In general, efficiency is the ratio of useful energy and the total one supplied to the system (or the one estimated by the system's nominal power). Table 2.6 presents some useful units used in the resolution of problems.

Notes

1 For example, when subatomic beta particles decay, an electron and a nucleus are produced. In the 1920s, physicists measured the energy of decay products and verified that it was not conserved. In 1930, Pauli proposed the existence of a third decay product that had not been measured. In 1933, Fermi called it 'neutrino' ('small neutron' in Italian). The physicists were so convinced of its existence – due to energy conservation laws – that they were not surprised when, in 1956, Fred Reines and Clyde Cowan discovered it (Harrison, 2005).

2 A force is a push or a pull exerted on a body aiming to change its rest or rectilinear uniform motion state. Force F is defined by the product of mass (m) and the acceleration (a). The standard unit of mass in the International System is the kilogram (kg), which corresponds to the mass of a prototype in iridium platinum, approved by the General Conference of Weights and Measures from 1889 and deposited in the Pavillon de Breteuil, in Sevres, Paris. The acceleration unit is the metre per square second (m/s^2), which corresponds to the acceleration of an animated body from a uniformly accelerated movement, the velocity of which varies 1m/s at each second. The force unit is the newton (N), the amount of force required to give a 1kg mass an acceleration of 1m/s^2.

3. $1J = 1N.m$ or $kg.m^2/s^2$.

4 Mathematically, one has

$$W = \int_{y_1}^{y_2} F_z \, dy = mg(y_1 - y_2) = mgh.$$

5 Work is mathematically defined by the integral of force (F_z) by the displacement ('z') of a point A to a point B:

$$W = \int_A^B F_z \, dz.$$

In the simpler case of a constant force, $W = F \times x$. If the force is not applied in the direction, the movement occurs, the component of the force is used in the direction of the movement.

6 Quantitatively, heat transfer can be obtained by calculating the energy balance of a system or by using an empirical formula, $\dot{Q} = UA\Delta T \, \dot{Q}$ (where $\dot{Q}$ is the heat transfer rate, U is a coefficient empirically defined from experimental data, A is the transference area and ΔT is the difference in temperature between the system and its surrounding).

7 By using temperature, it can be demonstrated that the changes in internal energy per unit of mass is given by the equation

$$\Delta \hat{U} = \hat{U}_2 - \hat{U}_1 = \int_{T_1}^{T_2} C_v \, dT$$

where T is the temperature and C_v is a constant called heat capacity. The development of these formulae can be found in several references (e.g. Himmelblau, 1996).

8 On planet Earth, solar energy (direct by radiation or indirect in reservoirs and stocks) and gravitational (the Moon acting on tides) flows act, without mass transfer outwards the system. The Earth retains the energy in reservoirs (petroleum, natural gas, coal, fissile materials, geothermal heat) and energy stocks (biomass in general, hydraulic potentials).

9 Enthalpy may be given in a closed system by the formula $H = U + pV$. In an open system, $H = E + pV$, where E is the system energy.

10 For a pure substance (e.g. water vapour), the variations in enthalpy per mass unit may be calculated by

$$\Delta \hat{H} = \hat{H}_2 - \hat{H}_1 = \int_{T_1}^{T_2} C_p \, dT,$$

where T is the temperature and C_p is the constant heat capacity. The reference conditions may be obtained in vapour tables, as in Van Wylen and Sonntag (1985).

11 At 25°C and 1 atmosphere: $H_2 + \frac{1}{2}O_2 \rightarrow H_2O - 286kJ$.

12 At 25°C and pressures up to 0.0313 atm: H_2O (liquid) $\rightarrow H_2O$ (gaseous) $+ 44kJ$.

13 In a closed system, simple and understandable, the displacement of a piston (boundary displacement work) may be represented by

$$\delta W = F dx = (P/A) dx = P dV.$$

This behaviour can also be described by the Law of Gases, equation $PV = kT$, which relates pressure P and volume V to absolute temperature (T) in Kelvin scale. To convert it, use $T = 273.16 + T_c$, where T_c is the temperature in Celsius (°C) degrees. In the *Fahrenheit* scale, $T_F = 9/5 T_C + 32 = 9/5 (T - 273.16) + 32$.

14 HP (*horse-power*) is a power unit. In the metric system, 1hp is equivalent to 735.49875W. In thermopower plants, the unit *boiler horsepower* is used, corresponding to 33,475Btu/h or 9.8095kW, which is the necessary energy flow to evaporate 15.65kg of water at 100°C in one hour.

15 The quadruple expansion – use of four cylinders for engines – was invented as recently as 1910.

16 A calorie is equivalent to 4.1855 joules and is the amount of heat necessary to rise the temperature of a gram of water at sea level by one degree Celsius (from 13.5°C to 14.5°C).

17 Mathematically, $P = dE/dt = dW/dt$, where E is energy and W is work. *Instantaneous power* is the limiting value when the time interval tends to zero. When the energy flow is constant, power can be simplified as $P = W/t = E/t$.

18 Although the notation MBtu/d represents 'millions of Btu per day', a notation commonly found is 'MMBtu/day'.

19 The units based on the calorific power of fuels (toe, m³ of natural gas, kg of liquefied petroleum gas, ton of sugar cane bagasse, etc.) have values that vary according to the region and the time (in general, by country and per year). For more, see IEA (2008).

20 An extensive thermodynamic property can be transformed into an intensive (specific) one, by dividing it by the mass. In the case of energy, $E = E/m$.

21 The First Law of Thermodynamics can be represented as $[E_{entra}] - [E_{sai}] = [\Delta E_{system}]$ or

$$\sum_i Q - \sum_j Wj = \Delta E_{cinética} + \Delta E_{potencial} + \Delta U$$

where ΔU represents the variations in internal energy.

22 In a given time unit, the entering mass minus the leaving mass is equal to the mass that remains within the control volume. Mathematically,

$$\sum_{entering} \dot{m}_e - \sum_{leaving} \dot{m}_s = dm_{controlvolume} / dt,$$

where $\dot{m}$ is the mass flow per time (e.g. in kg/h).

23 The notation with a small upper dot represents a flow, a discharge expressed in mass and/or energy units divided by a time unit. In the case of enthalpy, a mass discharge conveys energy with it.

24 In the case of mechanical work, $n = W/W_0$, where W is useful work (e.g. conveying a given load along a certain distance) and W_0 is the energy of the fuel used by the engine. This energy, in turn, can be represented by $W_0 = m \times PCI$, that is, the mass of fuel used multiplied by the *lower heating value* of the same energy input (in, for example, MJ/kg).

References

Angrist, S. W. and Hepler, L. G. (1967) *Laws of Order and Chaos*. Basic Books, New York

Brucat, P. J. (2000) *The Chemical Origins of Reaction Enthalpy*. University of Florida, http://itl.chem.ufl.edu/2045/lectures/lec_9be.html

Cook, E. (1976) *Man, Energy, Society*. W. H. Freeman and Co., San Francisco, CA

Fludd, R., De simila naturae, *apud* Simanek, D. E. (2007) 'Perpetual futility. A short history of the search for perpetual motion'. Lock Haven University of Pennsylvania, www.lhup.edu/~dsimanek/museum/people/people.htm. Last accessed April 2009

Harrison, D. M. (2005) 'The concept of energy', University of Toronto, www.upscale.utoronto.ca/PVB/Harrison/ConceptOfEnergy/ConceptOfEnergy.html. Last accessed April 2009

Himmelblau, D. M. (1996) *Basic Principles and Calculations in Chemical Engineering.* Prentice Hall, London

IEA (2008) *Energy Balances of non-OECD countries.* International Energy Agency, Paris

Kroemer, H. and Kittel, C. (1980) *Thermal Physics,* 2nd edn, W. M. and Freeman Co., ISBN 0716710889.

Strzygowski *Asiens bildende Kunst* (1930) Figure 272, p285; *apud* Hans Peter, 2004, *Mathematical Gatherum* (www.hp-gramatke.net)

Van Wylen, G. J. and Sonntag, R. E. (1985) *Fundamentals of Classical Thermodynamics.* John Wiley & Sons, Hoboken, NJ

Chapter 3

Energy and Human Activities

The minimum energy necessary for an adult human being to stay alive for one day is approximately 1000kcal (= 10^6cal). A person fed with less than this amount of energy loses weight and may die. World War II prisoners in concentration camps received less than 1000kcal/day of food. An adult engaged in normal activities requires about 2000kcal per day and for a man conducting heavy manual work, 4000kcal daily. Table 3.1 shows the energy needs for a number of human tasks.

However, to satisfy the growing needs of humans a considerable increase in energy consumption is necessary. Throughout history, the development stages of man may be correlated with the energy consumed, as shown in Figure 3.1.

A million years ago, *primitive man* from Eastern Africa did not master fire and relied only on the energy of the food ingested (2000kcal/day). A hundred thousand years ago, the European *hunter* already consumed more food and burned wood to get warm and to cook. Later, *primitive agricultural man* from Mesopotamia (5000BC) used the energy of draught animals. In the early Modern Ages (AD1400), *advanced agricultural man* from Northeastern Europe also used coal for heating, and the mechanical energy from waterfalls and from the wind. In England, *industrial man* developed

Table 3.1 Energy needs for different activities (Cook, 1976)

Effort	Example	Energy consumption (kcal/hour)
Light to moderate	Be relaxed	20
	Light activities	50–60
	Walk, shower	125–240
	Light work (e.g. carpentry)	150–180
	March	280
Heavy	Break stones	350
	Row, swim, run	400–700
	Intensive sports	800–1000

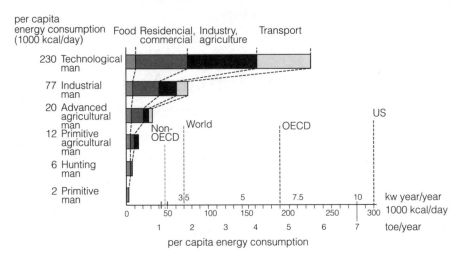

Figure 3.1 Development stages and energy consumption (Cook, 1976)

the steam engine by the 1800s. Later, in the 20th century, *technological man* improved the steam engine and developed internal combustion engines (Otto and Diesel cycles), electric engines and nuclear energy. In 2004, each of the 6.35 billion inhabitants of the planet consumed an average of 17.7 million kilocalories (or 1.77 tons of oil equivalent *per capita* per year), about one million times the amount the primitive humans consumed. Each African consumed an average of 0.67 tons of oil equivalent (toe) per year; each Chinese 1.25 toe per year. In turn, each inhabitant from the OECD-developed countries consumed 4.73 toe of energy in that year; each US citizen, 7.91 toe per year (IEA, 2006).

Noblemen of the Roman Empire quantified their wealth in number of slaves, which corresponded, in energy terms, to multiples of 2000kcal a day, or 0.73 million kilocalories a year. Using the same analogy nowadays, the average energy consumption per inhabitant in the world would be equivalent to 24 'slaves' (Box 3.1).

Box 3.1 Energy and slavery

A young adult, normally active, in a temperate climate, needs an amount of food energy of 2000kcal a day, which corresponds to a continuous flow of energy of about 100W (called 'human equivalent power' unit – HEP). We introduce here the idea that to satisfy the basic energy needs of a person would require the work of several hypothetical slaves, each of them consuming energy at a rate corresponding to 1 HEP. Therefore, the number of slaves necessary to supply several human basic needs is obtained. Table 3.2 lists these basic energy needs and the necessary number of hypothetical slaves.

Table 3.2 Basic energy needs of a hypothetical society dependent on slaves (Haffner, 1979)

Type of activity	Slaves per capita	Daily energy needs per capita	
		(watt)	*(kcal)*
Food	3	300	6000
Dwelling	3	300	6000
Clothes	1	100	2000
Transport	2	200	4000
Leisure	6	600	12,000
Total	15	1500	30,000

The energy cost of satisfying basic human needs

Several attempts have been made to quantify the minimum human need. One of the most sophisticated was made by the Fundación Bariloche (1977) with its World Latin-American Model. The Bariloche model explores the possible physical limits to establish a society in which the basic human needs are satisfied and, based on a simple econometric model, investigates the possibility of doing that with the present available economic resources. The desired levels assumed in the Bariloche model are: (a) 3000kcal and 100 grams of protein per person per day; (b) a home (50 square metres of dwelling area) per family; and (c) 12 years of basic education (i.e. school enrolment of all children between six and 17).

The quantitative definition of a representative 'basket' of basic human needs is difficult for several reasons. One of them is that basic needs vary with climate, culture, region, period of time, age and sex. Another one is that there is not a single level of basic needs, but a hierarchy of them. There are needs that have to be supplied for survival, such as a minimum of food, of dwelling and protection against fatal illnesses. The satisfaction of a greater level of needs (such as basic education) makes 'productive survival' possible. Even higher levels of needs such as trips and leisure emerge when people try to improve their quality of life beyond 'productive survival'. Obviously, the needs perceived as basic vary according to the conditions of life in any society. Despite the difficulties involved in defining and in classifying human needs, the three quantitative measures chosen in the Bariloche model may be considered as a basic nucleus for 'productive survival'.

The final aim of the World Latin-American Model is to find the necessary GNP (gross national product) per capita needed to satisfy basic human needs: this monetary income can be converted into energy units using adequate coefficients for the sectors considered. Thus the amount of commercial energy necessary to satisfy basic human needs is obtained. It is well known, however, that a large number of people in rural areas in developing countries have no access to commercial energy due to the lack of purchasing power, or for other reasons. In order to survive, these people depend on non-commercial sources of energy, mainly fuelwood, manure and agricultural waste that can be obtained at a negligible monetary cost. In many of these countries, non-commercial energy corresponds to a significant parcel of the total primary energy consumption and 7.5×10^3kcal/day is considered a significant number of that consumption. By adding this number to the amount of commercial energy needed to supply basic needs, the total energy cost to satisfy basic human needs is as indicated in Table 3.3: it varies between 27.8×10^3 and 36.4×10^3kcal/day per capita, that is, between 1.0 and 1.3 toe per capita per year.

Energy consumption as a function of income

One of the intrinsic characteristics of a dual society in developing countries is the fact that the elite and the poor differ fundamentally in their energy uses. The elite tries to mimic the lifestyle prevailing in industrialized countries and has similar luxury-oriented energy standards. In contrast, the poor are more concerned with setting enough energy for cooking and for other essential activities. For the poor, development means satisfying basic human needs, including access to employment, food, health services, education, housing, running water, sewage treatment, etc. The lack of

Table 3.3 Basic needs: energy consumption per capita
(Krugmann and Goldemberg, 1983)

Region	Year	Commercial energy (kcal/day)	Non-commercial energy (kcal/day)	Total energy (kcal/day)
Latin-America	1992	24.2×10^3	7.5×10^3	31.7×10^3
Africa	2008	20.3×10^3	7.5×10^3	27.8×10^3
Asia	2020	28.9×10^3	7.5×10^3	36.4×10^3

access to these services by most people is a fertile ground for political unrest and hopelessness that leads to emigration to industrialized countries in search of a better future. A large part of the energy for agriculture, transportation and domestic activities in poorer developing countries comes from the muscular effort of human beings and from draught animals. Other sources include biomass in the form of fuelwood, animal and agricultural waste. Fuelwood is actually the dominant source of energy in rural areas, especially for cooking. In rural areas, women and children usually pick up sticks as fuel to cook instead of buying wood. Figure 3.2 shows results of research into how energy is consumed by different income classes in Brazil. For families with incomes over 10 wage units (WU), oil products including liquefied petroleum gas (LPG) represent 65 per cent of the total energy consumed, whereas for families between 0 and 2WU they represent 35 per cent. In turn, for high income families, fuelwood and coal represent 8 per cent, whereas for poor families they represent 40 per cent.[1]

At the level of approximately 5WU, the direct consumption of energy undergoes a minimum due to the replacement of fuelwood (used with low efficiency) by liquefied petroleum gas (used with high efficiency). Above 5WU electricity and liquid fuels consumption increase, due to the greater use of electric appliances and transportation. People with incomes between 0 and 2WU consume 20×10^3kcal/day, whereas people with more than

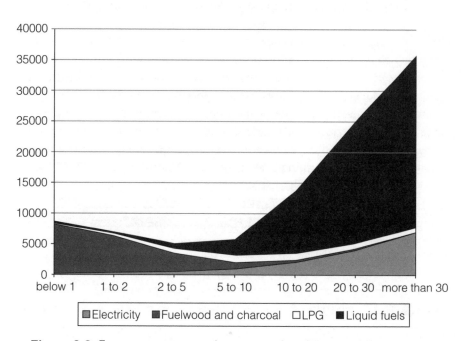

Figure 3.2 Energy consumption by income class (measured by minimum wages) in Brazil, 1988 (Almeida and Oliveira, 1995)

20WU consume 280×10^3kcal/day, that is, 14 times more. Half of the energy consumed is direct and the other half is indirect. The fraction of electricity and LPG increased, whereas the fraction of fuelwood and coal decreased. Country urbanization in this period greatly influenced this trend. The replacement of fuelwood by LPG and electricity is related to the availability of alternatives and to its relative price. Thus, when an energy input of higher quality is made accessible to a community it tends to migrate to that input as it can afford it (UNDP et al, 2002).

Figure 3.3 shows the energy consumption by type (commodity) and region in the world.

About 2 billion people in the world rely on fuelwood for their basic needs. If each person were to use kerosene, 50kg a year would be necessary, which

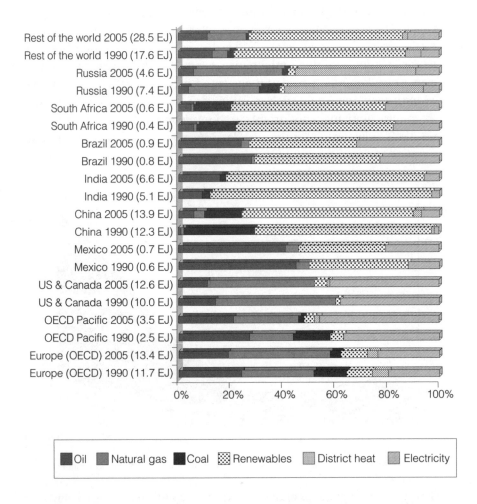

Figure 3.3 Household energy use by energy commodity (IEA, 2008)

Table 3.4 Comparison among cooking fuels

Fuel	Inferior calorific power (MJ/kg)	Necessary fuel in relative energy terms (LPG = 1)	Necessary fuel in relative weight terms (LPG = 1)
LPG	45	1.0	1.0
Kerosene	43	1.0	1.0
Coal	30	2.0	3.0
Dry fuelwood	15	40	12.0

would represent 100Mtoe of oil, or about 3 per cent of the world's consumption of this fuel. Clearly, this does not represent a resource limitation.

Neither does it represent an excessive weight in the balance of payment of most countries. Estimates for Nicaragua, Sri Lanka and Kenya indicate that it would represent less than 10 per cent of the value of their imports. However, the poorer part of the population does not manage to have access to more modern fuels by their own means (as shown in Table 3.5) and subsidies may be necessary.

Even then there might be problems with the logistics of distribution and transactions. The lack of this infrastructure is a bottleneck for the switch to new energy inputs. The increase in LPG prices may also lead to a decrease in its consumption and consequently to neglect of the already-established infrastructure.

Table 3.5 Relative prices of different fuels (Foley, 2000)

| Place and date | Relative price per weight | | | |
	Fuelwood	Coal	Kerosene	LPG
Bamako, Mali (1979)	1–1.7	5.3–6.0	–	–
Bangalore, India (1979–80)	1	2.2	5.5	7.8
New Delhi, India (1982)	1		3.6 (subsidized) or 7.6 (without subsidies)	–
Indonesia (1981)	1	18.4	5.2	21.9
Niamey, Niger (1983)	1	2.5	8.7	–
Nigeria (1983)	1–3.8	4.9	2.7–5.0	7.6
Senegal (1982)	1	2.5	8.7	1.5–3.1
Uganda (1982)	1	3.2	14.7	20.6
Yemen (1983)	1–2	1.6	1.0	1.0

Energy consumption in rural areas and in peri-urban households

The consumption of fuelwood is dominant in poorer families. About 43.5 per cent of the poorer families (up to 2.5WU) are in the rural area where access to fuelwood is easy. Even among families with higher incomes in rural areas, the consumption of fuelwood is considerable.

In more urbanized regions, poorer populations living in slums obtain their energy differently. In general, they resort to clandestine connections to electricity, exposing whole communities to the risk of fires (that frequently occur). They also use some fuelwood (whenever possible) or collected wood waste (from demolition, for example, which is dangerous both for the risk of fires and for the contamination by toxic gases from paints and varnishes). Other fuels used are LPG and kerosene, prime choices for the replacement of fuelwood. It is thus of paramount importance that energy supply to this vast parcel of the population be accessible in terms of cost.

Figure 3.4 shows the weight of energy in the cost of living of a Brazilian family as a function of income units. Those who get less than 1WU cannot afford to buy electricity besides food. This is the reason for the high rate of clandestine connections to the energy grid (Table 3.6).

Table 3.6 Major lighting sources in Brazilian households (Néri, 2001)

		Electric	Diesel or gasoline generator	Gas lamp	Candle or oil lamp	Dwellings (×1000)
Total		92.26	0.07	7.29	0.37	26,799
Per income	20% poorest	77.99	0.01	21.27	0.74	6435
	20% richest	99.27	0.00	0.64	0.10	5090
Per region	Rural Southeast	81.83	0.67	16.47	1.03	1630
	Urban Southeast	99.25	0.00	0.75	0.00	7524
	Sao Paulo Metropolitan Region	99.80	0.00	0.00	0.20	4284
	Fortaleza Metropolitan Region	96.82	0.14	3.04	0.00	598
	Rural Northeast	53.54	0.00	44.67	1.79	3353
	Urban Northeast	97.99	0.00	1.81	0.19	4485

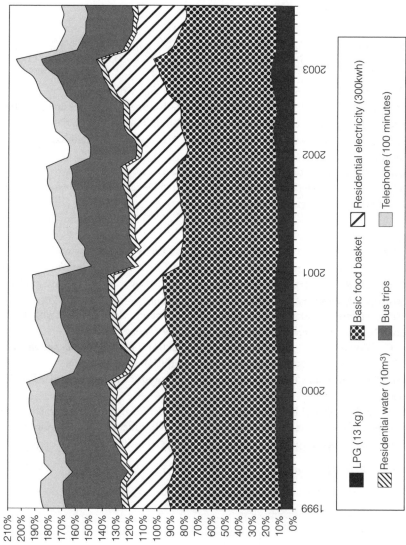

Figure 3.4 Cost of the major inputs in percentual function of the wage unit in Brazil between 1999 and 2003 (Lucon et al, 2004)

Note

1   At the time of the research, a WU was US$50. Although the last data available are from 1988, the research outcomes are still very representative.

References

Almeida, E. and Oliveira, A. (1995) 'Brazilian Life Style and Energy Consumption', in *Energy Demand, Life Style Changes and Technology Development*. World Energy Council, London

Cook, E. (1976) *Man, Energy, Society*. W. H. Freeman, San Francisco

Foley, G. (2000) 'The Economics of Fuelwood Substitutes. An Assessment of the Impact on Domestic Fuelwood Demand of Replacing Fuelwood with Conventional Fuels', *Food And Agriculture Organization*. UN, www.fao.org/docrep/r6560e/r6560e03.htm

Fundación Bariloche (1977) *Catástrofe o nueva sociedad? Modelo Mundial Latinoamericano*. Fundación Bariloche, International Development Research Centre, IDRC, Ottawa, 064s, www.fundacionbariloche.org.ar

Haffner, E. (1979) *Optimum Power Requirement of Civilized Humans*. Hampshire College, Amherst, Mass., EUA

IEA (2006) *Key World Energy Statistics*. International Energy Agency, www.iea.org

IEA (2008) Worldwide Trends in Energy Use and Efficiency, *Key Insights from IEA Indicator Analysis*. International Energy Agency, www.iea.org/Textbase/publications/free_new_Desc.asp?PUBS_ID=2026

Krugmann, H. and Goldemberg, J. (1983) 'The Energy Cost of Satisfying Basic Human Needs', *Technological Forecasting and Social Change*, 24, 45–60

Lucon, O., Coelho, S. T. and Goldemberg, J. (2004) *LPG in Brazil: Lessons and Challenges*. Energy for Sustainable Development (VIII) 3, 82–90

Néri, M. (2001) *Lampião, 'Gatos' & Robin Hood*, Conjuntura Econômica, IBRE/FGV 60, 60

UNDP, UNDESA, World Energy Council (2002) *World Energy Assessment: Energy and the Challenge of Sustainability*, www.energyandenvironment.undp.org/undp/index.cfm?module=Library&page=Document&DocumentID=5037

Chapter 4

Energy Sources

One million years ago the human population was probably less than half a million individuals, easily allowing nature to supply its needs in energy and food. When scarceness threatened, populations moved to other regions and, generally speaking, there was no concern about *environment support capacity*, that is, the natural conditions for resources regeneration.

Nonetheless, the intensive use of wood for buildings, ships, military purposes and heat generation led to the destruction of forests in several environmentally sensitive regions on the planet, especially islands and mountains. This is what occurred on Easter Island in the pre-Columbian period, and in ancient Greece and Rome. By the late Middle Ages a large proportion of the European forests had been cut down. With the growing consumption of energy, new sources of *primary energy* besides fuelwood were explored, such as the hydraulic potential of rivers, coal for heating and generating steam, oil and its byproducts to power internal combustion engines, and uranium for generating thermonuclear power.

Classification of the sources of energy

Primary sources of energy are usually classified as *commercial* (or *marketed*, when they are the object of monetary transactions, as is the case of coal, oil and natural gas) and *non-commercial* (freely obtained, such as sunlight). With an oil barrel cost of US$50 and the present world energy matrix, the energy-related direct monetary transactions in the world are of about US$1 trillion dollars (UK£billion) annually.

Primary energy is subjected to transformations, generating *secondary energy*, which is the form consumed by human beings to meet their needs:

- *electricity* generated from power plants, either hydro (moved by hydraulic energy), thermoelectric (moved by fossil fuels, geothermal heat, biomass or nuclear fission), or from wind farms and photovoltaic panels;
- *oil products* (such as diesel oil, fuel oil, gasoline, kerosene and liquefied petroleum gas);

- *'modern' biomass* (such as the biogas from landfills and biofuels);
- process *heat* and from district heating, obtained by combustion in boilers.

A primary source of energy may be considered *renewable* when natural conditions allow its replacement in a short time span. Renewable sources are basically:

- *solar* (radiation emitted by the Sun);
- *tidal* (tide variations due to the gravitational power of the Moon–Earth–Sun system) and *marine currents* (generated by difference in temperature in the oceans);
- geothermal (originating from inside the Earth);
- potential hydraulic energy (concentrated in waterfalls or by the force of rivers);
- wind energy (winds, generated by differences in pressure); and
- *biomass* (fuelwood, charcoal, organic waste, agricultural products).

Non-renewable sources of energy are those which nature is unable to replace in a time span compatible with its consumption by human beings. Non-renewable are:

- coal;
- oil;
- natural gas;
- other fossil fuels (such as peat); and
- uranium (for the production of nuclear power).

This classification may be considered simplistic, as it does not separate the theoretical aspects of *renewability* with the practical reality of *environmental sustainability*. Some examples are:

- there is a lot of fuelwood obtained from deforestation, conducted at such an accelerated rate that the environment is unable to replace it; this is the typical case of Haiti, with overpopulated regions;
- some hydropower plants (which produce power from hydraulic potentials) flooded huge areas, destroying forests and other important ecosystems; furthermore, the hauling and accumulation of soil sediments shorten the service life of these plants;
- nuclear power advocates argue that the option should also be considered renewable, as it consumes small amounts of fuel to generate large amounts of power. This is not true as there are stages in the nuclear power life cycle (mining and uranium enrichment, waste storage and

plant decommissioning, for example) that impact considerably and require significant amounts of energy.

The physical reality cannot contradict the laws of thermodynamics: every energy process has losses, altering the previous situation and consequently impacting on the environment. Nevertheless, it is unproductive to stick to the semantics of the word 'sustainable'. Objective criteria are necessary to agree on what is a renewable source and what is not. A way of classifying energy balance items is shown in Table 4.1.

By following this convention and by applying it to the International Energy Agency data, it is possible to represent the world energy matrix in Figure 4.1.

The definition allows better understanding of the environmental limits and impacts deriving from an energy system *lifecycle* (Figure 4.2), that is, the stages that comprise its production, consumption and post-consumption.

Table 4.1 Classification of energy sources

Sources		Primary energy	Secondary energy
Non-renewable	Fossil	coal oil and oil products natural gas	thermopower, heat, transportation fuel
	Nuclear	fissile materials	thermopower, heat
Renewable	'traditional'	primitive biomass: deforestation fuelwood	heat
	'conventional'	mid-sized and large hydraulic potential	hydropower
	'modern' (or 'new')	small hydraulic potential	
		'modern' biomass: reforested fuelwood, energy crops (sugar cane, vegetal oils)	biofuels (ethanol, biodiesel), bagasse thermopower, heat
		others solar power	heat, photovoltaic power
		geothermal wind tidal and wave	heat and electricity electricity

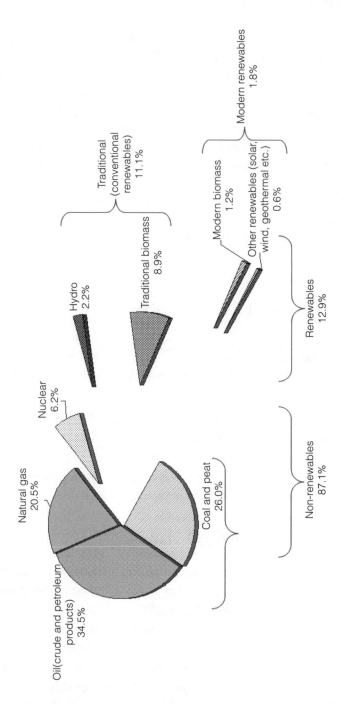

World total primary energy supply (2006): 11,740 Mtoe

Figure 4.1 World energy by primary sources, 2006 (IEA, 2008b)

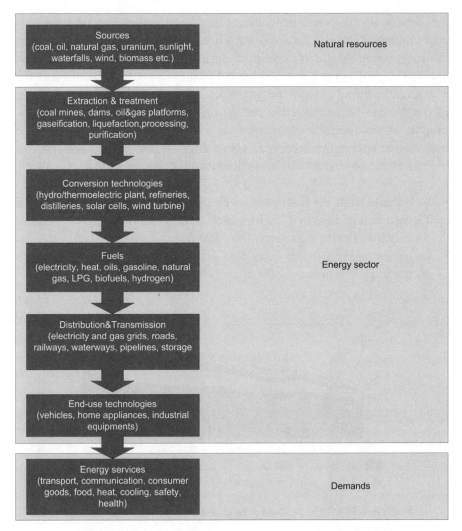

Figure 4.2 Lifecycle of an energy system (IAEA, 2006)

Energy balances

Energy balances are important tools for analysing the situation of a given region (such as a country) at a given period (usually a year). Table 4.2 shows, as an example, the world energy balance conducted by the International Energy Agency (IEA, 2006a). The major *sources of primary energy* (coal, oil, natural gas, nuclear, hydraulic, renewable fuels and bio-mass waste, other renewable 'modern' sources such as geothermal and solar) and *secondary energy* (electricity and heat) form the column headings. The first column shows shares of the *total primary energy supply* (produc-tion minus exports plus imports plus positive variation of stocks); later their *transformations* (in power generation plants, heat generation, oil refineries, coal processing, losses) for obtaining *secondary energy* or *fuel consumption* in the main *sectors* (industry, transport, agriculture, commerce and services, residential), the latter being subdivided into *energy use and non-energy use* (for manufacturing plastics, for example). Moreover, the balance provides electricity and heat production per source. Balances are similar to photographs which, periodically compared (year after year), illustrate the evolution in energy production and consumption (Figures 4.3 and 4.4).

Energy balances data can be obtained from different sources, such as:

- world data from the International Energy Agency (IEA, 2008), the US Department of Energy (US EIA-DoE, 2008) and from private companies such as British Petroleum (BP, 2008);
- countries (and in many cases also sub-national regions) also publish their energy balances periodically.

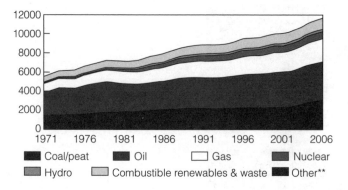

Figure 4.3 World primary energy supply by source (IEA, 2008b)

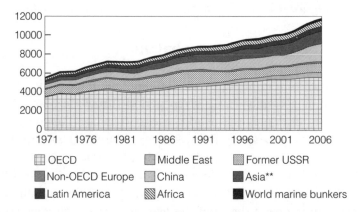

Figure 4.4 Total fuel (secondary energy) consumption by region (IEA, 2008b)

Table 4.2 World energy matrix in 2006 (IEA, 2008a)

		Coal and peat	Crude oil and oil products	Natural gas	Nuclear	Hydraulic	Geo-thermal, solar, etc.	Com-bustible renewables and wastes	Electricity	Heat	Total
Total Supply of Primary Energy – TPES (Mtoe)	production (+) imports (–) exports (+) stock changes	3053.54	4028.66	2407.82	728.42	261.14	66.25	1184.91	– 0.65	9.88	11,739.96
Transformations, own use losses (Mtoe)	(–) transfers (+) statistical differences (+) electricity plants (+) combined heat and power plants (+) heat plants (+) gas works (+) petroleum refineries (+) coal transformation (+) liquefaction plants (+) other transformation (+) own use (+) distribution losses	–2355.30	–547.29	–1174.38	–728.42	–261.14	–55.01	–144.79	1346.07	263.42	–8084.44

Table 4.2 continued

	Coal and peat	Crude oil and oil products	Natural gas	Nuclear	Hydraulic	Geo-thermal, solar etc.	Com-bustible renewables and wastes	Electricity	Heat	Total
(=) Total Fuel Consumption – TFC (Mtoe)	550.57	329.54	434.28			0.42	187.83	560.17	117.64	2180.46
industry sector (iron and steel, chemical and petro-chemical, non-ferrous metals, non-metallic minerals, transport equipment, machinery, mining and quarrying, food and tobacco, paper pulp and printing, wood and wood products, construction, textile and leather, non-specified industrial uses)										

transportation sector (international aviation, domestic aviation, road, rail, pipeline transport, domestic navigation, world marine bunkers, non-specified)	3.78	2104.86	71.28				23.71	22.80		2226.43
other sectors (residential, commercial and public services, agriculture and forestry, fishing, non-specified)	114.21	471.71	592.90			10.81	828.57	763.75	155.66	2937.62
non-energy use (industry and transformation, transport, other sectors)	29.69	575.27	134.99				0.53			739.94
Electricity generated (GWh) electricity plants	7148666	981486	2724024	2766367	3036471	194158	130147		1310	16982629
CHP plants		114561	1082869	26663		8032	109234		481	1947811
Heat (TJ) electricity plants		438821	3423306	22399		9524	320968	1459	125999	6339750
CHP plants	4235929	513508	3281187			15663	250248	5760	542623	7577451

Just like accounting balances (indispensable tools for managing companies), energy balances are fundamental for energy planning, since they allow analysing aspects such as:

- retrospective and prospective behaviours (future trends);
- share of each fuel (e.g. oil) or group of energies (renewables) in the matrix;
- self-sufficiency in energy, foreign dependence and foreign trade (production, imports and exports);
- efficiency in processes for transforming primary energy into secondary;
- distribution of final energy consumption per end-use sector (industry, transport, residences, commerce and services, etc.).

Energy production and consumption can also be linked to other indicators and factors, allowing the calculation of:

- energy intensities (dividing energy consumption by economic production and/or population);
- bulk emissions of greenhouse gases and other pollutants (multiplying energy consumption by emission factors);
- the technological profile of the power generation plants from the distribution in the region, by type (hydropower, thermonuclear, gas thermopower, wind) and size (below 30MW of installed capacity).

Analyses of energy matrixes allow more detailed discussions of the problem, examples of which are:

- the 'combustible renewables and waste' category refers to biomass, a very broad definition encompassing both traditional and modern sources; however, in the transportation sector (basically by road) it means biofuels (bioethanol and biodiesel), which are modern sources of renewable energy;
- biomass consumption in the residential sector in less developed countries is predominantly fuelwood (collected[1] or deforested) and, in some cases, such as China, animal wastes (dung, dry manure, gas from domestic biodigestors); in turn, in more developed countries, such as Finland, energy consumption from residential biomass derives predominantly from replanted fuelwood;
- some industrial categories are very *energy-intensive* (i.e. consume large amounts of energy per unit of product output); that is, in the case of the steel industry (iron and steel sector); aluminium (non-ferrous metals) and mining.

Energy balances do not always present disaggregated data. Even so, it is possible to notice some intrinsic characteristics in certain countries. For example, Central African and Caribbean countries very much depend on fuelwood (an energy source still obtained at almost zero-cost) for residential consumption, and on oil product imports for transportation and power generation.

An energy matrix thus shows the production structure and consumption of a region at a given period. To fully understand it, it is necessary to analyse the relation between energy *resources and supply.*

Energy resources and reserves

Energy used by man originates from four different sources:

1. radiant energy emitted by the Sun (with a power of $174,000.10^{12}$W), which originated fossil fuels, biomass, winds and hydraulic potentials;
2. gravitational energy resulting from the interactions of the Earth with the Moon and with the Sun (power of 3.10^{12}W);
3. geothermal power originated inside the planet (32.10^{12}W); and
4. nuclear power (the resources of which are abundant yet exhaustible[1]).

However, little of this energy is effectively usable. For example, from all the solar power inciding on living matter, only 40.10^{12}W are fixed by photosynthesis. Part of the resources are the *reserves*, determined or estimated amounts for natural energy deposits at a given place, based on prospection (geological, hydrological, wind regime) and engineering data, available with current extraction and production technologies, as well as costs. Reserves can be:

- *proved* (also called 1P), which can be economically exploited with reasonable certainty (about 90 per cent);
- *probable* (including the proved ones and thus called 2P): exploited with a 50 per cent probability, with current commercial technologies or at an advanced stage of pre-commercial development; and
- *possible* (including the proved and probable ones, 3P): reserves that have about 10 per cent probability of exploitation, under favourable circumstances.

The exact definition of proved reserves varies from country to country and from company to company exploiting the resources, since the announcement of a new discovery (or speculation on it) may have a strong

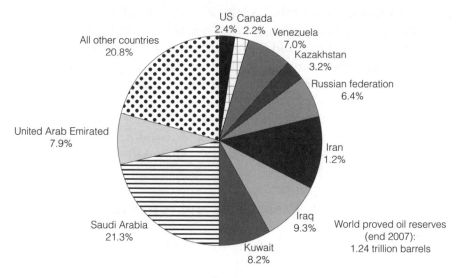

Figure 4.5 World proved oil reserves in billions of barrels, end of 2007
(BP, 2008)

repercussion on stock prices, strategic and geopolitical position. For this reason, many countries do not announce their reserves in detail, and there is a great international effort to standardize definitions and to provide proper information about the discoveries. Oil is an extremely versatile, easily transported and stored fuel, the most important and strategic energy source on the planet. Nevertheless, most oil reserves are concentrated in just a few countries.

Of the estimated two trillion (UK billion) oil barrel reserves the planet originally had, between 45 and 70 per cent have been exploited so far. From 1965 to 2005, 0.92 trillion (UK billion) oil barrels were produced. About 1.2 trillion barrels remain to be exploited, and this stock is likely to be exhausted in about 50 years.

Expressed in remaining years, the ratio Reserves/Production (R/P) defines the remaining proved reserves static at the end of a given year, the value of which is divided by the production (exploitation) in that same year, also considered constant in the future. Table 4.3 presents the R/P ratio of the largest oil, natural gas and coal reserves in the world.

Since security in energy supply is a vital aspect in a country's geopolitics, internal reserves strongly determine its position in both international trade and environment negotiations. The Organization of the Petroleum Exporting Countries (OPEC) was created in the 1970s to obtain better international prices for its member countries. The Middle East is the largest producer and a region of vital strategic importance. Many countries rely on large and unexplored coal reserves, enough for two or three centuries, but

Table 4.3 Proved reserves in some countries and regions in late-2007 (BP, 2008)

	Oil			Natural gas			Coal		
	Billion or 1000 million barrels (= 0.1364Gtoe)	% total	R/P ratio	Trillion cubic metres (=0.9Gtoe)	% total	R/P ratio	Mt (= 0.68Mtoe)	% total	R/P ratio
US	29.4	2.4	11.7	5.98	3.4	10.9	242,721	28.6	234
Canada	27.7	2.2	22.9	1.63	0.9	8.9	6578	0.8	95
Mexico	12.2	1.0	9.6	0.37	0.2	8.0	1211	0.1	99
Total North America	69.3	5.6	13.9	7.98	4.5	10.3	250,510	29.6	224
Brazil	12.6	1.0	18.9	0.36	0.2	32.3	7068	0.8	*
Venezuela	87.0	7.0	91.3	5.15	2.9	*	479	0.1	60
Total S. & Cent. America	111.2	9.0	45.9	7.73	4.4	51.2	16,276	1.9	188
Kazakhstan	39.8	3.2	73.2	1.90	1.1	69.8	31,300	3.7	332
Norway	8.2	0.7	8.8	2.96	1.7	33.0			
Russian Federation	79.4	6.4	21.8	44.65	25.2	73.5	157,010	18.5	500
UK	3.6	0.3	6.0	0.41	0.2	5.7	155	♦	9
Total Europe & Eurasia	143.7	11.6	22.1	59.41	33.5	55.2	272,246	32.1	224
Iran	138.4	11.2	86.2	27.80	15.7	*			

Table 4.3 continued

	Oil			Natural gas			Coal		
	Billion or 1000 million barrels (= 0.1364Gtoe)	% total	R/P ratio	Trillion cubic metres (=0.9Gtoe)	% total	R/P ratio	Mt (= 0.68 Mtoe)	% total	R/P ratio
Iraq	115.0	9.3	*	3.17	1.8	*			
Kuwait	101.5	8.2	*	1.78	1.0	*			
Oman	5.6	0.5	21.3	0.69	0.4	28.6			
Qatar	27.4	2.2	62.8	25.60	14.4	*			
Saudi Arabia	264.2	21.3	69.5	7.17	4.0	94.4			
Syria	2.5	0.2	17.4	0.29	0.2	54.7			
United Arab Emirates	97.8	7.9	91.9	6.09	3.4	*			
Yemen	2.8	0.2	22.7	0.49	0.3	–			
Total Middle East	755.3	61.0	82.2	73.21	41.3	*	1386	0.2	*
Algeria	12.3	1.0	16.8	4.52	2.5	54.4			
Libya	41.5	3.3	61.5	1.50	0.8	98.4			
Nigeria	36.2	2.9	42.1	5.30	3.0	*			
South Africa							48,000	5.7	178
Total Africa	117.5	9.5	31.2	14.58	8.2	76.6	50,991	5.8	186
Australia	4.2	0.3	20.3	2.51	1.4	62.8	76,600	9.0	194

China	15.5	1.3	11.3	1.88	1.1	27.2	114,500	13.5	45
India	5.5	0.4	18.7	1.06	0.6	35.0	56,498	6.7	118
Indonesia	4.4	0.4	12.4	3.00	1.7	45.0	4328	0.5	25
Malaysia	5.4	0.4	19.4	2.48	1.4	40.9			
Total Asia Pacific	40.8	3.3	14.2	14.46	8.2	36.9	257,465	30.4	70
TOTAL WORLD	1237.9	100.0	41.6	177.36	100.0	60.3	847,488	100.0	133
of which:									
European Union	6.8	0.5	7.8	2.84	1.6	14.8	29,570	3.5	50
OECD	88.3	7.1	12.6	15.77	8.9	14.4	356,910	42.1	168
Former Soviet Union	128.1	10.4	27.4	53.53	30.2	67.7	225,995	26.7	463
Canadian Oil Sands	152.2								
Proved reserves and oil sands	1390.1								

which generate high pollution levels. The R/P ratio of oil is far smaller, sufficient only for a few decades, making many countries prospect and develop other energy options.

The *United States Geological Survey* estimates that the total oil reserves are about three times the number of the known ones, yet a large part of this potential may remain unexplorable until 2050 (USGS, 2007). Some reserves not considered are bitumen and energy recycling of tyres and plastic, besides the environmental treaty-protected reserves in the Antarctic continent. Reserves previously not considered as such became viable, due to the positive investment returns from the high oil prices, as well as geopolitical security reasons.[2]

Table 4.4 estimates the world energy potential ('reserves'), from renewable and non-renewable sources.

Energy consumption per inhabitant

The world annual average consumption of energy per capita in 2004 was 1.77 tons of oil equivalent (toe or $1.77 . 10^7$kcal). There is, however, a huge difference (of more than a factor of ten) between the energy consumption per capita of industrialized countries – where 18.3 per cent of the world population live – and developing countries – where the remaining 81.7 per cent live. The US alone, with 4.6 per cent of the world population, consumes 20.7 per cent of all the energy produced in the planet. While Bangladesh consumed 0.16 toe per inhabitant, Iceland consumed 11.9 toe per inhabitant (IEA, 2008c).

The annual consumption per capita in 2003 was 4.73 toe in the OECD industrialized countries and only 0.91 toe in developing countries (non-OECD), including non-commercial energy sources (IEA, 2008c). Table 4.5 presents the differences in energy consumption and in their growth.

Table 4.6 shows the shares of the primary energy sources used in industrialized countries and developing countries.

This table shows relevant aspects in the regional energy matrixes, such as the strong dependence on oil, the significant share of natural gas in power generation in the developed countries, nuclear power in Europe, the relatively small share of biomass in total consumption of industrialized countries, as compared to the developing ones (especially Africa), and, finally, the fact that the development of 'new renewable' technologies is incipient but is already present in the rich countries' matrixes.

Table 4.4 World energy potential, 2001 (UNDP, UNDESA, WEC, 2004)

Source	Primary energy (10¹⁸J)	Primary energy (10⁹ toe)	Total %	Proved reserves (10⁹ toe)	Static reserves/ production ratio (year)	Resources/ production ratio (year)	Dynamic resources/ production ratio (year)
Fossil fuels	332	7.93	79.4	778			
Oil	147	3.51	35.1	143	41	~200	125
Natural gas	91	2.16	21.7	138	64	~400	210
Coal	94	2.26	22.6	566	251	~700	360
Renewables	57	1.37	13.7		Renewable		
Hydro	9	0.23	2.3				
Traditional biomass	39	0.93	9.3				
'Modern' renewables	9	0.21	2.2				
Nuclear	29	0.69	6.9	55	82f	~300 10,000+	
Total	418	9.99	100.0				

Table 4.5 Primary energy supply by region, growth rate and energy per capita, 2006 (IEA, 2008)

	Primary energy (Mtoe)	*Annual growth 1971–2006*	*Population (million)*	*Consumption (toe per capita)*
OECD	5537	1.4%	1154.5	4.80
Non-OECD	6020	3.1%	5113.4	1.18
Middle East	523	6.8%	177	2.95
Former USSR	1017	0.7%	286.1	3.55
East Europe non-OECD	108	0.6%	54.7	1.97
China	1897	4.6%	1295.2	1.46
Asia, other non-OECD	1330	3.9%	2017.7	0.66
Latin America and the Caribbean	531	2.8%	431.6	1.23
Africa	614	3.3%	851	0.72
World	11,740	2.2%	6267.9	1.87

Notes

1   Uranium can be found in the whole of the Earth's crust; high-degree ores (2 per cent or 20,000ppmU) are used for energy production. Considering all the conventional reserves, there would be 10 million tons (Mt) of uranium to exploit which, with the present use (665,000 tU/year), would be possible for about 150 years with 370GWe of power produced. Nearly 5.47Mt U reserves were known and considered recoverable in 2007 (WNA, 2008).

2   That is the case, for example, of the tar sands of Western Canada, the world's second largest oil reserve. However, the exploitation of these sands requires a lot of energy besides causing great local and global environmental impacts, such as large deforested areas, exposed mines, acidification and greenhouse gases. Canada exploits oil contained in these sands and sells energy to the US. Therefore, although having ratified the Kyoto Protocol, its greenhouse gas emissions increased by about 25 per cent between 1990 and 2005. In turn, the US seeks new boundaries for exploring hydrocarbons (oil and natural gas) in the remote regions of Alaska, also with high environmental costs.

Table 4.6 Primary energy total, by source and region in 2006 (IEA, 2008a, b)

2006	Total primary energy		Non-renewable					Renewables			
	Gtoe	%	Total	Coal and peat	Crude oil and petroleum products	Natural gas	Nuclear	Total	Hydro	New renewables (geothermal solar, etc.)	Biomass (traditional and modern)
World	11.73	100.0	87.1%	26.0%	34.3%	20.5%	6.2%	12.9%	2.2%	0.6%	10.1%
OECD	5.54	47.2	93.4%	20.6%	39.9%	21.9%	11.1%	6.6%	2.0%	0.8%	3.8%
North America OECD	2.77	23.6	93.6%	21.2%	40.9%	22.7%	8.7%	6.4%	2.1%	0.7%	3.6%
Pacific OECD	0.88	7.5	96.3%	25.0%	43.0%	15.0%	13.3%	3.7%	1.2%	0.7%	1.8%
Europe OECD	1.88	16.1	91.8%	17.5%	37.0%	23.8%	13.5%	8.2%	2.2%	0.9%	5.0%
Non-OECD	5.19	44.2	78.7%	28.5%	27.8%	20.4%	2.1%	21.3%	2.3%	0.4%	18.6%
Africa	0.60	5.1	51.4%	16.9%	21.7%	12.3%	0.5%	48.6%	1.3%	0.2%	47.2%
Latin America and the Caribbean	0.51	4.3	69.8%	4.4%	44.7%	19.8%	0.9%	30.2%	10.6%	0.4%	19.2%
Asia (exc. China) non-OECD	1.29	11.0	71.6%	25.5%	31.1%	13.9%	1.2%	28.4%	1.5%	1.2%	25.8%
China	1.90	16.2	85.9%	64.0%	18.6%	2.6%	0.8%	14.1%	2.0%	0.2%	11.9%
Europe non-OECD	0.11	0.9	89.1%	28.8%	31.6%	21.3%	7.5%	10.9%	4.8%	0.1%	5.9%
Former USSR	1.01	8.6	96.6%	18.1%	19.7%	52.1%	6.7%	3.4%	2.1%	0.0%	1.3%
Middle East	0.50	4.3	99.2%	1.8%	54.9%	42.5%	0.0%	0.8%	0.4%	0.2%	0.2%

References

BP (2008) Statistical Review of World Energy, 2008. British Petroleum, www.bp.com

IAEA (2006) *Brazil: A Country Profile for Sustainable Development*. International Atomic Energy Agency, Vienna

IEA (2008a) *Energy Balances of OECD Countries*. International Energy Agency, Paris

IEA (2008b) *Energy Balances of non-OECD Countries*. International Energy Agency, Paris

IEA (2008c) Key World Energy Statistics 2008. International Energy Agency, Paris

Hubbert, M. K. (1971) 'The Energy Resources of the Earth', *Scientific American*, 60, 224

UNDP, UNDESA, WEC (2004) World Energy Assessment 2004 Update, www.undp.org/energy/weaover2004.htm

US EIA-DoE (2008) Energy Information Administration, www.eia.doe.gov

USGS (2007) United States Geological Society, www.usgs.gov

WNA (2008) Supply of Uranium (June 2008). World Nuclear Association, www.world-nuclear.org/info/inf75.html

Chapter 5

Energy and Development

The search for solutions for energy problems requires an understanding of what are the existing alternatives and choosing the best one. These choices may affect the local consumption patterns and the life quality of populations.

Development has different focuses: economic, social and environmental are probably the most important. Although there is an apparent direct relationship between economic development and energy consumption, these parameters are not indissolubly linked. This is a very important fact because it shows that there are alternative development paths for society without a corresponding increase in energy consumption. In other words, it is possible to *decouple* economic growth from consumption. The evidence is both historical and by making comparisons between developed and developing countries.

The best historical evidence available refers to the UK and the US during their initial stages of industrialization, when energy consumption rose faster than economic income. Then the situation changed: the mechanization in agriculture, the increased use of the automobile and the rationalization of industrial activities allowed these nations to grow more quickly with less energy. The same has happened to developing countries, due to the so-called saturation effects (Box 5.1).

Box 5.1 Reduction in energy intensity: saturation effects

After the 1970s, the industrialized countries reduced part of their demand for fossil fuels through the 'saturation effects' in the consumption of certain goods. For some of these countries, long-term data are available, allowing the construction of curves for the historical evolution of energy intensity over more than a century. The result is well known: there has been an increase in energy intensity as the infrastructure and heavy industry developed, reaching a peak followed by a progressive decrease. The latecomers in the industrialization process, such as Japan, reached a peak of energy intensity smaller than that of their predecessors, indicating a previous adoption of industrial processes and innovative and more energy-efficient modern technologies (Figure 5.1).

For developing countries, there are data available only for the last decades. There are two methodological problems limiting its usefulness:

(a) the contribution of energy outside commercial transactions (e.g. in households) is very significant in several countries and statistics are not accurate; the end-use efficiency of non-commercial sources is usually smaller than that of commercial sources, leading to overestimated energy intensity data; and
(b) the calculation of the GDP using official conversion rates of the American dollar or its purchasing parity power (PPP) can make a considerable difference, of as much as four times.

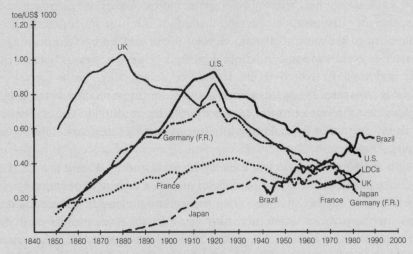

Figure 5.1 Long-term historical evolution of industrialized countries' energy intensity (Martin, 1988)

A study (Mielnik and Goldemberg, 2000) on the evolution of the energy intensities for 41 (18 developed and 23 developing) countries in the period 1971–94, utilizing GDP-PPP and adding the commercial primary energy to the non-commercial energy, indicated that:

- energy intensity in most of the industrialized countries is decreasing;
- energy intensity in developing countries is increasing and is usually smaller than that in industrialized countries; and
- the grouping around an average value became more marked along time, indicating that the energy systems have common important aspects in global terms. This is not very surprising for industrialized countries, but for the developing ones it indicates that the modern sector is similar to those in industrialized nations, dominating economic activities and energy consumption.

Comparisons between developed and developing nations also allow important analyses on the way energy is consumed. In principle, more developed regions consume more power per capita. However, it is possible to identify different consumption profiles in the same group of countries, as in Figure 5.2. Later in this chapter some methods of assessing the economic development of nations and social classes are presented.

Gross Domestic Product (GDP) and National Accounting

The *Gross Domestic Product* (*GDP*) is the most widely used indicator to measure the performance of national economies.[1] In practice, the GDP is equivalent to the sum of the products of the quantities by values, of each respective good and service, within a given country (or region) over a one-year period (365 days).

GDP measures the performance of the economy in relation to the goods and services produced in the country, both the production factors owned by native citizens of the country and those owned by foreigners. This is particularly important concerning the management of a country's energy system and for this reason it is used as a base in energy statistics.

Since prices may increase (due to inflation) or decrease (deflation) from one period to another, it is necessary to establish a measure that neutralizes the temporal price variations and allows assessment of the evolution of production over time. Hence the *nominal GDP* (which uses the prices practised at the date of assessment, without taking the variation in prices into account) is differentiated from the *real GDP* (also called real-term GDP). The real GDP utilizes an index (referring to a given base-year) that neutralizes the fluctuation in prices practised in the subsequent years. Both notations should present a reference date that makes the analysis viable.

GDP deflator is the result of the division of the nominal GDP by the real GDP multiplied by 100. By using the GDP deflator, a historical series of nominal GDP (or current prices) can be transformed into a historical series of real GDP (or constant prices), and thus one obtains a more precise assessment of the evolution in the production of assets and services of an economy along the period observed. This way, the GDP evolution in the period 1995–2005 can be expressed in '2005 US$' or in 'constant US$'.

In order to compare the products of different countries and regions a common monetary unit is used, as well as a currency exchange rate indexed to a reference date. In general, the indexers refer to the North-American (US dollars) or European (euro, EUR) currency and a 'full' date, such as the years 1995, 2000 and 2005.

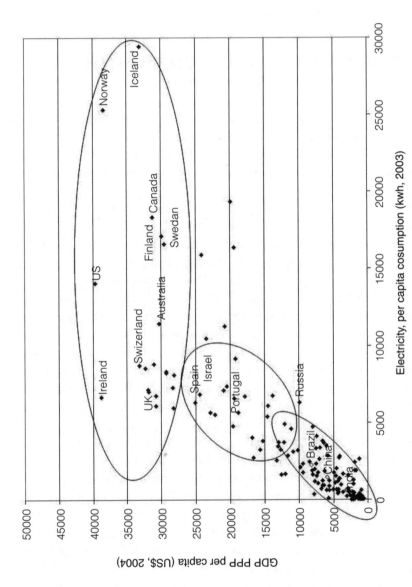

Figure 5.2 Power consumption (2003) and gross domestic product at the purchasing power parity, 2004 (data from IEA, 2006)

Divided by the population, the GDP per capita is obtained, representing how much each resident inhabitant produced and consumed in a given region and year.

Another conversion factor used is the Purchasing Power Parity – PPP. Since the cost of living is different from country to country, the PPP factor represents how much of the currency of a given country is necessary to buy locally what would be bought in a reference country in the same period. The most common index is the purchasing power of one US dollar. The use of the PPP allows converting the GDP of a country to the GDP per capita more adequately to the population reality. Table 5.1 shows the values of the GDP of some countries and regions in the year 2003, measured in (year 2000) US dollars.

As can be seen, the GDP with purchasing power parity reduces the gap between the products of poorer and wealthier regions. Also worth noting is

Table 5.1 Values of the Gross Domestic Product for 2003, both real and converted by the purchasing power parity, total and per capita, converted into US dollars of year 2000 (data from IEA, 2008)

Country or region	Real GDP (2000) US$ billion	GDP PPP (2000) US$ billion	Real GDP per capita (2000) US$	GDP PPP per capita (2000) US$
Africa	773	2207	825	2354
Latin America and the Caribbean	1796	3425	3947	7527
China	2315	8916	1756	6761
Non-OECD Asia excluding China	2139	7661	1009	3614
Non-OECD (Eastern) Europe	162	477	3028	8916
Former-USSR	568	2266	1997	7968
Middle East	838	1456	4427	7691
North America, OECD	12,775	13,313	2384	2485
Pacific, OECD	6303	5281	31,374	26,287
Europe, OECD	10,090	12,564	18,692	23,275
Developed countries (OECD) total	29,169	31,158	24,722	26,407
Developing countries (non-OECD) total	8591	26,407	1603	4928
World	37,759	57,565	5777	8807

that neither the transactions conducted in the so-called 'informal economy' nor domestic work (e.g. home cooking) are considered in the GDP, which only includes the production occurred in the period and does not account for sales of second-hand goods produced in previous periods.

National Accounting is the economic area that measures fundamental macroeconomic aggregates. One of the major macroeconomic aggregates is the *product*. The GDP, already discussed, refers to the gross domestic product. Another type of product is the Net National Income (NNI), which represents the monetary value that society can use. Between the GDP and the NNI, several events occur, such as the depreciation of goods, forwarding and receipt of foreign resources, payment of taxes to the government and subsidies received from it (Box 5.2).

Box 5.2 Quantifying Economic Aggregates

The most common approach to measuring and quantifying GDP is the expenditure method, defined by

$$[GDP = C + I + G + (X - Y)]$$

where:

- [C] is the consumption, or the final purchase of goods (durable and non-durable; physical products capable of being delivered to a purchaser and involves the transfer of ownership from seller to customer, e.g. commodities) and services (intangible products, such as consultancies, commissions or property rights);[1]
- [I] stands for gross investment, or the choice by the individual to risk his savings with the hope of gain, either a material (e.g. equipment, real estate properties) or financial assets (such as money that is put into a bank or the market);
- [G] is the government spending (government expenditure) for consumption (purchases of goods and services for current use, purchases of goods and services intended to create future benefits, such as infrastructure investment or research spending) or transfer payments (such as social security payments, pensions, healthcare, defence, education, interests);
- [(X − Y)] is the net balance of trade, that is, exports [X] minus imports [Y] of any good (e.g. a commodity) or service, legitimately commercially moved from one country to another; there are two basic types of exports/imports: industrial/consumer goods and intermediate goods and services.

Gross and Net: 'gross' means depreciation (loss in value) of capital stock (i.e. an existing number of items of extensive value at that point in time, which may have been accumulated in the past, such as the energy generation infrastructure) is not taken into consideration. Depreciation can be understood as the loss in value of an asset due to usage, passage of time, wear and tear, technological outdating or obsolescence, depletion or other such factors.

Net (National/Domestic) Product is thus the Gross (National/Domestic) Product minus Depreciation (D), respectively:

$$[NNP = GNP - D] \text{ and } [NDP = GDP - D].$$

National and Domestic: as seen, the Domestic (or Internal) Product is the monetary value of the final goods and services produced (also by foreign companies) within a country's borders in a given period. In turn, the National Product (NP) is the monetary value of the production conducted exclusively by national production factors (resident), these being or not within the geographic limits of the country (i.e. including national companies abroad). The NP comprises the domestic (internal) product, plus income earned by its citizens abroad (ICA, or net contribution of the production factors of non-residents to the product), minus income earned by foreigners (IEF, or the net contribution of the production factors of residents to the rest of the world product) in the country. Thus,

$$NP = DP + (ICA - IEF).$$

For gross products,

$$GNP = GDP + (ICA - IEF)$$

and for net production,

$$NNP = NDP + (ICA - IEF).$$

A product at factor costs (fc) is the necessary product price to pay for the production factors; that is, price without government interferences (taxes and subsidies, $[T]$ and $[S]$ respectively) that compose the final market prices (mp). Thus,

$$[GDPfc = GDPmp - T + S], \text{ similarly to } [GNPfc], [NDPfc] \text{ or } [NNPfc].$$

The Net National Income (NNI) is the total monetary value available to society, encompassing the income of households, businesses and the government. It is defined as the Net National Product (NNP) at factor costs (i.e. minus indirect taxes plus subsidies from the government).

The development of a given country is influenced by all these factors. For example:

- the government may opt for subsidizing strategic economic sectors, both for obtaining greater competitiveness, aggregating value to its exports and for protecting local producers;
- taxation (taxes, tariffs, contributions) increases the price of goods, transferring income from society to the government;
- capital goods and infrastructure undergo depreciation, losing value over time;
- part of the revenue of a country is sent abroad by multinational companies, investors and residents.

As mentioned, GDP is the total goods and services produced by the residents (inhabitants, producing units, etc.) and, therefore, is the sum of the values added by the different sectors plus taxes, net subsidies, to the products not included in the production value. On the other hand, the gross domestic product is equal to the sum of the final goods and service consumptions at market prices, also equal to the primary revenues. The inputs used in productive activity are work, land (e.g. raw materials and natural resources) and capital goods (such as installations and equipment). Capital goods undergo depreciations along time, which also have to be accounted. Thus the *Net Product* is defined: it is the Gross Product minus the depreciation of the capital stock. An example is energy generation, transmission and distribution infrastructure, which has a given service life and needs repair or replacement.

The government intervenes in the economy, either taxing (collecting taxes and other types of tributes) or stimulating (making subsidies and other types of subventions available). All these factors directly interfere in the final revenue available to the society in the country. While taxes take part of the revenues (transferring them to the state) from the private economy (family and entrepreneurial entities), *subsidies* provide private activities with resources from the National Treasury.

Direct taxes are those paid by the tax payer, as is the case of Income Tax; the *indirect* ones are passed on to the tax payer when goods and services are sold, as is the case of taxes on added value.

Subsidies are basically benefits granted by governments under two hypotheses:

- financial contribution by a government or public organism within the country; and
- any form of income or prices maintenance which directly or indirectly contributes to increasing exports or to reducing imports of any product.[2]

Subsidies directly affect the countries' relative competitiveness and are thus constant issues in international trade dispute resolution organisms, especially the World Trade Organization – WTO.

Indirect taxes and subsidies form the *market price* of the goods and services traded in the economy. If they are discounted, the production at factor costs is obtained, that is, the income that reverts to the families and to the private companies.

There are three possible ways to calculate the GDP, all of them leading to the same value:

- on the side of production – the gross domestic product is equal to the production value minus the intermediary consumption plus taxes, net subsidies, over products not included in the production value;
- on the side of demand – the gross domestic product is equal to the final consumption expenditure plus the gross formation of fixed capital plus the variation in stocks, plus the exports of goods and services minus their imports;
- on the side of income – the gross domestic product is equal to the remuneration of employees plus the total taxes, net subsidies, over production and import, plus the gross mixed revenue plus the gross operating surplus.

The *Gross National Product*, or GNP, is similar to the GDP, but it computes the production of national companies abroad and deduces the domestic production of the foreign ones. Thus, the GNP corresponds to the market value of the set of goods and services produced in a certain period using asset inputs of the national companies of the country, both if the goods and services have been produced in the country itself or in other countries. In the case of a multinational company, the revenues are considered as if they belonged to the country where the headquarters are and not where the wealth was generated (and where the resources have been used). What determines the GNP is that the inputs are owned by the citizens of that country.

Actually, there is little difference between the GNP and the GDP of a country when these are considered from a historical or global perspective. Although the GNP is more used in the literature concerning development, the GDP is more often employed in the statistics of the economic state of affairs. One of the reasons for this is that the GDP is closely aligned with other indicators, such as industrial production, employment, productivity and investment, and is thus a more adequate measure of the current economic activity.

When comparing the standards of living in different countries, the Gross National Product per capita (GNP/capita) is used, which results from the division, in a certain year, of the GNP by the population of a country. Until 1999 the GNP per capita was presented as a development indicator by the World Bank, which divided the countries into groups, as seen in Table 5.2. Some countries such as Israel, Kuwait, Singapore and the Arab Emirates are considered developing by the UN, yet their income is compatible with those of high GNP per capita.

The variation in product values in the different countries in the world is considerable and comparison is thus difficult. Countries with similar nominal income may present different incomes assessed by the purchasing power parity, that is, of access to goods and services (Figure 5.3). Taiwan, for example, has a lower nominal income than that of Kuwait, but higher purchasing power parity. Myanmar has a nominal income per capita close to that of the Congo, but a much higher standard of living if measured by the purchasing power parity.

Moreover, within a given country there may be wide gaps. Income per capita is an average that does not reflect the access of each resident in the country to inputs, masking the income distribution conditions among a country's population.

Table 5.2 Subdivision into income classes according to the World Bank (2007)

Income category	GNP per capita (1999) US$	Countries and regions
low	up to 765	nearly the whole of Saharan and Sub-Saharan Africa, India, Pakistan, Indonesia, Mongolia
middle-low	766–3035	Russia, China, Kazakhstan, Iran, Turkey, Romania, Thailand, Algeria, Egypt, Morocco, Namibia, Peru, Colombia, Paraguay, Bolivia, Ecuador, Cuba
middle-high	3036–9385	Brazil, Mexico, Colombia, Chile, Argentina, Uruguay, South Africa, Libya, Saudi Arabia, Poland, Hungary, Malaysia, the Philippines, South Korea
high	9386 or more	US, Canada, Western Europe, Australia, New Zealand, Japan

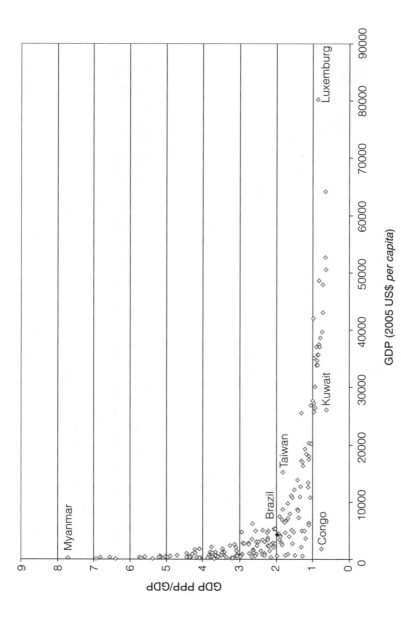

Figure 5.3 GDP per capita in the world, in 2005 nominal US dollars, and its relation with the GDP measured by the purchasing power parity – PPP (data from IMF, 2006)

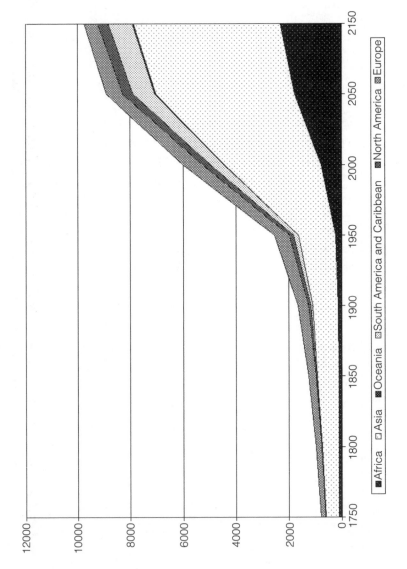

Figure 5.4 Projections for population growth (in billions) of developed and developing regions (WRI, 1998)

Economic growth

Promoting economic growth is the general aspiration of the great majority of developing countries' populations and the performance of their political leadership is judged by their success in managing it.

As the economic growth has to follow populational growth, great challenges are faced by governments: increasing employment, capacity building and education, reducing inequalities, expanding the infrastructure and public services, increasing the efficiency in exploiting natural resources and controlling pollution. Difficulties grow exponentially, as this is how population growth behaves, at a more accelerated rate in developing countries (Figure 5.4).

A very much used indicator to appraise the development of a country along time is product growth (Table 5.3).

In general, the world economy increased in the last 15 years, allowing greater gains for low-income countries. The developed countries had a smaller growth, but their total GDPs (and GNPs) are still high and allow maintaining of the social welfare state. Some economies emerged, as in the case of China (which developed its manufacturing industry) and India (which opted for the service sector). Russia has been recovering from the losses of the USSR crash, thanks to oil and natural gas exports.

Box 5.3 Exponential growth

Exponential growth is a particular case of increases that may well apply to populational, economic and energy data. It is therefore fundamental to know its application when analysing the relations between energy, environment and development. Some examples are a country's demographic growth, the increase in energy consumption at a given sector or the incidence of interests on investments. Exponential growth can be calculated by using the formula:

$$VF = VI \, (I + i)^n$$

where *VI* is the initial value, *VF* is the final value, *i* is the growth rate and *n* is the number of periods in question. The ratio $(I + i)^n$ can be calculated or found in financial mathematics tables.

For example, if the amount of $100.00 (= *VI*) is invested in an investment fund for two years (*n* = 2) at interests of 20 per cent annually (*i* = 0.2), at the end of the period, $104.04 (= *VF*) will be obtained.

Another calculation can be that of an increase in production or consumption of energy in a region over time. For example, the power

Table 5.3 Annual increase in the Gross Domestic Product by region (data from World Bank, 2007)

	GDP (billion 2000 US$)				Annual GDP increase		
	2006	2000	1990	1971	1971–90	1990–2000	2000–06
Africa	773	591	460	263	3.0%	2.5%	4.6%
Latin America and the Caribbean	1796	1474	1088	625	3.0%	3.1%	3.3%
China	2315	1367	553	133	7.8%	9.5%	9.2%
Non-OECD Asia excluding China	2139	1554	925	320	5.7%	5.3%	5.5%
Non-OECD (Eastern) Europe	162	123	124	64	3.5%	-0.1%	4.7%
Former USSR	568	377	577	404	1.9%	-4.2%	7.1%
Middle East	838	639	444	255	3.0%	3.7%	4.6%
North America, OECD	12,775	11,071	8011	4329	3.3%	3.3%	2.4%
Pacific, OECD	6303	5632	4727	2153	4.2%	1.8%	1.9%
Europe, OECD	10,090	8975	7172	4321	2.7%	2.3%	2.0%
Developed countries (OECD) total	29,169	25,677	19,910	10,802	3.3%	2.6%	2.1%
Developing countries (non-OECD) total	8591	6126	4171	2063	3.8%	3.9%	5.8%
World	37,759	31,802	24,081	12,865	3.4%	2.8%	2.9%

generation of 100TWh (= *VI*), growing 4 per cent annually (= *i*) in ten years (= *n*), will total 148TWh.

The growth formula may also be used to calculate the growth rate by using it as follows:

$$i = (VF/VI)^{(1/n)} - 1.$$

For example, the world energy consumption was 15,379TWh (= *VF*) in 2000 and 5247TWh (= *VI*) in 1971 (therefore, *n* = 2000 − 1971 = 29). The annual growth is $i = [(15,379/5247)^{(1/29)} - 1] = 0.0377 = 3.77$ per cent.

The time necessary to reach a given growth can also be determined by applying logarithms and rewriting the expression:

$$n = \ln (VF/VI) / \ln (i).$$

As an example, the time necessary for a given factor (such as gasoline consumption) to double (*VF* = 2 *VI*), assuming the projected growth of 1 per cent (= *i*) is $n = \log 2 / \log (0.001) = 69$ years. If *i* = 5 per cent, the doubling time falls to 14 years. If *i* = 10 per cent, it will be seven years.

Disparities in income distribution

Economic growth, however, cannot be measured by the income 'per capita' in all countries because many of them have dual society characteristics, formed by small islands of abundance surrounded by a sea of poverty. The elites, which are a small minority, and the rest of the population, who are poor, differ in both their incomes per capita and their needs, aspirations and ways of life. For all practical ends, the two groups live in two separate worlds.

In 1992, the fifth poorest part of the population in the planet represented 1.4 per cent of the world GNP; the fifth richest part represented 82.7 per cent of the GNP (Figure 5.5).

In 2000, the situation did not change much. A large share of the planet population lives on US$2 a day, or less (Figure 5.6).

Even more shocking than this global information is the income gap within a given country. Brazil is a typical example of a dual society, which can be seen in its income distribution in relation to Japan and to Bangladesh. In Figure 5.7, the area below the curves is equivalent to the population in these countries.

A way of appraising the gap in income distribution is the Gini index, which measures the length at which the income or consumption

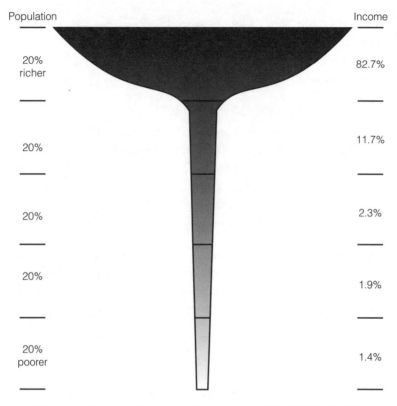

Figure 5.5 World income distribution, 1992 (IPCC, 2001)

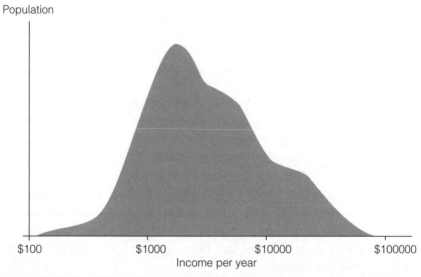

Figure 5.6 Population distribution (area =100 per cent or about six billion people) in function of the world income in 2000 (GapMinder, 2006)

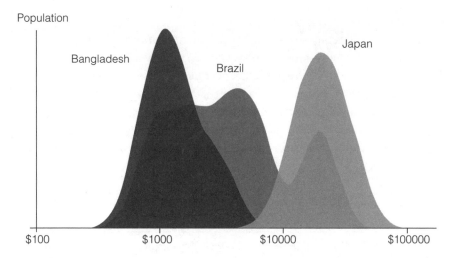

Population

Figure 5.7 Income distribution among the population in different countries in 2000 (GapMinder, 2006)

distribution among individuals or households of a certain country and year deviates from a perfect equalitarian distribution (Box 5.4).

Box 5.4 The Gini index

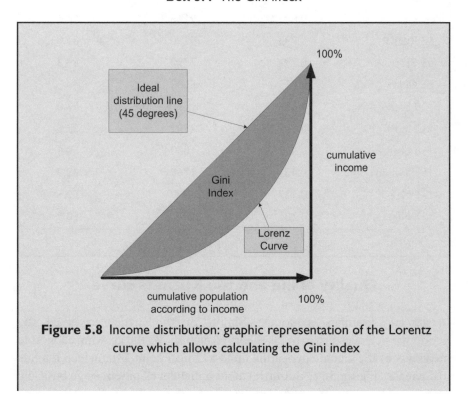

Figure 5.8 Income distribution: graphic representation of the Lorentz curve which allows calculating the Gini index

The Gini index is calculated from the *Lorentz curve*, which highlights the percentages accumulated from the income received against the accumulated number of recipients of that income. The Gini index measures the area between the Lorentz curve and a hypothetical line of absolute equality, expressed as a percentage of the maximum area under the line. Graphically, the rate is expressed by the area highlighted in Figure 5.8. The smaller the dark area, the closer to ideal income distribution (Gini equal to zero) will be a given economy. The more unequal, the more Gini tends to 1.

Table 5.4 Income per capita and Human Development Index (HDI) and Gini index by country

Ranking by the HDI (2003)	HDI	GDP per capita (GDP PPP US$ / capita)	Gini index
1 Norway	0.963	37,670	25.8
10 US	0.944	37,562	40.8
11 Japan	0.943	27,967	24.9
28 Korea	0.901	17,971	31.6
37 Chile	0.854	10,274	57.1
53 Mexico	0.814	9168	54.6
62 Russia	0.795	9230	31.0
63 Brazil	0.792	7790	59.3
85 China	0.755	5003	44.7
120 South Africa	0.658	10,346	57.8
127 India	0.602	2892	32.5
158 Nigeria	0.453	1050	50.6
159 Rwanda	0.45	1268	28.9
174 Mali	0.333	994	50.5
177 Niger	0.281	835	50.5

Quality of life and the Kuznets curve

In 1971, Ukrainian economist Simon Smith Kuznets received the Economic Sciences Prize for his theory, which shows the growing economic inequality of the income per capita up to a critical point, after which it tends to decrease (Figure 5.9). Countries at an initial development stage basically depend on investments in physical capital (equipment, infrastructure, machinery) and the inequality directs the growth by allocating resources to the sectors that invest more, to the detriment of basic services such as health and education. The great market imperfections increase inequalities to such an extent that investments start to be destined to human capital (service sectors and advanced industries), reducing inequalities since the largest share of the economically active population moves to more specialized and better paid sectors (from agriculture to industry and from industry to services), migrating from rural areas to cities. This argument is frequently used to justify a 'provisional right to degradation', since the basic needs of the population have to be met by development.

The theory is much criticized for being based on comparisons between countries at a given date, and not on the follow-up of a country's performance along time. Latin America, for example, would be half way along the curve, given its high levels of inequalities. Another criticism of the Kuznets curve concerns the environmental quality: the fact that a country needs to pollute more at its first development stages is not an absolute truth, and neither will this tendency be reverted when it is at a higher development level and the local society destines more resources to fight pollution. The use of natural resources does not decrease with the increase in income. Nevertheless, these observations do not invalidate Kuznets's theory, which is fit for some topics (such as air pollution) but not for others (such as greenhouse gas emissions).

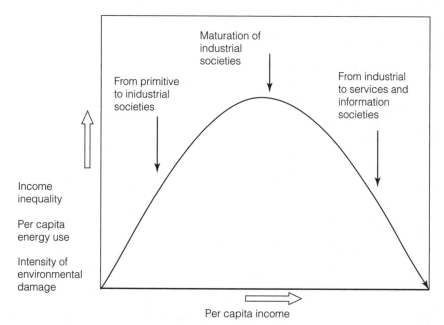

Figure 5.9 Kuznets curve

Concerning energy, the Kuznets curve is not a compulsory path, either, since the relations between economic activity and the use of primary energy are complex. In the development process, a certain society may learn from the errors of others, by *leapfrogging* and avoiding the impacts deriving from the intermediary maturation process. Visually, the leapfrogging process creates a kind of 'plateau' in the Kuznets curve (Figure 5.10).

At the same level of income per capita, the developing countries now have better opportunities than the developed ones used to have in the past. Some *leapfrogging* examples are:

- in isolated communities, the transition from collected fuelwood to electricity, by the use of photovoltaic panels and without the need of using diesel generators (which is under way in Ghana, Africa);
- in large urban centres the use of bus corridors instead of automobiles (as in the cases of Curitiba, Brazil, and Bogota, Colombia);
- for individual transportation, the development of flexible-fuel *(flex)* vehicles, a new automotive technology that makes the large scale introduction of bioethanol viable (as is the case of Brazil);
- in industries, the adoption of state of the art technologies in manufacturing and in specialized labour by means of solid education policies (as is the case of South Korea);

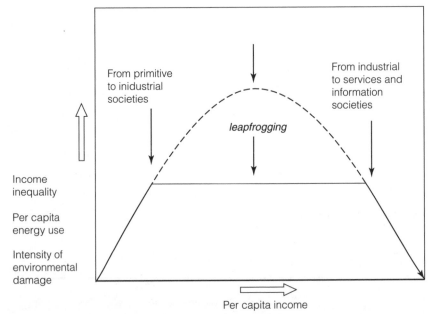

Figure 5.10 Kuznets curve and the leapfrogging effect

- in development plans, opting for an economy based on the services sector (as is the case of India); and
- in the end use, the immediate adoption of more efficient domestic appliances (as is the case of China).

In this way, the *leapfrogging* success is founded on the previous understanding of the impacts deriving from the possible choices for a certain society. In the long run, policies for controlling pollution have an effect on a country's income, as depicted in Figure 5.11.

Human Development Index (HDI)

A number of social indicators, such as life expectancy, literacy and total fertility rate, seem to be strongly correlated to per capita energy consumption.

For this reason, a more complex indicator than the GNP per capita or the GDP per capita is sometimes used to try and incorporate such correlations; the most widely used is the Human Development Index (HDI), which was created to address some of the problems with the use of income per capita as a development measure. The HDI is a combination of:

- longevity – measured by life expectancy;
- education – measured by a combination of adult literacy (75 per cent weight) and average years of education (25 per cent weight); and

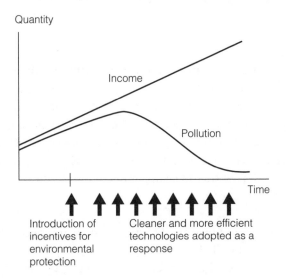

Figure 5.11 Schematic representation of the effect of introducing environmental protection policies on the income (Goldemberg, 1997)

- income – standard of living measured by the purchasing power, on the basis of the GDP per capita adjusted to the local costs.

Each of these indicators is given a value between 0 and 1, and an average of the resulting numbers in a global rate is attained. For example, in 2003, the minimum life expectancy was 25 years and the maximum was 85 years; the longevity component for a country where life expectancy is 55 years would be 0.5. A similar procedure is used for education (minimum of 0 per cent and maximum of 100 per cent of literacy and for school enrolment, with their respective relative weights of 0.75 and 0.25) and for the standard of living (GDP per capita PPP between US$100 and US$40,000).

Since the calculation criteria of the HHDI change along time, the UN Development Program (UNDP, 2004) recommends caution in temporal analyses. Even so, the situation has been improving for the great majority of countries as a consequence of open economies, democratic regimes and expansion of public services, as is the case of energy. Figure 5.12 illustrates this situation. Some countries have smaller income per capita but a relatively good HDI. That is the case of Cuba, which developed a good education and health infrastructure.

However, there is a limit to this consideration. In places with extreme poverty there is no development and there will hardly be a good standard of living. Since 2002, the World Bank tries to measure poverty by means of statistical research using local prices as well as goods and services not traded internationally, instead of the GDP per capita with purchasing power parity.

Some indicators for poverty are:

- 'extreme poverty', or a population living with less than one US dollar (1985 base) a day, adjusted by the purchasing power parity (i.e. the consumption level necessary to minimally provide for life maintenance);
- *'Poverty Gap'*, average distance of the poverty line expressed in percentile or the amount of resources necessary to take the whole population to a level above the poverty line by theoretically perfect financial transfers – this measure reflects the depth of poverty and its incidence (WRI, 2006).

A country with good income distribution does not necessarily present a good HDI, as shown in Table 5.4.

There is a strong relation between access to energy and the Millennium Development Goals, proposed by the United Nations (Box 5.5).

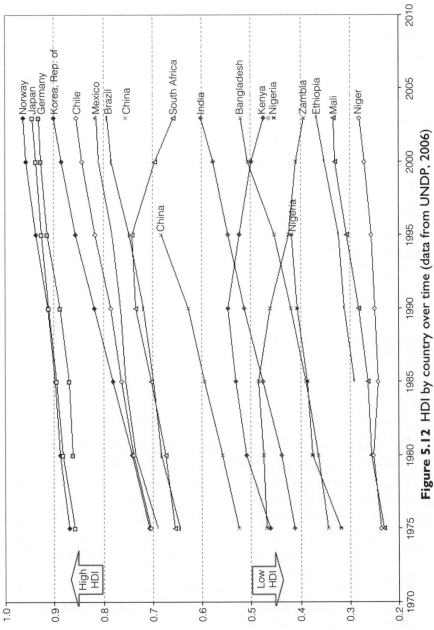

Figure 5.12 HDI by country over time (data from UNDP, 2006)

Table 5.4 Income per capita, Human Development Index (HDI) and Gini index by country (UNDP, 2006)

Ranking by the HDI (2003)	HDI	GDP per capita (GDP PPP US$ / capita)	Gini index
1 Norway	0.963	37,670	25.8
10 US	0.944	37,562	40.8
11 Japan	0.943	27,967	24.9
28 Korea	0.901	17,971	31.6
37 Chile	0.854	10,274	57.1
53 Mexico	0.814	9168	54.6
62 Russia	0.795	9230	31.0
63 Brazil	0.792	7790	59.3
85 China	0.755	5003	44.7
120 South Africa	0.658	10,346	57.8
127 India	0.602	2892	32.5
158 Nigeria	0.453	1050	50.6
159 Rwanda	0.45	1268	28.9
174 Mali	0.333	994	50.5
177 Niger	0.281	835	50.5

Box 5.5 Millennium Development Goals

The Millennium Development Goals are part of the Millennium Declaration, an international agreement adopted by 189 nations in 2000, under the auspices of the UN. On the basis of goals, deadlines and measurable indicators, the goals have to be pursued and met by 2015, to face the major world development challenges. The results are followed up by the UN Development Program (UNDP, 2007). The goals synthesize many of the most important commitments agreed separately by the countries in the 1990s, and explicitly recognize the interdependence between growth, poverty reduction and sustainable development. Evidently, these goals are closely linked to the availability of universal and good quality energy. The goals are to:

- eradicate extreme poverty and hunger;
- achieve universal primary education;

- promote gender equality and empower women;
- reduce child mortality;
- improve maternal health;
- combat HIV/AIDS, malaria and other diseases;
- ensure environmental sustainability; and
- develop a global partnership for development.

Adequate energy services are essential to meet these goals. UN Secretary-General Kofi Annan, in the preparatory meetings for the Johannesburg Development Summit in 2002, brought a structure containing key topics to guide the discussions. Until then, there was no international or intergovernmental process to facilitate the talks on these priorities. The priority areas of action are water, energy, health, agriculture and biodiversity. Called WEHAB – Water, Energy, Health, Agriculture, Biodiversity (United Nations, 2002) – all these priorities are strongly interrelated, especially with the access to energy, as shown in Figure 5.13.

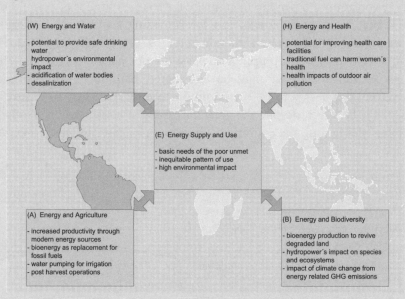

Figure 5.13 Energy and the UN priority areas for development

The relationship for energy-development

The importance of energy for development is illustrated in Figures 5.14 to 5.16, which show the relation between commercial energy consumption per capita and the indicators composing the HDI. The most evident is income (Figure 5.14). To overcome the barrier of 1 ton of oil equivalent per year (toe/capita.year) seems to be an important landmark to development and social change. Low energy consumption is not obviously the only cause of poverty and underdevelopment, yet it is a good indicator for many of its causes, such as unsatisfactory education, inadequate healthcare and sacrifices imposed on women and children. As commercial energy consumption per capita increases to values above 2 tons of oil equivalent, social conditions improve considerably.

There may be the same HDI for countries with different income per capita, which means that a lower income is compensated by greater longevity and an increase in education. That is the case of Cuba, for example. Figure 5.15 graphically presents HDI as a function of total primary energy consumption per capita annually for a large number of countries in 2003. For comparison effects and for providing an idea of the relative development in some countries, values for 1980 were also included. For commercial energy consumption above 4 toe per person a year, the HDI value (greater than 0.8) may be considered high for most countries. Therefore, this seems to be the minimum energy necessary to ensure an acceptable life level, despite the great variations in consumption standards and lifestyles among the countries. There are also cases in which a certain

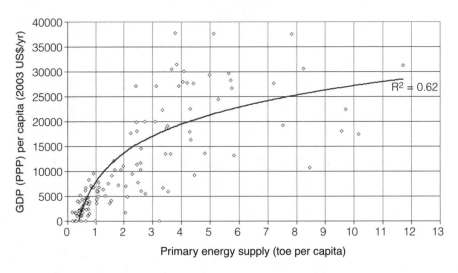

Figure 5.14 Income as a function of commercial energy per capita

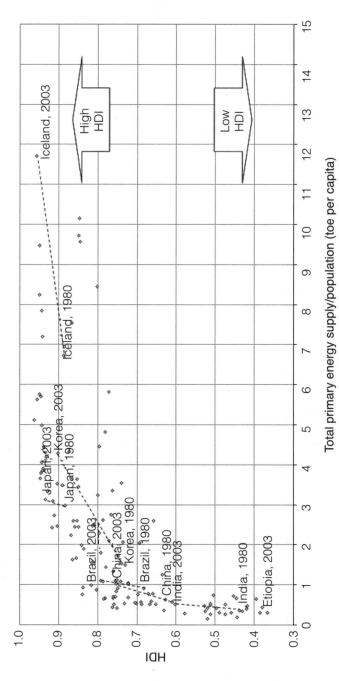

Figure 5.15 HDI as a function of energy consumption per capita, by country

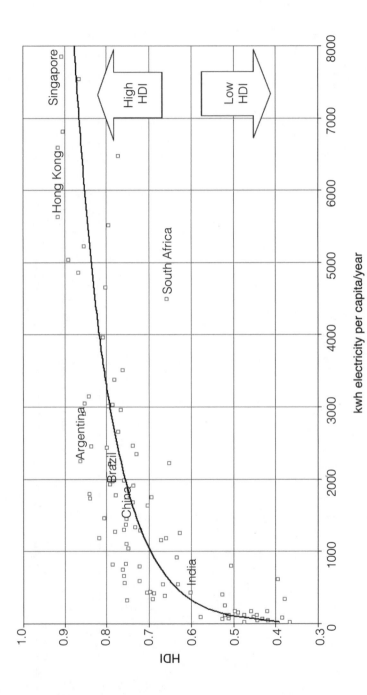

Figure 5.16 HDI in function of (direct and indirect) energy consumption per capita, per non-OECD country, 2003

economy prioritizes less energy-intensive economic sectors: Japan, Hong Kong and Singapore are examples.

The correlation between HDI and energy consumption is even more marked, as can be seen in Figure 5.16. This reflects a larger share of direct energy consumption.

It can be noticed that countries with high or near high HDI present direct and indirect power consumptions above 2000kWh a year. Some points out of the curve are the small oil-producing Arab countries (Oman, Arab Emirates and Kuwait, with high consumption and high HDI) and South Africa, with high industrial consumption and mid-HDI. In places where the services sector predominates, as is the case of Singapore and Hong Kong, HDI and consumptions are high. In sub-Saharan Africa and places such as Bangladesh, HDI and consumption are very low.

Direct energy is the energy on which a person has direct control, such as driving a car or switching on an electrical appliance. Indirect energy, in turn, is that incorporated in products over which the person has no direct control on the amount consumed, such as an ice-cream or aluminium can. In energy balances, the energy in the residential sector may be considered direct and the one consumed in productive activities (industry and agriculture) are indirect. The transportation sector has direct and indirect shares of energy, and the separation is more difficult. In terms of direct energy, a minimum family consumption should be around 100kWh per month, or 300kWh per capita a year for a family of four.

Energy intensity: energy and economic product

The growth in the GNP of a country occurs by an increase in population, in the number of households, automobiles, domestic appliances and other factors. If the productive and consumption structure is maintained, at a first approximation it can be evident that energy consumption has grown together with the increase in income.

The ratio energy consumption (E) economic product (P) is defined as the economy *energy intensity* (I) and given by the formula $I = E/P$, which can be expressed for a given reference year, for example, in tons of oil equivalent (toe) of total primary energy by US dollars of GDP (or GNP).

Energy intensity can be analysed *statically* (by comparing the performance of different regions in a given year) or *dynamically* (evolution along time for one or more regions). Long-term temporal series of energy intensity for different countries show that it changes along time, reflecting the combined effects of alterations on the economic product structure (included in the GDP), as well as on the combination of energy generation sources, on their consumption structure and on the efficiency of their end use.

From the definition of energy intensity, percentile changes can be obtained that allow elasticity analyses (Box 5.6).

Box 5.6 Elasticity coefficients

Elasticity is a relative measure between variations, a general concept applied to any functional relation between two variables $y = f(x)$. Often used in economy, elasticity refers to the increment in a variable in relation to the increment in another. The more usual formula[3] is

$$Ex,y = \frac{\text{percent variation in } y}{\text{percent variation in } x} = \frac{(\Delta y / y)}{(\Delta x / x)}$$

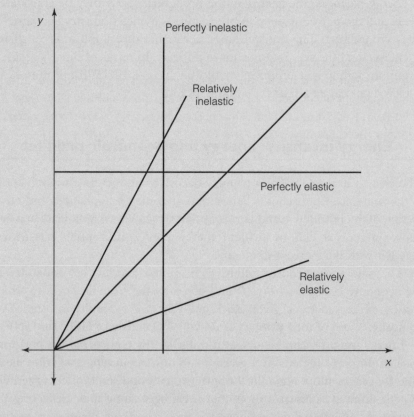

Figure 5.17 Graphic representation of elasticities

Some examples are:

the increase in energy consumption in function of the increase in GDP (elasticity–income);[4]

the reduction in the use of gas for cooking when its price rises (elasticity–price);[5]

the replacement of gasoline with ethanol in flex vehicles, in function of their relative prices (elasticity–substitution);

estimations of the effects of a tax on goods consumption (incidence of indirect taxation);

distribution of wealth in function of governmental policies (such as subsidies) and relationship among countries. Usually, the more expensive a product gets (i.e. the more its price increases), the smaller its consumption. The higher the income, the higher the consumption of goods. However, elasticity assesses the relations between these proportions (Figure 5.17).

If $Ex, y = 0$, the proportion is absolutely inelastic (e.g. cooking salt in relation to its price). If $Ex, y < 1$, the proportion is relatively inelastic. If $Ex, y > 1$, the proportion is absolutely elastic, and if Ex, y tends to infinite, the proportion is absolutely elastic. The long-term elasticity is generally greater than in the short-term, since investments in production or the development of competitive replacements are more intense in a broader horizon. This is also valid for demand: consumers tend to save more when prices rise constantly.

The elasticity between energy consumption and income may be calculated by:

$$\frac{\Delta I}{I} = \frac{\Delta E / E}{\Delta P / P}.$$

Table 5.5 supplies numbers for $\Delta I/I$ in the periods 1971–90 and 1990–2006 for different regions in the world, using the total energy supply as an energy indicator and the GDP adjusted by the purchasing power parity as a product indicator. In case the periods are respectively 20 and 17 years, the annual variation in energy intensity has also been calculated.

It can be noted that:

- there are economic crisis cases that reduced energy consumption and income (e.g. Former Soviet Union); energy intensity improved, but at the expenses of a reduction in production;
- the income grew relatively more than the use of energy, both in developed and in developing countries; however, gains in efficiency between 1971 and 1990 were greater than those in 1990–2006;
- in places where energy intensity was above one, much more energy was produced than was obtained in terms of economic return (as is the special case of the Middle East in the first period);
- in China, there was a strong growth in GDP, but with reduction levels in energy intensity comparable to those in developed countries; these gains, nevertheless, were more easily obtained, since there were great improvement potentials (other Asian developing countries had similar reductions in energy consumption, but their economic product did not grow as much as that of China);
- in Africa before 1990 there was a flow of energy-intensive industries which increased the energy more than the income;
- after 1990 the performance of Latin America and the Caribbean was inferior to the average of the developing countries: energy intensity increased; the growth in GDP did not follow the increase in energy use.

As seen earlier in this chapter, more developed countries reached a smaller energy intensity over time, that is, they directed their productive structure to less energy-intensive (and usually less pollutant) activities. Developing countries present higher energy intensities, culminating in the case of the indirect energy exporting countries (embedded in their products). The poorer countries consume little energy, but more efficiently, and, therefore, may be considered mid-energy intensive. As a country develops, its energy intensity initially grows for the greater consumption and for the greater presence of primary goods industries for export, such as ores and metals. After that, capital goods industries – such as machinery and equipment, as well as petrochemicals – start to predominate. Later, there are more specialized industries (such as *software* and fine chemistry) and the service sector, which consume less energy and generate a larger economic product.

Notes

1 Some prefer to split the general consumption term into private consumption and public sector (or government) spending. Another way of measuring GDP is through income accounts. The so-called GDP(I) is the sum of:

- compensation of employees (wages, salaries, employer contributions to social security and other such programmes);

Table 5.5 Variations in primary energy, economic product by the purchasing parity power (GDP PPP) and energy intensity in 1971–90 and 1990–2006 (data from IEA, 2008)

Region	Primary Energy (E) Mtoe			GDP PPP bln 2000 US$			ΔE/E in the period		ΔP/P in the period		Elasticity ΔI/I in the period per year		Elasticity ΔI/I	
	2006	1990	1971	2006	1990	1971	1971–90	1990–2006	1971–90	1990–2006	1971–90	1990–2006	1971–90	1990–2006
OECD	5537	4523	3391	31,158	20,826	11,474	0.33	0.22	0.82	0.50	0.41	0.27	2.2%	1.7%
Non-OECD	6020	4104	2068	26,407	12,189	5968	0.98	0.47	1.04	1.17	0.94	0.45	5.0%	2.8%
Middle East	523	229	52	1455	720	432	3.44	1.28	0.67	1.02	5.17	1.93	27.2%	12.1%
Former USSR	1017	1348	788	2266	2372	1663	0.71	-0.25	0.43	-0.04	1.66	-0.57	8.7%	-3.6%
East Europe non-OECD	108	141	86	477	350	173	0.64	-0.23	1.02	0.36	0.62	-0.23	3.3%	-1.4%
China	1897	891	395	8918	1926	464	1.25	1.13	3.15	3.63	0.40	0.36	2.1%	2.2%
Asia, other non-OECD	1330	760	346	7661	3381	1319	1.20	0.75	1.56	1.27	0.77	0.48	4.0%	3.0%
Latin America and the Caribbean	531	340	203	3425	2096	1131	0.67	0.56	0.85	0.63	0.79	0.66	4.2%	4.1%
Africa	614	395	198	2207	1344	785	0.99	0.55	0.71	0.64	1.40	0.78	7.3%	4.9%
World	11,740	8627	5458	57,565	33,015	17441	0.58	0.36	0.89	0.74	0.65	0.40	3.4%	2.5%

- gross operating surplus ('profits', such as rents and interests);
- gross mixed income (for unincorporated, small businesses);
- taxes (less subsidies) on production and imports that the government has levied (or paid).

The international standard for measuring GDP is contained in the book *System of National Accounts* or SNA (United Nations Statistical Division, 2008), which provides a set of rules and procedures for the measurement of national accounts. The 1995 ESA (European System of Accounts, 2008) is used by members of the European Union and is broadly consistent with the 1993 SNA in definitions, accounting rules and classifications.

2 A subsidy is considered specific when limited to certain companies, industries, production sectors or geographic regions. By the international trade rules, it may be considered forbidden in case it is linked to exporting performance or to the preferential use of domestic products to the detriment of foreign products. Some subsidies are allowed, as is the case of pre-competitive research and development activities.

3 In general, the elasticity of a magnitude y in relation to a magnitude x is given by $E_{x,y} = (\partial x/\partial y).(y/x)$.

4 Energy (E, in general the total supply of primary energy or power consumption) can be related to the product (P, generally adopting the GDP). The elasticity of income related to energy consumption can be calculated by $\gamma = (\Delta E/E)/(\Delta GDP/GDP)$. If $\gamma = 1$, the consumption of energy grows proportionally to the GDP; if $\gamma < 1$, energy consumption grows less quickly than the GDP and if $\gamma > 1$, energy consumption grows more quickly than the GNP. For example, if the energy consumption grows by 4 per cent a year and, in the same period, the GNP has grown by 5 per cent a year, the proportion is relatively inelastic, since $\gamma = 4/5 = 0.80$. If the GNP grows only by 3.2 per cent a year, it will be inelastic: $\gamma = 4/3.2 = 1.25$.

5 For example, an elasticity-price (β) for energy consumption (E) can be defined as: $\beta = (\Delta E/E)/(\Delta P/P)$, where P is the price of energy.

References

European System of Accounts (2008) '1995 ESA', http://circa.europa.eu/irc/dsis/nfaccount/info/data/esa95/esa95-new.htm

GapMinder (2006) Income distribution 2003. Gapminder website, www.gapminder.org/projectsView-2.htm

Goldemberg, J. (1997) 'Leapfrogging strategies for developing countries'. In Environment, Energy, and Economy: Strategies for Sustainability, Yoichi Kaya and Keiichi Yokobori (ed.), United Nations University Press, Tokyo

IEA (2006) *Energy Balances of non-OECD Countries*. International Energy Agency, OECD, Paris

IEA (2008) *Energy Balances of non-OECD Countries*. International Energy Agency, OECD, Paris

IMF (2006) International Monetary Fund, World Economic Outlook Database, September 2006, www.imf.org/external/pubs/ft/weo/2006/02/data/weorept.aspx?

IPCC (2001) Climate Change 2001: Working Group III: Mitigation. Intergovernmental Panel on Climate Change

Martin, J. M. (1988) 'L'intensité énergétique de l'activité économique dans les pays industrialisés, *Economies et sociétés – Cahiers de l'ISMEA* 22(4), April; *apud* José Goldemberg, J. (1997) 'Leapfrogging strategies for developing countries'. In *Environment, Energy, and Economy: Strategies for Sustainability*, Yoichi Kaya and Keiichi Yokobori (ed.), United Nations University Press, Tokyo, www.unu.edu/unupress/unupbooks/uu17ee/uu17ee00.htm#Contents

Mielnik, O. and Goldemberg, J. (2000) 'Converging to a Common Pattern of Energy Use in Developing and Industrialized Countries', *Energy Policy* 28, 503–508

UNDP 2004 Human Development Report 2004 – Technical Notes. United Nations Development Program, p258

UNDP (2006) Human Development Report, http://hdr.undp.org/reports/global/2004/pdf/hdr04_HDI.pdf

UNDP (2007) Millennium Development Goals, www.undp.org/mdg/tracking_home.shtml

United Nations Statistical Division (2008) 'National Accounts', http://unstats.un.org/unsd/sna1993/toctop.asp

United Nations (2002) *A Framework for Action on Energy*, by the WEHAB Working Group – J. Gururaja, UNDESA, S. McDade, UNDP, and I. Freudenschuss-Reichl, UNIDO, www.un.org/jsummit/html/documents/summit_docs/wehab_papers/wehab_energy.pdf

World Bank (2007) Statistics, http://siteresources.worldbank.org/DATASTATISTICS/Resources/table4-1.pdf

WRI (1998) World Resources 1996–97, World Resources Institute

WRI (2006) World Resources Institute, www.worldresources.org

Chapter 6

Energy: The Facts

The environment in which we live changes continuously due to natural causes over which we have little control. The seasons of the year are the most evident of these changes, mainly in regions of high latitudes (north or south). There are many other natural changes, such as the solar spots on the surface of the Sun, volcanic eruptions, earthquakes and tsunamis, hurricanes, floods and forest fires.

Life on Earth has shown a surprising capacity to bear these changes. Mankind in particular has adapted well to climate changes after its last glaciation, about 10,000 years ago, when most of the northern hemisphere was covered in ice and snow. However, most of the great changes in our environment occurred slowly along time, over many centuries.

Recently there have been considerable changes in the environment, caused by human actions. These changes, called *anthropogenic*, were insignificant before the Industrial Revolution in the 19th century, but became a reason for concern owing to the increase in population and to the predatory use of natural resources, notably fossil fuels in industrialized countries.

The presence of man on Earth is quite recent in geological terms and depends on very specific environmental conditions: climate, temperature, existence of water and other forms of life. Disturbances beyond these limits, even with the notable capacity for adapting, are dangerous.

The concept of environment derives from pro-nature movements in modern society. From the economic point of view, nature is both a resource supplier and a recipient of wastes. Without inputs from natural resources there is no economic production.

The way in which energy is produced and used is the cause for many of the environmental impacts witnessed. In this chapter, these problems will be discussed in order to identify how production and use of energy are involved, and proposals for energy policies that may reduce or prevent environmental changes.

Environmental impacts due to energy production and use

In a short period (about 150 years after the Industrial Revolution), the environmental impacts of anthropogenic origin are comparable to the ones caused by natural effects in terms of magnitude. These problems are extremely important nowadays: in the considerations of the Russian scientist Vernadsky,[1] humans have become a force of geological proportions. For example, natural forces (such as winds, erosion, rain and volcanic eruptions) move about 50 million tons of materials a year. The Earth's population of six billion people consume an average of 8 tons of mineral resources a year, moving about 48 billion tons. A century ago, the population was 1.5 billion and consumption was smaller than 2 tons per capita: the total impact was 16 times smaller. As a result, new sorts of problems or areas of interest in the environmental field evolved into matters of study and concern.

Energy consumption is most probably the main source of environmental impact at all levels. In a micro scale, it is the cause of respiratory diseases due to the primitive use of fuelwood. At a macro level, it is the major source of greenhouse gas emissions, which intensify climate changes and cause biodiversity losses. In some situations, energy does not play a dominant role but it is still important; that is the case, for example, of coastal and marine degradation due to oil leakages and to other environmental disasters (Table 6.1).

Table 6.1 Environmental impacts, dimensions and causes

Impact and magnitude	Main cause
LOCAL	
Urban air pollution	Emissions of sulphur dioxide (SO_2), carbon monoxide (CO), nitrogen oxides (NO_x) and particulate matter (PM) in fossil fuels burning, especially oil and coal. Evaporative emissions of hydrocarbons (HCs) and other volatile organic compounds (VOCs) by solvents and fuel transfer operations. Formation of low-altitude ozone (O_3) by the solar light action on NOx and HCs.
	Emissions of heavy metals such as lead (Pb), cadmium (Cd), mercury (Hg) and other toxic and carcinogenic substances (such as dioxins and furans) when burning coal, oils and solid wastes.

'Occupational' air pollution	Emissions of PM and CO by the use of solid fuels (biomass and coal) for heating and cooking in indoor environments. Toxic emissions from industrial and manufacturing processes. Exposition of certain professional categories to intense air pollution.
Pollution of superficial waterbodies (rivers, lakes, estuaries) and groundwater; contamination soils	Leakages of oil byproducts. Use of fertilizers and pesticides in agriculture. Percolation of domestic (e.g. landfill leachate), industrial or commercial (e.g. filling stations leakage) wastes. Abandoned industrial and mining areas, without appropriate decommissioning operations (cleanup, isolation and storage, recovery). Environmental accidents and emergencies (with different magnitudes and reaches).

REGIONAL

Acid rain	Deposition of sulphuric (H_2SO_4) and nitric (HNO_3) acids, formed by the reaction of water (rain, snow, etc.) with SO_2 and NO_2 generated by fossil fuel burning.
Pollution of seas and transboundary waterbodies	Oil leakages and other leakages in interstate or international waters. Contamination of underground aquifers by the percolation of toxic substances.

GLOBAL

Greenhouse effect	Emissions of carbon dioxide (CO_2) by fossil fuels burning and by deforestation of native forests. Methane emissions (CH_4) by incomplete fuel burning and by (anaerobic) digestion of waste.
Persistent organic pollutants (POPs) and radioactive waste	Accumulation of heavy metals (such as the mercury emitted by coal thermopower plants, entering in the food chain) in living organisms, of man-made toxic compounds (such as PCBs – polychlorinated biphenyls found in fluids utilized in electric equipment) and of radioactive substances (deriving from nuclear accidents, tests and leakages).
Loss of biodiversity, changes in the oceans and desertification	Deforestation for producing fuelwood and charcoal, as well as land cleaning for agriculture, coastal and marine degradation due to oil leakages into the sea, carbon dioxide (CO_2) emissions causing acidification of the oceans. Ecosystems flooded by hydropower reservoirs. Use of agrochemicals by energy or food monoculture.

The manifestation of the impacts caused by changes in socio-economic standards (Table 6.2) may be either immediate (such as air pollution by black smoke) or chronic (such as bioaccumulation of toxic substances in organisms or a rise in ocean level due to the increased greenhouse effect).

In general, all these problems have several causes such as populational increase, industry, transportation, agriculture and even tourism. Impacts are also intrinsically related to changes in consumption patterns and their consequent pressures on natural resources.

The viewpoint that nature should serve mankind does not justify development at any cost or the lack of consideration of environmental impacts due to their multiple types and intensities. It is necessary to frequently take decisions and, especially for the energy sector, the use of indicators may be an important *analysis tool,* such as the ones exemplified in Table 6.3.

Emission inventories

A particular case of analyses tools are the *emission inventories,* important tools for energy-environmental planning (Box 6.1). The knowledge of emission intensities along time and their sources allows a better pollution control, as it is possible to identify sectors, regions and typologies, both

Table 6.2 Characteristic time horizons in the Earth system (IPCC, 2006)

System	Process	Years necessary
Socio-economic	Changes in energy end-use technologies	1–10
	Changes in energy supply technologies	10–50
	Infrastructure	30–100
	Policies, social rules and governance	30–100
Ecologic	Life of plants	1–1000
	Adaptation of plants to the new atmospheric conditions (e.g. CO_2 concentration)	1–100
	Organic matter decay	0–500
Climate	Increase in temperature with the increase of CO_2 in the atmosphere	120–150
	Heat and CO_2 transfer to the bottom of the oceans	100–200
	Rise in the ocean levels by the increase in temperature	up to 10,000
Atmospheric	50% decay of a CH_4 load emitted	8–12
	50% decay of a CO_2 load emitted	50–200
	Mix of greenhouse gases	2–4

Table 6.3 Analysis tools: indicators for the impacts of energy production and use

Type of environmental indicator	Function of	Example
Pollutant emissions in a given period from a given process	• *load effectively measured according to scientifically validated methods* • *load estimated in inventories*	• millions of tons of carbon dioxide emitted a year • tons of oil leaked in a given accident • grams of particulate matter emitted per hour from an industrial stack
Pollutant concentrations at a given media and at a certain moment	• *effectively measured, continuously or by samplings* • *estimations by modelling*	• micrograms of ozone per cubic metre of air in the city centre, 2006 average measured in air quality monitoring stations • pH in a river affected by acid rain
Public health	• survey of *statistical data* on mortality or on morbidity (diseases) attributed to a given cause	• cases of hospital care due to respiratory diseases caused by urban air pollution, in given region and period
Biomonitoring	• populational counting, toxicity assessment and other impacts in organisms	• specimens of a certain river, upstream and downstream, a thermopower plant that releases hot water from cooling towers
Inter-relations among indicators	• relationship among the use of resources, cost-benefit analyses, impacts and other environmental, economic and social effects	• area flooded by installed capacity in hydropower plants • water consumption for cooling thermopower plant turbines

industrial and non-industrial, such as transportation, fuel storage, forest burnings and many others. Comparisons can also be established among different fuels and technologies (such as coal, natural gas and biomass-fired thermopower plants), policies on fuels (such as the reduction in sulphur content) or even international negotiations on limiting greenhouse gas emissions.

An emission inventory should be sufficiently geo-referenced, with a spatial coverage compatible with its impact. It is justified to inventory the effect of greenhouse gases emitted by a country, but for local pollutants a reduced scope (such as 'PM_{10} surrounding a given site' or 'hydrocarbons in the municipality') is preferable for public health effects.

Box 6.1 Emission inventories

Emission inventories are basically the sum of pollutant emissions. Emissions are usually estimated by using the formula

$$E = EF \times A \times (I - ER)$$

where *E* is pollutant *P* emission, *EF* is the emission factor, *A* is the activity rate and *ER* is the overall emission reduction efficiency (percentage) in removing (controlling) pollutants.

As there are significant uncertainties at all the stages of an inventory, this should be considered a dynamic process and subject to constant refinements. An emission inventory, for example, for emissions from fuel consumption, can be conducted through top-down or bottom-up approaches. In the first case, the activity is considered the fuel consumed (taken from, for example, a country energy balance). In the bottom-up, the emissions of each source or sector are added up, as if they were bricks forming a building. The ideal situation occurs when top-down and bottom-up inventories reach the same value, that is, there is 100 per cent closure. Table 6.4 shows examples of emission factors of a global pollutant (CO_2) and of local pollutants emitted by thermopower plants and vehicles.

ER may be considered null for gross pollutant load purposes. In the case of CO_2, instead of *ER*, a fraction of oxidized carbon (i.e. which forms soot) is used, usually 1 per cent. Biomass CO_2 emission is considered zero (or near zero) since carbon is considered fully incorporated by biomass during its growth. The US Environmental Protection Agency (US EPA, 2001) provides information on emission factors.

Table 6.4 Air pollutant emission factors from fuel combustion by process in the US (US EPA, 2001)

Process	Fuel	$PM_{2.5}$ kg/TJ	PM_{10} kg/TJ	SO_x kg/TJ	NO_x kg/TJ	COV kg/TJ	CO kg/TJ	CO_2 t/TJ
Boiler	coal (7%S)	119	340	70	980	2	155	95
Boiler	fuel oil (2.5%S)	120	184	10	131	nd	14	77
Turbine	natural gas	nd	nd	–	53	2	7	56
Boiler	bagasse	nd	32	–`	2	nd	nd	renewable
Generator, internal combustion engine	diesel (2%S)	169	169	8	240	nd	52	74

Modelling

Estimating gross emissions in order to know their impacts is not enough. The path of a plume follows several stages from its source to the final receptor (Figure 6.1):

- gross pollutant emission loads often goes through a control system (filters, precipitators, cyclones, scrubbers), which abate a considerable percentage from these emissions before they leave the stack, the exhaustion or any other end-of-pipe system;
- once released into the environment, pollutants are dispersed (by the action of meteorological, topographic as well as gases and fluid dynamics conditionants); in some cases, chemical reactions occur in the atmosphere;
- receptor (humans, animals, plants, buildings) is exposed to pollutant concentrations for a certain period (from a few minutes to many years); in some cases, the pollutant may bioaccumulate in the organism; and
- pollutant triggers a negative reaction in the receptor (such as diseases).

The path of the pollutants from the source to the final receptor may be simulated by *models*, based on emission inventories, on local air quality data and on meteorological parameters (such as wind direction and intensity,

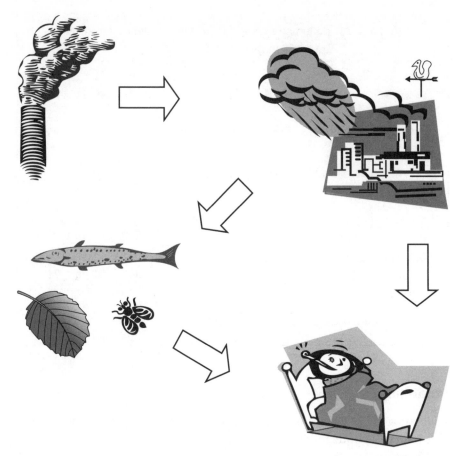

Figure 6.1 Stages of pollutants impact: emissions, atmospheric dispersion, intake by receptors and possible bioaccumulation, pathologies

rains), topographic (existence of physical barriers, stack height), type of gases and particulate matter (affecting the configuration of the 'plume' leaving the stack). Figure 6.2 exemplifies a plume and a pollutant dispersion model.

Since it is important to assess pollution control and to establish new directives and norms, models are frequently required for environmental approval of large pollutant enterprises, such as thermopower plants, in order to prevent major impacts on local communities. There is a wide variety of models: Gaussian (impacts by primary pollutants emitted directly into the atmosphere), numerical (when there are chemical reactions), statistical (when there is no full understanding of the processes involved) and physical (reduced replicas and wind tunnels).

These examples refer to atmospheric pollution, which is the most common aspect in energy processes. Nevertheless, the concepts of emissions,

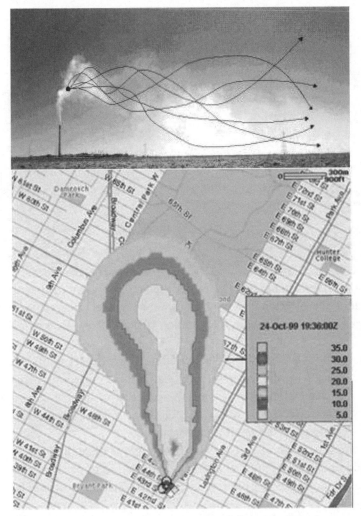

Figure 6.2 Pollution plume and concentration of a given substance: results of dispersion models (US DoT, 2007; CSIRO, 2004).

loads, concentrations and dispersion are also valid for water (underground, surface, marine) and soil pollution.

Qualification of environmental impacts in function of income

Impact assessment is an even more complex task than the emissions inventory as it involves complex issues. The gravity of the environmental impact can differ greatly for different populations. This is shown in Figure 6.4: the poor suffer more intensely from the effects of diseases due to the lack of

Figure 6.3 Contamination of waterbeds (plume representing the increase in pollutant concentration in underground water) by fuel leakages (load caused by emissions) in a vehicle filling station (adapted from Alvarez, 2007).

basic sanitation, while the rich concentrate their concerns on the climate changes caused by the increase in global carbon emissions. Mid-income populations have already overcome the problem of lack of sanitation, but are very much affected by urban air pollution, in large cities with growing industrialization and deficient transportation.[2]

An empirical example of the Kuznets curve is presented in Figure 6.5, with sulphur dioxide (SO_2) emissions as a function of per capita income in Mexico. As can be seen, pollution increases with the income and later tends to decrease.

A series of economic factors help to counteract the factors leading to environmental degradation:

- as societies turn richer, there is a shift to a less natural resource-intensive production, more efficient and with better technological capacity;
- the societies' preferences (mainly the democratic ones) also turn to environmental conservation and improvement; and
- the most impacting production, in turn, is relocated to developing countries, where there are less restrictions and, therefore, less costs incorporated in the products (causing the so-called 'environmental dumping').

However, the idea that the increasing income allows reducing or eliminating pollution is far too simplistic, as can be seen in terms of

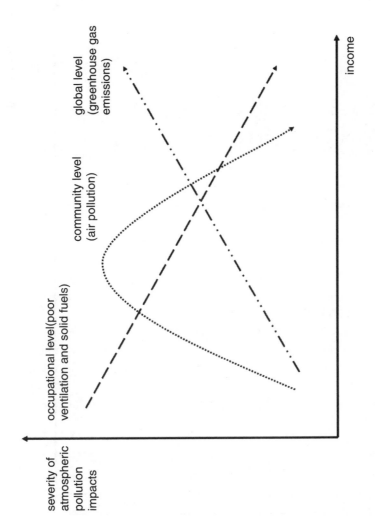

Figure 6.4 Transition of the environmental impact risks of air pollution in function of income levels (UNEP, 2006)

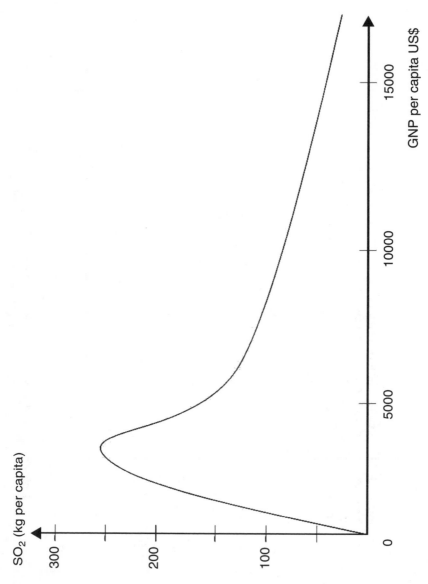

Figure 6.5 SO_2 emissions in function of income in Mexico (Grossman and Krueger, 1991)

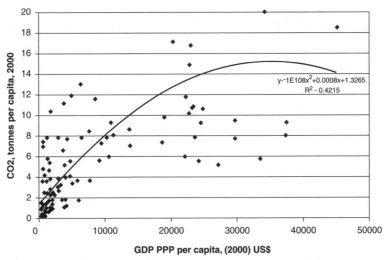

Figure 6.6 CO_2 emissions as a function of income (adjusted by the purchasing power parity – PPP) by country in 2000 (WRI, 2009)

carbon emissions as a function of per capita income, from country to country.

It can be argued that climate change affects mainly the poor, but environmental priorities are very much related to the timescale and the hierarchy of basic needs.[3] Populations without economic means to provide for their basic and immediate needs are not particularly concerned with phenomena that will occur more frequently in the future.

Economists constantly try to refine methods to assess the costs of pollution and, therefore, the benefits of their abatement. This approach is called *damage function* and considers impacts such as mortality and morbidity among humans, damages to ecosystems, to agriculture and to infrastructure, pollutant concentrations and exposition to risk agents and others. The impacts are quantified and calculated in function of medical costs avoided, gains in productivity or even society's willingness to pay for these benefits. The estimates are conservative generally, since not all parameters are quantifiable. The costs caused by individuals and paid by society as a whole are called *externalities* (Box 6.2).

Box 6.2 Environmental externalities

Environmental externalities are non-valued costs in market transactions, paid by society as a consequence of an activity conducted by certain private agents. The influence of the state is necessary to internalize such costs, to conciliate economic activities with environmental protection. When internalized, the social costs increase the price of products and reduce the demand; when this does not occur, society pays for the difference (Figure 6.7).

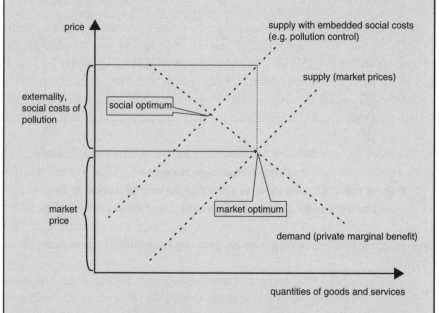

Figure 6.7 Microeconomic representation of the externality concept on the supply and demand curves

Personal suffering and non-compensated work are not adequately captured by the analyses of externalities. Estimated values are usually greater when studies are based on the *willingness to pay* for the benefits by a part of society, since these benefits are varied and comprehensive. For the case of air pollution, in general, the benefits are many times greater than the costs of its mitigation.[4] Studies in general may be transferred and adjusted from one place to another. That is the case, for example, of child mortality due to occupational pollution.

The internalization of external costs in general occurs by means of public policies and by legislation on the basis of the *polluter-pays principle*, by which the one that causes pollution is to pay for its costs. The principle means *attributing to* the polluter the cost of the prevention measures and/or of combatting pollution, as decided and established by the government. It is very important to stress that this principle does not *justify* the compensation of the damages caused by pollution, or that the polluter should pay *exclusively* for the costs of the impact prevention measures. This is the root of many of the constant conflicts that occur among developmentalists and conservationists. Another frequent problem with the principle occurs in its international aspect, for example, in cases in which a given country provides subsidies to polluting industries (OECD, 1975).

Frequently, entrepreneurs advocate the point of view of scientific uncertainty and of the inevitability of the environmental impact due to the 'necessary development' – a way of being exempted from possible liabilities. On the other hand, environmentalists – some with certain exaggeration – evoke the *precautionary principle* (against risk), which aims to prevent today a suspected future impact, in order to guarantee a safety margin from the risk line.

Some processes present an intrinsic risk of environmental impacts of such magnitude that its occurrence is unacceptable. That is the case, for example, of thermonuclear power generation risks of accidents with explosions and leakages of radioactive substances. For these cases, the legislation is supported by the *principle of objective responsibility*, by which one cannot be exempted from causing an accident, independently of the causes.

Local urban pollution

In general, local pollution is the one that generates the first conflicts and concerns. This is not a recent problem: during the Roman Empire, there were already dispositions for the nuisances caused by the sewage discharged into water courses and by the smoke from households and small manufacturers. The ancient Romans melted large amounts of lead to manufacture water pipes, contaminating vast regions. In the Middle Ages, the use of coal in London was intensified, and in the late 16th century air pollution problems were already well documented. With the Industrial Revolution, air pollutant concentrations reached devastating levels in several English towns, increasing the number of deaths and diseases, especially when there was smoke and fog, forming the so-called *smog*. In 1875, cases of cancer in stack-sweeping workers were registered. An English Law from 1875 contained a section which provided on the reduction of smoke in urban areas and another from 1926 focused on industrial emissions. For many centuries, pollution was an issue at municipal level and it was not rare to witness scenes of towns immersed in smoke (Figure 6.8).

In 1943, a critical *smog* episode occurred in Los Angeles, leading the California government to ban emissions with blackening above a certain level and to control emissions that caused distress to the population. This led to the first studies on environmental quality standards on the basis of the

Figure 6.8 Pollution in Donora, Pennsylvania, US, 1910 and 1948 (University of San Diego, 2007)

(opposite page)

Figure 6.9 The Great London Smog, 1952: photographs and daily sulphur dioxide concentrations and related deaths (De Angelo, 2008; Bell, 2009; Nielsen, 2002)

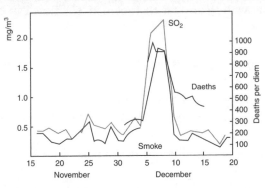

effects on human health. Another episode occurred in London in 1952 (Figure 6.9), killing 4000 people and establishing strict laws for pollution control and land use.

Other laws followed in other North American and Western European countries, establishing agencies to monitor, regulate and assess environmental quality. In 1963, the US issued the Clean Air Act, which introduced emission standards for vehicles, even under strong opposing pressure from the automotive industry. The Act was amended in 1967, with emission standards for stationary sources and the definition of Air Quality Control Regions (AQCR). Another amendment, from 1970, classified the air pollutants into two different categories:

- *regulated* pollutants (*criteria air pollutants*, the case of SO_2, NO_x, CO, PM and lead), with negative effects to health and social welfare; and
- *hazardous air* pollutants (a complex and diversified list, frequently updated, including, among others, mercury, benzene, arsenic, cadmium and PCBs (polychlorinated biphenyls), substances persistent in the environment, carcinogenic and bioaccumulative), with evidences of severe and irreversible damage to health (*toxicity, carcinogenicity, teratogenicity*, that is, intoxication potentials, to cause cancer and mutations) and to the environment (*bioaccumulation* in the organism and *biomagnification* along the food chain and through generations).

Later, legislation started to incorporate other photochemical pollutants: *smog precursors* (product of nitrogen oxides and hydrocarbon reactions in the atmosphere, in the presence of sunlight). As from the 1990s, environmental legislation also started to provide compulsory reductions of pollutant emissions on the basis of the *best available technology,* incorporating preventive concepts for the industry. Other strategies are based on environmental quality targets, product performance standards (especially vehicles), taxation on emissions, allocation of maximum quotas (limits) for industrial pollutant releases, exchange of emission credits and other instruments.

There is not one and only one air pollution problem, but several different phenomena, with their own characteristics. These can be described by four dimensions:

1 horizontal, in which it is verified how much the Earth surface is involved;
2 vertical, depth at which the atmosphere is involved;
3 time scale, in which problems unfold and on which their controls operate; and
4 organizational scale required for their resolution (Table 6.5).

Table 6.5 Scales and categories of air pollution problems (Stern et al, 1984)

Scale	Categories of air pollution problems				
Horizontal	local	urban	regional	continental	global
Vertical	stack height	first mile	tropo-sphere	strato-sphere	atmo-sphere
Temporal	hours	days	months	years	decades
Organization required for their resolution	municipal	metropolitan	state or national	national or international	inter-national

Pollution is intrinsically related to population growth and to changes in consumption patterns. In the 20th century, as a consequence of the rural exodus and of industrial development, the urban population grew significantly, aggravating its problems. Over time, the cities expanded and conurbated into large metropolises, and now in the world nearly a billion people live in cities with over a million inhabitants, mainly in developing countries (Table 6.6).

The high intensity of activities in metropolises leads to several pressures on the environment: water consumption, waste generation, noise and air pollution. Of these, air pollution is the local problem most intrinsically linked to energy consumption. Large metropolises are particularly subjected to local air pollution caused by industry, energy generation and transportation. Particulate matter concentrations are a relevant indicator for the inefficient and poorly controlled use of coal and oil products, as can be seen in the data of the major Asian cities (Figure 6.10).

Table 6.6 Population in cities with over a million inhabitants
in 2002 (WRI, 2009)

Region	Million inhabitants
World	873
Developed countries (OECD)	116
Developing countries	757
Countries of low per capita GDP	299
Asia (except for the Middle East)	420
Central America and the Caribbean	47
Middle East and Northern Africa	99
South America	128
sub-Saharan Africa	88

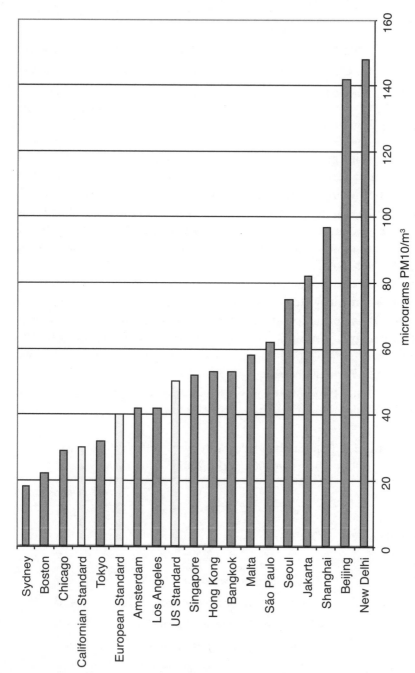

Figure 6.10 PM$_{10}$ concentrations in Asian cities, 2003, and other cities in the world, 1997 (Sinton et al, 1995; Ontario Ministry of the Environment, 1998)

Next, Figure 6.11 shows that the incidence of diseases attributed to air pollution is higher in developing countries consuming low-quality coal and oil products.

The main urban air pollutants, as well as their main characteristics and exposure criteria provided by WHO, are presented in Table 6.7. Except for (low-altitude or tropospheric) ozone,[5] all the other pollutants are called *primary*, that is, they are directly emitted by the processes – usually combustion.

The duration of each pollutant impact and its reach vary a lot with climate, topographic and exposure conditions. Synergistic and antagonistic effects also occur, either increasing or reducing their impact. An example is the emission of sulphates, sulphur composites which adsorb (in their surface) toxic substances (such as benzene) and heavy metals, forming fine particulate matter (Figure 6.12). High sulphur diesel oil burning is a specific example, with a direct effect on the high environmental concentrations of fine particulate matter ($PM_{2,5}$) in large cities.

When assessing the pollutant effects, it is very important to differentiate concentrations from loads:

- *concentrations,* actually sampled or estimated by modellings, are the proportion of pollutants observed or expected in a given air volume (or another means), reflecting the environment situation either volumetrically (e.g. in 'parts per million in volume', ppmv) or by mass (e.g. in 'micrograms per cubic metre', $\mu g/m^3$) of pollutants;
- *pollutant loads* are amounts emitted (by stacks, vehicle exhaust tailpipes and other exhaust systems) in a given period; they are usually

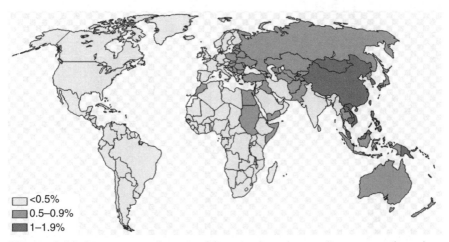

Figure 6.11 Proportion of service life years lost due to diseases attributed to air pollution in 2003 (Sinton et al, 1995)

Table 6.7 Main air pollutants (UNEP, 1992; WHO, 2005a)

Pollutant	Major anthropogenic sources	Impact, duration and scale	Symptoms	WHO (2005) exposure criteria
Sulphur dioxide SO_2	Combustion of coal and oil byproducts; industrial processes using sulphur	Toxic and very acid, few days; from local to regional	Respiratory distress, lack of air, harmed pulmonary function, increase in susceptibility to infections, diseases of the lower respiratory tract (especially in children), chronic pulmonary diseases and pulmonary fibrosis	500mg/m³ for 10 min; 20mg/m³ for 24h
Carbon monoxide CO	Incomplete burning of fossil fuels and of biomass	Toxic and acid, month; occupational and local	Interferes with the blood oxygen (chronic anoxia)	100mg/m³ for 15 min; 60mg/m³ for 30 min
Nitrogen oxides NO_x (NO and NO_2)	Fuel burning at high temperatures (especially the ones containing nitrogen in their composition)	Toxic, acid and precursor of O_3, from hours to a few days; from local to regional	Eyes and nose irritation, respiratory tract diseases, lung damage, decreased pulmonary function and heart stress	400mg/m³ for 1 hour; 150mg/m³ for 24 hours
Particulate matter PM	Incomplete burning of fossil fuels and of biomass, presence of sulphur in fuel forming sulphates (SO_4^-)	Toxic and irritating, from hours to a few days; from occupational to regional	Irritation, altered immunological response, systematic toxicity, decreased pulmonary function and heart stress.	$PM_{2.5}$ (fines): 10mg/m³ annual average and 25mg/m³ for 24h

Hydrocarbons HCs	Fuels evaporative emissions	Toxic, irritating and precursors of O_3, from months to years; from local to global (as is the case of methane, CH_4)	Acts in combination with SO_2. The effect depends on the biological and chemical properties of individual particles	PM_{10}: 20mg/m³ annual average and 50mg/m³ for 24h
Tropospheric ozone O_3	Secondary pollutant, not emitted by processes, but formed by the photochemical oxidation (solar light) of NO_x and HCs in the atmosphere	Toxic and irritating, month; from local to regional	Decreased pulmonary function, heart stress or failure, emphysema, pulmonary and respiratory tissue fibrosis and aging	100mg/m³ for 8h
Heavy metals, especially lead (Pb) and mercury (Hg)	Coal and oil byproducts burning with additives	Very toxic, month; from local to regional	Kidney diseases and neurological damage, affecting mainly children	0.5–1.0mg/m³ for years

represented in units of mass per time, directly (such as 'tons/year') or indirectly, associated to outflows (e.g. in kg/Nm^3 and outflows in $Nm^3/hour$ – where Nm^3 stands for 'normal cubic metre'); these emissions can be *potential* (gross, without end control) or *remaining* (final, after going through emission control equipments, such as filters).

Whereas information on concentrations reflects the *environment quality*, information on loads reflects the *discharge* of pollutants into the environment. In general, environmental control is based on loads (by means of emission limits), environmentally calibrated by concentrations.

A pollutant concentration in the atmosphere indicates the degree of exposure of *receptors* (humans, animals, plants, materials) as the final result of the process of discharging its pollutant *loads* into the atmosphere from its emission sources and its *interactions* in the atmosphere, both physical (dilution) and chemical (reactions). The system is shown in Figure 6.13.

Even under stable emissions, air quality may change in function of the meteorological conditions that determine a higher or lower pollutant dilution in the environment. Air quality worsens with relation to CO, PM and SO_2 parameters during the winter months, when the meteorological conditions are less favourable for pollutant dispersion. Ozone, in turn, presents

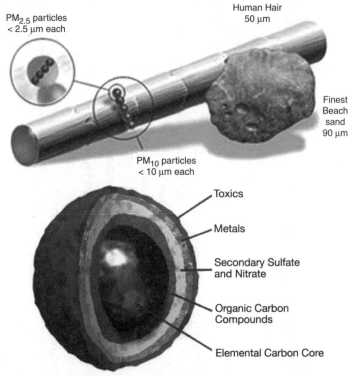

Figure 6.12 Fine particulates (CARB, 2008;CATF, 2008)

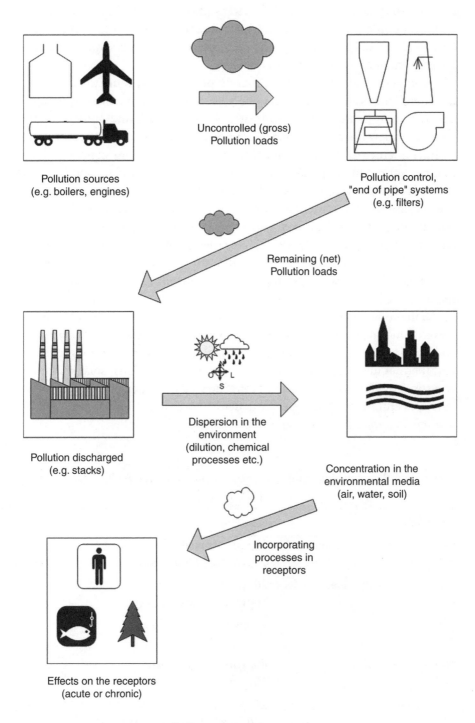

Figure 6.13 Pathways of pollutants

higher concentrations in spring and summer, due to higher sunlight intensity. The interaction between the sources of pollution and the atmosphere defines the final air quality level, which in turn determines the occurrence of adverse air pollution effects on receptors. Table 6.8 presents the World Health Organization air-quality standards.

Air-quality standards refer to different periods of exposure to pollutants: in general one hour, one day and one year. They determine the pollutants' concentration limits in order to protect human health and are constantly revised, as new scientific evidence of impacts and new forms of controlling pollutants emerge. *Primary standards* determine pollutant concentrations that may affect the population health when exceeded; the secondary ones foresee the minimum damage to humans and to the environment, and are used to guide environmental protection policies.[6] Critical episodes of air pollution occur with high concentrations of pollutants in the atmosphere, determining progressive levels for controlling emitters. In the last stage, industrial activities may be halted and the traffic of vehicles may be restrained. Figure 6.14 exemplifies the concentration data in certain regions.

As mentioned, air pollutant concentration at a certain place depends on topographic (presence of mountains, valleys, buildings and other barriers) and meteorological (winds and air circulation, rains, temperature gradients and thermal inversions) characteristics, chemical reactions, solar radiation and types of sources of emission (concentrated or dispersed). Some pollutant concentration effects are particularly hazardous. This is the case of *thermal inversions* (Box 6.3) and of the *emission plumes* effect.

Table 6.8 Air-quality standards recommended by the WHO Guidelines (WHO, 2006a)

Air pollutant	Standard
Particulate matter, ultrafines $PM_{2,5}$	$10\mu g/m^3$ annual mean $25\mu g/m^3$ 24-hour mean
Particulate matter, fines PM_{10}	$20\mu g/m^3$ annual mean $50\mu g/m^3$ 24-hour mean
Ozone O_3	$100\mu g/m^3$ 8-hour mean
Nitrogen dioxide NO_2	$40\mu g/m^3$ annual mean $200\mu g/m^3$ 1-hour mean
Sulphur dioxide SO_2	$20\mu g/m^3$ 24-hour mean $500\mu g/m^3$ 10-minute mean

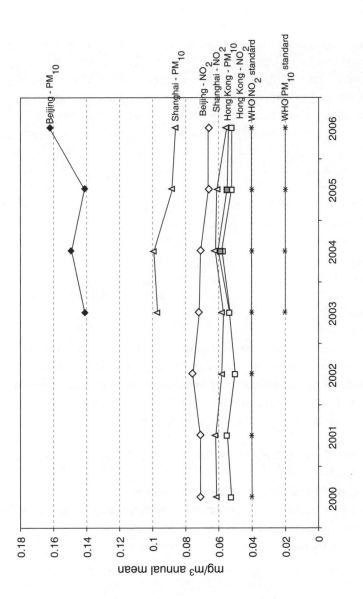

Figure 6.14 Annual pollutant concentrations in selected Chinese cities (Clean Air Initiative for Asia, 2008)

Box 6.3 Thermal inversions

In the troposphere, the temperature decreases almost every time the altitude is increased. In some cases, the temperature may increase with the altitude; when this occurs, we are faced with a temperature inversion or, more simply, *thermal inversion* (Figure 6.15).

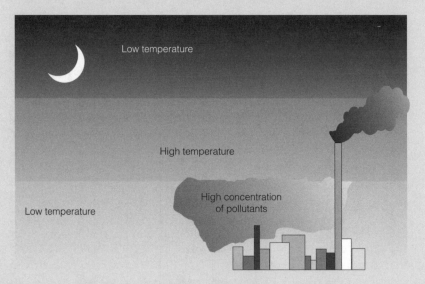

Low temperature

High temperature

High concentration of pollutants

Low temperature

Figure 6.15 Thermal inversion (Davis, 2004)

Thermal inversion is a natural phenomenon that may occur on any day of the year and at any hour of the day. Although in itself it does not pose any risk to human health, it may become dangerous when there are undispersed high pollutant concentrations in the atmosphere layer where it occurs. The causes for a thermal inversion are varied, such as:

- radiation (rapid cooling of the Earth surface during the nights, mainly the cloudless ones);
- advection (transport of cold air to hot zones);
- subsidence (descent of large masses of usually cold air, caused by high-pressure systems); and
- frontal meteorological phenomena (that foster advection).

Due to the interruption of vertical movements, which tend to disappear quickly, thermal inversion indicates the stability of the atmosphere layer, even if it is not necessarily the cause of high pollutant concentrations. These concentrations may be associated with more significant meteorological conditions and with larger extensions. The elements characterizing a thermal inversion are thickness (difference in height between the top and the base of the thermal inversion); intensity (difference in temperature between the top and the base of the thermal inversion); and the temperature and disruption time of the thermal inversion (temperature necessary for the thermal inversion to disappear, that is, for the top temperature to be close to that of the base). Throughout the day, solar rays warm the surface of the Earth which, in turn, warms the closest atmosphere layers. If there is an inversion, the cold air that is below warms slowly until it reaches the same temperature as the air above, which causes the thermal inversion to disappear.

Emission plumes (Figure 6.16) are representations of substance concentrations belched by industrial stacks, thermopower plants and incinerators. The shape of these plumes depends on dispersion conditions: winds, temperature, etc. Before an environmental licensing organism authorizes the installation of such processes near populated areas, it is necessary to model their effects, anticipating the impact and requiring dispersion devices, together with final control of pollutant emissions.

Other pollutant concentration effects occur in traffic jams. Certain populations are more exposed to this sort of pollution: traffic agents, drivers in general, children in school buses and establishments opening onto polluted streets. The proximity to a diesel vehicle exhaust pipe may increase the particulate matter concentrations inside an automobile by over a thousand times (CATF, 2009).

The air pollution problem of a given place may have its origin in a vast array of emissions. The sum of the known loads along a certain period corresponds to the *emission inventory*, which is an important indicator of the performance of pollution sources (despite not necessarily representing its impact, since emissions may be quite dispersed). An example of an inventory is in Figure 6.17, showing how the emissions of local pollutants significantly decreased in the US as a consequence of better technologies (both in production and in pollutant control), of using of cleaner inputs (such as lower-sulphur and lead free oils) and of prioritizing products with higher value and less environmental impacts added.

Energy systems are the main source of SO_2 emissions (especially by poor quality coal and oil byproducts), NO_x (thermal NO_x generated by combustion at temperatures above 1300°C and fuel-NO_x from the use of heavy oils, with high nitrogen content), HCs (evaporative emissions from fuel tanks and vehicle engines, as well as incomplete fuel burning processes)

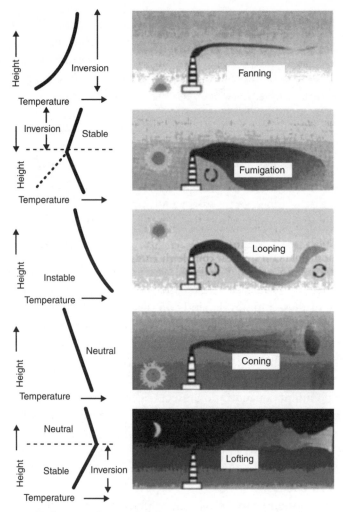

Figure 6.16 Different effects of pollutant concentration by plume emissions, function of the temperature profile (Davis, 2004)

and CO (incomplete hydrocarbon burning). Particulate matter is a more complex class of pollutants, as it involves both dusts and combustion wastes (tar, soot, sulphates). Figure 6.18 shows pollutants by source in Europe.

A serious problem is coal burning in thermopower plants and in industries. This fuel contains large amounts of sulphur and heavy metals such as mercury (Hg). In 1995, about 5500 tons of mercury were emitted globally by natural processes and by human activities (US DoE, 2009). Natural gas-fired power plants emit relatively less pollutants, except for NO_x. Biomass boilers, when well controlled, also basically emit NO_x and PM. Without control, the amounts of particulate matter increase considerably.

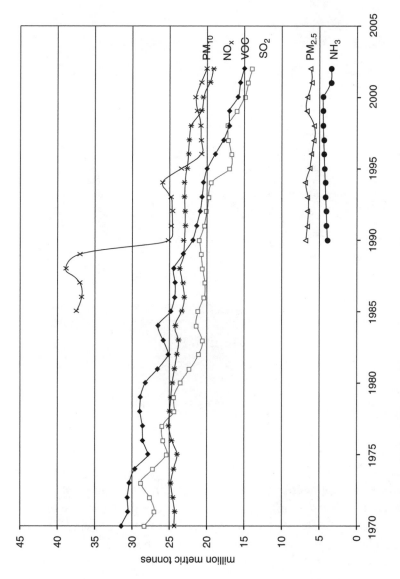

Figure 6.17 Emission inventory of local pollutants in the US (US EPA, 2006)

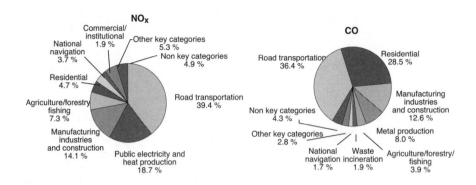

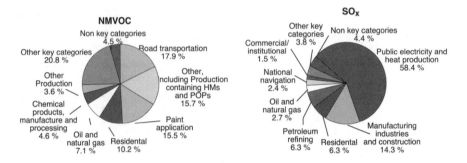

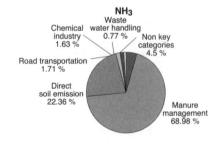

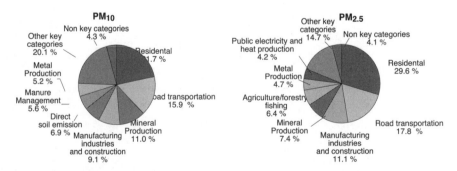

Figure 6.18 *Contribution of key categories to EU-27 emissions of NOₓ, CO, NMVOCs, SOₓ, NH₃, PM₁₀ and PM₂.₅ in 2006 (EEA, 2008)*

Regional pollution

Polluted air in large urban centres may contain traces of volcanic eruptions, forest burning and desert sands coming from thousands of miles away – this is called *background pollution* (Figure 6.19). The air may also be affected by industries, thermopower plants and vehicles located in other states or even countries.

Ozone (O_3) is a secondary pollutant formed from photochemical reactions (i.e. under sunlight) in its precursors, volatile hydrocarbons (such as gasoline) and nitrogen oxides (NO_x). The reactions are difficult to predict, depending on several factors. Ozone pollution may occur far away from where its precursors were emitted. Therefore, a large traffic jam may emit large amounts of NO_x and HCs, which may be carried away by wind to distant regions, where they will react and form ozone miles away from where the precursors were emitted and many hours later. Thus, ozone is not only a local pollutant but also regional, transboundary, which may be detected by satellite assessments. As it is a dispersed pollution, ozone control has to be conducted on its precursors.

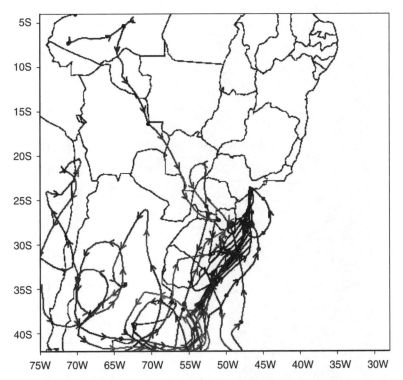

Figure 6.19 Background pollution: particulate matter burnings in the Amazon and its path up to the city of Sao Paulo (Andrade, 2002)

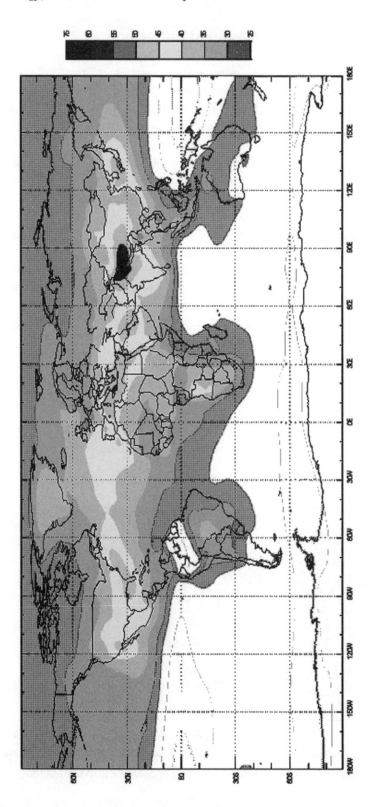

Figure 6.20 Annual average of ozone concentrations, parts per billion in volume, 2000 (UNEP, 2006)

In the troposphere (below 10km of altitude), ozone in high concentrations causes damage to vegetation, harm the lungs and is the main smog formation agent.

Tropospheric and stratospheric ozone should not be confused. The substance is the same, but while the former is a toxic pollutant, the latter is of critical importance for life on Earth, as it filters the Sun's ultraviolet rays (UV-A and UV-B). This occurs in the stratosphere, at altitudes above 25km. In this range, the phenomenon of the ozone layer hole occurs, caused by CFCs and other man-made gases. There is no compensation between the lack of one and the excess of the other type of ozone.

Acid rain

Besides ozone, acid rain may be considered the major transboundary pollution source. Damage to lakes by acidification occurred in Sweden more than 40 years ago, when the decreasing fish population in rivers and lakes was related to changes in water acidity. Acidity is measured by the H^+ (hydrogen ions) concentration in pH units. The pH is defined as the negative logarithm (on a ten basis) of the H^+ concentration. A 7pH is the neutral point, that is, the pH of pure water containing both positive and negative ions. Substances with pH below seven are acid and those above seven are basic. Typical values of pH are presented in Table 6.9.

The pH of acid rainfall in Western Europe and the US are typically found in the interval 4–5 (Figure 6.22), endangering several regions (Figure 6.23).

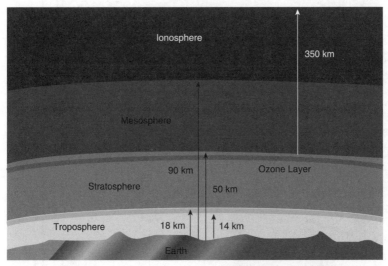

Figure 6.21 Atmosphere layers: troposphere and stratosphere

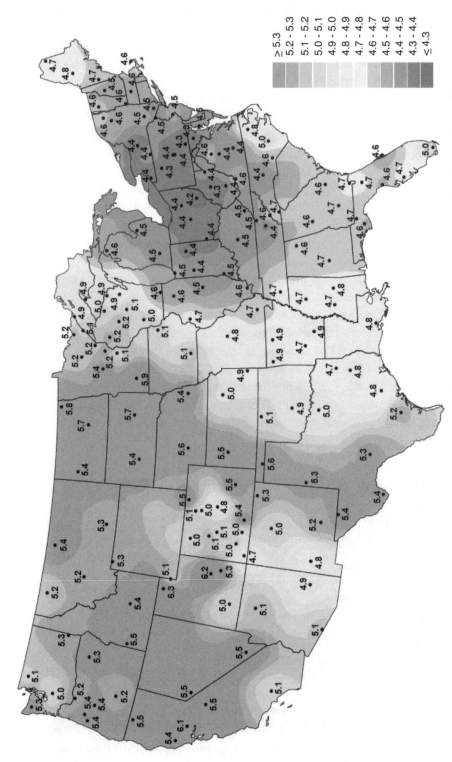

Figure 6.22 Hydrogen ion concentration as pH from measurements in the US, 1999 (NADP, 1999)

Table 6.9 Typical values of pH and their consequences
(Hollander, 1992; VWQD, 2004)

14.0	upper limit, basic substances
12.2	lime
11.3	ammonia
9.0	maximum limit for healthy ecosystems
8.0	sea water
7.0	blood, pure water
6.5	milk
6.0	molluscs and trout start to die
5.6	rain water
5.5	freshwater frog eggs, tadpoles, crustaceans die
4.5	river water in Scandinavia and Eastern US
4.2	fish die
4.0	citric juices
3.0	vinegar
2.4	Coca-Cola
2.2	acid rains close to great SO_2 and NO_x emitters (US)
1.7	mist and fog
0.3	battery acid
0.0	lower limit, acid substances

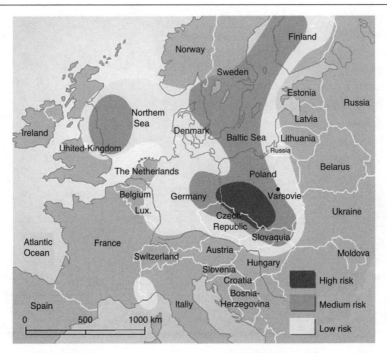

Figure 6.23 Acidification risks in Europe, 1990 (UNEP/GRID-Arendal, 1993)

There are many consequences of acid rain. Some animal species are very vulnerable to acidification; for example, crustaceans and molluscs, their exoskeletons consisting of calcium, do not manage to get formed, thus altering the whole food chain. Trout, salmon and coral reefs are also considerably affected, as well as several vegetable species. Alterations in pH and in temperature affect fish that have trigger mechanisms which determine their survival, sex and other characteristics. Furthermore, acid rain corrodes buildings and monuments, chiefly those of building materials containing calcium, as in the case of marble ($CaCO_3$).

The chemistry of the acid rain production process is only partially understood. Several mechanisms may cause the formation of acid and the dominant chemical reactions depend on location and on weather conditions, as well as on the composition of the local atmosphere. Sunlight, soot and metal waste may also accelerate the acid formation process under certain circumstances (Figure 6.24).

The major precursors of acid rain are sulphur (SO_2) and nitrogen (NO_2) dioxides, by means of two mechanisms:

1   the dry precipitation of oxides deposited on vegetation (mainly pines and other conifers that do not lose their leaves in winter), monuments and buildings;

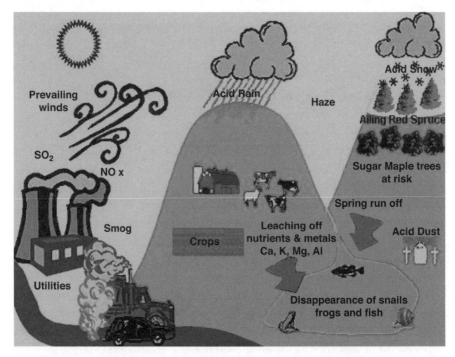

Figure 6.24 Acid rain cycle (VWQD, 2004)

2 wet precipitation, which occurs when oxides are dissolved in the rainfall or atmospheric water vapours, forming sulphuric (H_2SO_4) and nitric (HNO_3) acid.

Every year, about 100 million tons of SO_2 derive from fossil fuel burning, against 2.8Mt from forest burnings and 8Mt from volcanoes (Berresheim et al, 1995). The end-products of fossil fuel burning, SO_2 and NO_x, may be taken very far away from the emission point by the wind. This causes acid rain in places far from the primary pollution source – a regional problem that may cross national boundaries. The anthropogenic emissions of these precursors have systematically decreased in OECD countries, but have increased elsewhere, particularly in Asia (UNEP, 2007).

The anthropogenic SO_2 and NO_x flows are concentrated in a few industrial regions. Frequently, countries receive a considerable amount of pollution originated elsewhere; for example, 90 per cent of the sulphur precipitation in Switzerland in 1980 came from other countries and only 10 per cent was produced in the country itself. A severe problem now occurs in Asia, where the fast industrial expansion requires large amounts of energy, especially from coal and oil. The perspectives are for a large increase in acidic deposition in Asia in the coming decades, especially in regions close to those which use coal intensively: Eastern China, Korea, Eastern India, Thailand, Malaysia and the Philippines (Downing et al, 1997; World Bank, 2006). Acid rain, therefore, is a type of regional pollution with global effects, as shown in Figure 6.25.

Global aspects: the greenhouse effect

The Earth's atmosphere is almost fully transparent to incident solar radiation. A small fraction of this radiation is reflected back to space, but most of it hits the planet surface, mainly as visible light, where it is absorbed and re-emitted as thermal radiation in all directions by infrared rays. However, the atmosphere contains gases that are not transparent to thermal radiation, acting as a blanket around Earth and heating it, in the same way as a greenhouse remains sufficiently warm in winter, to allow the growth of out-of-season vegetables and flowers (Figure 6.26).

As a consequence of the action of the so-called *greenhouse gas effect* (GHG, mainly carbon dioxide and methane), the planet loses less heat into space. The existence of the atmosphere and of the GHG allows life on the planet. They act as stabilizers against sudden changes in temperature between night and day. Without the GHG, it is estimated that the average temperature on the Earth's surface would be 15–20°C below zero. Whereas

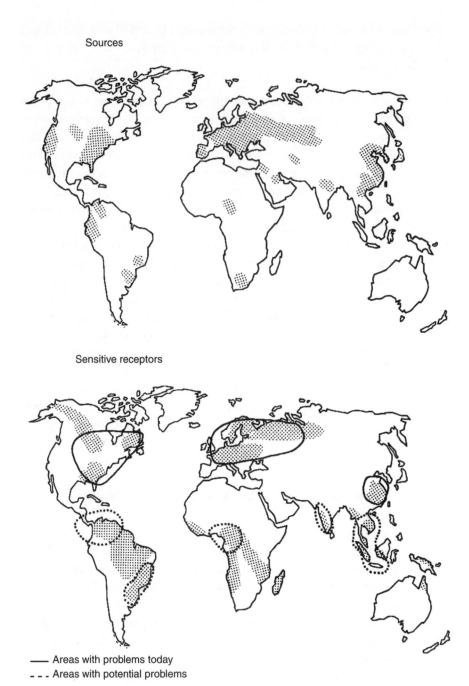

Sources

Sensitive receptors

——— Areas with problems today
- - - Areas with potential problems

Figure 6.25 Acid rain: emitters and receptors (adapted from MSAD, 2006)

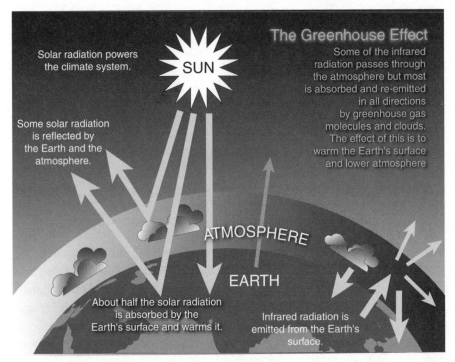

Figure 6.26 The 'greenhouse effect' (Le Treut et al, 2007)

the Moon and Mars do not have an atmosphere and suffer from large differences in temperature throughout the day, Venus has a very thick 'cover', keeping its temperatures permanently high.

The heating produced depends on the concentration and properties of each gas in contributing to it, and on the amount of time in which the gases remain in the atmosphere. Aerosols (small particles) from volcanoes, from sulphate emissions by the industries and from other sources may absorb and reflect radiation as well. In most cases, aerosols tend to cool the climate. Aerosols and ozone (both tropospheric and stratospheric) are also factors that cause an increase in the greenhouse effect; however, the effect is much smaller and scientific uncertainty is even larger. Moreover, there are changes in surface albedo – a reflectivity measure – altered, for example, by change in land use and by the deposition of black particles on white snow. The combined effect of these factors is assessed by means of *radiative forcing,* a term representing an external distress on the energy balance of the Earth's climate system.

Svente Arrhenius (1896) suggested that the *anthropogenic* CO_2 emissions result in Earth warming, but this concept remained as an academic issue until the mid-20th century. Any changes made by human beings in the radiant balance of the Earth, including those deriving from an increase

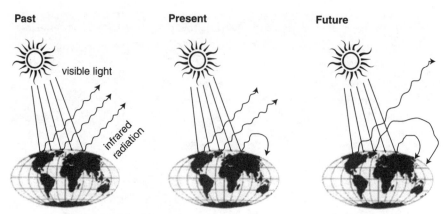

Figure 6.27 Changes in the greenhouse effect mechanism

in the amount of greenhouse gases or aerosols, will tend to change the atmosphere and ocean temperature, as well as the associated currents and types of climate. These changes are overlapped on the natural climate changes and, to distinguish them, it is necessary to identify 'signals' against the 'background noise' of the natural climate variability.

This is not an easy task. The best information available on global climate changes are the scientific assessments by the Intergovernmental Panel on Climate Changes (IPCC[7]), which published its first report in 1990. The fourth version was published in 2006 and its major conclusions are in Box 6.4.

Box 6.4 Intergovernmental Panel on Climate Change Fourth Assessment Report (AR4) Conclusions – The Physical Science Basis (IPCC, 2007)

- The concentration of carbon dioxide – CO_2, the most important greenhouse effect gas – increased from the 280 parts per million (ppm) in the pre-industrial era to 379ppm in 2005, by far exceeding the natural range (180–300ppm) observed in the last 650,000 years by samples in ice cores. The growth rate between 1995 and 2005 was 1.9ppm a year. The world average emission between 2000 and 2005 was 26.4Gt CO_2/year (or 7.2Gt Ceq/year) from fossil fuel burning, as compared to 23.5Gt CO_2/year in the 1990s. The second largest emission sources were the changes in land use, with 5.9Gt CO_2/year in the 1990s.
- The average methane (CH_4) concentration in the atmosphere increased from the pre-industrial 715 parts per billion (ppb) to 1774ppb in 2005; the natural variation in the last 650,000 years was 320–790ppb. The different emission sources are not yet well defined.

- In the case of nitrous oxide (N_2O), the pre-industrial atmospheric concentrations were 270ppb and, in 2005, they were 319ppb. The growth has been constant since 1980 and the main source is from agricultural activities.
- The combined radiative forcing of CO_2, CH_4 and N_2O is +2.30W.m^{-2}, which very probably has not occurred in the last 10,000 years (Figure 6.28).

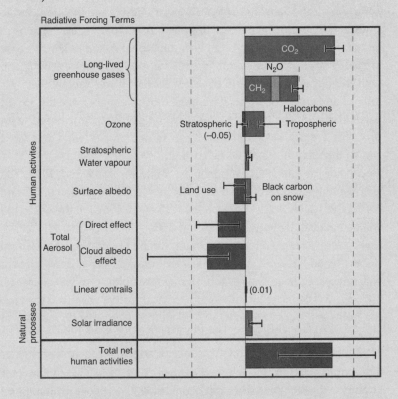

Figure 6.28 Main components of the radiative forcing of climate change between 1750 and 2005 (Forster et al, 2007)

- The 11 years between 1995 and 2006 broke records in average temperature, assessed since 1850. Between 1906 and 2005, the Earth's average temperature increased by 0.74°C. The linear increase in temperature per decade in the last 50 years nearly doubled the one observed in the last 100 years. In the last century, the increase in average temperature in the Arctic doubled that of the planet's average.
- Glaciers and mountain snow, as well as polar ice caps, decreased in a disseminated way. In the Arctic, the spring defrost has increased by 15 per cent since 1900. The dynamic defrosting effects contribute even more to the rise in ocean levels.

- The oceans absorb more than 80 per cent of the heat inciding on Earth and their average temperatures increased in depths of up to 3000m, leading to a volumetric expansion and to the increase in sea level. The sea level rose 17cm in the 20th century, being 1.8mm a year in 1961–2003 and 3.1mm a year in 1993–2003.
- Rainfalls increased in the West of the Americas, Northern Europe and North and Central Asia. Droughts increased in the Mediterranean, South Africa and Sahel (between the Sahara desert and the more fertile lands in the South) and parts of Southern Asia. There is evidence of an increase in cyclone activity, mainly in the North Atlantic. The increase in strong precipitation events is consistent with global warming and with the higher atmospheric concentration of water vapour.
- Intense and longer droughts have been more frequent since the 1970s, particularly in the tropics and subtropics. Also associated with droughts are the alterations in ocean temperatures, wind standards and an increase in mountain defrosting.
- According to the IPCC modellings, between 1999 and 2099, the average temperature of the planet will increase by between 0.3°C and 6.4°C; the sea level will rise between 0.18 and 0.59m and the ocean pH will be reduced by between 0.14 and 0.35.
- The models also predict that warming will be greater on land than on oceans – and higher in the northern latitudes; perennial snow and ice will decrease; heat waves and strong precipitations will increase; cyclones will be more intense; extra-tropical storms will move towards the poles and ocean currents will be altered (the Atlantic meridional ocean current will decrease by about 25 per cent).
- Therefore, to stabilize the CO_2 concentrations in the atmosphere at 450ppm, increasing the average temperature by 0.5°C, in the 21st century considerable effort will be necessary to reduce emissions by 2460Gt CO_2 (or 670Gt Ceq) to 1800Gt CO_2 (490Gt Ceq).
- Past and future CO_2 emissions caused by human activities will continue to contribute to global warming and an increase in ocean levels for more than a millennium, due to the timescale necessary to remove these gases from the atmosphere.

One of the most important examples of global warming occurred in the summer of 2003 when, for the first time recorded, the perennial snows of Mount Kilimanjaro in Tanzania, the last ice cap in Africa, have melted. Figure 6.29 illustrates the causes for the rise in ocean levels:

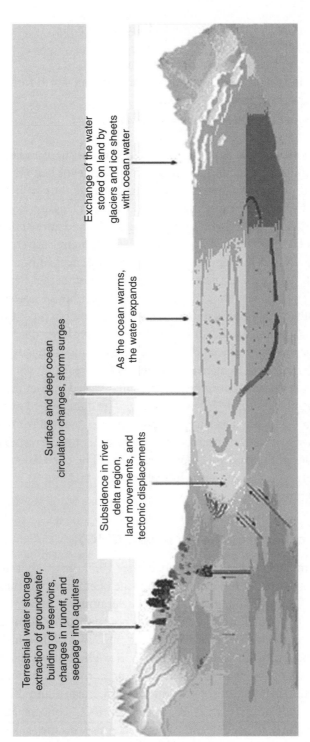

Figure 6.29 Causes of rise in ocean level

1   surface water storage, underground water extraction, reservoirs building and seepage in aquifers;
2   silt deposits, land and tectonic movements;
3   changes in surface and deep current circulation, storm formation;
4   water expansion in warmed oceans;
5   defrosting of the water stored in glaciers.

In addition, changes have occurred in the atmosphere and the ocean circulation standards, affecting the great ocean conveyor belt (Figure 6.30).

The phenomena associated with climate change thus go beyond warming: extreme events are more intense and frequent (Figure 6.31).

The Earth's average surface temperature data and atmosphere temperatures obtained by satellite altitudes of several kilometres are consistent. The IPCC 4th Assessment Report states that the evidences of human influence on global climate are increasingly stronger, and that there is between 90 and 99 per cent probability that the increase in 'greenhouse gases' concentrations has substantially contributed to global warming in recent years. In the past 400,000 years, the Earth's climate witnessed large changes in a few decades, for example, glaciation. These rapid changes suggest that the climate may be sensitive to internal or external factors. Analyses of ancient ice layers indicate that temperatures in the planet varied little in the last 10,000 years – possibly less than 1°C per century. The data in the last 40 years are the most accurate; the data of past centuries are obtained from ice samples from the Arctic and the Antarctic, at different depths corresponding to the precipitations of the land and snow at the time. The correlation between the CO_2 concentration in the atmosphere and the increase in temperature is evident (Figure 6.32).

CO_2 and other greenhouse gases (GHG)

The experimental evidence established after 1950 proves that the composition of the atmosphere has changed since the beginning of the industrial era and that the pace of change has been accelerating. Typical of the average situation of the planet are the data on carbon dioxide concentration in the atmosphere at the Mauna Loa observatory, in Hawaii, US, which is isolated from external emission factors (Figure 6.33). The fast oscillations are due to the seasons of the year. There is a strong correlation between the CO_2 concentrations in the atmosphere and the temperature, and the evolution is not linear, indicating that from a certain CO_2 concentration, abrupt changes are likely to occur. Anthropogenic emissions may take the climate back to the instability observed before the ice age. CO_2 from fossil fuel

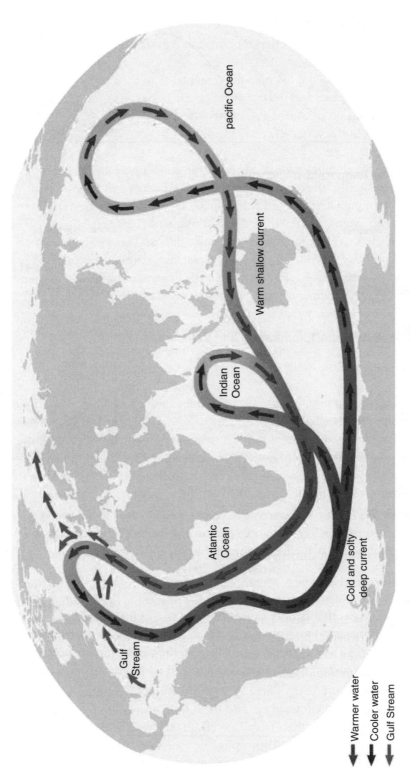

Figure 6.30 The Great Ocean Conveyor (UNEP/GRID-Arendal, 2006)

Increase in Average Temperature

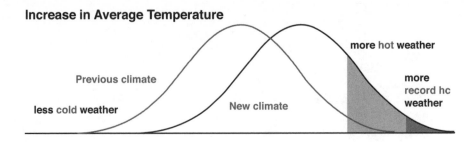

Increase in Temperature Variance

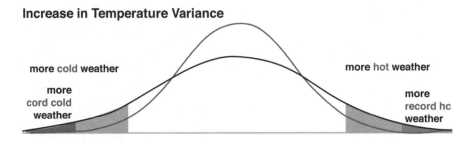

Increase in Average Temperature and Variance

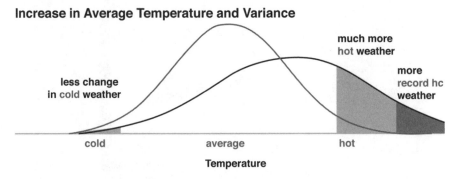

Figure 6.31 Effects in extreme temperatures: increase in the average temperature, top; increase in temperature variation centre; synergetic result of the two effects, bottom (NASA, 2007; figure adapted from IPCC, 2001)

burning is the gas that mainly causes the increase in the greenhouse effect, due to the large amounts involved, which affect the carbon balance on Earth (Table 6.10 and Figure 6.34). Whereas the combustion processes are immediate, the carbon recovery by the soil and by biomass is slow, affecting the cycle.

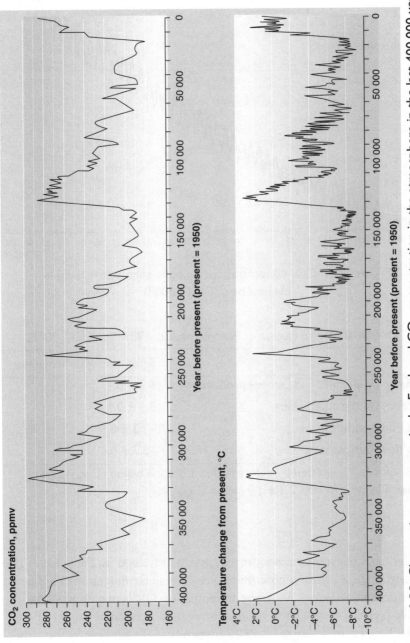

Figure 6.32 Changes in temperature in the Earth and CO_2 concentration in the atmosphere in the last 400,000 years, analysis of the ice core at the Vostok base, Antarctic (UNEP, 2008b).

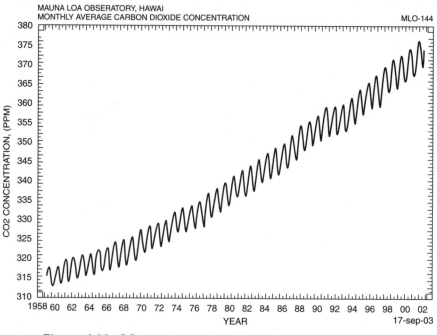

Figure 6.33 CO_2 concentrations (in ppm, parts per million) in Mauna Loa (CDIAC, 2003)

Table 6.10 Global carbon emissions balance, 1989–98 (IPCC, 2001)

	Billion tons of carbon a year
Emissions (fossil fuels and cement production)	6.3 ± 0.4
C increase in the atmosphere	3.3 ± 0.1
Ocean flow–atmosphere	−2.3 ± 0.5
Earth flow–atmosphere*	−0.7 ± 0.6

* Net value being emitted by deforestation 1.6 ± 0.8 billion tCeq/year and absorbed by new forests 2.3 ± 1.8 billion tCeq/year

The most relevant greenhouse effects are presented in Table 6.11. The capacity of these gases in contributing to global warming is assessed by an indicator called Global Warming Potential, or *GWP*, which provides the relative contribution of each gas, per mass unit, compared to that of CO_2. As can be seen in Table 6.11, *GWP* depends on its lifetime in the atmosphere and on its interactions with other gases and with water vapour. Some substances have a much-extended lifetime in the atmosphere, increasing their *GWP*; it is the case of chlorofluorocarbons – CFCs.[8]

Table 6.11 Major greenhouse gases (IPCC, 2001)

Greenhouse gas (GHG)	Formula	Greenhouse effect potential (GWP)	Concentrations (ppbv) pre-industrial	Concentrations (ppbv) in 2007	Lifetime in the atmosphere (years)	Anthropic sources
Carbon dioxide	CO_2	1	278,000	383,000	variable	Fossil fuels, deforestation
Methane	CH_4	21	700	1770	12	Wastes, livestock
Nitrous oxide	N_2O	310	270	311	120	Fertilizers, industrial processes
CFC-12	CCl_2F_2	6200–7100	0	0.503	102	Refrigeration, expanding agents
HCFC-22	$CHClF_2$	1300–1400	0	0.105	12	Refrigeration
Perfluoromethane	CF_4	6500	0	0.070	50,000	Aluminium production
Sulphur hexafluorine	SF_6	23,900	0	0.032	3200	Dielectric fluid

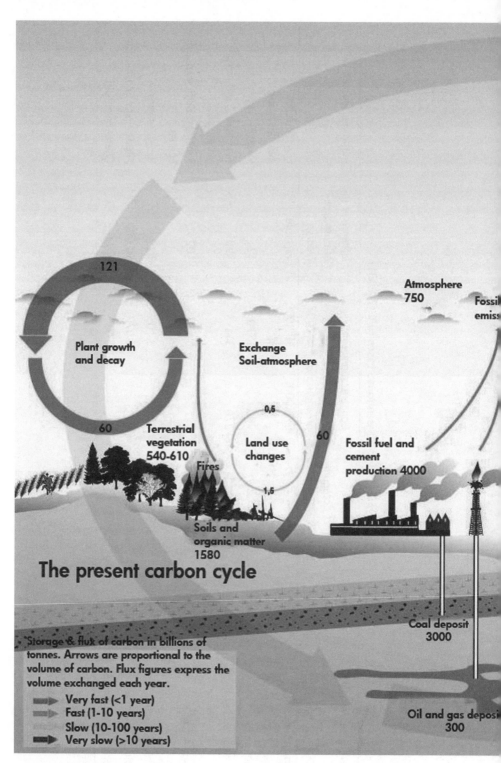

Figure 6.34 The global carbon cycle (UNEP/GRID-Arendal, 2005)

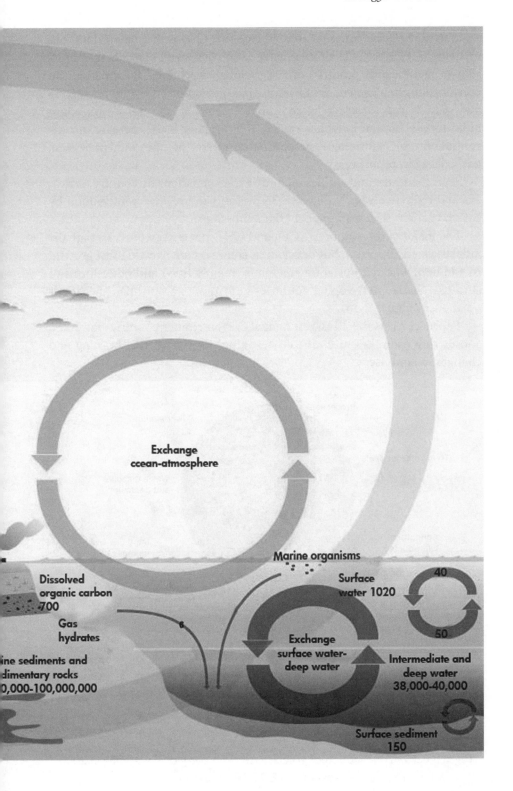

Exchange
ocean-atmosphere

Marine organisms

Dissolved
organic carbon
700

Surface
water 1020

40

Gas
hydrates

Exchange
surface water-
deep water

50

ine sediments and
dimentary rocks
0,000-100,000,000

Intermediate and
deep water
38,000-40,000

Surface sediment
150

Due to the large amounts emitted globally, CO_2 is the main GHG, but methane (CH_4) has a 21 times greater *GWP* (also with considerable emissions), significantly contributing to global warming. Information on emissions is often shown, as in *tons of carbon equivalent* (tCeq) or *tons of carbon dioxide equivalent* (tCO₂eq) units.[9] One of the most important indicators of human influence on the environment is the increase in concentrations of substances in the atmosphere in the industrial age, particularly in recent years.

Several authors and entities quantify GHG emissions by country, sector, gas and reference year.[10] Figure 6.35 presents the relative contribution by gas and activity sector for global GHG emissions.

The major carbon emitters (CO_2 and CH_4) per energy processes are the industrialized countries, but developing countries are showing fast growth. In addition, with deforestation emissions (mainly fires) and other forms of land-use change, developing countries emit more carbon than the developed ones (Figure 6.36).

Table 6.12 lists the 20 largest annual carbon emitter countries for 2003, considering estimates of emissions resulting from fossil fuel burning and changes in land use.

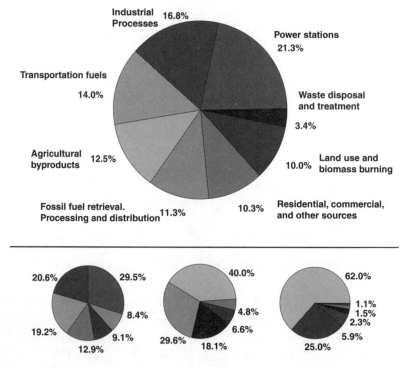

Figure 6.35 Contribution of greenhouse gases for global warming in 2000 (data from EDGAR, 2009)

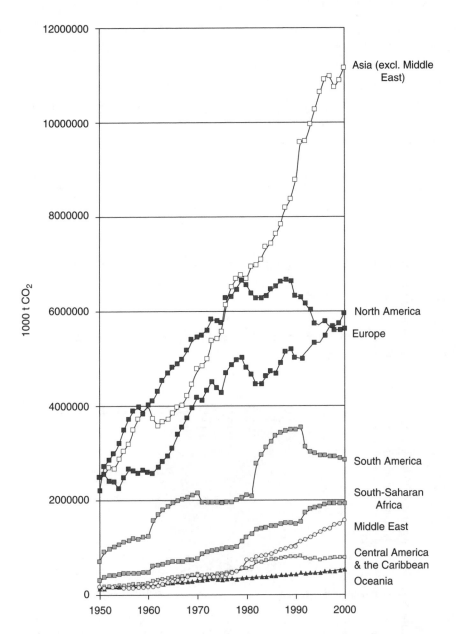

Figure 6.36 CO_2 emissions including land use change by region (WRI, 2009)

The 'per capita' contribution to emissions shows expressible differences among countries, reflecting both consumption habits and production patterns. Figure 6.37 underlines the predominance of developed countries and the weight of the oil and coal producers.

After a growth period, as from the 1980s, the countries in North America and Europe stabilized and even reduced their CO_2 per capita

Table 6.12 Ranking of the 20 largest carbon emitters, with and without land use change (data from CDIAC, 2003; UNFCCC, 2006)[11]

Country	A Fossil fuel burning, 2003 million tons of carbon (Ceq)	B = A x 44/12 Fossil fuel burning, 2003 (Mt CO$_2$eq)	C CO$_2$ per fossil fuel ranking	D GHGs (MtCO$_2$eq) without land use change	E GHGs (MtCO$_2$eq) with land use change	F = E − D GHGs (MtCO$_2$eq) by the land use change	G Latest reference year	H = B + F Total CO$_2$ (MtCO$_2$eq) in 2003, with land use	I Ranking with land use
US	1580	5793	1	6894	6072	−822	2003	4971	1
China	1131	4147	2	4057	3650	−407	1994	3740	2
Russia	408	1496	3	1873	1664	−209	1999	1287	4
India	348	1276	4	1214	1229	15	1994	1291	3
Japan	336	1232	5	1339	1230	−109	2003/1995	1123	5
Germany	219	803	6	1018	982	−36	2003	767	7
Canada	154	565	7	740	696	−44	2003	521	10
UK	152	557	8	651	650	−1	2003	556	9
South Korea	124	455	9	289	263	−26	1990	429	11
Italy	122	447	10	570	488	−82	2003	365	14
Mexico	114	418	11	383	525	142	1990	560	8
Iran	104	381	12	385	417	32	1994	413	12

France	102	374	13	557	505	–52	2003	322	16
South Africa	99	363	14	380	361	–19	1994	344	15
Australia	97	356	15	515	550	35	2003	391	13
Ukraine	86	315	16	527	471	–56	2003	259	19
Spain	84	308	17	402	362	–40	2003	268	18
Poland	83	304	18	370	319	–51	2002	253	20
Saudi Arabia	83	304	19	nd				304	17
Brazil	81	297	20	659	1477	818	1994	1115	6
Total	5507	20,192	–	na	na	na	na	na	–
World	6925	25,392	–	na	na	na	na	na	–

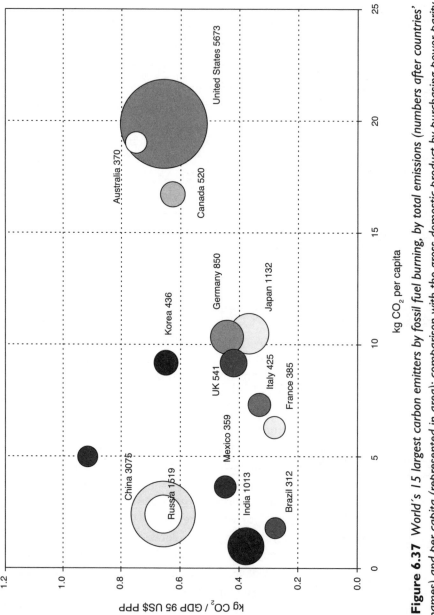

Figure 6.37 *World's 15 largest carbon emitters by fossil fuel burning, by total emissions (numbers after countries' names) and per capita (represented in area); comparison with the gross domestic product by purchasing power parity (GDP PPP) in 2001 (data from IEA, 2004)*

emissions, both by gains in efficiency and by transfer to other regions of energy-intensive industries, such as metallurgy, non-ferrous metals, mining, paper and pulp and others (Figure 6.38).

Box 6.5 The Intergovernmental Panel on Climate Change (IPCC), Convention on Climate Change (UNFCCC) and the Kyoto Protocol

Before the scientific evidence of the influence of human activities on the climate, in 1988 the World Meteorological Organization and the UN Environment Program established the Intergovernmental Panel on Climate Change (*IPCC*). The repercussion of the IPCC's first assessment report, published in 1990, led to the adoption of the *UNFCCC - UN Framework Convention on Climate Change*. The *UNFCCC* was open for signing at the Eco-92, the 'Earth Summit' in Rio de Janeiro (UN Conference on Environment and Development – UNCED) and has been in force since 21 March 1994, among 180 countries that meet periodically (at the so-called Conferences of the Parties, or *CoPs*).

The 1992 Climate Convention final objective is the stabilization of the atmospheric concentrations of greenhouse gases at levels considered safe ,and in compatible timescale with the ecosystem's capacity of recovery and natural adaptation (UNFCCC, 2009). One of the principles of the Convention is that of common but differentiated responsibilities. Under such principle, industrialized countries (or Parties of the Convention Annex I)[12] contribute – and contributed more in the past – to the impact on the climate and must thus compromise to reduce greenhouse gas emissions. Also, developing countries (Non-Annex I Parties) will have a longer deadline and less stringent commitments, with no compulsory goals for reducing emissions – at least until 2012. In order to account for the reductions, the Parties submit documents to the Convention (National Communications) with their greenhouse gas emission inventories. After several rounds of discussions and negotiations, in 1997 the countries adopted the Kyoto Protocol, by which the *Annex I* Parties (industrialized countries) commit to individual emission reduction *targets* for the period 2008–12. Targets vary from country to country, but jointly they agreed with reducing emissions, by at least 5 per cent in relation to the 1990 levels, of the major greenhouse gases: CO_2, CH_4, N_2O, HFCs, PFCs and SF_6. The US has not yet ratified the Kyoto Protocol, citing 'loss of economic competitiveness'. In order to reduce the emission mitigation costs, the Kyoto Protocol established three *mechanisms*:

1   Joint Implementation;
2   Emissions Trading; and
3   Clean Development Mechanism – CDM.

In agreement to the latter, Annex I countries help developing countries with investments and can log the reductions obtained as their own. The Protocol operating function is still the object of meetings among the Parties and there is a very complex sector: change in land use and forests, by deforestation, forestation and reforestation. The official emission statistics, informed by the countries in their National Communications and compiled by the *UNFCCC*, are complex, since each country's emissions can refer to different base years and often do not cover all gases (such as CFCs) and sources (such as deforestation emissions, for example).[13] The Kyoto Protocol also approaches the *adaptation* to climate change issues, especially by the more vulnerable developing countries, such as insular countries and the ones experiencing desertification.

Table 6.13 shows the emissions data presented to the UNFCCC by Brazil, China and India, comparing the total 122 Non-Annex I developing countries with the Annex I developed countries. The considerable weight of land use change can be verified in Brazil, basically from deforestation.

Some Annex I countries are far from achieving their goals. According to the UNFCCC, 2007, among the countries that mostly increased their greenhouse gas emissions in the period 1990–2004 are: Turkey (+72.6%), Spain (+49.0%), Portugal (+41.0%), Greece (+26.6%), Canada (+26.6%) and Australia (+25.1%). The latter two had an increase for producing 'dirty' energy, from bituminous sands and coal. The first ones were due to the fast economic growth not followed by enough increases in energy efficiency. Developed countries such as the Netherlands (+2.4%), Belgium (+ 1.4%), France (–0.6%) and Sweden (–3.5%) managed to stabilize their emissions to the 1990 levels, thanks to efficiency actions. Others went beyond: UK (–14.3%) and Germany (–17.2%). The collapse of the USSR brought significant reductions in some countries in Eastern Europe, more for economic reasons than for an increase in efficiency: Russia (–32.0%), Ukraine (–55.3%) and Latvia (–60.4%). Such reduced emissions are called 'hot air'.

Among the developing countries in the Non-Annex I group, the emerging economies of China, India, Brazil and South Africa are highlighted, and their GHG per capita emissions, excluding land use, are in Table 6.14.

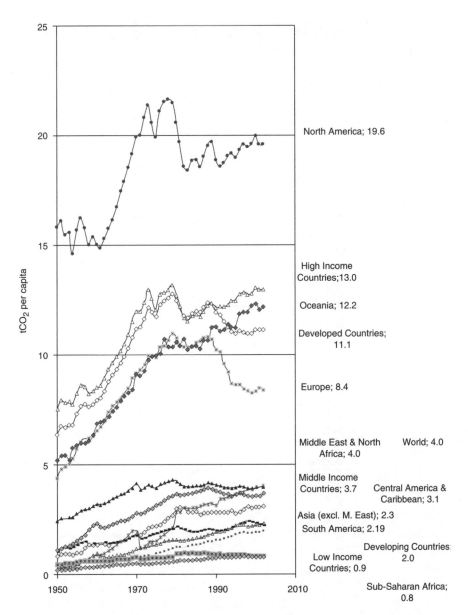

Figure 6.38 Carbon dioxide emissions by inhabitant and region (data from CDIAC, 2009; and FAO, 2009)

Land use change

The UN Food and Agriculture Organization (FAO, 2005) estimates that the world forests store 283 billion tons (Gt) of carbon in their biomass, not to mention the organic matter deposited in the soil. These stocks grew about 1.1Gt every year, due to continuous deforestation and forest

Table 6.13 Greenhouse gas emissions informed by the national communications to the UNFCCC, without land use, by country or group of countries (UNFCCC, 2005)

Country	Reference	Gas (without land use)				Sector (without land use)				Total Tg CO_{2eq}	
		CO_2	CH_4	N_2O	HFCs PFC SF_6	Energy	Agriculture	Industries	Wastes	Without land use	With land use
Brazil	1994	38.4%	36.2%	25.3%	nd	37.6%	56.0%	3.2%	3.1%	659	1477
China	1994	75.8%	17.7%	6.5%	nd	74.1%	14.9%	7.0%	4.0%	4057	3650
India	1994	64.2%	31.3%	4.6%		61.3%	28.4%	8.5%	1.9%	1214	1229
Non-Annex I	1994 or latest year available	63.1%	25.7%	11.2%	nd	63.9%	25.9%	6.0%	4.3%	4374	12,493
Annex I	1990	80.1%	12.3%	6.5%	1.1%	86.0%	7.1%	4.7%	2.2%	18,371	16,824
	2003	82.7%	10.0%	5.6%	1.7%	85.8%	5.6%	5.6%	3.0%	17,288	15,734

degradation for land use change and natural processes connected to human activities, such as fires and plagues. The carbon stored in a hectare of tropical forest is larger than that of other types of vegetation, as can be seen in Table 6.15.

In 2005, there was an average of 0.62 hectare[14] of forests per capita in the world. However, two billion people live in 64 countries with an average below 0.1 hectare per capita and seven countries do not have forests. Ten countries have two-thirds of all the forests on Earth (Figure 6.39).

Table 6.14 GHG emissions (in CO_2eq) excluding land use change for 1994 (or closest year informed), in the major developing countries and regions Non-Annex I (UNFCCC, 2005)

	t CO_2 eq per capita	
Africa	2.4	
South Africa		9.1
Asia-Pacific	2.6	
China		3.3
India		1.3
Latin America and the Caribbean	4.5	
Brazil		4.1
Other Non-Annex I		5.1
122 Non-Annex I countries		2.8

Table 6.15 Changes in forest areas and in the carbon stored, 1990–2005 (FAO, 2005)

	In planted forest areas (million ha)			In carbon stored in forests (Gt Ceq)		
	1990	2000	2005	1990	2000	2005
Africa	12	13	14	66	64	62
Asia	46	55	64	41	35	31
Europe	22	25	27	42	43	44
North and Central America	11	17	18	41	42	42
Oceania	2	3	4	12	10	10
South America	8	10	11	105	100	99

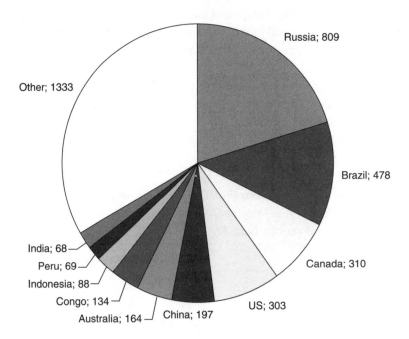

Figure 6.39 Countries with the largest forest areas
(million of hectares) in 2005 (FAO, 2005)

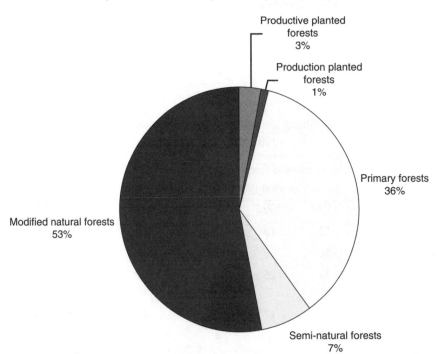

Figure 6.40 Forest characteristics in 2005 (FAO, 2005)

Primary forests (i.e. native species without significant human interference) correspond to 36 per cent of the total (Figure 6.40), but six million hectares have been lost or modified since 1990.

It is difficult to assess the initial extension of the ecosystems in the period preceding agriculture. A total 4628 million hectares (Mha) of forests are estimated to have existed at the pre-agricultural age (being 1277Mha of tropical forests), against a present total of about 3952Mha (UNEP, 1992). The European native forests were devastated between 7000 and 3000 years ago. In the Mediterranean basin, they decreased even more because Greek and Roman civilizations used wood to cast metals, build ships and for other uses, which was in addition to substantial agricultural and herding expansion. In areas where there were tropical forests, the impact records go back thousands of years, possibly until 23,000 years ago in the Peruvian Amazon. The present forests are distributed as shown in Table 6.16.

The annual deforestation rate is 13 million hectares a year and, considering reforestation, 7.3 million hectares a year (the Panama area). In the period 1990–2000, the liquid decrease was 8.9 million hectares a year. In the greenhouse gas emissions inventories, there is a very important sector, difficult to deal with: land use change.[15] In developed countries the total greenhouse gas emission is smaller considering land use, whereas in Brazil (besides Southeastern Asia and in many African countries) the opposite occurs. This reflects the predominance of reforestation activities in the former and deforestation in the latter. The reforestation activities reabsorb the carbon from the atmosphere by photosynthesis, reducing the total emissions of the country which produced them. This does not mean an automatic recovery of original forests, or of the biodiversity lost, but a

Table 6.16 Forests by sub-region in 2005 (FAO, 2005)

	2005 Area (1000ha)	Total world	Annual change, 1990–2000 1000ha		Annual change, 2000–2005 1000ha	
Africa	635,412	16.1%	−4375	−0.64%	−4040	−0.62%
Asia	571,577	14.5%	−792	−0.14%	1003	0.18%
Europe	1,001,394	25.3%	877	0.09%	661	0.07%
North and Central America	705,849	17.9%	−328	−0.05%	−333	−0.05%
Oceania	206,254	5.2%	−448	−0.21%	−356	−0.17%
South America	831,540	21.0%	−3802	−0.44%	−4251	−0.50%
World	3,952,025	100.0%	−8868	−0.22%	−7317	−0.18%

simple accounting of the carbon stored, mostly in fast-growing trees such as *eucalyptus* and *pinus*. As an example of biodiversity, Brazil has 7780 native tree species, whereas Iceland has only three. Moreover, the selective cutting of noble trees does not appear in land-use change data. The forest statistics are also imprecise concerning the changes dynamic, that is, the natural regeneration of the deforested areas and the losses by natural disasters. Natural forests are continuously being lost in many developing countries due to deforestation, inadequate regeneration, the advancement of the agricultural boundaries, urbanization and pollution. The alteration in local climate leads to a *savannization* process of the forest edges and to the selection of more resistant species within these ecosystems. This issue will be further discussed.

Occupational pollution

There are several categories of occupational pollution, but air pollution in enclosed environments deserves special attention. Three types of problem are related to this topic:

1 *traditional* pollution, due to the use of solid fuels (fuelwood, coal, wastes) for heating and cooking in enclosed environments, which produces smoke, particulate matter (PM), carbon monoxide (CO) and other gases, mainly affecting the poor in rural areas;
2 *occupational pollution itself* harms miners (especially coal miners) and industrial workers with diseases such as silicosis and mercury poisoning;
3 *modern pollution* (also called *sick building syndrome*) affects people who live in confined spaces and are exposed to chemical and biological contaminants (such as aldehydes from insulating foam, paints, coatings and solvents, asbestos from building materials, viruses and bacteria in air conditioning).

In some cases, due to occupational issues, certain parcels of the population are more exposed to local air pollution. That is what occurs to drivers (even within vehicles), traffic wardens and other people who work and live near busy roads.

Occupational pollution due to the energy use of traditional biomass

More than half the world's population depend on fuelwood to cook; domestic cooking accounts for more than 60 per cent of the total energy used in sub-Saharan Africa and exceeds 80 per cent in several countries. In 2002, about 2.4 billion people, mostly in developing countries, were harmed by this type of pollution (IEA, 2004). Latin America alone accounted for 79 million people. The use of solid fuels does not differ from country to country solely in amount, but also in type. Table 6.18 shows that Asian countries use a high proportion of dung and straw, whereas in Africa and in Latin America, fuelwood is more frequently used.

The use of fuelwood for energy ends has a global environmental dimension (greenhouse gas emission), as well as a regional and a local dimension (air pollution) and considerable occupational impact (pollutant concentrations in enclosed environments). Biomass burning by the poor for cooking has been identified by WHO as the major health problem, owing to the air pollution in enclosed environments, in the world today. In 2002, the simple act of cooking killed about two million people and accounted for 2.7 per cent of all the costs of medical assistance. Occupational pollution deriving from the use of solid fuels is one of the most serious health risk factors in the world, even worse than air pollution in urban centres. An important indicator is the disability-adjusted life years, or DALYs, shown in Figure 6.41.

Globally, 38.5 million DALYs (2.6 per cent of the total) are attributed to the use of solid fuels in 2002 by the WHO. In Africa, this percentage rises to 3.6 per cent (WHO, 2004). This type of pollution particularly affects less developed countries, both in terms of mortality and in terms of morbidity (Figure 6.42).

Life conditions that expose people to high air pollution levels in enclosed environments are well documented. WHO estimates that nearly 1.5 billion people live in an unhealthy atmosphere. Women (who usually conduct all the house chores), elderly people and children staying indoors are the population segment most continuously exposed to air pollution in enclosed environments. In 2002, the proportion reaches one woman out of three persons in the Southeast Asia regions and West Pacific region (WHO, 2006b).

Among all the endemic diseases, including diarrhoea, occupational pollution is the most disseminated cause of chronic diseases. The exposure to the high smoke rates of fuelwood (frequently ten or more times above the limits recommended) occurs in all the developing countries and, in turn, has been associated to acute respiratory infection, especially pneumonia, and to several other diseases. Acute respiratory infection is actually the main danger for children's health in developing nations, accounting for 4.3 million estimated deaths a year.

In rural areas and city peripheries, homes frequently consist of small buildings of multiple use, where the same room or a few rooms are used for cooking, sleeping and working. In many cases, the total internal volume is smaller than 40m³; and can be less than 20m³, with minimal ventilation.

Table 6.17 Occupational pollution and its effects on human health (WHO, 2005b, c, 2006b)

Pollutant		Major sources of occupational pollution	Mechanism	Effects on health
Fine particulate matter, particulate matter, particles in suspension and smoke	$PM_{2.5}$ PM_{10} PM	burning of coal, oil and byproducts (especially diesel), fuelwood burning, tobacco, resuspension of sitting dust	bronchial tubes irritation, reduction in mucus	respiratory infections, cancer, aggravation of heart conditions
Carbon monoxide	CO	burning of coal, oil and by-products (specially in vehicles), tobacco	combination with haemoglobin, reducing oxygen circulation in blood	cardiovascular diseases, alterations in the central nervous system, perinatal death, low weight at birth
Sulphur oxides (especially dioxide)	SO_x (SO_2)	coal burning	irritation of the respiratory tract and eyes, formation of sulphates, which are combined with other substances forming PM	lung damage, infections, irritations, cancer
Ozone	O_3	solar rays action on NO_x and HCs	irritation in the eyes and respiratory tract	precocious aging, infections, respiratory distress
Hydrocarbons (HCs)		incomplete burning and evaporation of fuels and other volatile compounds	irritation	cancer, respiratory problems

Polycyclic aromatic hydrocarbons (PAHs)		combustion and cooking oil vapours, tobacco	carcinogenesis	cancer
Arsenic, fluorine	As, F	coal burning	chronic intoxication	cancer
Volatile organic compounds (VOC)		fuel burning, tobacco, solvents, paint and gloss, cooking oil vapours	carcinogenesis	lung cancer
Aldehydes		building materials, furniture, cooking, vehicular emissions	respiratory tract and eye irritation	infections, asthma, cancer
Pesticides, asbestos, lead		Consumption products, dusts	acute and chronic intoxication, irritation of the respiratory tract, saturnism	death for contamination, cancer

Table 6.18 Use of solid fuels in developing countries (ESMAP, 2003)

	Fuelwood	Charcoal or coal	Dung	Leaves, sticks	Any solid fuel *
Brazil**	16.2				16.2
Nicaragua	65.9	1.2			67.1
South Africa	31.4	8.1	1.2		37.9
Vietnam	67.5	17.9		59.6	89.1
Guatemala	73.8	12.4			81.8
Ghana	62.2	46.4			96.2
Nepal	77.7	0.5	28.4	32.3	95.5
India	72.0	3.1	37.2		77.7

Notes: * the parcels may exceed the sum due to the use of multiple energy inputs in the same home; **the Brazilian research does not distinguish fuelwood from charcoal and coal.

The resulting pollution rates in the household and in the kitchen represent a proportion of particulate matter equivalent to smoking several packs of cigarettes a day, and is far more intense than the air pollution levels sampled in the urban centres. Table 6.19 shows that the WHO daily exposure norms are usually exceeded by a large margin in developing countries.

Table 6.19 Emissions of traditional cookstoves in indoor environments (Kammen, 1995; Smith et al, 2000) as compared to the World Health Organization (WHO, 2006b) exposure limits and with average concentrations of urban pollutants

Fuel and cookstove combination	CO (ppmv)	Particulate matter (mg PM_{10}/m^3)
Dung/traditional cookstove, peak	220–760	18.3
Fuelwood/traditional cookstove, peak	140–550	15.8
Charcoal/traditional cookstove, peak	230–650	5.5
Charcoal/improved cookstove, peak	80–200	2.6
Kerosene fuel and cookstove, peak	20–65	0.3
Fuelwood in hut, daily average	Nd	3.0
Bangkok, urban road, 2000	Nd	0.24
Berlin, centre, 2000	Nd	0.003
WHO 1-hour exposure standard	46	0.2

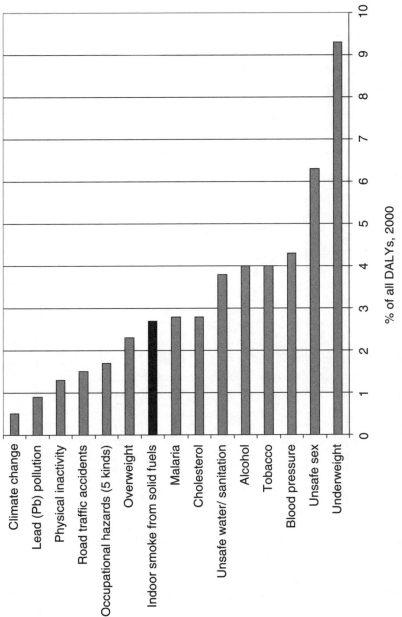

Figure 6.41 Occupational pollution deriving from the use of solid fuels versus other risk factors in the world (WHO, 2002b)

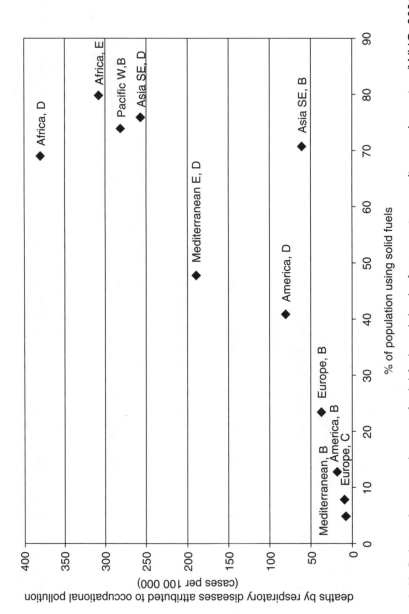

Figure 6.42 Relation between the use of solid fuels and deaths from respiratory diseases, by region (WHO, 2006b)

Notes: Population extracts according to the WHO, in function of mortality, are: I. very low for both children and adults; 2. low for both children and adults; 3. low for children and high for adults; 4. high for both children and adults; 5. high for children and very high for adults.

It is a complex task to estimate the environmental and social externalities, both positive and negative, deriving from the use of fuelwood. Sustainably collected (at lower rates than the natural recovery capacity), fuelwood is actually a renewable fuel. Fuelwood can be efficiently burnt, in equipment with pollutant emission control and with optimized burning. However, the accelerated consumption of fuelwood leads to deforestation, mainly in critical regions (*environmental hotspots*) such as Haiti and many cities' peripheries, where the population is especially sensitive to the cost of energy. In certain sensitive ecosystems, such as islands and mountains, irreversible devastation causes other serious problems, such as erosion and scarcity of food. The competition for forests leads to social conflicts for the ownership of land in different countries around the world – Bangladesh, Guatemala, Papua New Guinea and Angola.

Notes

1   Vladimir Ivanov Vernadsky (1863–1945) studied the biosphere (a concept named in 1875 by Austrian geologist Edward Suess), defining its boundaries (between 2km of the Earth's crust and 30km of atmosphere) and conceptualizing its evolution along the eras as an open system. According to his last paper (*Several Words on the Noosphere*, 1944), the present stage of resources exhaustion requires a rational convergence of efforts – the conditions for maintaining the so-called noosphere, sphere of human thought (a term created by French philosopher and mathematician Edouard Le Roy in 1922). These efforts basically dealt with equity, democracy, conflict resolution, population distribution around the planet, international governance, and freedom in scientific research and the exploration of new forms of energy (Behrends, 2005).

2   An empirical example to the world in 2003 can be found at Smith and Ezzati (2005).

3   Hierarchy of needs is a concept proposed by Abraham Maslow (in the essay *A Theory of Human Motivation*, 1943), by which 'the lower level needs should be satisfied before the higher level needs'. The five levels of needs are represented in a pyramid, being:

1. at the base, the basic physiological needs;
2. safety (employment, religion, science, safety itself);
3. social needs (love, belonging);
4. esteem needs; and
5. finally, at the top, self-actualization needs. For more, see Engel et al (1993).

4   There are several studies available at the World Bank's Clean Air website (World Bank, 2009). In the US, the benefits of the 1990 Clean Air Act are estimated to be US$690 billion by 2010, US$610 billion in terms of avoided mortality (UNEP, 2006).

5   One should not confuse tropospheric ozone (formed at low altitudes, up to 14km) with the stratospheric one (present at altitudes between 15 and 50km). The former is toxic to living beings; the latter filters ultraviolet sunlight (UV-A and UV-B).

6 Exceedances to air quality reference values should be seen in function of the time at which the excess occurred (hour, day, year), frequency (number of times) and intensity (the concentration gauged). For example, Sao Paulo and Los Angeles are sunny metropolises with lots of vehicles, subject to ozone standard exceedances. Even if the number of excesses (days a year) is similar, the value of the exceedances (O_3 concentrations) in Los Angeles is usually much higher.

7 The *Intergovernmental Panel on Climate Change* was jointly established by the World Meteorological Organization, WMO, and by the UN Environmental Program, UNEP, in 1988. Hundreds of scientists from a large number of countries participate in the Panel and in the different processes for assessing impacts, mitigation strategies and adaptation to climate changes.

8 CFCs, HCFCs, SF_6 and halons are compounds with high greenhouse effect potential (*GWP*), containing chlorine, fluorine, bromine or iodine. They are not associated directly to energy use, but destroy the stratospheric ozone layer that filtrates the ultraviolet rays striking the Earth and increase the incidence of skin cancer and other dangers to organisms. Very stable and atoxic, they were widely used in refrigeration and air conditioning systems, propellants in aerosols, foam-expansion and fire extinguisher agents. Production of these gases was phased-out by the Montreal Protocol, 1987, but their concentrations are still high in the atmosphere, as well as their permanence time in the environment.

9 For conversion, use the molecular mass: $1tCeq = 1tCO_2eq \times 12/44$. For the other gases, emissions are multiplied by the *GWP* to first be converted into tCO_2eq. Thus, $1tCH_4 = 21tCO_2eq = (21 \times 12/44)tCeq$. Similarly, $1t\,N_2O = (310 \times 12/44)tCq$.

10 One of the most important is *CDIAC, Carbon Dioxide Information Analysis Center*, from the US Department of Energy (CDIAC, 2009), which has data since the 19th century listed by country. Another is the *EDGAR, Emission Database for Global Atmospheric Research*, from the European Community, published by the Dutch Environmental Agency (EDGAR, 2009).

11 CO_2 emissions by fossil fuel from CDIAC (2003). Emissions, with and without land use from (UNFCCC, 2006); non-Annex I countries only include CO_2, CH_4 and N_2O; Annex I countries also include CFCs, HFCs, PFC and SF_6. Land use considered the same in the latest reference year and in 2003. Alternatively, land use change may be considered the annual variation in vegetal cover by country by the UN *Food and Agriculture Organization (FAO, 2005)*. Calculations follow the IPCC criteria, by which the carbon stored in products (*harvested wood products – HWP*) is not computed.

12 The Annex I Parties form the OECD countries (Germany, Australia, Austria, Belgium, Canada, European Community, Denmark, Spain, US, Finland, France, Greece, Ireland, Iceland, Italy, Japan, Liechtenstein, Luxemburg, Monaco, Norway, New Zealand, the Netherlands, Portugal, UK and Northern Ireland, Sweden, Switzerland and Turkey) and, with greater flexibility for the commitments but with the responsibility of providing resources to developing countries, the transition economies of the ex-USSR and Eastern Europe (Belarus, Bulgaria, Croatia, Slovakia, Slovenia, Estonia, Russian Federation, Hungary, Latvia, Lithuania, Poland, Czech Republic, Romania and Ukraine). The other countries are the *Non-Annex I*, among which are the great economies of China, India and Brazil.

13 According to the UNFCCC (2005b), having 1994 as the base year (or the closest year to it, in case this is not available to the country), non-Annex I countries emitted

11,735,437Gg total in CO_2 equivalent units, being 63% CO_2, 26% CH_4 and 11% N_2O. The other GHGs have not been inventoried.

14 One hectare (1ha) is equivalent to 10,000m², or a 100m × 100m square, or 0.01 square kilometres (km²), or the approximate area of a football pitch. More unit conversions are presented in Annex 2 at the end of this book.

15 There are several notations in the UNFCCC for this sector, among which are *LUCF (Land Use Change and Forestry), LULUCF (Land Use, Land Use Change and Forestry) and AFOLU (Afforestation, Forestation and Land Use)*.

References

Alvarez, P. J. J. (2007) Ethanol in fuel: microscopic & macroscopic implications for groundwater pollution. International ethanol and underground water seminar: from production to consumption, 8–10 October, Brazilian British Centre, São Paulo, Brazil

Andrade, M. F. (2002) PM trajectory from the Amazon forest burning to São Paulo City on 15 June 1999. Institute of Astronomy and Geophysics, University of São Paulo (USP). Personal communication, April 2002, mftandra@model.iag.usp.br

Arrehnius, S. (1896) On the influence of Carbonic Acid in the Air Upon the Temperature on the Ground. Philosophical Magazine, 41, 237–276

Behrends, T. (2005) The Renaissance of V. I. Vernadsky, The Geochemical News. The Geochemical Society (ISSN 0016-7010), http://gs.wustl.edu/archives/gn/gn125.pdf, pp 9–14

Bell, M. L. (2009) Health impacts of the London smog of 1952. Yale School of Forestry & Environmental Studies, http://environment.yale.edu/bell/research/london_smog_1952.html

Berresheim, H., Wine, P. H. and Davies, D. D. (1995) Sulphur in the Atmosphere. In Composition, Chemistry and Climate of the Atmosphere, ed. H. B. Singh, Van Nostrand Rheingold

CARB (2008) Particulate Matter Pollutant Monitoring, California Air Resource Board, www.arb.ca.gov/aaqm/partic.htm

CATF (2008) Diesel Soot Health Impacts – Diesel & Health in America – Clean Air Task Force, www.catf.us/projects/diesel/dieselhealth

CATF (2009) No Escape from Diesel Exhaust – Findings – Clean Air Task Force, www.catf.us/projects/diesel/noescape/findings.php

CDIAC (2003a) Ranking of the world's countries by 2003 total CO_2 emissions from fossil-fuel burning, cement production, and gas flaring. Oak Ridge National Laboratory, http://cdiac.esd.ornl.gov/trends/emis/top2003.tot

CDIAC (2003b) Carbon Dioxide Information Analysis Center and World Data Center for Atmospheric Trace Gases. Fiscal Year 2002 Annual Report. ORNL/CDIAC-139, July 2003. Carbon Dioxide Information Analysis Center and World Data Center for Atmospheric Trace Gases. Oak Ridge National Laboratory, Oak Ridge, Tennessee, http://cdiac.ornl.gov/epubs/cdiac/cdiac139/2002annrpt.html

CDIAC (2009) Fossil-Fuel CO_2 Emissions. Carbon Dioxide Information Analysis Center, http://cdiac.ornl.gov/trends/emis/meth_reg.html

Clean Air Initiative for Asia (2008) Asia–Beijing 2008: Annual Pollutant Concentration. CAI-Asia Center, Pasig City, Philippines, www.cleanairnet.org/caiasia/1412/article-72777.html

CSIRO (2004) Pollution Dispersion Team, CSIRO Atmospheric Research, www.dar.csiro.au/dispersion/index.html

Davis, R. E. (2004) Man's atmospheric environment. University of Virginia, www.evsc.virginia.edu/~evscta/EVSC250/images_250/fan.jpg

De Angelo, L. (2008) London smog disaster, England. Encyclopedia of Earth. Environmental Information Coalition, National Council for Science and the Environment, www.eoearth.org/article/London_smog_disaster,_England

Downing, R. J., Ranankutty, R. and Shah, R. J. (1997) RAINS-ASIA: An Assessment Model for Acid Deposition in Asia. The World Bank, Washington DC

EDGAR (2009) Emission Database for Global Atmospheric Research, Milieu- en Natuurplanbureau – MNP, www.mnp.nl/edgar

EEA (2008) Annual European Community LRTAP Convention emission inventory report 1990–2006. European Environment Agency, http://reports.eea.europa.eu/technical_report_2008_7/en

Engel, F. E., Blackwell, R. D. and Miniard, P. W. (1993) Consumer Behavior, 7th edn, Cryden Press, London, pp 118–119

ESMAP (2003) Household Energy Use in Developing Countries. A Multicountry Study October 2003. Joint UNDP/World Bank Energy Sector Management Assistance Programme. Report 27588

FAO (2005) Global Forest Resources Assessment 2005. Progress towards sustainable forest management. FAO Forestry Paper 147. Food and Agriculture Organization of the UN, Rome, www.fao.org/docrep/008/a0400e/a0400e00.htm

FAO (2009) FAOSTAT, UN Food and Agriculture Organization, http://faostat.fao.org/default.aspx

Forster, P., Ramaswamy, V., Artaxo, P., Berntsen, T., Betts, R., Fahey, D. W., Haywood, J., Lean, J., Lowe, D. C., Myhre, G., Nganga, J., Prinn, R., Raga, G., Schulz, M. and Van Dorland, R. (2007) Changes in Atmospheric Constituents and in Radiative Forcing. In Climate Change 2007: The Physical Science Basis. Contribution of Working Group I to the Fourth Assessment Report of the Intergovernmental Panel on Climate Change, Solomon, S., Qin, D., Manning, M., Chen, Z., Marquis, M., Averyt, K. B., Tignor, M., Miller, H. L. (eds.), Cambridge University Press, Cambridge, UK, and New York, NY, US.

Grossman, G. M. and Krueger, A. B. (1991) Environmental impacts of a North American Free Trade Agreement. National Bureau of Economic Research Working Paper 3914, NBER, Cambridge MA

Hollander, J. M. (1992) The Energy Environment Connection, Island Press, Washington DC

IEA (2004) World Energy Outlook 2004. International Energy Agency, OECD, www.iea.org//textbase/nppdf/free/2004/weo2004.pdf

IPCC (2001) Climate Change 2001: the Scientific Basis. Intergovernmental Panel on Climate Change, Working Group I, Third Assessment Report, WG1-TAR, http://grida.no/climate/ipcc_tar/wg1/index.htm

IPCC (2006a) Changes in Atmospheric Constituents and in Radiative Forcing. Working Group I Report 'The Physical Science Basis', WG1 AR4 Report, http://ipcc-wg1.ucar.edu/wg1/Report/AR4WG1_Print_Ch02.pdf

IPCC (2006b) Fourth Assessment Report. Working Group I Report 'The Physical Science Basis' (4AR-WGI). Intergovernmental Panel on Climate Change, http://ipcc-wg1.ucar.edu/wg1/wg1-report.html

IPCC (2007) Climate Change 2007: the physical basis. Contribution of Working Group I to the Fourth Assessment Report of the Intergovernmental Panel on Climate Change. Cambridge, UK, and New York, US. Available at www.ipcc.int

Kammen, D. M. (1995) From Energy Efficiency to Social Utility: Lessons from Cookstove Design, Dissemination and Use. In J. Goldemberg and T. B. Johansson (eds.), Energy as an Instrument for Socio-Economic Development, UNDP, New York.

Le Treut, H. R., Somerville, U., Cubasch, Y., Ding, C., Mauritzen, A., Mokssit, T., Peterson, T. and Prather, M. (2007) Historical Overview of Climate Change. In: Climate Change 2007: The Physical Science Basis. Contribution of Working Group I to the Fourth Assessment Report of the Intergovernmental Panel on Climate Change, Solomon, S., Qin, D., Manning, M., Chen, Z., Marquis, M., Averyt, K. B., Tignor, M., and Miller, H. L. (eds.), Cambridge University Press, Cambridge, UK, and New York, NY, US.

MSAD (2006) Maine School Administrative District, www.msad54.k12.me.us/MSAD54Pages/SAMS/SamsTechnology/arain%20images/threats.jpg

NADP (1999) National Atmospheric Deposition Program/National Trends Network, http://nadp.sws.uiuc.edu, http://nadp.sws.uiuc.edu/isopleths/maps1999/phlab.pdf

NASA (2007) The Impact of Climate Change on Natural Disasters. Earth Observatory, http://earthobservatory.nasa.gov/Study/RisingCost/rising_cost5.html

Nielsen, J. (2002) The Killer Fog of '52, www.npr.org/programs/atc/features/2002/dec/londonfog/lioygraphic.html

OECD (1975) Le principe polleur-payeur. Definition, analyde, mise en oeuvre. Organisation de Coopération et Dévelopment Économiques. Paris

Ontario Ministry of the Environment (1998) Air Quality in Ontario, www.ene.gov.on.ca/envision/techdocs/4054e.pdf

Sinton, J. E., Smith, K. R., Hu, H. and Liu, J. (1995) WHO/EHG/95.8 Human Exposure Assessment Series, Office of Global and Integrated Environmental Health, World Health Organization, Geneva

Smith, K. R., Samet, J. M., Romieu, I. and Bruce, N. (2000). Indoor air pollution in developing countries and acute lower respiratory infections in children. Thorax 55, 518–532

Smith, K. R. and Ezzati, M. (2005) 'How environmental health risks change with development. The epidemiologic and environmental risk transitions revisited'. Annu. Rev. Environ. Resourc. 30, 291–333, http://ehs.sph.berkeley.edu/krsmith/publications/2005%20pubs/ARER.pdf

Stern, A. C., Boubel, R. W., Turner, D. B. and Fox, D. L. (1984) Fundamentals of air pollution, 2nd edn. Orlando: Academic Press, pp 35–45; 96–99

UNEP (1992) The World Environment 1972–1992. Tolba, Mark (ed.), United Nations Environment Programme, Chapman and Hall, London

UNEP (2006a) GEO Yearbook 2006. UN Environment Programme, www.unep.org/geo/yearbook/yb2006/

UNEP (2006b) GEO Yearbook 2007. UN Environment Programme, www.unep.org/geo/yearbook/yb2007/

UNEP (2007) Geo Yearbook. UN Environment Programme, Nairobi

UNEP (2008) Temperature and CO_2 concentration in the atmosphere over the past 400,000 years – Maps and Graphics at UNEP/GRID-Arendal, http://maps.grida.no/go/graphic/temperature-and-co2-concentration-in-the-atmosphere-over-the-past-400-000-years

UNEP/GRID-Arendal (1993) Acid Rain in Europe. UN Environment Programme, http://maps.grida.no/go/graphic/acid_rain_in_europe

UNEP/GRID-Arendal (2005) Carbon cycle. UNEP/GRID-Arendal Maps and Graphics Library, http://maps.grida.no/go/graphic/carbon_cycle

UNEP/GRID-Arendal (2006) Maps and Graphics at UNEP/GRID-Arendal. UN Environment Programme, http://maps.grida.no/go/graphic/

UNFCCC (2005) Sixth compilation and synthesis of initial national communications from Parties not included in Annex I to the Convention. Addendum. FCCC/SBI/2005/18/Add.2, http://unfccc.int/resource/docs/2005/sbi/eng/18a02.pdf

UNFCCC (2005) Key GHG data. Greenhouse Gas Emissions Data for 1990–2003 submitted to the UN Framework Convention on Climate Change, http://unfccc.int/essential_background/background_publications_htmlpdf/items/3604.php

UNFCCC (2006) Key GHG Data. Greenhouse Gas Emissions Data for 1990–2003 submitted to the UN Framework Convention on Climate Change, unfccc.int/resource/docs/publications/key_ghg.pdf

UNFCCC (2007) Changes in GHG emissions without LULUCF, 1990–2004, UN Framework Convention on Climate Change, http://unfccc.int/files/inc/graphics/image/gif/graph1_2006.gif

UNFCCC (2009)   UN Framework Convention on Climate Change Website, http://unfccc.int

University of San Diego (2007) Conservation 1900-1960. History Department, http://history.sandiego.edu/gen/nature/environ4.html

US DoE (2006) Fossil fuel energy: Mercury emission control R & D. US Department of Energy, www.fossil.energy.gov/programs/powersystems/pollutioncontrols/overview_mercurycontrols.html

US DoE (2009) Fossil fuel energy: Mercury emission control R & D. US Department of Energy, www.fossil.energy.gov/programs/powersystems/pollutioncontrols/overview_mercurycontrols.html

US DoT (2007) Weather Applications and Products Enabled Through Vehicle Infrastructure Integration (VII). US Department of Transportation, Federal Highway administration, http://ops.fhwa.dot.gov/publications/viirpt/sec7.htm

US EPA (2001) Uncontrolled emission factor listing for criteria air pollutants. Emission Inventory Improvement Program. US Environmental Protection Agency, www.epa.gov/ttnchie1/eiip/techreport/volume02/ii14_july2001.pdf

US EPA (2006) US National Emission Trends – updated 18 July 2005, www.epa.gov/ttn/ chief/trends/trends02/trendsreportallpollutants07182005.zip

VWQD (2004) Acid Rain. Vermont Water Quality Division, www.anr.state.vt.us/dec/waterq/bass/htm/bs_acidrain.htm

WHO (2002a) Fuel for life: household energy and health. World Health Organization, Geneva, ISBN 978 92 4 156316 1

WHO (2002b) World Health Report 2002: Reducing Risks, Promoting Health Life. World Health Organization, Geneva, www.who.int/whr/2002/en/

WHO (2004) Indoor smoke from solid fuels. Assessing the environmental burden of disease at national and local levels. World Health Organization, Geneva

WHO (2005a) Air quality guidelines global update 2005. Report E87950 on a Working Group meeting, Bonn, Germany, 18–20 Oct. World Health Organization

WHO (2005b) Indoor smoke from household solid fuels – Chapter 18. Comparative Quantification of Health Risks: Global and Regional Burden of Disease due to Selected Major Risk Factors, World Health Organization, www.who.int/healthinfo/global_burden_disease/cra/en/index.html and www.who.int/publications/cra/chapters/volume2/1435-1494.pdf

WHO (2005c) Situation Analysis of Household Energy Use and Indoor Air Pollution in Pakistan. WHO/FCH/CAH/05.06

WHO (2006a) Air quality guidelines for particulate matter, ozone, nitrogen dioxide and sulphur dioxide. Global update 2005. Summary of risk assessment. WHO/SDE/PHE/OEH/06.02. World Health Organization, Geneva, www.who.int/phe/health_topics/outdoorair_aqg/en/index.html and http://whqlibdoc.who.int/hq/2006/WHO_SDE_PHE_OEH_06.02_eng.pdf

WHO (2006b) Air quality guidelines for particulate matter, ozone, nitrogen dioxide and sulphur dioxide. Global update 2005. Summary of risk assessment. WHO/SDE/PHE/OEH/06.02. World Health Organization, Geneva, www.who.int/phe/health_topics/outdoorair_aqg/en/index.html and http://whqlibdoc.who.int/hq/2006/WHO_SDE_PHE_OEH_06.02_eng.pdf

WHO (2006c) Fuel for life: household energy and health. World Health Organization, Geneva, ISBN 978 92 4 156316 1

World Bank (2006) RAIN-ASIA: An assessment model for acid deposition in Asia, World Bank, Washington DC, *apud* TERI, www.teri.res.in/teriin/news/terivsn/issue1/specrep.htm

World Bank (2009) Clean Air Net, http://www.cleanairnet.org

WRI (2009) Earthtrends database. World Resources Institute, http://earthtrends.wri.org/searchable_db/index.php?theme=3&variable_ID=666&action=select_countries

Chapter 7

Energy and the Environment: The Causes

Most environmental issues – air pollution, acid rain and global warming, loss of biodiversity and desertification – are caused by our present energy system, based on fossil fuel combustion and on traditional biomass burning. For the first time in history, our planet's natural resources are insufficient to meet everybody's needs, both in terms of supply (such as forests, fisheries, mines) and final waste disposal (soil, waters, atmosphere).

Indicators

An important environmental impact indicator is the *human disruption index*: the ratio of the flow of pollutants created by humans (anthropogenic) related to the natural flow, which is the baseline value. It is also possible to have an idea of the relevance of the contribution of energy production and use, as shown in Table 7.1, which features the contribution of anthropogenic action to the total emissions of the most significant pollutants. The planet's resources are no longer enough to meet current and future demand, and one of the ways of representing this idea is the 'ecological footprint' (Box 7.1).

Box 7.1 'Ecological footprint'

Formerly known as '*carrying capacity*', the '*ecological footprint*' emerged in the early 1990s at the University of British Columbia, Canada (Rees, 1992). It is an analysis comparing human demands with nature's ability to provide environmental services and regeneration. Resource accounting is similar to that of Life Cycle Assessment (LCA), but converted into a base unit. Thus, the use of energy, materials, pressure on the atmosphere and water, the impact on forests and other factors are converted into a standard measure, usually land equivalent hectares or even 'Earth Planets'. The Earth's carrying capacity is about 1.3 hectares per inhabitant (1.8ha/person

Table 7.1 Contribution of the major pollutants: human disruption index (UNDP, WEC, UNDESA, 2004)

Impact	Base value	Human disruption index	Disruption quota by cause			
			Commercial energy	Non-commercial energy	Agriculture	Industry
Lead emitted into the atmosphere	12,000 t Pb/year	18	41% fossil fuel combustion, gasoline additives included	Negligible	Negligible	59% ore and metal processing, waste incineration
Oil dumped into the oceans	200,000 t oil/year	10	44% oil extraction, processing and transport	Negligible	Negligible	56% oil contaminated waste disposal
Cadmium emitted into the atmosphere	1400 t Cd/year	5.4	13% fossil fuel combustion	5% traditional fuel burning	12% agricultural burning	70% waste incineration processing
Sulphur emitted into the atmosphere	31 million t S/year	2.7	85% fossil fuel combustion	0.5% traditional fuel burning	1% agricultural burning	13% foundries and waste incineration
Methane emitted into the atmosphere	160 million t CH$_4$/year	2.3	18% fossil fuel production, transport, storage and usage	5% traditional fuel burning	65% rice crops, livestock, poultry farms and changes in land use	12% sanitary landfills
Nitrogen compounds (NO$_x$, NH$_4$) emitted	140 million t Neq/year	1.5	30% fossil fuel combustion	2% traditional fuel burning	67% fertilizers, agricultural burning and changes in land use	1% waste incineration

Mercury, flow into the atmosphere	2500 t Hg /year	1.4	20% fossil fuel combustion (mostly coal)	1% traditional fuel burning	2% agricultural burning	77% metal processing, manufacturing and use, waste incineration
Nitrous oxide, flow into the atmosphere	33 million t N_2O /year	0.5	12% fossil fuel combustion	8% traditional fuel burning	80% fertilizers, changes in land use	Negligible
Particulate matter emitted into the atmosphere	3.1 billion t PM/year	0.12	35% fossil fuel combustion	10% traditional fuel burning	40% agricultural burning	15% foundries, resuspension
Hydrocarbon emissions (except for methane)	1 billion t HC/year	0.12	35% fossil fuel processing and combustion	5% traditional fuel burning	40% agricultural burning	20% fugitive emissions
Carbon dioxide, flow into the atmosphere	550 billion tCO_2/year	0.05	75% fossil fuel combustion	3% deforestation energy fuelwood	15% deforestation for changes in land use	7% industrial processes

if marine areas are considered). In 2003, the planet capacity was exceeded by 20 per cent. Each North American 'used' 9.6ha; each Chinese, 1.6ha (WWF, 2006). The per capita 'footprint' represents a way of comparing individual consumption and life styles, as well as the limits of environmental supply. Although this method is subject to criticism for its simplification, it is very useful in terms of environmental education on natural limits, excessive consumption behaviours, social inequalities, differences among countries and changes in patterns over time. Many non-governmental organizations (NGOs) provide calculation tools, such as the members of the *Global Footprint Network* (GFN, 2007).

Somewhat similar to the ratio between production and oil reserves, the 'ecological footprint' concept measures how much water and land area a human population requires for producing the resources it consumes and to absorb its wastes with the available technologies. As seen in Figure 7.1a, the break-even point was reached around 1990 and nowadays the human 'footprint' is almost 25 per cent above what the planet can naturally regenerate, that is, it would take the Earth one year and three months to regenerate what we consume in a single year. The ratio may also be expressed in area per inhabitant: on the demand side, population and consumption per capita grow; on the supply side, available resources decrease (Figures 7.1a, b).

This deficit of natural assets may be called *ecological exhaustion*, and the sustainability concept lies exactly in eliminating this exacerbated loss and, at the same time, in knowing better the shares of this accounting. The first fact verified is that developed countries consume more per inhabitant and have a larger 'footprint' (Figures 7.2 and 7.3).

The second fact is that there is not enough room for everybody to consume at this rate, which leads to three possibilities:

1 maintenance of inequalities and exclusion;
2 fierce competition for resources; or
3 sustainable base levelling, with the due compensations for 'debits' and 'credits' (Figure 7.4).

Contribution by sources

A better understanding of pollution sources and their emissions is essential for formulating policies capable of reducing or abating them. The main sources are power production, transportation, industry, building and

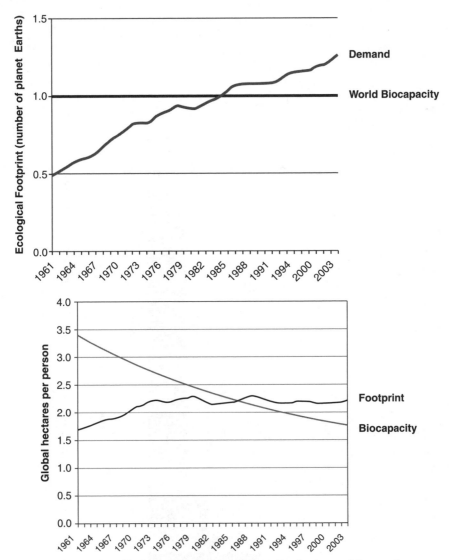

Figure 7.1 *'Ecological footprint' of Planet Earth, demand for goods and biocapacity (a, b) (WWF, 2008)*

deforestation. The ecological footprint is also categorized by its causes, in which the weight of factors associated with energy production and use can be felt: the growing carbon emissions from fossil fuels and increasing generation of nuclear waste. As observed, energy is also partially responsible for deforestation and land use.

Among the main causes of the footprint is the predominance of fossil fuels in electricity generation and in industrial use, as shown in Figure 7.6. Another fact verified is the heavy reliance on petroleum in the transportation sector.

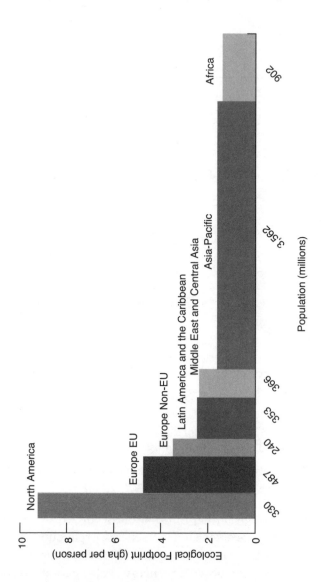

Figure 7.2 Ecological footprint and population by region, 2005 (WWF, 2008)

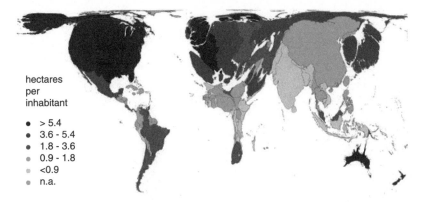

Figure 7.3 Ecological footprint in 2003 (WWF, 2008)

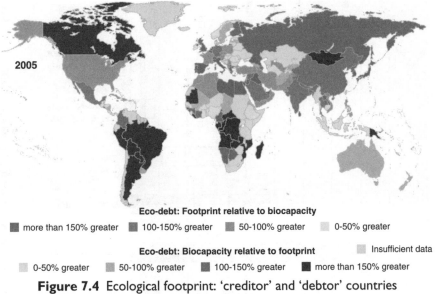

Figure 7.4 Ecological footprint: 'creditor' and 'debtor' countries (WWF, 2008)

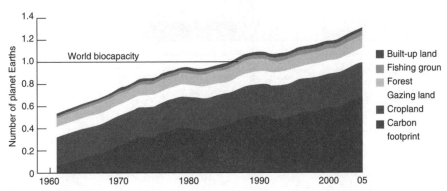

Figure 7.5 Ecological footprint by component (WWF, 2008).

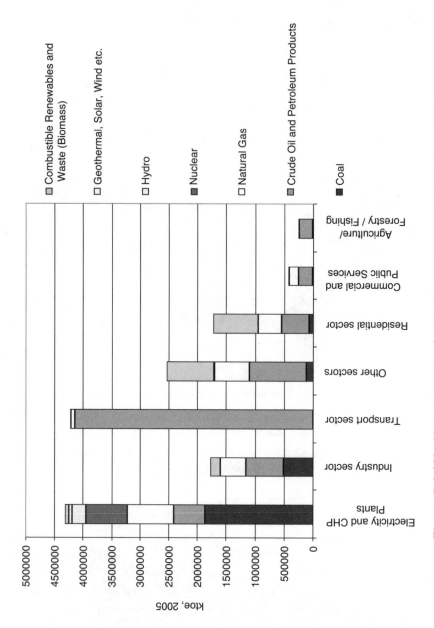

Figure 7.6 World energy use by fuel and sector, 2005 (data from IEA, 2008)

In 2003, industrialized countries accounted for 51 per cent of the world consumption of commercial energy. The contribution of the major pollution sources and of other environmental impacts connected to energy production and end-use will now be analysed.

Electricity production

Electricity production accounts for a little less than 20 per cent of the global primary energy consumption and still two billion people have no access to this service throughout the world – a reason to prioritize electrification programmes. However, electricity production from fossil fuels predominates and is the main source of pollutants. Figure 7.7 shows that electricity production still has a prevalent weight of CO_2 emissions from the burning of fossil fuels in the world.

Figures 7.8 and 7.9 show some emission factors for main pollutants emitted by thermoelectric plants. These factors vary significantly among studies, due to their comprehensiveness, fuels and technologies used.

Liquid effluents and solid wastes deriving from power generation must also be taken into account. The most important are the acidic runoffs from coal mines, oil leakages and radioactive wastes. Biomass wastes are also a problem, but they are more easily reused to generate electricity, for example, sugar cane bagasse. In most cases, electric power plants have to be located near water bodies for cooling the turbines, and they affect their surroundings. Thermoelectricity plants impact watercourses, especially by *consumptive use* (i.e. with no effluent returning to the water body, due to evaporative losses, as in Figure 7.10) and to *thermal pollution* caused by effluents flowing back to the water body at high temperatures, affecting species that depend on a narrow temperature range to live, thrive and migrate. Lastly, higher temperatures allow for the proliferation of alien species, such as tropical molluscs in Europe (Boyes and Elliot, 2008).

Impacts from fossil sources

Coal and fuel oil are the most polluting energy sources, especially when fuel does not undergo desulphurization (sulphur removal) and there is no final emission control, mainly of particulate matter. In addition, coal mines emit large amounts of methane (CH_4) into the atmosphere. Oil refineries, the storage of their products and fuel transfer stations emit CH_4 and other hydrocarbons (HCs), which are precursors of tropospheric ozone (O_3, low-level urban pollutant) and enhance the greenhouse effect.

Natural gas emits much less sulphur and particulate matter, but its problem lies in the emission of nitrogen oxides (NO_x, especially NO_2), which

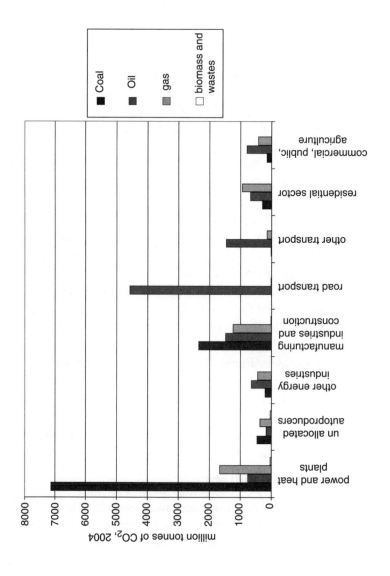

Figure 7.7 CO_2 emissions by sector, 2004 (IEA, 2006a)

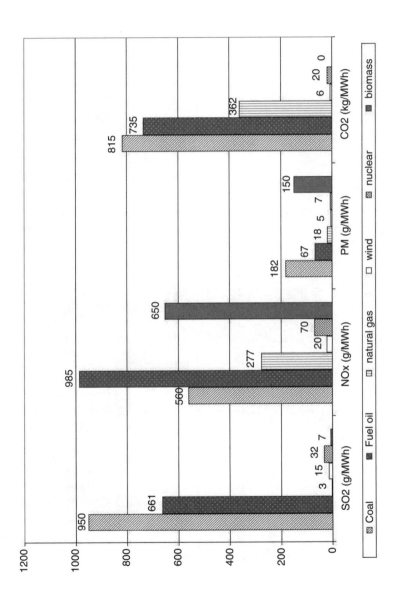

Figure 7.8 Atmospheric pollutant emissions released by electricity generation in Germany (Krewit et al, 1998)

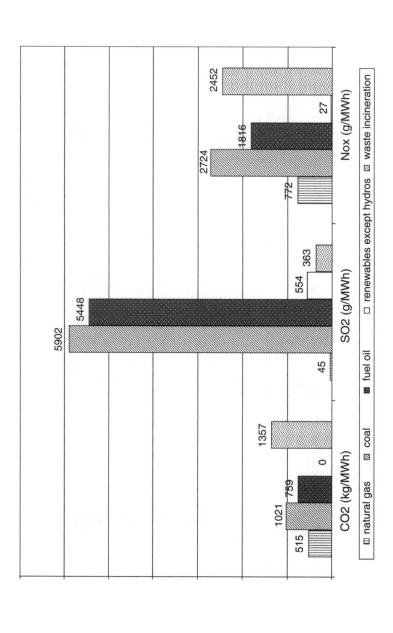

Figure 7.9 Atmospheric pollutant emissions released by electricity generation in the US (US EPA, 2004)

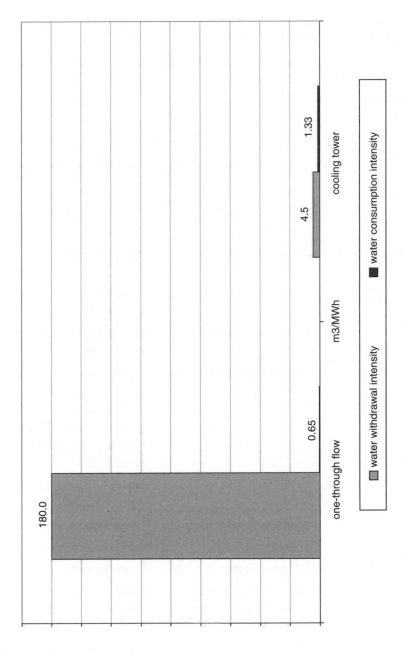

Figure 7.10 Water intensities in thermal plants (Vassolo and Doll, 2005)

also forms secondary O_3. In the natural gas production and utilization cycle there are HC emissions with a large share of CH_4. Since it is a fossil fuel, the natural gas cycle also adds CO_2 to the atmosphere.

Impacts from 'modern' renewable sources

The impacts from renewables must also be observed along their life cycles and energy balances, leading to distinct values. Impacts are diverse and their magnitude depends on local conditions. Table 7.2 identifies some of these impacts, by source.

Table 7.2 Environmental impacts of 'new renewable' energy sources

Energy source	Impact cause	Environmental impact
All	Use of fossil fuels along life cycle	Pollution, global warming
Modern biomass	Monoculture, use of pesticides	Biodiversity loss
	Deforestation and burning	Atmospheric pollution, biodiversity loss
	Excessive water usage	Lack of the resource for other ends
	Liquid effluents discharge	Massive death of fish and sea life in general, contamination of groundwater aquifers by nitrates and other toxic substances
	Use of fertilizers	Eutrophization (algae) in water courses
Wind	Equipment noise	Nuisances
	System installation	Aesthetic pollution
	Working blades	Death of migratory birds
Solar	Use of copper in the collectors and of lead in the batteries	Accumulation of toxic wastes in the environment
Small hydro	Reservoir formation	Interferences with the local fauna and flora, conflicts with tourism

The main environmental advantage of renewable energy sources is the mitigation of carbon dioxide emissions compared to the fossil alternatives, as shown in Figure 7.11.

Biomass is an environmentally-friendlier energy source in terms of carbon emissions since there is replanting and consequent reincorporation by photosynthesis, but the technology needs improvements for abating NO_x and PM. Emissions also depend on the life cycle boundaries and on the technologies considered. Biomass processes in cold-climate countries offer little benefit in terms of CO_2, since there is intense use of fossil energy in crop mechanization, in feedstock transport and in industrial production.

Hydroelectricity plants and their impacts

Hydro plants, except for micro hydro, use reservoirs to equalize the water flows that drive the electricity-generating turbines. These dams are built ideally in narrow gorges, with great depth and a relatively small flooded area. Examples are the Hoover Dam (near the Grand Canyon, which spurred the growth of Las Vegas) and the dams built in the Alps. As there are few places offering similar conditions, dams of lesser height and longer lengths are built, flooding vast superficial extensions. Hydroelectricity plants, mainly large ones (over 500MW installed capacity), interfere with the environment for building large dams, forming lakes by flooding vast areas, changing water flows and blocking fish migration. Relocation of affected populations is a considerable social problem in several cases. The impact of a hydroelectricity enterprise can usually be estimated by an indicator of the power produced by hectare of reservoir. The larger this number is, the lower the impact on the environment. Table 7.3 provides some examples from Brazilian hydroelectricity plants, highlighting the Balbina power plant, notorious as an environmental disaster.

Flooding is an important indicator for the environmental impact caused by dams, but it is not the only one. Among other impacts, populations are removed (traditional native populations included), river regimens are altered downstream (i.e. after the dam), there is sediment accumulation upstream, barriers to fish migration, proliferation of algae (eutrophication), water plants and mosquitoes, extinction of endemic species and loss of historical, archaeological and tourist heritages. Also to be considered are the risks associated with dam bursts.

All of these factors should be taken into consideration in the elaboration of previous environmental impact assessments, as well as in mitigation and compensation measures. The Brazilian government has classified the projects of future hydroelectricity plants by their size and complexity

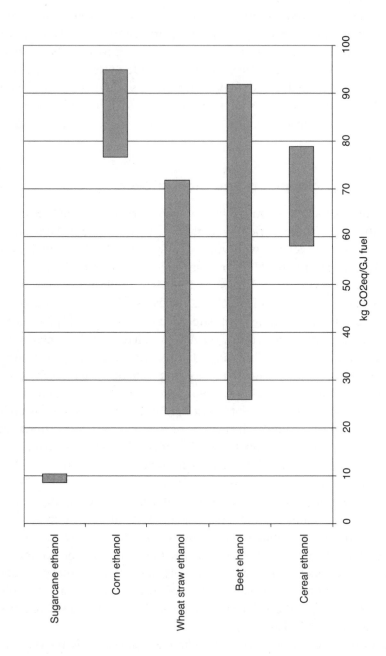

Figure 7.11 Greenhouse gas emissions by different types of ethanol fuel (Coelho et al, 2006)

Table 7.3 Hydroelectricity produced by hectare of flooded area in Brazil (Moreira and Poole, 1993; Lucon and Coelho, 2006)

Power plant (existing or under construction)	Installed capacity (MW)	kW/hectare
Xingó	5000	588.2
Segredo	1260	152.7
Itá	1620	116.7
Itaipu	12,600	93.6
Belo Monte	11,000	89.8
Machadinho	1200	45.8
Garabi	1800	22.5
Itaparica	1500	18.0
Tucuruí	3900	13.9
Três Irmãos	640	9.0
Porto Primavera	1800	8.4
Serra da Mesa	1200	6.7
Camargos	45	6.1
Manso	210	5.4
Samuel	217	3.3
Sobradinho	1050	2.5
Balbina	250	1.1
Average	–	21.7

(Table 7.4). It is worth noting that the greatest potential is concentrated in a few projects of high environmental complexity in the Amazon region.

During the electricity generation phase, hydroelectricity plants do not produce pollutants related to fossil fuels, except for CH_4, produced by the decomposition of the organic matter present in reservoirs (especially if vegetation is not removed before flooding). In the whole life cycle, however, there are CO_2 emissions in the construction and decommissioning stages.

Nuclear thermoelectricity

Nuclear power is neither based on hydrocarbon combustion, nor is it followed by the usual pollutants resulting from the burning of fossil fuels. Its problem lies in radioactive wastes, in safety issues and in carbon emissions in the whole life cycle, which includes decommissioning of mines and reactors as well as waste management.

Table 7.4 Environmental classification of Brazilian hydroelectricity plant projects (MME, 2003)

Region	Capacity (MW) according to environmental complexity			Number of projects according to capacity	
	Low	Medium	High	Up to 500MW	>500MW
Southeast	1081	1739	0	17	0
South	660	1840	0	5	2
Centre-West	343	822	0	11	0
Northeast	0	82	450	4	1
North	393	452	15,016	5	5
Brazil total	2477	4935	15,466	42	8

The use of nuclear power for electricity generation was a byproduct of the development of nuclear reactors for military purposes during and after World War II (1939–45). Nuclear power is based neither on mechanic nor on chemical energy (as is fossil fuels combustion). The source of nuclear power is the disintegration of the uranium atom nucleus, which releases a considerable amount of kinetic energy in fragments such as strontium (Sr) and xenon (Xe), which are usually radioactive. This process is called nuclear fission and may be produced by bombarding uranium atoms with adequate projectiles, such as neutrons (Figure 7.12). Nuclear fission is followed by neutrons or protons emission and by radiation, such as X-rays. The final radioactive fragments constitute the radioactive waste, one of the most serious problems resulting from the use of this source of energy.

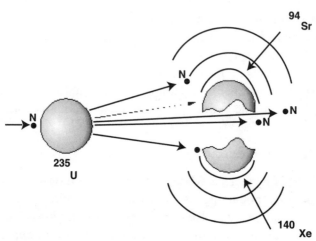

Figure 7.12 Fission of uranium into strontium and xenon

In the fission of a uranium atom by a neutron, three other neutrons are produced, which can produce other fissions, creating a chain reaction that leads to the fission of a huge amount of other atoms. If this process happens fast, it produces a nuclear explosion, which is basically a large number of uranium atoms undergoing fission in a short period (Figure 7.13).

It is also possible to 'burn' uranium slowly, limiting the heat of the radioactive fuel elements to hundreds of degrees in temperature. In *boiling water reactors (BWR)*, water circulates around those elements removing their heat and forming superheated vapour, which can drive a turbine, generating electricity in the same way as in a conventional coal, oil, gas or biomass combustion thermoelectricity plant (Figure 7.14). *Pressurized water reactors (PWR)* are the most used today; they keep water at high pressure and transfer heat to a secondary system through exchangers. In this system, water vaporizes and drives the turbines.

Uranium preparation requires a full 'fuel cycle', from extraction and purification of uranium salts and their conversion into a gas, up to uranium 'enrichment' in the fissionable isotope U^{235}. The latter constitutes only 0.7 per cent of the total mass, the remaining is U^{238}. It is necessary to use a uranium mix with at least 3 per cent of U^{235} in most commercial nuclear reactors. Enrichment consumes large amounts of energy; thus, depending on the source of this electricity, pollutant emissions can be significant in this process. Figure 7.15 shows the stages of nuclear power life cycle.

In the year 2006, nuclear power plants produced 15 per cent of the world's electricity, in a total of 18,930TWh (IEA, 2008). Most of the 443 nuclear power reactors operating in the world are in OECD countries

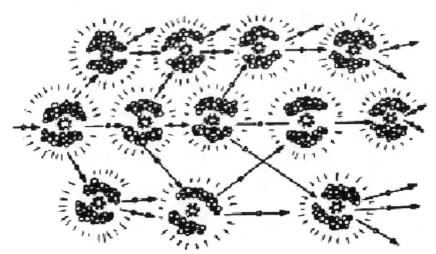

Figure 7.13 Nuclear chain reaction

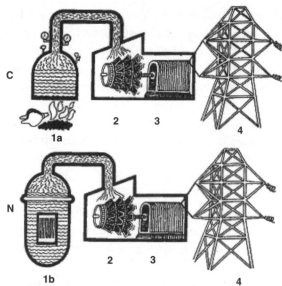

Figure 7.14 Thermoelectricity generated by conventional means and by a nuclear power plant

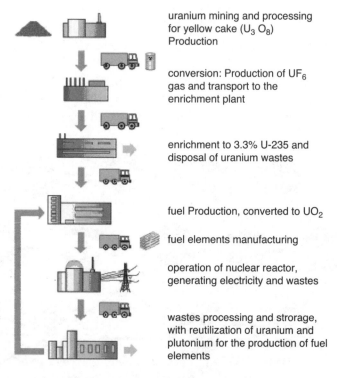

Figure 7.15 Nuclear power life cycle

(generating 84 per cent of the world's nuclear electricity) and in the former USSR. The total installed capacity is similar to that of hydro plants (IAEA, 2006a).

Most reactors were built along the 'golden age' of nuclear power, between 1975 and 1990. However, the construction of most of those reactors started before 1975 and was completed around 1985. After the incidents at Three Mile Island (US, 1978) and Chernobyl (USSR, currently in Ukrainian territory, 1986), serious concerns led to a stabilization of this figure (Box 7.2).

Box 7.2 Nuclear power, past and present

Enrico Fermi first experimentally achieved nuclear fission in 1934, bombarding uranium with neutrons. Four years later, Otto Hahn, Fritz Strassmann, Lise Meitner and Otto Robert Frisch conducted experiments bombarding uranium nuclei with neutrons, dividing the atoms in two, releasing additional neutrons in a chain reaction. This spurred nuclear fission and uranium enrichment research. In 1942 the first man-made reactor, known as Chicago Pile-1, was created in the US, later part of the Manhattan Project which built large reactors to breed plutonium for use in the first nuclear weapons. After World War II, reactor research was kept under strict government control and secrecy. In 1951 a nuclear reactor generated electricity for the first time (100kW Arco Reactor, Idaho, which experienced partial meltdown, in 1955). On 27 June 1954 the world's first nuclear power plant generating electricity for commercial use was officially connected to the Soviet power grid at Obninsk, USSR, from a 5MW water-cooled reactor. In 1956 at Sellafield, UK, the 45MW 196kW Calder Hall nuclear power station (gas-cooled reactor) started operating, and one year later the 60MW Shippingport station (pressurized-water reactor) opened in the state of Pennsylvania, US, the first American commercial nuclear generator (Pittsburgh became the world's first nuclear powered city in 1960). In 1954, the chairman of the United States Atomic Energy Commission declared that nuclear power would be 'too cheap to meter' and foresaw 1000 nuclear plants on-line in the US by 2000. Installed nuclear capacity initially rose quickly, from less than 1 gigawatt (or 1000MW) in 1960 to 100GW in the late 1970s and 300GW in the late 1980s. The 1973 oil crisis encouraged electricity-dependent countries such as France and Japan to invest in nuclear reactors. However, after the Three Mile Island (1979) and Chernobyl (1986) accidents, environmental and safety awareness increased, and nuclear capacity rose more slowly.

Table 7.5 Nuclear reactors on 31 December 2002 (IAEA, 2006b)

Country	Operating reactors		Reactors under construction		Electricity in 2002		Total in operation as of 31 Dec 2002	
	Units	Total MW(e)	Units	Total MW(e)	TW(e).h	Total%	Years	Months
Argentina	2	935	1	692	5.39	7.23	48	7
Armenia	1	376			2.09	40.54	35	3
Belgium	7	5760			44.74	57.32	184	7
Brazil	2	1901			13.84	3.99	23	3
Bulgaria	4	2722			20.22	47.30	125	2
Canada	14	10,018			70.96	12.32	461	2
China	7	5318	4	3275	23.45	1.43	31	6
Taiwan	6	4884	2	2700	33.94	20.53	128	1
Czech Republic	6	3468			18.74	24.54	68	10
North Korea			1	1040			0	0
Finland	4	2656			21.44	29.81	95	4
France	59	63,073			415.50	77.97	1,287	2
Germany	19	21,283			162.25	29.85	629	1
Hungary	4	1755			12.79	36.14	70	2
India	14	2503	7	3420	17.76	3.68	209	5

Iran			2	2111			0	0
Japan	54	44,287	3	3696	313.81	34.47	1070	4
South Korea	18	14,890	2	1920	113.07	38.62	202	7
Latvia	2	2370			12.90	80.12	34	6
Mexico	2	1360			9.35	4.07	21	11
Netherlands	1	450			3.69	4.00	58	0
Pakistan	2	425			1.80	2.54	33	10
Romania	1	655	1	655	5.11	10.33	6	6
Russia	30	20,793	3	2825	129.98	15.98	731	4
South Africa	2	1800			11.99	5.87	36	3
Slovakia	6	2408	2	776	17.95	54.73	97	0
Slovenia	1	676			5.31	40.74	21	3
Spain	9	7574			60.28	25.76	210	2
Sweden	11	9432			65.57	45.75	300	1
Switzerland	5	3200			25.69	39.52	138	10
UK	31	12,252			81.08	22.43	1301	8
Ukraine	13	11,207	4	3800	73.38	45.66	266	10
US	104	98,230			780.10	20.34	2767	8
Total	441	358,661	32	26,910	2574.17		10,696	4

The falling fossil fuel prices and electricity liberalization also contributed to increasing the financial risks of investing in nuclear power. Since 1996 the US does not have a new reactor operating, although the country is currently planning new plants. Activities continued in many countries, notably France, Japan, the former USSR and recently China. Many countries remain active in developing nuclear power and other nations plan to have their own capacity (Figure 7.16).

In Figure 7.17, the Chernobyl accident occurred between years 19 and 20.

Although the installed capacity has witnessed little expansion (Figure 7.18), operational conditions of reactors have improved, which increased the amount of power produced (Figure 7.19).

As a consequence, current power plants' capacity is close to saturation. In 2005, 21 reactors (with 21GWe capacity) were under construction, mainly in developing countries. Quantitatively, this is still not much in comparison to the expansion by other sources, but the decline in the nuclear industry is a complex phenomenon, which involves considerations of economics, security and geopolitics.

The increase in nuclear capacity slowed from 1995 onwards, mainly due to the economic advantages of fossil-fuelled thermoelectricity plants with smaller capital costs. The increase in safety requirements and decommissioning costs (demobilization of power plants and uranium mines, as well as waste management) also affects the economic feasibility of nuclear power. As opposed to other technologies and against optimistic predictions, nuclear power has not been shown to follow a *'learning curve'* process, where costs decrease with economies of scale (Box 7.3).

Box 7.3 The nuclear 'forgetting curve'

According to the learning curve concept, an advanced technology may be stimulated by adequate policies, including subsidies and subventions, making it more competitive in comparison to conventional technologies by means of economies of scale (Figure 7.20).

In spite of all the incentives, this has still not happened to nuclear power, which has its curve affected by perceived and internalized externalities (Figure 7.21). The decommissioning of nuclear installations

Figure 7.16 Commercial nuclear power plants in the world (Wikipedia, 2009)

status of commercial
nuclear power

Building first plant
Building new plants
Considering first plant
Considering new plants
Stable
Considering decommissioning
All plants decommissioned
No commercial reactors
Nuclear free area

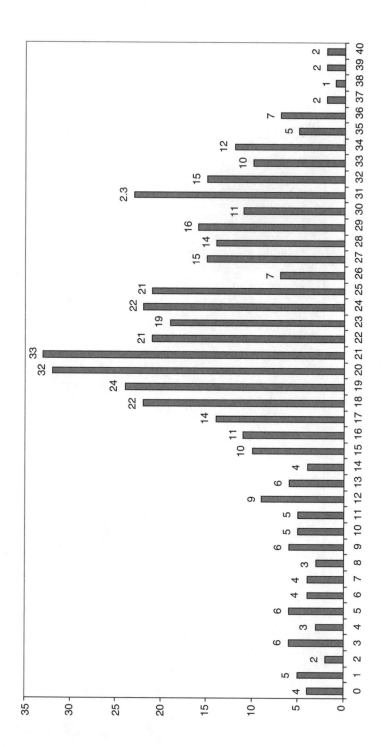

Figure 7.17 Nuclear reactors by age (years) as of 31 December 2005 (IAEA, 2006c)

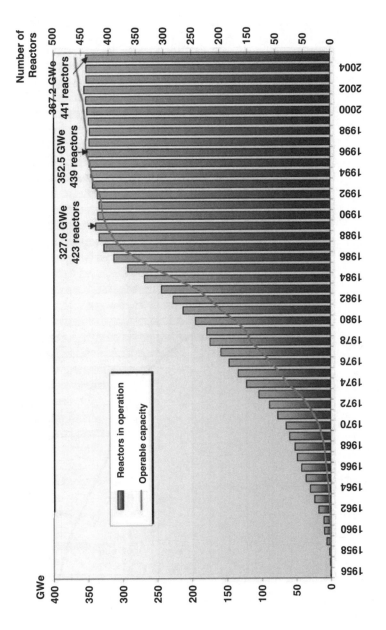

Figure 7.18 Operating reactors: installed capacity (MacDonald, 2006)

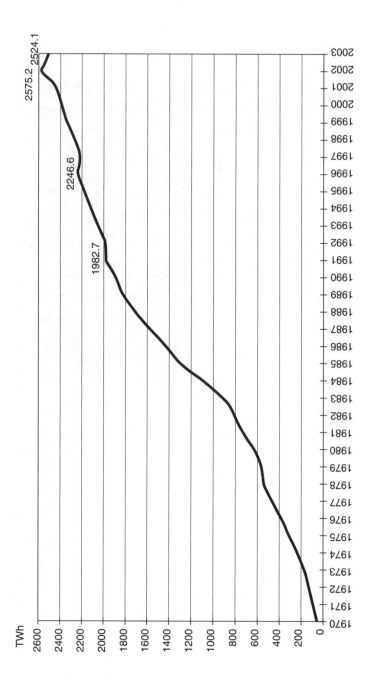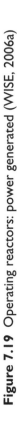

Figure 7.19 Operating reactors: power generated (WISE, 2006a)

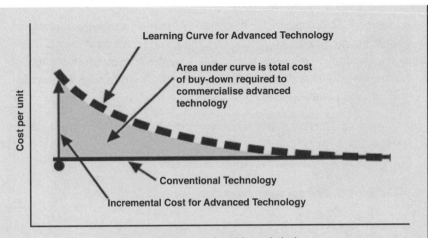

Figure 7.20 The learning curve concept

seems technically feasible, but it is expensive. The cost to decommission a 1000MW nuclear power plant was estimated at US$480 million, which aggravates the economic problems faced by this source of energy.

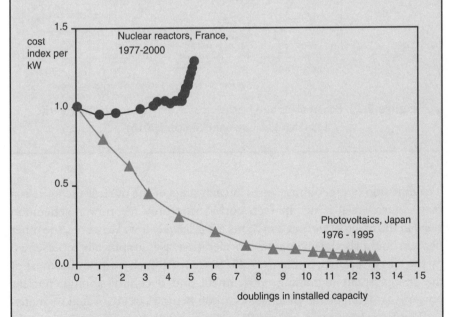

Figure 7.21 Cost of French nuclear reactors and Japanese photovoltaic solar panels in time (Nakicenovic, 2005)

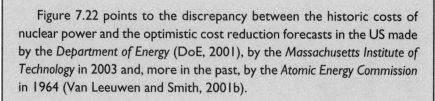

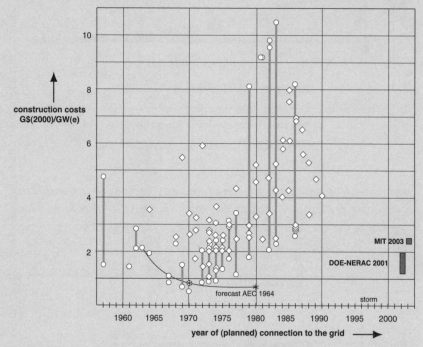

Figure 7.22 Projections and historic costs of nuclear reactors in the US (Van Leeuwen and Smith, 2001b)

The emission of greenhouse gases at each stage of the nuclear life cycle is a very controversial issue. In fact, considering only the power generation stage in the reactor, carbon emissions are relatively low. However, the other phases should also be taken into consideration, as is graphically represented by the energy balance in Figure 7.23. Since fossil fuels account for most of the energy spent in mining, enrichment and decommissioning, nuclear power is far from being 'practically carbon neutral', as advocated by many.

This issue has not yet been sufficiently clarified. Related studies are usually incomplete and assume different premises (location, technologies, number of reactors, service lifetime, stages involved and other parameters, such as uranium ore quality), and there is a lot of divergence concerning values. For comparison, Table 7.6 shows CO_2 emissions along the nuclear

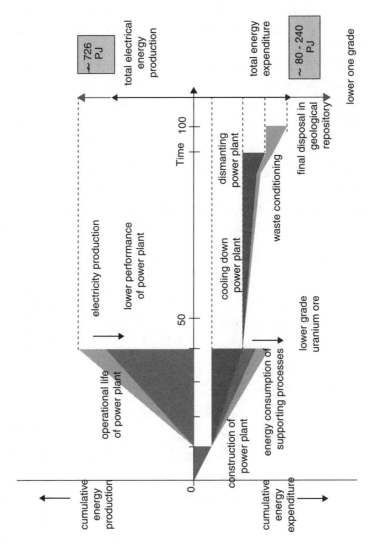

Figure 7.23 Schematic representation of the energy generated and used along the nuclear thermoelectricity life cycle (Van Leeuwen and Smith, 2001a)

power life cycle compared to other alternatives. In spite of the predominance of nuclear power in countries such as France, a common rule used by those in charge of energy planning is that power systems should not be dependent on sources that individually represent more than 15 per cent of the total system. Using this criterion, Bangladesh, the Philippines, Vietnam, Morocco, Chile – and probably Egypt and Pakistan – are not countries with good perspectives for installing large (1GW) nuclear reactors. This is a reason for the recent interest in new types of smaller power reactors (about 100MW), which offer improved safety features.

Nuclear power plants are very fuel efficient: whereas a 1000MWe conventional thermoelectric power plant burns between 2 and 2.4 million tonnes of fuel a year, a thermonuclear plant spends only 30 tonnes of uranium (Table 7.7). This 1000MWe nuclear power plant will generate 30 tonnes of high radioactive content waste (or 10 cubic metres), plus 800 tonnes of low and intermediate radioactive level waste. In case the waste is recycled, it will generate only 1 tonne of high content waste. All the nuclear power plants in operation in the world generate about 4000m³ of waste. In 30 years of operation, they will generate 120,000m³ or a cube with 50 metres each side. In volumetric terms, this is practically negligible, as

Table 7.6 CO_2 emissions per unit of energy generated during the nuclear life cycle

Source	Author	CO_2 kg / MWh
Nuclear	Vattenfall (2005)	2.8
	IAEA (2001)	2–6
	World Energy Council (WEC, 2004)	3–40
	Rogner and Khan (2002)	9–30
	Oko Institute (Fritsche, 1997)	34–60
	Tokimatsu et al (2006)	10–200
	WISE (1993 and 2005)	140–230
	Van Leeuwen and Smith (2001b)	120–437
Coal	Rogner and Khan (2002)	860–1290
Oil		689–890
Gas		460–1234
Hydro		16–410
Wind		11–75
Solar photovoltaic		30–279
Biomass		37–116

Table 7.7 Comparison among thermoelectricity plant fuels (Rosen, 1998)

Fuel	Power (kWh) generated by fuel kg	Amount required (tons a year) for a 1000MWe thermoelectricity plant
fuelwood	1	3,400,000
coal	3	2,700,000
fuel oil	4	2,000,000
uranium	50,000	30

compared to other energy alternatives (Figure 7.24), but significant in function of the potential risk involved (Figure 7.25).

Elements removed from a reactor after its use correspond to less than 1 per cent of the waste volume, but contain 95 per cent of the total radioactivity. The nuclear waste activity is reduced by 90 per cent in the first year, but 100,000 years are necessary for it to go back to the uranium ore levels (Figure 7.26). Uranium-235 (^{235}U) fission generates xenon and strontium, which in turn undergo decays until stable components are formed. Some of these intermediary products are very hazardous (carcinogenic) and persistent in the environment (absorbed by the bones): strontium-90 (^{90}Sr) and cesium-137 (^{137}Cs), with about 30-year half-lives – which make them active for hundreds of years (Nave, 2005).

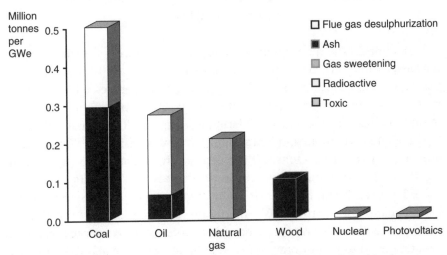

Figure 7.24 Waste produced in the fuel preparation and in the thermoelectricity plants operation (Rosen, 1998)

tonnes of nuclear wastes

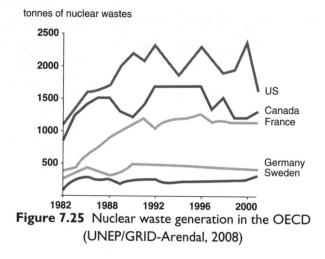

Figure 7.25 Nuclear waste generation in the OECD
(UNEP/GRID-Arendal, 2008)

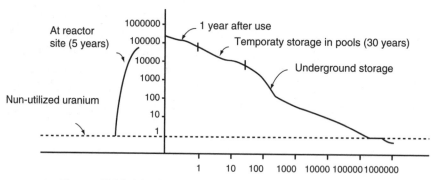

Figure 7.26 Nuclear fuel radioactivity along time (years)
(Environdec, 2006a)

Uranium-238 is more abundant and, when capturing a neutron in its nucleus, forms ^{239}U, decaying to generate plutonium (^{238}Pu), an element that serves to produce weapons. Plutonium can be reprocessed to generate more energy, reducing the amount of waste. In 2002, the amounts of plutonium stored in eight countries (Germany, Belgium, US, Russia, France, Japan, United Kingdom and Switzerland, without considering China) were estimated in about 885 tons, 80 per cent in civil reactors, 15 per cent in reprocessing plants and 5 per cent in other places (WISE, 2006). So far, waste has been stored in pools or drums, until a final deposit starts operating (Table 7.8). A 1000MWe thermopower plant produces 200kg of plutonium a year. The reprocessing of the waste could recover the material, making the 30 tonnes of uranium used annually generate about 3.5 million kWh, but the alternative is still considered anti-economic (until 1996, only 8 tonnes were reprocessed). About 1000 tonnes of plutonium generated by

Table 7.8 Known plutonium stocks on 31 December 2002 (WISE, 2006b)

	Germany	Belgium	China	US	Russia	France	Japan	Switzerland	UK
in civil reactors	48.9	20	nd	383	54	91.6	90	7	11
in reprocessing units	nd	0	nd	0	3	89.8	7	31	4 in
other places	5.4	–	nd	12	26	0.5	<0.5	<0.05	nd
Total	54.3	20	nd	395	83	181.9	97	38	<15

the nuclear power plants still wait for a decision about their final destination. The waste has to be stored for thousands of years in deep underground reservoirs, contained in cement, bitumen and resins or vitrification, and in stable geological formations on solid ground or on the sea bed. There is still no final storage for these materials. Despite proposals from different countries, the only nuclear waste permanent deposit is the Yucca Mountain in the US, which is to operate between 2010 and 2019. With a 70,000-ton capacity (half of what the existing American reactors will produce), it will cost between 100 and 200 billion dollars (US$1–2 bi per reactor), mostly paid by the government. A US$1/MWh fee on electricity has been charged since 1983 and has raised a total of about US$18 billion up to 2002. The total cost of nuclear power is estimated to be US$5.44/MWh, except for uranium mines decommissioning (EIA-DoE, 2002).

Nuclear power is often presented by its advocates as an efficient alternative for the greenhouse gas emissions problem. However, environmentalists in general are against nuclear reactors due to the risk of accidents, the uncertainty about the management of waste and hazards of atomic weapons proliferation (Box 7.4).

Box 7.4 Nuclear accidents and atomic weapons proliferation

The worst nuclear accident that ever occurred was in the Soviet Union (USSR) in 1986, in the city of Chernobyl. The reactor explosion exposed the whole northernmost region of Europe to high amounts of radiation (UNEP, 2006a). Today the catastrophe still has strong chronic effects and has caused a deceleration in nuclear programmes throughout the world. Besides the mega-accidents, minor 'incidents' routinely occur in nuclear installations – an issue to be considered. In France, for example, 56 incidents were reported in its reactors in the first half of 2000, for causes such as contamination, leakages, emergency systems failures and problems with waste inventories (WISE, 2005). A series of high severity accidents in nuclear (non-military) reactors can be found at WNA (2006). When analysing the impacts of power production, mainly the hazards issue has to be considered concerning the accidents. Hazard is defined as the probability of an undesirable event occurrence, multiplied by the consequence of the event. Even not considering the effects of military artifacts or the chronic deaths from contamination, the number of direct deaths due to accidents in nuclear power plants is relatively low in relation to coal (especially explosions in mines with high methane concentrations and very frequent accidents), to natural gas and LPG (explosions), to oil (fires) and even to hydropower plants (dam bursts; less frequent accidents but with a large number of victims) (WNA, 2006). Uranium is found in nature with low radioactivity levels, below 1 per cent. Even so, uranium mining contains the elements ^{235}U and ^{238}U, which cause lung cancer in miners and pollute water bodies with radioactivity (from uranium, radium and thorium) and heavy metals. ^{235}U enrichment to at least 3 per cent is an essential condition for power generation in current generators. In order to produce (non-'dirty') weapons, more sophisticated enrichments are necessary (above 20 per cent). Nuclear weapons production is technically accessible not only to countries that reached a reasonable industrialization level (US, England, France, China and Russia), but also to India, Pakistan, North Korea and possibly Israel and Iran. The efforts of the countries that have the technology and those of the International Atomic Energy Agency to strictly limit access to the full uranium fuel cycle, so as to avoid nuclear proliferation all over the world, do not manage to deter the arms black market and the systems for detecting radioactive substances are still inefficient[2]. Weapon proliferation is a matter of concern: every year, North Korea alone produces about 6.6kg of high-content plutonium (Albright, 1994). One gram of plutonium is enough to contaminate 10 million people. An accident at a state-of-the-art plant (*mixed oxide fuel, MOX*) with 600g of plutonium, with 99.9 per cent of effective contention, may contaminate 600,000 people. Without contention, 1g of plutonium (in a 'dirty bomb') may contaminate 10 million civilians. The bomb, equivalent to 24,000 tonnes of TNT which exploded in Nagasaki in Japan, on 9 August 1945, contained a sphere 8cm in diameter of about 4kg of plutonium in its nucleus (CCNR, 2006). Despite the attempts to control nuclear proliferation since 1945, more powerful weapons were invented and at least 12 countries are perceived as having nuclear weapons: United States (1945), the Soviet Union, now Russia (1949), United Kingdom (1951), France (1960), China (1964), India (1974), Pakistan (1998) and North Korea (2006); South Africa and Israel also developed nuclear arms, but there is no evidence of tests (NTI, 2006). Surface tests were banned in 1963, considerably reducing the radioisotopes concentration in the atmosphere. On the surface, decay is much slower.

The International Atomic Energy Agency was established to inspect the processes and control nuclear proliferation. In 1968, the Nuclear Non-Proliferation Treaty (NPT) limited arms transfer among countries for its 188 signatories. However, not all countries signed the NPT and some develop secret nuclear programmes, in which the boundary between pacific uses and arms production is not well defined. Moreover, there is the threat of the arms technology black market – including those using plutonium – and also of equipment for enriching uranium. This risk increased greatly with the fall of the USSR, which possessed more than 10,000 nuclear warheads, not to mention the waste from nuclear installations, which may be used for non-pacific ends (UNEP, 2006b, c).

Transportation

The globalization of economies and urbanization are factors that very much influence the transportation sector. If participation and consumption are assessed, developing countries have been far below the levels of industrialized countries for more than 30 years (Table 7.9), a cause for concern, since levelling these 'top' standards is unsustainable under the environmental point of view.

The transportation sector consumes over 60 per cent of all the oil byproducts produced in the world and grows more quickly than the other final consumption sectors, as shown in Table 7.10.

The vehicle fleet also grows all over the world, but very vigorously in developing countries (Figure 7.27).

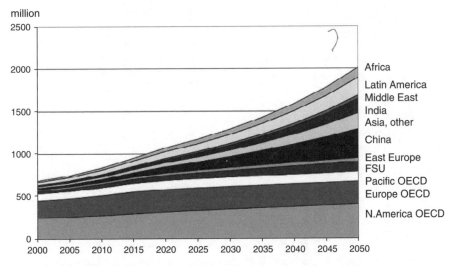

Figure 7.27 Vehicle fleet by region (Schipper, 2006)

Table 7.9 Industry and transportation participation in the final consumption of energy, 1973 and 2004 (IEA, 2006b)

	World 1973		World 2004		OECD 1973		OECD 2004		Non-OECD 1973		Non-OECD 2004	
	Mtoe	%	Mtoe	%	Mtoe	%	Mtoe	%	Mtoe	%	Mtoe	%
Total consumption	4608	100%	7644	100%	2839	100%	3828	100%	1769	100%	3817	100%
Transportation	967	21%	1975	26%	721	25%	1284	34%	246	14%	690	18%
Industry	1507	33%	2058	27%	955	34%	879	23%	553	31%	1179	31%

Table 7.10 Increase in energy final consumption, total and per sector, between 1973 and 2004 (IEA, 2006b)

Growth 1973–2004	World	OECD	Non-OECD
Total consumption	1.65%	0.97%	2.51%
Transportation	2.33%	1.88%	3.38%
Industry	1.01%	-0.27%	2.47%

Vehicle density by the population is far greater in the US. In 2002, Western Europe had the 1972 North-American density; China, the 1912 density (Worldwatch, 2005). Figure 7.28 gives an idea of the differences in this distribution, up to 100 times greater between North America and China or India. The in-use vehicle fleet in the world was of about 50 million in 1950 and grew to 551 million in 2005 (Worldwatch 2006), an average increase of 4.5 per cent annually. If this trend continues, before 2020 there will be one billion vehicles in the world.

The world automobile production rose by 3.2 per cent in the same period and, in 2005, was about 46 million vehicles a year. The increase was marked in the period 1950–70, then stabilized, decelerating until 2000 and rising again until 2005 (Table 7.11).

Bicycle production doubled that of automobiles between 1950 and 2002, from 11 to 104 million units/year – 61 per cent in China alone (Worldwatch, 2005); it is still too early to affect the increase in energy consumption in transportation. The energy consumption per passenger-kilometre varies from country to country, according to physical configurations, technologies and transportation modes (Figure 7.29).

Whereas in 1950 a North-American covered an average 14,600km a year, in 2003, this distance rose to 19,000km. The automotive industry consumes large amounts of raw materials, inducing indirect industrial emissions; despite the growing use of light materials, vehicles keep their 1970s weight, with about 824kg of steel, 149kg of iron, 126kg of aluminium and 116kg of plastics.

The increases in the number of vehicles and in the distances travelled require large investments in infrastructure: roads, terminals and useful space in the cities. The transportation systems may unfavourably affect the environment in different ways: taking useful space in cities, making soils

Table 7.11 Automobile production in the world (Worldwatch, 2007)

Year	Millions of automobiles produced	% increase a year over the period
1950	8.0	–
1960	12.8	4.8%
1970	22.5	5.8%
1980	28.6	2.4%
1990	36.3	2.4%
2000	41.3	1.3%
2005	46.0	2.2%

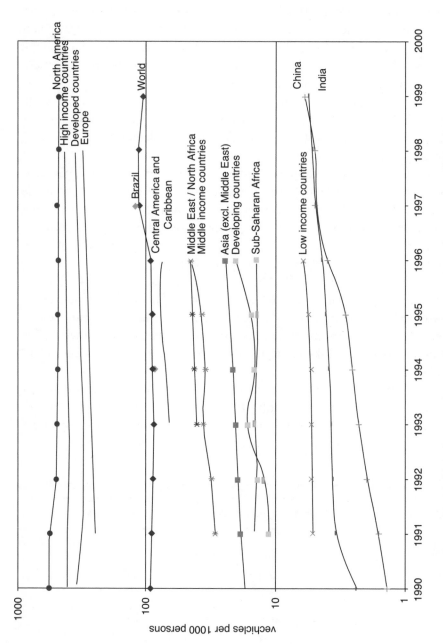

Figure 7.28 Vehicles per thousand people, by country and region (WRI, 2006)

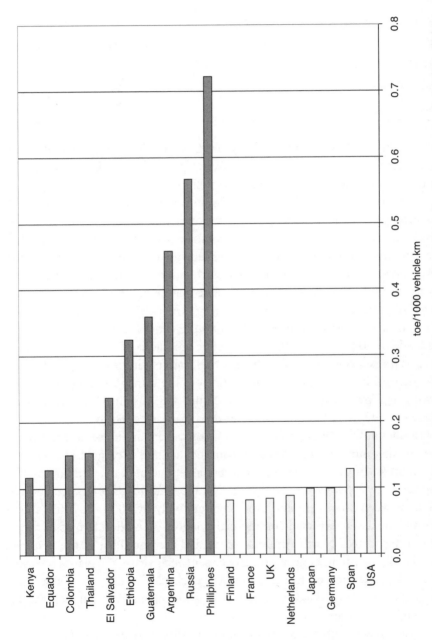

Figure 7.29 Energy intensity: energy used in road transport divided by the distance travelled (WRI, 2006)

Table 7.12 Energy used by transportation mode (Smith, 1978)

Mode	MJ/passenger.km	Assumed load factor
Bicycle	0.13	1.0
Walking	0.20	1.0
Bus	0.80	0.5
Train	1.10	0.5
Automobiles	3.00	0.5
Planes	6.50	0.5

impervious, disfiguring the scenery, cutting and inducing occupation in forested areas and other sensitive ecosystems, generating disturbances due to noise and mainly contributing to air pollution.

If the use of automobiles in developing countries reaches the OECD countries' level all over the world, environmental problems may become insoluble. As a result of the internal combustion engine, automotive vehicles generate different pollutant gases during their operation, the most representative being carbon dioxide and monoxide, methane and other hydrocarbons, nitrogen oxides, particulate matter, sulphur oxides and lead. Over 70 per cent of all CO emissions, more than 40 per cent of NO_x emissions, nearly 50 per cent of HC, about 80 per cent of all benzene emissions and at least 50 per cent of the atmospheric emissions of lead may be attributed to transportation. One of the most relevant environmental problems is the increase in CO_2 emissions deriving from the transportation sector, following energy consumption. In 2002, the US gasoline-fuelled vehicles alone emitted more than the whole of the Japanese economy.

Besides automobiles and trucks emissions, there are those deriving from the growing number of planes and from the increase in cargo and distances transported. In the 50 years of commercial jet aviation, the demand for air trips grew by 9 per cent annually, on average, and the sector expectation is a rise between 3 per cent and 5 per cent annually by 2020. In 2003, about 1.7 billion passengers used commercial aviation; 35 million tonnes of cargo were transported. North America accounted for one-third of the volume, but the Chinese market grows by 10 per cent each year (777 planes released in 2003), as compared to the 2 per cent each year in the US. Table 7.13 presents the data of aviation in the world, showing a recent fall after the 11 September 2001 attacks.

Aviation accounts for 3.5 per cent of the 1992 climate impacts – including vapours condensed at high altitudes, increasing the greenhouse effect (Worldwatch, 2005). The sector emits 2 per cent of the anthropogenic CO_2 and practically all the NO_x found between 8 and 15km of altitude (relevant

Table 7.13 Air trips per distance and passenger volume (Worldwatch, 2006)

Year	Billions of passengers km	% annual increase in the period
1950	28.0	–
1960	109	14.6%
1970	460	15.5%
1980	1089	9.0%
1990	1894	5.7%
2000	3038	4.8%
2003	2992	–0.5%

regional pollution). Short flights are increasing their participation (45 per cent of the European flights are of less than 500km); in these, take-offs consume 15 per cent of all the fuel necessary for the trip.

Industry

The industrial sector consumes 27 per cent of all the energy used in the world, 23 per cent of the energy in developed countries and 31 per cent in developing countries. The most energy-intensive industrial sectors are paper, chemical, primary metals (particularly aluminium) and the oil industry itself.

In the last three decades, there was a significant fall in the absolute amounts and in the percentile fraction of almost all the pollutants produced by the industry in the industrialized OECD countries, both deriving from better practices (both voluntary and compulsory) and by the transfer of more pollutant sectors to other countries, as a consequence of market globalization and of the specialization in the tertiary sector.

The manufacturing and building industry is still the third largest source of carbon emissions by fuel burning, with a total of 4.5Gt CO_2 in 2003. This amount has practically remained stable since 1971, reducing the industry weight in total emissions from 23 per cent in 1990 to 18 per cent in 2003.

Nevertheless, industries emit large amounts of global pollutants and, in a very concentrated way, local pollutants. This is a special reason for concern, since the effects on a certain community may be critical, both for the emission concentration and for the risk of accidents.

The occurrence of accidents in industry is much less frequent than in other activities, such as transportation. Likewise, the number of deaths is relatively smaller. However, big industrial accidents attract a lot of attention from the public and give great visibility to environmental concerns. Chemical and toxic waste from industrial activities accounted for the accidents in Bhopal (India, 1984; 2000 deaths, methyl-isocyanide released by an explosion at a pesticide industry), Seveso (Italy; 1976, dioxins released by an explosion in a chemical industry) and Minamata (Japan, in the 1960s; mercury released by factories contaminated fish and humans).

Besides the process phase itself, industrial activities indirectly contribute to a series of environmental damages at the resource extraction phases (mainly mining), storage and for generating potentially dangerous substances.

Steel production is a very relevant indicator. From 1950 to 2004, world production went from 190 million tonnes to 1.05 billion tonnes. Induced by China, in 2004 alone, the world steel production increased by 8.8 per cent (Worldwatch, 2005). The also-growing steel recycling (37 per cent between 1994 and 2003) is not enough to sufficiently mitigate the demand for ores, coal coke and, in developing countries, wood and fuelwood from deforestation.

Aluminium is another impacting industry, as it requires large amounts of power in its production. The production of 1 ton of aluminium consumes 15,771kWh of power, plus 308m^3 of natural gas, 238kg of heavy oil, 13kg of diesel and 186kg of coal. In 2000, the aluminium industry used 52% of hydropower, 31.6% of coal, 0.8% of oil, 9% of natural gas and 6.1% of nuclear power (IAI, 2003). China is the world leader, producing 4.5 million tonnes in 2003, and these values are estimated to double by 2010 (Hunt Jr, 2004).

For using heavy fuels (coal and oil) under high temperatures, industries emit large amounts of oxides responsible for acid precipitation (SO_x and NO_x) and for highly toxic heavy metals (such as arsenic, cadmium, mercury and lead) in the form of particulate matter. Furthermore, the industry usually consumes substantial amounts of power, which in most countries is generated by coal, oil and natural gas thermopower plants, with the environmental consequences previously discussed.

Buildings and civil construction

Households, commercial premises and buildings use a substantial amount of energy, not only in their construction, but also for the operation of their heating, refrigeration and lighting equipment and appliances. Figure 7.30 shows some indicative numbers on the way energy is consumed in the residential sector in developed countries.

There are wide gaps between countries. Very poor communities do not even heat water. In general, ambient heating is not necessary in tropical countries. Figure 7.31 discriminates consumption by end-use.

The environmental concerns resulting from construction are a consequence of the trends for the greater use of electric equipment – the larger size of dwellings, larger number of individual homes and more

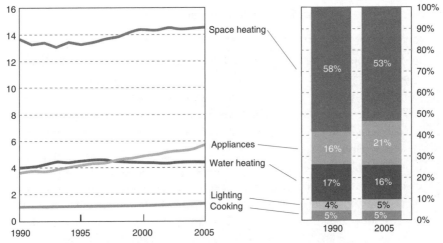

Figure 7.30 Residential energy use (IEA, 2008)

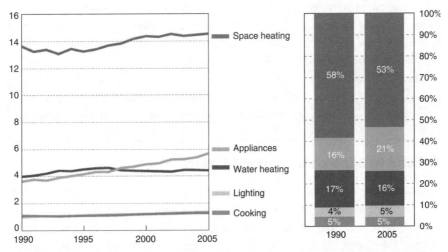

Figure 7.31 Household energy use by end-use, 19 countries (IEA, 2008)

Note: the IEA member countries are Australia, Austria, Belgium, Canada, Czech Republic, Denmark, Finland, France, Germany, Greece, Hungary, Ireland, Italy, Japan, Republic of Korea, Luxembourg, Netherlands, New Zealand, Norway, Portugal, Slovak Republic, Spain, Sweden, Switzerland, Turkey, United Kingdom and United States.

air-conditioning and heating installations are being used in commercial buildings. Building construction induces many types of environmental impacts due to the use of materials, waste generation and permanent change in land use. Moreover, there is occupational pollution, partially discussed before in the fuelwood and solid fuels aspect. Another very relevant type of occupational pollution is the Sick Building Syndrome (Box 7.5).

Box 7.5 The Sick Building Syndrome

In 1982, the WHO acknowledged the existence of the Sick Building Syndrome (SBS), after an episode of pneumonia contamination in a hotel in Philadelphia, with 182 cases and 29 deaths. After the oil crisis in the 1970s, the new building standards encouraged almost hermetically closed buildings, reducing energy consumption; however, without enough internal air renovation, there was a rise in the concentration of chemical and biological pollutants: building materials, cleaning materials, cigarette smoke, electro-electronic devices and even people-concentrated carbon monoxide and dioxide, ammonia and formaldehyde. The proliferation of viruses, fungi, algae, protozoa, bacteria and mites, was promoted by the inadequate cleaning of carpets, rugs, curtains and poor maintenance of air circulation and air-conditioning systems. The automation of air-conditioning systems controls only the temperature and relative humidity of the internal air, ignoring other parameters involving air quality and factors that affect the health of those occupying these environments. A building is 'sick' when about 20 per cent of its occupants present symptoms associated with the time spent in it: eyes, nose, skin and throat irritation, headaches, tiredness, lack of concentration and nausea. Other associated factors are missing work, reduction in productivity and in ambient quality.

Oil and marine coastal degradation

The sea is the final drain for most liquid waste and for a considerable fraction of solid waste resulting from human activities on Earth. More than three-quarters of the whole marine pollution comes from land sources by draining and discharge into rivers, bays, open coasts and from the atmosphere. The remaining sources of marine pollution are navigation, deep ocean mining and oil production, all related to energy. The oil that occasionally appears in the sea is due to some of the following five categories: natural sources; atmospheric pollution; marine transportation; coastal production; municipal and industrial waste and spills. The amount of oil in each of these categories is given in Table 7.14.

Table 7.14 Sources of oil in the sea (millions of tonnes annually) (Hollander, 1992)

Source	Probable range	Best estimate
Natural sources	0.025–2.5	0.25
Atmospheric pollution	0.05–0.5	0.3
Marine transportation	1.00–2.60	1.45
Coastal production	0.04–0.06	0.05
Municipal and industrial waste and spills	0.585–3.21	1.18
Total	1.7–8.8	3.2

About half of the 3.2 billion tonnes of oil consumed annually is transported by sea. Oil pollution is a highly visible form of marine pollution and, therefore, has resulted in a great public outcry and resulting corrective measures. The major accidents with tankers are listed in Table 7.15.

Both the number of incidents resulting in oil spill and the amount of oil spilt have systematically fallen since the 1970s.[1] Large accidents account for most of the spills; for example, 15 per cent of the oil spilt in 1978 was from a single accident, that of the *Amoco Cadiz* tanker (ITOPF, 2006). Nevertheless, oil pollution in the sea is not always caused by tankers, as shown in Table 7.16.

Other impacts associated with offshore oil exploration lie in the prospection phase, since explosives are used, interfering with whales' guidance systems. A typical seismic investigation takes from two to three weeks and covers distances of up to 1000km. Near the source, the sound intensity may reach 250dB (decibels) and, at 30km, 117dB – something close to a stone crusher (Alaska Marine Conservation Council, 2007).

Conversion in land use and deforestation

Energy fuelwood is not the major cause of deforestation and of the consequent desertification in developing countries. The exception occurs in sensitive areas, such as islands and high regions, where the vegetal cover is not enough to supply the energy needs of growing and needy populations. The major case for forest loss is the Brazilian Amazon deforestation; in the other extreme, China was the country with greater forest area expansion (Table 7.17).

Deforestation and desertification are caused by a combination of intense human exploration and of the local ecological frailty. The deforestation and desertification causes are:

- populational growth and migratory pressures;
- crop substitutions;
- political problems, mainly in Africa, which hinder the seasonal migration of livestock breeders across provincial and national boundaries;
- poor policies to promote populations' relocation because of inappropriateness of soil and other conditions; and
- national development strategies which excessively prioritize predatory activities, such as timber production, forest products, crops and meat for export. The latter two are the major causes of the Brazilian Amazon deforestation.

Table 7.15 Major accidents with tankers since 1967 (ITOPF, 2006)

Position	Name of tanker	Year	Place	Thousands of tonnes spilled
1	*Atlantic Empress*	1979	Tobago coast, Caribbean	287
2	*ABT Summer*	1991	700 nautical miles from Angola	260
3	*Castillo de Bellver*	1983	Saldanha Bay coast, South Africa	252
4	*Amoco Cadiz*	1978	Bretagne coast, France	223
5	*Haven*	1991	Genoa, Italy	144
6	*Odyssey*	1988	700 nautical miles from Nova Scotia, Canada	132
7	*Torrey Canyon*	1967	Scilly Islands, UK	119
8	*Sea Star*	1972	Oman Gulf	115
9	*Irenes Serenade*	1980	Navarino Bay, Greece	100
10	*Urquiola*	1976	La Coruña, Spain	100
11	*Hawaiian Patriot*	1977	300 nautical miles from Honolulu, Hawaii	95
12	*Independenta*	1979	Bosphorus Sound, Turkey	95
13	*Jakob Maersk*	1975	Porto, Portugal	88
14	*Braer*	1993	Shetland Islands, UK	85
15	*Khark 5*	1989	120 nautical miles from the Morocco Atlantic coast	80
16	*Aegean Sea*	1992	La Coruña, Spain	74
17	*Sea Empress*	1996	Milford Haven, UK	72
18	*Katina P*	1992	Maputo coast, Mozambique	72
19	*Nova*	1985	Kharg Island, Iran Gulf	70
20	*Prestige*	2002	Spanish coast	63
35	*Exxon Valdez*	1989	Prince William Sound, Alaska, US	37

Table 7.16 Oil spills and their causes, 1974–2005 (ITOPF, 2006)

Cause		<7 tons	7–700 tons	>700 tons	Total
Operations	Loading and unloading	2820	328	30	3178
	Storage	548	26	0	574
	Others	1178	56	1	1235
Accidents	Collisions	171	294	97	562
	Stranding	233	219	118	570
	Hull failures	576	89	43	708
	Fires and explosions	88	14	30	132
Other/unknown causes		2180	146	24	2350
Total		7794	1172	343	9309

Table 7.17 Countries with greater forest losses and gains, 2000–05 (FAO, 2006)

	Larger net losses (1000ha/year)		Larger net increases (1000ha/year)
Brazil	3103	China	4058
Indonesia	1871	Spain	296
Sudan	589	Vietnam	241
Myanmar	466	US	159
Zambia	445	Italy	106
Tanzania	412	Chile	57
Nigeria	410	Cuba	56
Congo	319	Bulgaria	50
Zimbabwe	313	France	41
Venezuela	288	Portugal	40
Total	8216	Total	5104

Even without government incentives, deforestation is a lucrative business: a hectare of virgin forest has its market price more than doubled after being converted into pasture by burning the forest, not to mention the income derived from the timber cut and sold. Some types of wood – such as mahogany – are worth high export market values. Forest plantations are increasing, but only count on 3.8 per cent of the total world forest areas, or 140 million hectares. About 22 per cent of the planted forests are for water and soil conservation and 78 per cent for productive ends, including energy. The forest plantation areas grew about 2.8 million hectares a year in the period 2000–05, being 87 per cent for productive ends. An interesting fact is the private participation in the forests: about 84 per cent of the planet forests belong to the public sector. The proportion is high both in Europe (90 per cent) and in Asia (above 92 per cent) and Africa (above 95 per cent). In South America, they are 76 per cent; in North America, they are 67 per cent; and in Central America, 42 per cent. The proportion does not mean that the forests are being protected. In 2005, three billion cubic metres of fuelwood were removed in the world, a number similar to that of 1990 and around 0.69 per cent of the world total reserves; about half of this extraction is for energy use (FAO, 2005).

In Brazil, the forest sector contributed to about 4.5 per cent of the GDP in 2002, something about US$28 billion (IBAMA, 2005). The country lost about 2.3 million hectares of forest between 1990 and 2000, especially along the so-called 'deforestation arch' and in stripes ('fishbone'), with up to 100km along the roads. The country deforestation was estimated to be 11,224km^2 in 2007, according to official data (Figure 7.33). The reductions in deforestation has basic economic causes, with the removal of subsidies to forest products exploration in the 1990s and, more recently, fluctuations in the *commodities* prices (mainly soybean and meat) in the international market.

The main reason for deforestation all over the world is the change in land use, for the expansion of crops and grazing areas. Table 7.18 illustrates this statement with the case of Northern China.

Even though the use of fuelwood is not the main cause of deforestation, there are 'hotspot' areas in the world in which its contribution is of major importance. As previously discussed, this occurs mainly in Africa, where a large part of the population depends on fuelwood for cooking. Charcoal production can also cause the degradation of vast forest areas. This is the case in Northern Thailand, which produces charcoal for Bangladesh. It is also the case of the states of Northern Brazil, to supply the steel industry. Many times the industry consumes 'biomass waste' from sawmills that deforest, a process that still occurs in several charcoal works and metallurgy industries. Other industries that frequently use

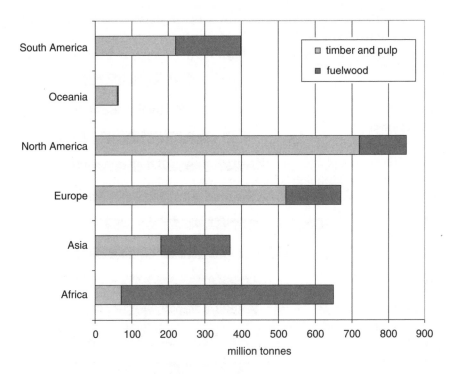

Figure 7.32 Extraction of wood and fuelwood, 2005 (FAO, 2005)

Table 7.18 Different areas prone to desertification and its causes in Northern China (Zhenda et al, 1989)

Lands prone to desertification and its causes	Total land area Areas (km²)	Desertification (%)
Intensive cultivation in steppe	44,700	25.4
Intensive grazing in steppe	49,900	28.3
Unsustainable extraction of fuelwood	56,000	31.8
Technogenic factors	1300	0.7
Poor use of water sources	14,700	8.3
Dunes invasion by the force of the wind	9400	5.5
Total	176,000	100.0

fuelwood without considering its origin are ceramics, gypsum and food industries.

Besides desertification, deforestation significantly contributes to global heating for CO_2 emission. Each hectare of tropical forest contains about 500 tonnes of stored CO_2 which go into the atmosphere due to deforestation.

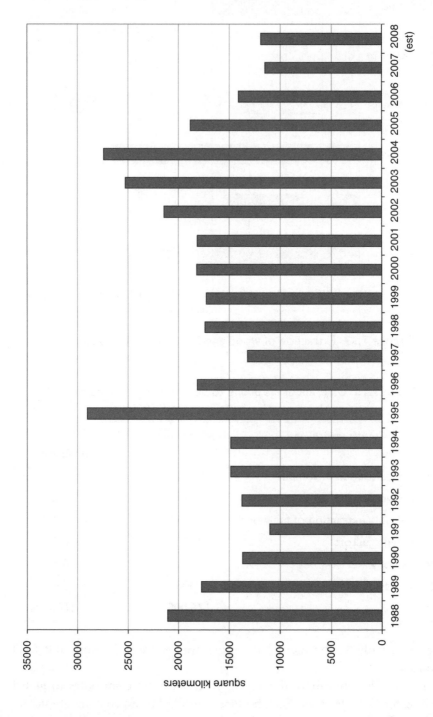

Figure 7.33 Annual deforestation in the Brazilian Amazon Forest, with an estimate for 2008 (MMA, 2007; INPE, 2008)

The amount of carbon stored per hectare of forest varies considerably according to the biome (FAO, 2005). Deforestation and ecosystems fragmentation also account for the loss of biodiversity – one in four mammals is endangered (Worldwatch, 2005) – as well as for the loss in quality of the drinking water that supplies the planet.

The use of energy fuelwood

While in developed countries most of the timber is used for industrial ends, in developing countries it is used as fuelwood (Table 7.19).

About 5 per cent of the world's energy still derives from traditional fuelwood. However, this ratio reaches 50 per cent in Haiti and Nepal, and two-thirds in places such as Congo, Eritrea, Ethiopia, Mozambique and Tanzania. Several countries depend on fuelwood energy, obtained at low economic cost in relation to other fuels. The contribution of fuelwood in the countries' economies is relatively little. According to FAO (2006), in 2001, 1.9 billion cubic metres of traditional fuelwood (75 per cent in developing countries) were produced in the world, which corresponds to 53 per cent of all the energy and non-energy fuelwood. These commercial transactions are estimated in about US$4–26 billion a year, or at most 0.006 per cent of the world GDP. The price of fuelwood is approximately US$5–25/m^3 in developed countries and US$1–10/m^3, or even less, in the developing ones. A large portion of the fuelwood is collected for private immediate use, and so is out of market transactions and is difficult to estimate. Some poor families spend a large share of their incomes to buy energy (Figure 7.34) or dedicate a great deal of their total time to collect fuelwood (Figure 7.35).

There is a considerable fuelwood deficit in the world. In 2010, the world fuelwood deficiency reaches about 960 million cubic metres a year due to populational increase – the energy equivalent to 240 million tonnes of oil a

Table 7.19 Percentage of all the timber used for traditional and modern power production in 1997 (FAO, 2005)

Region	Fuelwood / timber
World	53
Europe	18
North America	15
Developing countries	76
Africa	89
Asia	79
South and Central America	59

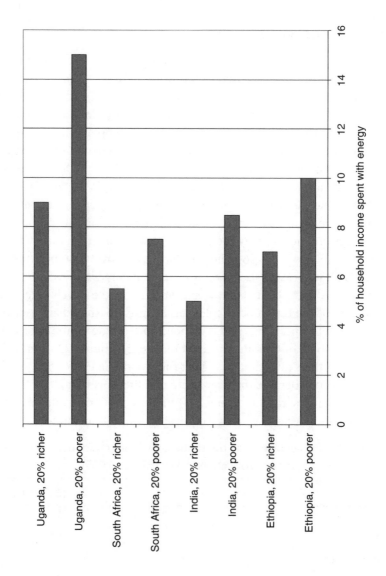

Figure 7.34 Energy-related expenditures by class of income, 2002 (WHO, 2006)

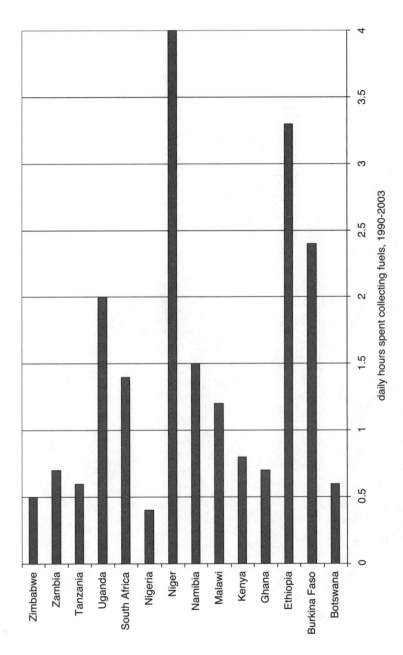

Figure 7.35 Time spent for obtaining energy (WHO, 2006)

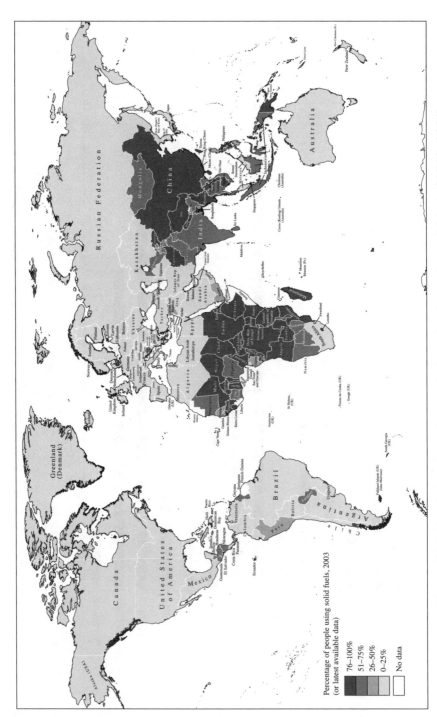

Figure 7.36 Population dependent on fuelwood and on other solid fuels (WHO, 2006)

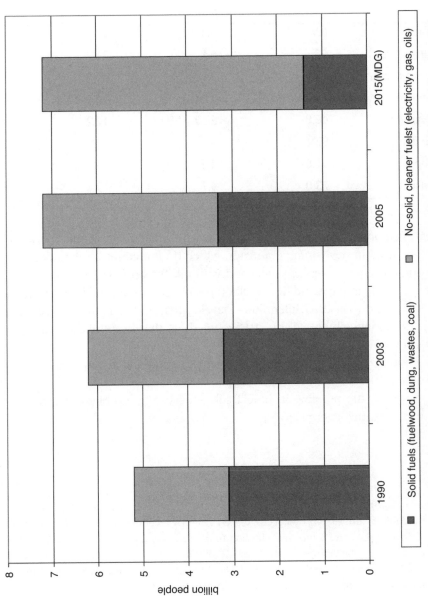

Figure 7.37 World Health Organization projections of population dependent on fuelwood and on other solid fuels, related to the Millennium Development Goals (WHO, 2006)

Table 7.20 Fuel switch by country, percentage in households (Esmap, 2003)

	No change – only solid fuels	Partial change, between solid and non-solid energy inputs	Full change – only among modern non-solid energy inputs
Brazil	6.9	9.4	83.4
Nicaragua	67.1	nd	31.7
South Africa	13.9	24.0	61.8
Vietnam	67.0	22.1	10.9
Guatemala	48.8	32.9	17.2
Ghana	92.1	4.1	2.8
Nepal	91.0	4.5	4.4
India	73.0	4.7	19.6

year, or approximately US$40 billion worth. Since most of this fuelwood will be used in developing countries, which do not count on the necessary strong currency to replace fuelwood with oil, the crisis will probably continue. Today in the world, three billion people depend on solid fuels (Figure 7.36), and one of the Millennium Development Goals is that of reducing this dependence by a half by 2015, something that is not likely to happen (Figure 7.37).

Poorer countries have less economic conditions to substitute fuels (Table 7.20).

Some of the possible technical solutions to this problem will be presented next: the 'energy ladder'.

Notes

1 In 1973, the International Convention for the Prevention of Pollution from Ships, modified by the 1978 protocol (MARPOL 73/78), accounted for the reduction in oil spilled on the seas. A massive adhesion to the protocol has helped to reduce oil discharge due to tanker operations from 710,000 tonnes a year in 1981 to an estimated 190,000 tonnes a year in 1989. By 1990, MARPOL 73/78 had been signed by 57 nations, covering 85 per cent of the world merchant fleet.

2 For more, see Biever (2005).

References

Alaska Marine Conservation Council (2007) Risks of oil & gas drilling, www.akma-rine.org/our-work/protect-bristol-bay/risks-of-oil-gas-drilling and www.akmarine.org/our-work/protect-bristol-bay/Impacts_of_Seismic_Surveys_AMCC.pdf

Albright, D. (1994) How much plutonium does North Korea have? Bulletin of the Atomic Scientists, September/October, pp 46–53 (vol. 50, no. 05), www.thebul-letin.org/article.php?art_ofn=so94albright

Biever, C. (2005) Improved X-ray vision to stop nuke smugglers. *New Scientist*, www.newscientist.com/article.ns?id=mg18825225.800

Boyes, S., Elliott, M. and Ducrotoy, J. P. (2008) Lerneinheit: Case Study – Thermal Pollution – Severity of This Pollution – ChemgaPedia, www.chemgapedia.de/vsen-gine/vlu/vsc/en/ch/16/uc/vlus/thermalpollution.vlu/Page/vsc/en/ch/16/uc/pollution/ca sestudies/thermal/thermalseverity.vscml.html

CCNR (2006) Canadian Coalition for Nuclear Responsibility, www.ccnr.org/max_plute _aecb.html#1 and www.ccnr.org/bomb_Pu.html

Coelho, S. T., Goldemberg, J., Lucon, O. and Guardabassi, P. (2006) Brazilian sugar-cane ethanol: lessons learned. Energy for Sustainable Development, vol. X, no. 2, June, pp26–39

EIA-DoE (2002) 'Nuclear Fuel Data'. Energy Information Administration, Form RW-859, www.eia.doe.gov/cneaf/nuclear/spent_fuel/ussnfdata.html

ENVIRONDEC (2006) Environmental Risk Assessment, www.environdec.com/reg/ 026/Chapters/Chap6/Chap6.htm

ESMAP (2003) Household Energy Use in Developing Countries. A Multicountry Study, October 2003. Joint UNDP/World Bank Energy Sector Management Assistance Programme. Report 27588

FAO (2006) State of the World's Forests 2005. United Nations Food and Agriculture Organization, Rome, www.fao.org/docrep/007/y5574e/y5574e00.htm

Fritsche, U. (1997) Comparing greenhouse gas emissions and abatement costs of nuclear and alternative energy options from a life cycle perspective. Oko Institut, www.oeko.de/service/gemis/files/info/nuke_co2_en.pdf

GFN (2007) Global Footprint Network, www.footprintnetwork.org

Hollander, J. M. (1992) *The Energy–Environment Connection*, Island Press, Washington DC

Hunt, W. H. Jr (2004) The China Factor: Aluminum Industry Impact. TMS online, www.tms.org/pubs/journals/JOM/0409/Hunt-0409.html

IAEA (2001) Nuclear power advantages, www.iaea.org/Publications/Booklets/ Development/devnine.html and www.iaea.org/Publications/Booklets/Development/ fig_18.html

IAEA (2006a) Power Reactor Information Systems – PRIS, http://www-pub.iaea.org/ MTCD/publications/PDF/cnpp2003/CNPP_Webpage/pages/AnnexII/AnnexII.htm

IAEA (2006b) Nuclear reactors database, www.iaea.org/cgi-bin/db.page.pl/ pris.charts.htm

IAI (2003) Year 2000 Aluminum LCI report for the International Aluminum Institute – March 2003. International Aluminium Institute, www.world-aluminium.org/iai/ publications/documents/lca.pdf

IBAMA (2005) O estado das florestas (The state of the forests). Brazilian Institute for the Environment, http://www2.ibama.gov.br/~geobr/Livro/cap2/floresta.pdf

IEA (2006a) CO$_2$ emissions from fuel combustion. International Energy Agency, Paris

IEA (2006b) Key World Energy Statistics, www.iea.org

IEA (2008a) Worldwide Trends in Energy Use and Efficiency – Key Insights from IEA Indicator Analysis. International Energy Agency, www.iea.org/Textbase/publications/free_new_Desc.asp?PUBS_ID=2026

IEA (2008b) Energy Balances of non-OECD Countries. International Energy Agency, Paris

INPE (2008) PRODES Project. Brazilian National Institute of Space Research (Instituto Nacional de Pesquisas Espaciais), http://www.obt.inpe.br/prodes/index.html (in Portuguese)

ITOPF (2006) Oil spill statistics. International Tanker Owners Pollution Federation Limited, www.itopf.com/stats.html

Krewitt, W., Mayerhofer, P., Friedrich, R., Trukenmüller, A., Heck, T., Greßmann, A., Raptis, F., Kaspar, F., Sachau, J., Rennings, K., Diekmann, J. and Praetorius, B. (1998) 'ExternE – Externalities of Energy. National Implementation in Germany'. IER, Stuttgart; 1998. *Apud* Nuclear Energy Institute – Clean-Air Energy, www.nei.org/filefolder/ExternE_Germany_-_Lifecycle_Emissions.ppt

Lucon, O. and Coelho, S. T. (2006) Environmental Impacts of energy. In Brazil: a country profile for sustainable development. International Atomic Energy Agency, Vienna. ISBN: 92-0-104906-4

MacDonald, A. (2006) Nuclear Expansion: Projections and Obstacles in the Far East and South Asia. The World Nuclear Association 2004 Annual Symposium, www.world-nuclear.org/sym/2004/macdonald.htm

MMA (2007) Monitoramento e Controle Ambiental, Resultado do Prodes 2006–07, Brazilian Environment Ministry, www.mma.gov.br/estruturas/imprensa/_arquivos/relat_desmat_amazonia_2006_2007.pdf

MME (2003) Executive Summary of the 2003–2012 Ten Year Expansion Plan. Brazilian Ministry of Mines and Energy (original in Portuguese: *Sumário Executivo do Plano Decenal de Expansão 2003/2012*, CCPE, Ministério de Minas e Energia, Brasil). *Apud* IAEA (2006) Brazil: A Country Profile on Sustainable Energy Development. International Atomic energy Agency, http://www.iaea.org/OurWork/ST/NE/Pess/assets/BRAZIL_FINAL_24April06.pdf

Moreira, J. R. and Poole, A. D. (1993) 'Hydropower and Its Constraints'. In Johansson, T. B., Kelly, H., Reddy, A. K. N. and Williams, R. H. (eds.), Renewable Energy – Sources for Fuels and Electricity, Island Press

Nakicenovic (2005) Energy scenarios for sustainable development, www.iiasa.ac.at/Research/ECS/IEW2004/docs/Nakicenovic_2004IEW.ppt

Nave, R. (2005) HyperPhysics. Georgia State University, http://hyperphysics.phyastr.gsu.edu/hbase/hph.html

NTI (2006) Profiles. Nuclear Threat Initiative, www.nti.org/e_research/profiles/

Rees, W. E. (1992) 'Ecological footprints and appropriated carrying capacity: what urban economics leaves out', Environment and Urbanisation. 4(2), Oct., http://eau.sagepub.com e http://eau.sagepub.com/cgi/reprint/4/2/121

Rogner, H. H. and Khan, A. (2002) Comparing energy options, www.iaea.org/Publications/Magazines/Bulletin/Bull401/article1.html

Rosen, M. (1998) Managing Radioactive Waste: Issues and Misunderstandings. The Uranium Institute 23rd Annual international Symposium. World Nuclear Association, www.world-nuclear.org/sym/1998/restore/ros-rest.htm

Schipper, L. (2006) Vehicle Efficiency and CO_2 Emissions: Troubling Trends embarq.wri.org/documents/Schipper-VehicEfficiency.pdf

Smith, C. B. (1978) Efficient electricity use, 2nd edn, Pergamon, New York

Tokimatsu, K., Kosugi, T., Asami, T., Williams, E. and Kaya, Y. (2006) Evaluation of lifecycle CO_2 emissions from the Japanese electric power sector in the 21st century under various nuclear scenarios. Energy Policy 34, pp833–852

UNDP, UNDESA, WEC, 2004, World Energy Assessment 2004 Update, www.undp.org/energy/weaover2004.htm

UNEP (2006a) Ground deposition of 137Cs after the Chernobyl Accident, http://maps.grida.no/go/graphic/ground_deposition_of_137cs_after_the_chernobyl_accident

UNEP (2006b) South Eastern Europe to Central Asia: Political Transition and Environmental Risks, http://maps.grida.no/go/graphic/south_eastern_europe_to_central_asia_political_transition_and_environmental_risks

UNEP (2006c) Spent fuel generation, http://maps.grida.no/go/graphic/annual_world_nuclear_reactor_construction_spent_fuel_generation

UNEP/GRID-Arendal (2008) Nuclear waste generation, http://maps.grida.no/go/graphic/nuclear_waste_generation

US EPA (2004) Clean Energy, www.epa.gov/cleanenergy

Van Leeuwen, J. W. S. and Smith, P. (2001a) Nuclear power – the energy balance energy insecurity and greenhouse gases, www.stormsmith.nl/Chap_1_CO-2_emission_of_the_nuclear_fuel_cycle.PDF and www.stormsmith.nl/Chap_3_Power_Plant_rev4.PDF

Van Leeuwen J. W. S. and Smith, P. (2001b) Nuclear power – the energy balance, www.stormsmith.nl

Van Leeuwen, J. W. S. and Smith, P. (2001c) The power plant, www.stormsmith.nl/Chap_3_Power_Plant_rev4.PDF

Vassolo, S. and Doll, P. (2005) Global-scale gridded estimates of thermoelectric power and manufacturing water use. Water Resources Research, vol. 41, W04010, doi:10.1029/2004WR003360, 2005, www.geo.uni-frankfurt.de/ipg/ag/dl/f_publikationen/2005/Vassolo_Doell_WRR2005.pdf

Vatenfall (2005) Life Cycle Assessment, www.vattenfall.com/files/environment/lca_2005.pdf

WEC (2004) World Energy Council Nuclear Study. *Apud* NEI, 2004, Putting nuclear in its place. Nuclear Engineering International, www.neimagazine.com/story.asp?sectioncode=76&storyCode=2025148

WHO (2006) Fuel for life: household energy and health. World Health Organization, Geneva, www.who.int

Wikipedia (2009) http://en.wikipedia.org/wiki/Nuclear_power_by_country, http://en.wikipedia.org/wiki/Nuclear_power_by_country

WISE (1993) No leading-role for nuclear power in preventing the greenhouse effect. News Communique on April 8, http://www10.antenna.nl/wise/index.html?http://www10.antenna.nl/wise/389/3791.html

WISE (2005) Nuclear Energy – Safety. Incidents Reported by the French Nuclear Safety Authorities: Breakdown, www.wiseparis.org/english/ourgraphs.html

WISE (2006a) Declarations of the Permanent Missions to the IAEA, published under reference no. 549 of the IAEA 'Information Circular'

WISE (2006b) Plutonium investigation. Figures and Graphs, World Information Service on Energy, www.wise-paris.org/english/ourgraphs.html

WNA (2006a) Safety of Nuclear Power Reactors – Appendix. World Nuclear Association, www.world-nuclear.org/info/inf06app.htm

WNA (2006b) The Hazards of Using Energy. World Nuclear Association, www.world-nuclear.org/info/inf06app.htm

Worldwatch (2006) Vital Signs 2005, www.worldwatch.org

Worldwatch (2007) Vital Signs 2006–2007, www.worldwatch.org

WRI (2006) World Resources Institute, www.wri.org

WWF and GFN (2006) Living Planet Report 2006. World Wildlife Foundation and Global Footprint Network, WF Gland, Switzerland, www.footprintnetwork.org /newsletters/gfn_blast_0610.html

WWF (2008) Living planet report 2008. World Wide Fund For Nature (formerly World Wildlife Fund), Gland, Switzerland, www.wwfint.org/news_facts/publications/living_planet_report/index.cfm

Zhenda, Z., Shu, L. and Xingmin, D. (1989) Desertification and rehabilitation in China. Institute of Desert Research, Academia Sinica, Lanzhou. Science Press, Beijing

Chapter 8

Technical Solutions

The main cause of environmental problems deriving from energy use, identified in Chapter 6, is the use of fossil fuels in power production, in the transportation, industry and building sectors. Hydropower production and nuclear energy also pose some special problems, as does biomass. The use of fuelwood in developing countries is a source of local pollution and deforestation, and accounts for a considerable parcel of the greenhouse gas emissions. The most obvious way of solving these problems is to totally or partially remove their causes. This is a very difficult task, yet not impossible. In the energy area, there are three possible ways of solving problems:

1. *energy efficiency* (or *energy conservation*), to obtain an equivalent well-being with less natural resources;
2. *renewable energies*, which save fossil fuels from exhaustion; and
3. new *technological advances*, which manage to achieve commercial scale use.

These categories are complementary, as it is possible to develop a new technology for obtaining renewable energy with simultaneous gains in efficiency. Solar energy offers great possibilities in this sense. A more efficient energy use must be made whenever possible, as this extends the life of the finite sources of fossil fuels, reduces environmental impacts and in general offers economic advantages in terms of investment returns.

Energy efficiency

Many are the advantages of energy efficiency:

- the cost of energy economy is usually smaller than that of its generation;
- security of supply increases and resources which are finite are saved;
- there are micro and macroeconomic gains associated with an increase in productivity and in industrial competitivity;
- the access to energy services is increased; and
- environmental impacts are reduced, especially the emission of pollutants and greenhouse gases.

As an example, without the energy savings obtained between 1973 and 1998, energy consumption in the OECD would have been 50 per cent higher (Figure 8.1).

It is very important for developing countries to benefit from the adoption of energy efficiency measures, with the possibility of saving up to 65 per cent of their energy between 2006 and 2026. This is already happening: the new efficiency standards for equipment in China should save 200TWh of electricity until 2009, equivalent to the total residential consumption of the country in 2002. In the steel sector, the potential gains in efficiency in China, India, Brazil, Mexico and South Africa – the five developing countries which are the largest emitters of greenhouse gases – are estimated to be between 33 per cent and 49 per cent (World Bank, 2006). In the next 20 years, the OECD countries are expected to achieve reductions in energy use between 25 and 35 per cent and from 30 to more than 45 per cent in developing countries (UNDP, UNDESA, WEC, 2004). Rationalization of energy use did not evolve at times when energy was abundant and cheap, but during crises. Among these, the following can be mentioned:

- during World War II, when the German fear of depending on petroleum stimulated research in the coal gasification area;
- the soaring oil prices in the 1970s and the Western countries' fear of an exaggerated dependence on Middle East imports;

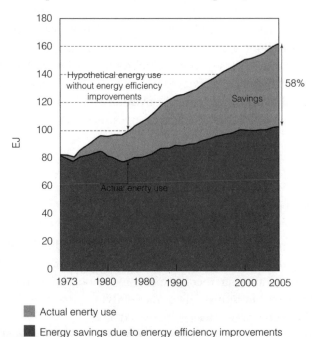

Figure 8.1 Efficiency gains in OECD, 1973–2005 (IEA, 2008a)

- the power crisis due to a prolonged draught in Brazil in 2001, which led to a reduction in consumption and to a replacement of older equipment by more efficient equipment.

Besides cost reduction, the productive sector realized that technological changes for energy savings and recovery as a byproduct also reduces environmental impacts. The reduction in energy use may also lead to a decrease in water consumption and that of other inputs, generating more savings. Another important reason is the strategic positioning enterprises in markets, aiming to improve the competitivity of a company in the future.

Energy efficiency potentials

There are several possibilities of increasing the efficiency of the use of primary sources of energy, but they are limited by a number of restrictions (Figure 8.2): *physical* (theoretical), *technical, economic* and *market*:

- the *theoretical potential* represents what may be achieved on the basis of physical laws – particularly the laws of thermodynamics – and the existing natural resources; within this potential, gains can be obtained by the replacement of inputs, reuse of materials and heat, elimination of friction and reduction in losses in general;
- the *technical potential* represents energy savings resulting from the use of more efficient technologies and services available without taking economic considerations into account;
- the *economic potential* considers the most efficient technologies which make sense with prices in a market which works perfectly, with wide competition among investors and availability of information among all users for decision making;
- the *market potential* is what is expected to be obtained given the commercial conditions (such as the supply of products and services supply, the cost of energy, consumers' preferences), market barriers and imperfections (such as lack of information between agents who sell and buy) and social barriers (in which externalities such as ecologic as well as health impacts are not taken into account); considering all these factors, the estimated market potential is obtained for the conditions effectively available.

The present situation and the estimated potentials are premises from studies on energy scenarios, which are generally simulations of future situations in which problem-solving measures are proposed. The weak point of the models lies exactly in their premises that, if not well equated and adopted, will lead to unrealistic results.

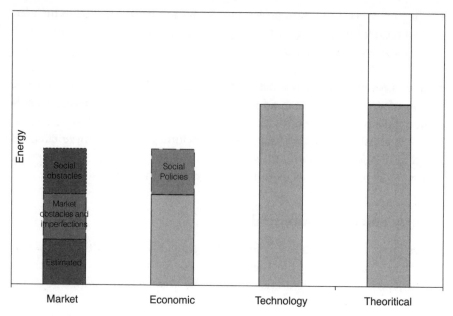

Figure 8.2 Energy efficiency potentials

Barriers to energy conservation

Energy efficiency is a component of economic efficiency, but not always the dominant one. Even though the Energy Service Companies (ESCOs) specialists consider efficiency something special, the productive sector simply considers energy as a production ingredient, besides capital, labour and raw materials. Issues related to energy frequently require specific knowledge, which is quite distant from the enterprise's final activity. The situation gets even more difficult when the income of a company, of an economic sector and even of a country derive mainly from selling energy products. In these cases, there is opposition to energy conservation, as efficiency measures represent, at least in principle, a decrease in profits. That is the case, for example, of:

- manufacturers of vehicles for the luxury segment;
- power utilities, which sell electricity for profit (except for sectors with subsidized prices, such as low-income populations);
- large oil companies; and
- international bodies, such as the Organization of the Petroleum Exporting Countries (OPEC).

According to Poole and Geller (1997), the main barriers against energy conservation, in addition to the loss of income on the part of the utilities, are:

- the low price of energy for certain sectors, which does not reflect the generation costs;
- the lack of priority for energy, considered a fixed cost in companies devoted to other activities;
- the difficulty for the consumer in taking decisions and the risks at the moment of transition to a more efficient system, since costs on a life-cycle basis are not evident;
- the lack of information provided by manufacturers and by sellers of products that consume energy;
- the small availability of efficient equipment in the market;
- the lack of financing by third parties (and the occasional renegotiation of contracts) when consumers do not use their own means to pay for the transition;
- the short-term economic-financial view, mainly in inflationary cultures or with high interest rates; and
- the lack of laws and regulatory marks that make energy efficiency compulsory.

These considerations do not generally take the investment return rate of energy efficiency actions into account, the perspectives of which are usually very positive (Box 8.1).

Box 8.1 Some economic definitions

Several economic merit indicators may be used to measure the profitability of investments in energy efficiency:

(a) the simple and discounted rate of return;
(b) the cost of the energy saved;
(c) the internal rate of return; and
(d) the life cycle cost, simple and annualized.

a) The *simple rate of return* period (SRR) measures the necessary time to recover the investment made, resulting from the ratio between the initial investment in energy efficiency and the energy savings obtained each year. For example, where the initial investment is US$30,000 and the energy savings are US$10,000 a year, the simple rate of return equals 3, that is, the time to recover the capital invested will be equal to three years:

$$\text{SRR} = \text{initial investment (\$)/savings per year (\$)}$$
$$= \text{investment return (years)}.$$

In this case, the annual savings are expressed in monetary units, discounting inflation (US$ or, for didactic purposes, 'dollars'), and correspond to the multiplication of the 'energy price (in US$/kWh) by the annual energy savings (in kWh)'.

Despite its simplicity and ease of application, the simple rate of return does not consider the value of money in time, that is, the capital cost, which is an essential element in an investment assessment process. For this reason, the *discounted rate of return* (DRR) is used, which measures the value of the necessary time to recover the investment made. For this, the cost of capital value is considered, that is, the discount rate (*d*) and the investment lifetime (*n*) to calculate the period of time in which the investment in energy efficiency will be recovered. The following formula is used:

$$DRR = n \times CRF\,(d,\,n)\,\frac{\text{initial investment (\$)}}{\text{savings per year (\$)}} = \text{investment return (years)}$$

in which CRF(*d*, *n*) is the capital recovery factor, which represents the annualized value (during the lifetime of the investment in energy efficiency) of the present value of the initial investment, assuming a certain discount rate.

The CRF formula is:

$$CRF = \frac{d\,(1+d)^n}{(1+d)^n - 1}.$$

The higher the discount rate *d* (i.e. the higher the cost of capital, the interest charged for loans), the higher will be the return period discounted from the capital and the longer will be the time to recover the investment made. For example, let us consider a US$30,000 initial investment resulting in US$10,000 energy savings a year. Being the discount rate equal to 8 per cent a year and the investment lifetime equal to five years, the following capital recovery factor is obtained:

$$CRF = \frac{0.08 \times 1.469}{0.469} = 0.251.$$

In this way:

$$DPR = 5 \times 0.251 \times \frac{30,000}{10,000} = 3.76 \text{ years.}$$

Keeping the same conditions, but considering a discount rate equal to 15 per cent a year, the following result would ensue:

$$CRF = \frac{0.15 \times 2.011}{1.011} = 0.298$$

$$DRR = 5 \times 0.298 \times \frac{30,000}{10,000} = 4.48 \text{ years.}$$

(b) The *saved energy cost* (SEC) is a measure that expresses the cost equivalent to an energy unit saved, considering the discount rate and the service life of the investment in energy efficiency. The SEC results from the division between the annualized cost of the investment in energy efficiency and the annual energy savings obtained. The importance of the SEC lies in the fact of allowing an economic comparison between investments in energy efficiency and investments in energy supply. The result will be in US\$/kWh and will allow comparing the Saved Energy Cost to the cost of energy:

$$SEC = CRF\,(d, n) = \frac{\text{initial investment (\$)}}{\text{annual energy saving (kWh)}}.$$

For example, consider an initial investment is US\$30,000, which results in energy savings of 180MWh/year (i.e. 180.000kWh/year). With the discount rate equal to 8 per cent a year and the investment lifetime equal to five years, a CRF equal to 0.251 is obtained. Therefore:

$$SEC = 0.251 \times \frac{\text{US\$30,000}}{180\text{MWh}} = \$0.042/\text{kWh.}$$

(c) The *internal rate of return* (IRR) is the discount rate value that reduces the present liquid value of an investment to zero, that is, the value of the discount rate for which the sum of all the energy savings on the initial date of the project must be equal to zero. In case the IRR is higher than the cost of capital, the investment presents a competitive discount rate and can be made. The IRR is calculated iteratively by the formula

$$0 = \sum_{n=0}^{n} \frac{\text{energy savings}}{(1 + IRR)^n}.$$

For example, for a US\$30,000 energy efficiency investment resulting in US\$10,000 energy savings a year for five years, the IRR is 19.86 per cent.

(d) The *life cycle cost* (LCC) is the present value of all expenditures related to the energy efficiency investment. This indicator is important to compare alternatives with the same service life time, as it allows choosing the alternative that presents the smaller LCC. However, it does not allow comparing alternatives of investments presenting different service live times:

$$\text{LCC} = \text{initial investment (\$)} + \frac{\text{annual energy cost (US\$)}}{\text{CRF } (d, n)}.$$

For example, let us consider a US$50,000 investment resulting in a US$10,000 annual energy cost. Supposing a 12 per cent discount rate and a ten-year investment lifetime, CRF will be 0.177. Thus:

$$\text{LCC} = 50,000 + \frac{10,000}{0.177} = 50,000 + 56,497 = 106,497.$$

The *annualized life cycle cost* (ALLC) is the annual sum of the investment in energy efficiency and the annual energy cost. The ALLC actually corresponds to the annual cost of investment and of operation for an equipment that consumes energy:

$$\text{ALLC} = \text{initial investment (US\$)} \times \text{CRF}(d, n) + \text{annual cost of energy.}$$

For example, let us consider a US$50,000 investment resulting in a US$10,000 annual energy cost. Supposing a 12 per cent discount rate and a 10-year investment lifetime, a CRF equal to 0.177 ensues. Therefore:

$$\text{ALLC} = 50,000 \times 0.177 + 10,000 = 18,850.$$

Keeping the same conditions, but considering a 20-year investment service life, the following result would be obtained:

$$\text{CRF} = 0.134 \text{ e ALLC} = 50,000 \times 0.134 + 10,000 = 16,700.$$

Energy efficiency related actions and policies have their focus where the major potential gains are, the main ones being:

- small-scale power generation and cogeneration;
- transportation;
- industrial heat and stationary electric motors;
- lighting, especially incandescent light bulbs;

- refrigeration, air conditioning and heating;
- cooking, mainly with fuelwood.

Technological advances in power production

The environmental impacts resulting from power production may be reduced by improving the efficiency of generation technologies, thus reducing the emission of pollutants at the source. The conventional systems for power generation (steam turbines and boilers) hardly ever have efficiencies greater than 35 per cent and significantly contribute to environmental degradation. *Combined cycle systems* recover the heat lost in the process, increasing the efficiency of the present systems to values over 50 per cent (Figure 8.3).

Technological advances have already overcome the 60 per cent efficiency barrier in power generation. It is important to note that the *total* efficiency of the system may be greater than the ones presented in Figure 8.4, also considering the use of heat for other purposes.

Figure 8.5 shows efficiencies in coal-fired thermoelectric power plants in different countries and years. Opportunities for improving Chinese and Indian plants are evident. As a comparison, in Japan, a 36 per cent average efficiency in thermopower plants had already been achieved in 1965. In 2004, the Japanese thermopower plants had an average efficiency of 40.4 per cent, and some of its units reached efficiencies of up to 52 per cent (Tohoku Electric Power, 2006). Denmark had a 36 per cent average efficiency in 1960 and 52 per cent in 2000. Some plants reached 58 per cent in that year (Noer and Kjaer, 2005).

Advanced technologies include supercritical steam generators, together with boilers operating under high pressures (over 220 bar), so that there is

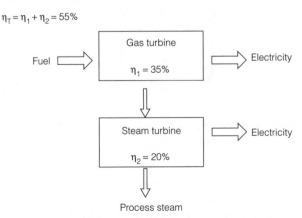

$$\eta_T = \eta_1 + \eta_2 = 55\%$$

Gas turbine

Fuel ⟹   ⟹ Electricity

$$\eta_1 = 35\%$$

Steam turbine   ⟹ Electricity

$$\eta_2 = 20\%$$

Process steam

Figure 8.3 Combined cycle generators

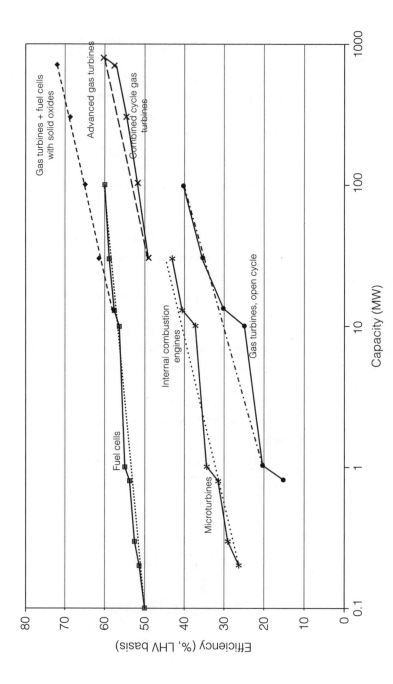

Figure 8.4 Efficiency of different power generation technologies

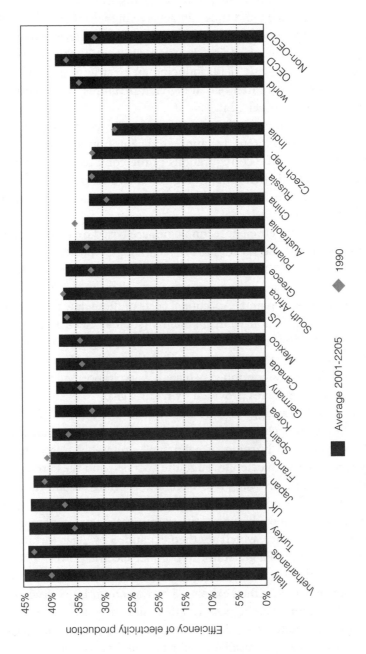

Figure 8.5 Efficiency of coal thermopower plants in different countries

no separation between water and steam and losses are reduced, increasing efficiency. The present tendencies are the replacement of Rankine thermodynamical cycles[1] by steam turbines by Brayton-Rankine combined cycles, with gas and steam turbines, which achieve efficiencies of up to 60 per cent. New materials, such as nickel alloys, withstand higher temperatures and pressures than steel, and thus can achieve higher efficiencies. Other methods are at an advanced stage of research and development, including magnetohydrodynamic cycles, in which electrically-charged plasma moves in an intense magnetic field, inducing an electric current. Other research includes the study of fuel cells at high temperatures, which could reach efficiencies of over 70 per cent.

Natural gas thermopower plants typically emit NO_x, which may be reduced up to a point by more efficient burners (*low-NO_x burners*), improvements in the configurations of the combustion chamber and optimization of the air-fuel ratio. In regions where air pollution is critical, other much more expensive control devices may be required, such as ammonium injection.

Several highly efficient technologies are based on coal use, an abundant source of energy. Some are proven technologies in use, as is the case of circulating fluidized bed combustion plants. Others are in a demonstration phase in large-scale units. In many cases there is the possibility of retro-fitting the present plants. Additional costs of these new technologies, as well as the use of emission control systems (such as electrostatic precipitators, gas and filter washers), usually increase their capital cost by up to 20 per cent. Even so, due to the present availability of coal and its low cost, this fuel will probably continue to have a very important role in the future, despite the advantages provided by natural gas.

In an integrated gasification combined cycle plant (*IGCC*), the fuel (usually coal, but also petroleum or biomass) is *gasified*. Gasification is basically a controlled burning of solid fuel, preferably pulverized, with little oxygen. Steam is injected through the coal bed and the carbon is combined with the oxygen, releasing hydrogen and forming carbon monoxide.[2] This (CO and H_2) blend is called *syngas*, a fuel that is then pumped and driven into a combustion chamber with compressed air, generating hot gases under high pressure, which are then expanded by a gas turbine, moving an air compressor and a generator to produce electric power. The hot exhaust gases from the gas turbine (basically CO_2)[3] are subsequently used to produce steam, which is then expanded by a steam turbine, driving a generator to produce more electric power. The gasification process produces a lot of heat that is used to pre-heat the water that will generate the turbine's steam. The surpluses may be used for ambient heating (district heating) in cold climates. The hydrogen of *syngas* may also be separated and used in a fuel cell

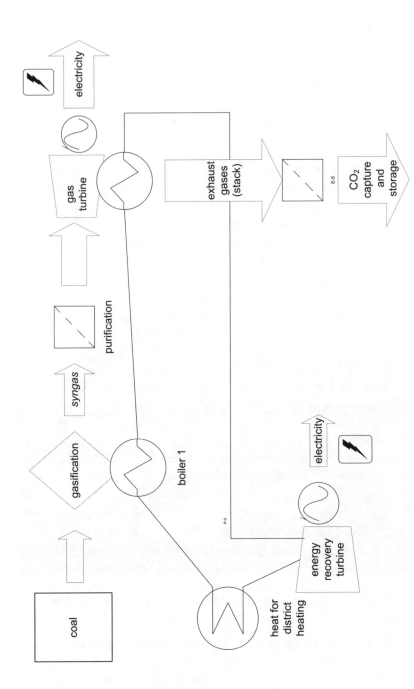

Figure 8.6 Integrated coal gasification and cogeneration cycle (adapted from WTE, 2006)

vehicle. *Syngas* can also be converted into other hydrocarbon fuels for transportation and industrial uses. Integrated gasification combined cycle installations (IGCC, Figure 8.6) produce less CO_2 for the same amount of power produced,[4] which reflects the gas turbine's higher efficiency.

In order to complete the integrated cycle and even more so to mitigate carbon emissions, the underground capture and storage is in advanced study phase (Box 8.2).

Box 8.2 Carbon Capture and Storage (CCS)

Carbon capture and storage (CO_2 Carbon Capture and Storage, or CCS) at the very source, in order to improve oil and natural gas exploitation, or in abandoned deposits deep in the ocean is a technical option to be considered when the main concern is the greenhouse gases effect (IPCC, 2005). If no leaking occurs, no gas will be emitted into the atmosphere from the source (Figure 8.7).

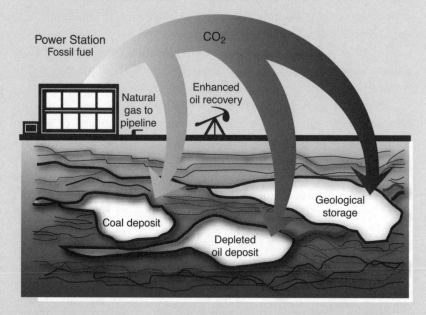

Figure 8.7 Carbon capture and storage diagram (Reeve, 2000)

About one-third of all the CO_2 emissions from fossil fuel-based energy sources derive from thermopower plants, a priority source of control. The idea of capturing CO_2 from the gases exhausted from power plants stacks did not develop from concern about the greenhouse effect, but rather as a possible source of commercial carbon gas, for the beverage and dry ice industries. Several CO_2 recovery plants were built and operated in the US, but most of them were closed for economic problems caused by the fall in prices of crude oil in the 1980s. Once CO_2 is captured, the problem is removing it. The commercial use is extremely limited and thus there is no economic incentive for capturing large amounts of CO_2. Apart from this, there is the risk of CO_2 leaking back into the atmosphere and, depending on the case, of altering the sea water composition. In high concentrations, CO_2 is toxic and may cause deaths, as occurred in the Republic of Cameroon in 1986, when CO_2 leakage from volcanic origin in Lake Nyos killed over 1700 people, as well as livestock and wild animals (Camp, 2006). CO_2 capture processes usually require a large amount of energy, reducing the conversion efficiency of the plant and the available power, and therefore increasing the amount of CO_2 produced per power unit generated. The most interesting method seems to be removing nitrogen from the air before the combustion process, as it has lower energy cost. Figure 8.8 compares several CO_2 capture technologies and their energy cost (ratio between the liquid powers developed by the plant with and without CO_2 controls).

The CCS technology, combined with hydrogen production, is part of a fossil fuels 'decarbonization' proposal (Figure 8.9), which may still be considered futuristic.

Although the CCS technology is usually linked to coal and natural gas thermopower plants, nothing prevents it from being applied to biomass power generation (as is the case of sugar cane bagasse). In this case, the CO_2 liquid emissions would be negative, as the carbon in the atmosphere has been synthesized in the plants, transformed into energy and injected underground. Although such ideas are interesting, in practice they face great difficulties. One of them would be to transport the CO_2 from the source to its final deposition, be it through a gas duct network (which would cause problems with landowners and ecologically sensitive areas) or by road/railway transportation (which would overload the transportation infrastructure and require more energy).

Renewable energies

There is a wide variety of technologies to produce power from renewable sources. The main ones are listed in Table 8.1, with qualitative information on their present technological and commercial stage.

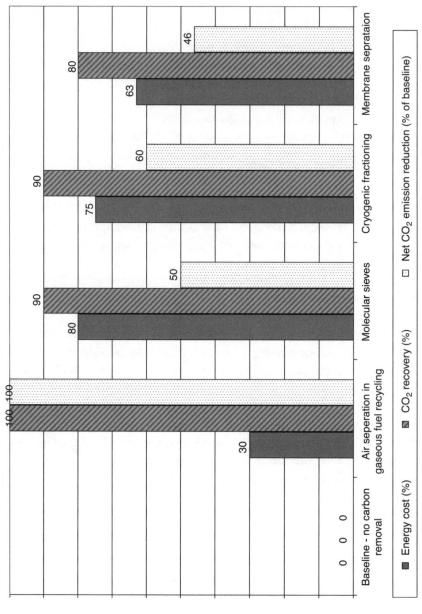

Figure 8.8 Energy cost and efficiency in carbon recapture (IPCC, 2005)

Table 8.1 Summary of the 'status' of renewable energy technologies (update from IEA, 1994)

	Technology	Technical 'status'	Present commercial 'status'
Biomass	Agricultural wastes	R–D	A
	Bagasse cogeneration	M	E
	Energy 'farms'	R–D	A
	Municipal Solid Waste (MSW) incineration	M–D	A
	Biogas from domestic sewage	D	A
	Biogas from industrial effluents	M–D	A
	Biogas from landfill	M–D	A
Geothermal	Hydrothermal	M	E
	Geopressurized	D	NE
	Hot dry rocks	R–D	NE
	Magma	R	NE
Hydropower	Small scale	M	E
	Large scale	M	E
Oceanic	Tides	M	A?
	Tide current	R–D	NE
	Coastal waves	R–D	A?
	Sea waves	R–D	A?
	Ocean thermal (OTEC)	R–D	A
	Salinity gradient	R	NE
Solar	Solar thermopower	R–D	NE
	Solar thermal	M	E
	Solar architecture	M–D	E
	Photovoltaic	M–D	A
	Thermochemical	M–R	A?
	Photochemical	R	NE
Wind	Inland	M	A
	On the sea	M	A
	Air pumps	M–D	A

Notes:
1) For technical *status*: (R) under research phase; (D) under development; (M) mature technology.
2) For commercial *status*: (E) economically viable; (NE) non-economic; (A) economically viable in certain areas or market niches; (A?) possible economic viability in certain market niches.

Table 8.2 Status of the renewable energy technologies in 2001 and 2004 (update from REN21, 2006; UNDP, UNDESA, WEC, 2004)

Technology	Increase in installed capacity 2001–04 (%/year)	Capacity in operation at the end of 2004	Capacity factor (%)	Power produced in 2004	Investment (2001 US$/kW)	Energy cost[5] 2001	Energy cost[5] Future potential
Biomass							
Electricity	1.7	~44GWe	25–80	~179TWh (e)	500–6000	3–12 ¢/kWh	4–10 ¢/kWh
Heat	1.6	~22GWth	25–80	>765TWh(th)	170–1000	1–6 ¢/kWh	1–5 ¢/kWh
Ethanol	14.2	33 billion litres		671PJ		8–25 $/GJ	6–10 $/GJ
Biodiesel	16.4	3.9 billion litres		71PJ		15–25 $/GJ	10–15 $/GJ
Wind power	28.4	59GWe	20–40	91TWh (e)	850–1700	5–13 ¢/kWh	3–10 ¢/kWh
Photovoltaic (PV)	53.3	5.4GWe	6–20	3.6TWh (e)	5000–18,000	25–125 ¢/kWh	5–25 ¢/kWh
Solar thermal power	~ 0	0.4GWe	20–35	0.9TWh (e)	2500–6000	12–18 ¢/kWh	4–10 ¢/kWh
Thermal solar heat	51.2	88GWth	8–20	197TWh (th)	300–1700	3–20 ¢/kWh	2–10 ¢/kWh
Hydropower							
Large and medium	1.2	741Gwe	35–60	2564TWh (e)	1000–3500	2–8 ¢/kWh	2–8 ¢/kWh
SHPs	34.6	66Gwe	20–90	244TWh (e)	700–8000	4–10 ¢/kWh	3–10 ¢/kWh
Geothermal							
Electricity	4.2	9.3GWe	45–90	60TWh (e)	800–3000	2–10 ¢/kWh	1–8 ¢/kWh
Heat	32.2	28GWth	20–70	127TWh (th)	200–2000	0.5–5 ¢/kWh	0.5–5 ¢/kWh
Marine							
Tides	nd	0.3GWe	20–30	0.6TWh (e)	1700–2500	8–15 ¢/kWh	8–15 ¢/kWh
Waves	–	test phase	20–35		2000–5000	10–30 ¢/kWh	5–7 ¢/kWh
Currents	–	test phase	25–40		2000–5000	10–25 ¢/kWh	4–10 ¢/kWh
Ocean thermal	–	test phase	70–80		8000–20,000	15–40 ¢/kWh	7–20 ¢/kWh

Figure 8.9 'Decarbonization' of fossil fuels: hydrogen and CCS
(Nakicenovic, 2004)

The medium-term costs, capacity factors and energy produced in 2001
and 2004 for renewable energies are presented in Table 8.2.

Renewable energy is rapidly developing, as shown in Table 8.3, which
presents the data for the 2005–07 period.

Table 8.3 Renewable energy technologies indicators in the period
2005–07 (REN21, 2007)

Indicator	Unit	2005	2006	2007
Annual investments	US$ bi	39	55	66
Renewables total capacity				
(excluding large hydroplants)	GW	182	206	237
(including large hydroplants)	GW	930	970	1010
Wind, capacity	GW	59	74	93
Solar PV grid-connected, capacity	GW	3.4	5.0	7.8
Solar PV, annual production	GW	1.8	2.5	3.8
Solar heating, capacity	GWth	88	103	121
Ethanol	bil. litres	33	38	44
Biodiesel	bil. litres	3.9	6.0	8.0

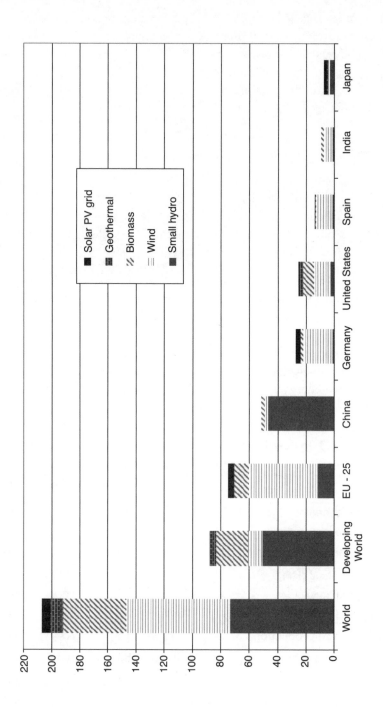

Figure 8.10 'Modern' Renewable Power Capacities, Developing World, EU, and Top Six Countries, 2006 (REN21, 2008)

Figure 8.10 shows the installed electrical capacity of renewable energies in different regions of the world. Whereas developing countries exploit their hydraulic and biomass potentials, the developed ones foster mainly wind power. The total 200GW-installed capacity represents about 5 per cent of the total world power generation.

Biomass, wind power, solar thermal and photovoltaic (PV) energy will be further discussed in more detail.

Biomass

Biomass has a great potential to contribute to the total world energy supply in the future, as shown in Table 8.4. Figure 8.11 shows some of the bioenergy transformation routes from different types of biomass.

Gaseous biomass can be used in stationary systems directly feeding engines and/or turbines, or in boilers to generate steam. It can also be used in transportation, in modified engines, as reformed hydrogen or in fuel cells. Biomass with high humidity levels (manure, sewage and garbage) may be converted into biogas through anaerobic digestion (by methanophilic bacteria with little oxygen). Biogas contains about 75 per cent CO_4; the rest is CO_2 and impurities. These contain sulphidric acid (H_2S) and, in some cases (such as in internal combustion Otto cycle

Table 8.4 Projections of worldwide contribution of renewable energies made by the International Institute for Applied Sciences – IIASA (*apud* Grimm, 2004)

Mtoe	2001	2010	2020	2030	2040
Biomass	1080	1313	1791	2483	3271
SHP (small hydropower plants)	9.5	19	49	106	189
Large and medium-sized hydro	222.7	266	309	341	358
Wind	4.7	44	266	542	688
Solar photovoltaic (PV)	0.2	2	24	221	784
Solar thermal, heat	4.1	15	66	244	480
Solar thermal, electricity	0.1	0.4	3	16	68
Geothermal	43.2	86	186	333	493
Marine (tides, waves, currents)	0.05	0.1	0.4	3	20
Total renewable	1364.5	1745.5	2694.4	4289	6351
Total consumption	10,038.3	10,549	11,425	12,352	13,310
Renewable/Total (%)	13.6	16.6	23.6	34.7	47.7

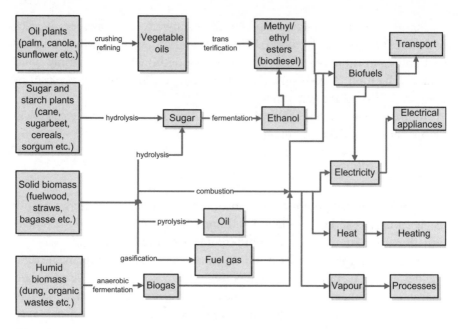

Figure 8.11 Bioenergy transformation routes

Table 8.5 Biomass characteristics

Fuel	Moisture content (%)	High heating value (kWh/kg dry matter)	Ashes (% of dry matter)
Fuelwood (unbarked)	50–60	5.1–5.6	0.4–3.0
Bagasse	70	1.8	1.7
Dry bagasse	0–20	5.0	1.0–3.0
Pellets	<10	>4.7	<0.7
Coal	6–10	7.2–7.9	8.5–10.9

engines), a chemical neutralization operation (desulphurization) is necessary. This adds costs to the system. There are several technologies for producing energy from solid biomass, increasing in complexity depending on the feeding system, type of fuel, combustion chamber(s) configuration, gases recirculation, heat exchangers, emission control systems and other characteristics. Some examples are:

a. simple boilers for domestic heating (Figure 8.12);
b. boilers with lower fuelwood feeding for greater demands;
c. boilers for incineration (Figure 8.13);

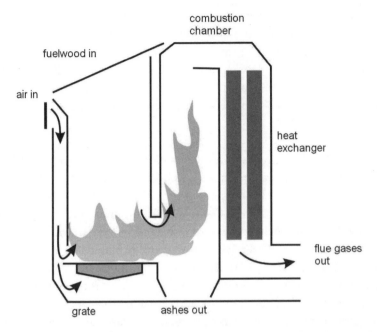

Figure 8.12 Simple heating boiler fed on the upper part (downdraft) by wood waste (wood chips and pellets)

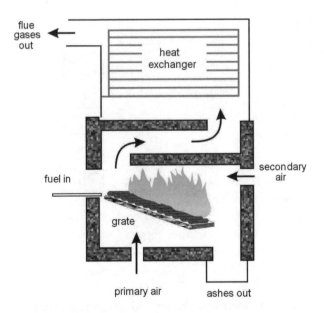

Figure 8.13 Boiler with incineration grate

d. boilers for burning straw;

e. boilers with a pulverized biomass injector;

f. fluidized bed boilers (Figure 8.14);

g. biomass gasifiers, encompassing systems with a simple boiler that produces fuel gases (CO and CH_4, deriving from incomplete burning, Figure 8.15) up to a complete integrated gasification and cogeneration plant (Figure 8.16).

Besides biofuels, power and heat generation by burning fuelwood, bagasse and other agricultural waste is a very well-known technology used in many countries. In 2003, the US generated a total of 29,001GWh of electricity from biomass, of which 18,331GWh was from paper industry black liquor and 9162GWh from fuelwood wastes (US DoE, 2006). In Brazil, sugar cane bagasse generated 6964GWh whereas lixivium produced 4220GWh in electricity in 2004 (MME, 2006). A biomass thermopower plant consists of different units: fuel storage, combustion unit, steam production, power generation, process heat generation and additional use of steam.

Traditional systems are being progressively replaced by new ones. Old low-pressure boilers (below 20 bar, 2MPa) had efficiencies below 10 per cent. Small improvements, using extraction-condensation steam turbines and higher temperatures, with pressures of up to 80 bar and efficiencies over 30 per cent, were introduced. In Brazil, sugar and ethanol plants have

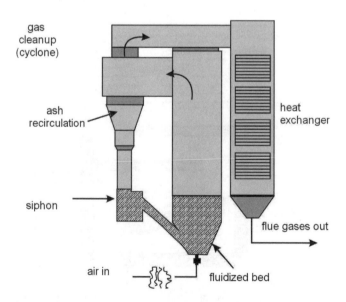

Figure 8.14 Fluidized bed boiler with cyclone for cleaning gases and heat exchanger

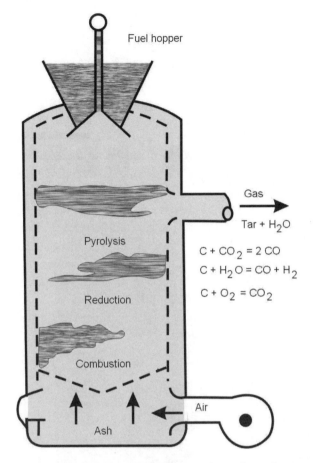

Figure 8.15 Biomass gasification and pyrolysis diagram

become self-sufficient in their electricity and heat needs by means of cogeneration, no longer depending on fossil fuels. Electricity surpluses are sold to the grid by the so-called *self-producers*, who already have an installed capacity of 500MW, with a tenfold expansion potential. The electricity production is now 80kWh per ton of sugar cane; the best technology available allows reaching 120kWh/ton of sugar cane and, in the future, with gasification, 300kWh/ton of sugar cane. Complex systems, integrating gasification and cogeneration in energy farms (Box 8.3), are encouraging signs for a significant role of biomass in the energy matrix of several countries.

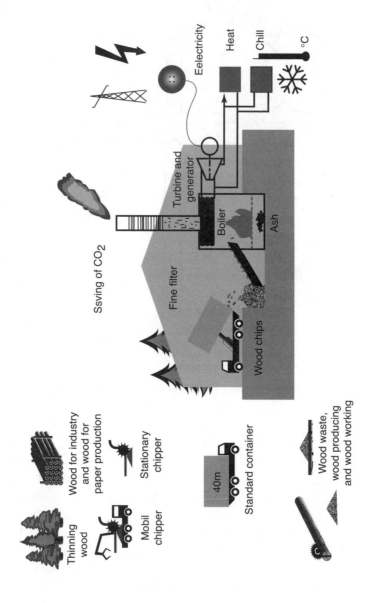

Figure 8.16 Layout of a cogeneration process from biomass (wood chips and straw)

Box 8.3 Energy farms

Advanced technologies have been proposed to gasify solid biomass, using the gas in turbines to generate electricity with efficiencies over 40 per cent. This efficiency is not surprising, since combined cycle generators are in operation, working with natural gas, with similar and higher efficiencies. The merit of the biomass integrated gasifier and gas turbine systems (BIG/GT, Figure 8.17) is the possibility of operating with high efficiency in small generation units, at a convenient range for the economic use of biomass, between 20 and 100MW in capacity. Figure 8.17 illustrates the WBP/SIGAME project, with total capacity of 32MW, producing 238GWh a year from an energy farm with 6800ha eucalyptus, and a production of 35m^3 fuelwood/hectare.year.

The higher generation capacity limit is determined by the cost of transporting biomass over long distances. The system is still under the research and development phase, but if the technology meets the expectations the global implications may be significant, with biomass contributing power at a similar scale to that of nuclear power and hydropower globally. The fuel is wood chips, produced in large 'energy farms', the handling of which would be particularly relevant in promoting rural development and for generating jobs in developing countries.

Wind power

Although apparently very simple (Figure 8.18), wind power production technology has become highly sophisticated, with important developments in the areas of control, aerodynamics and materials. Variable speed and positioning of the rotor and blades with different 'attack' angles allow the rotor to spin at an optimal speed when submitted to a wide range of wind conditions, increasing power production, reducing material fatigue and maintenance costs. The increase in the size of blades and rotors reduces the rotation frequency, the noise and impacts on migratory birds. New, more resistant and durable materials allow placing large systems (offshore wind farms) far from communities and with fewer environmental constraints. Wind farms can have more than 300 generators, each with a generation capacity of 5MW and blades with more than 80 metres in length.

After the year 2000, the costs of the power produced fell significantly, mostly as a result of technical and organizational improvements. Manufacturers learned how to exploit economies of scale of mass production

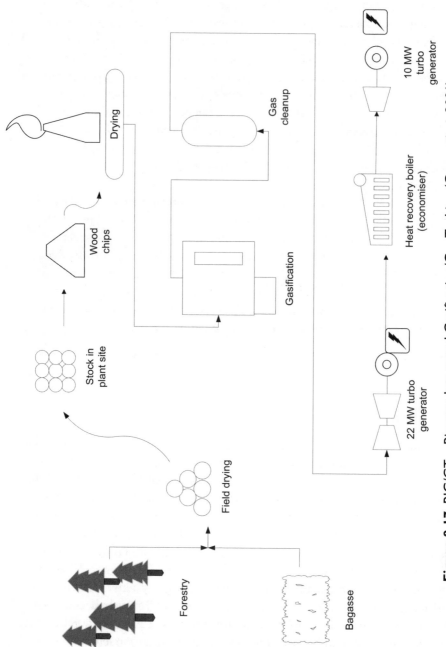

Figure 8.17 BIG/GT – Biomass Integrated Gasification/Gas Turbine (Carpentieri, 2001)

Figure 8.18 Simplified diagram of a wind generator (US DoE, 2008)

for standardized wind turbines, and the entrepreneurs in the sector improved the location of wind machines to produce more power with the same technology. The trends in the cost of power from wind are provided in Figure 8.19.

Worldwide installed capacity reached 59GW in 2005, with a 24 per cent growth in 2007 (Figure 8.20).

The installed capacity of wind power is comparable to that of other sources in countries such as Denmark and Germany (Figure 8.21), thanks to government policies supporting this technology.

Solar energy

Thermal water heating systems

Solar equipment for heating water is usually passive; solar light is absorbed in a panel at the top of a building, through which water circulates. The warmed water is then stored and distributed. Some passive systems are pre-fabricated as one piece. The collectors are panels covered with glass, under which water circulates in metallic tubes usually made of copper. Active systems are more adequate for cold climates, in which water freezes;

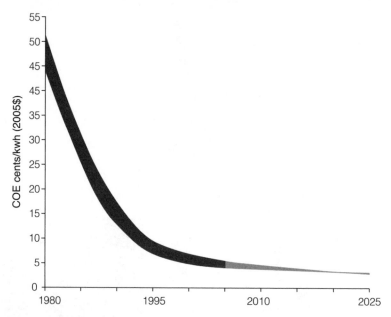

Figure 8.19 Past costs and future projections (US dollar cents per kWh, 2005 base) for wind-derived power (NREL, 2006a)

they use pumps that move water and other liquids, which go through heat exchangers (Figure 8.22). Both use an auxiliary electric or gas system to heat the water in the reservoir when it falls below 50°C (122°F).

There are also plastic solar collectors, placed on blankets to heat swimming pools. Other applications for solar energy, such as air conditioning, are under development. The principle is the same of a refrigerator: a liquid at 90°C (194°F) expands, cooling an insulated chamber. Solar stoves are also frequently used in demonstration projects, especially for poorer countries. However, their use is very limited and the user ends up preferring the traditional fuelwood cooking stove, which produces more heat in less time. When replacing natural gas, a compact system for water heating may abate around 4.5 tons of CO_2 a year, which makes many countries subsidize the use of solar panels. Solar water heaters became very popular in China, which has 65.4 per cent of the world installed capacity – 104GWh in 2006 (Figure 8.23). Solar panels may replace large investments in additional power production needed to supply the electricity used at peak times – the case of electric showers in Brazil (Box 8.4).

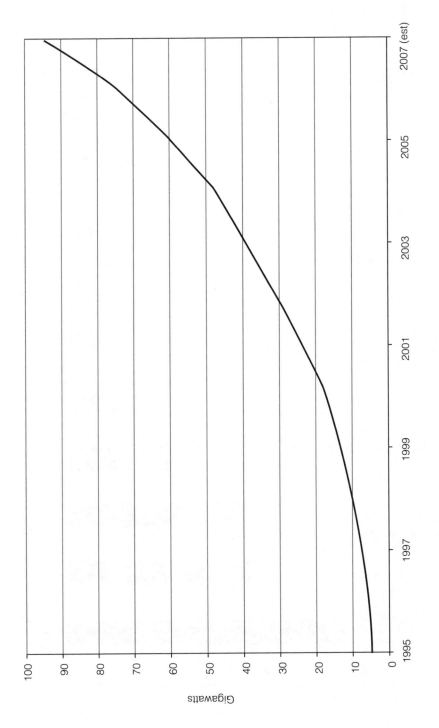

Figure 8.20 Wind Power, Existing World Capacity, 1995–2007 (REN21, 2008)

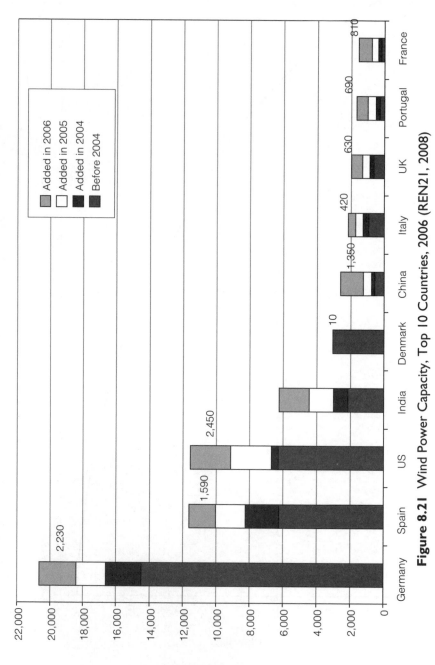

Figure 8.21 Wind Power Capacity, Top 10 Countries, 2006 (REN21, 2008)

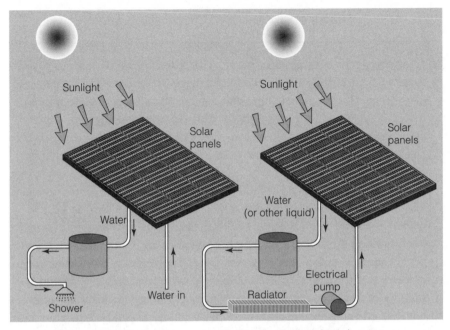

Figure 8.22 Solar systems: (left) passive and (right) active

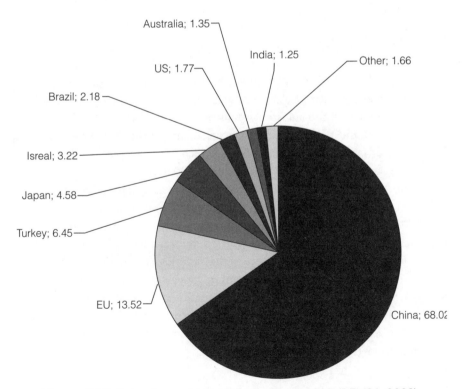

Figure 8.23 Solar thermal installed capacity in 2007 (REN21, 2008)

Box 8.4 Solar energy in China and in Brazil

Solar energy has been used for many years to heat water. Countries such as Israel and cities such as Barcelona have strict laws and incentive programmes for this technology, which efficiently replaces the use of fossil fuels and fuelwood for heating. In hot climates, solar heating may replace approximately 75 per cent of the water heating demand. In the cold climate of Europe, this proportion falls to about 20 per cent, or even less.

China managed to popularize a low-cost solar water heating system, with prices starting at US$190 (80 per cent cheaper than Western ones): US$120–150/m², against US$700–800/m² in Europe. In China, at least 30 million users had thermal heaters in 2006. Besides being cheap, the system is efficient, and can work under a cloudy sky and temperatures below zero. Labour is cheap (the sector employs one-eighth of the renewable industry in the country, or 250,000 people). A single company, located in the city of Dezhou, accounts for 14 per cent of the national collector market, with an annual growth of 20 per cent in sales, and is expected to grow by 80–100 per cent. The main reason for thermal solar heater expansion in the country was the cost, coupled to the high price of oil and coal (Planet Ark, 2006).

In the case of Brazil, solar water heaters are an excellent alternative to replace electric showers, which, albeit cheap, consume a lot of energy, mainly in the peak hours in the early evening, requiring large investments in generation (mainly with hydropower plants) and increasing its environmental impacts. Solar heating can also be used in swimming pools and in commercial and industrial installations. Nevertheless, in 2002, there were only 1.2m² of solar heaters per inhabitant in the country – against 67.1m² per inhabitant in Israel. In Brazil, which has an average of 280 sunny days a year, the initial cost of a system with a 300-litre capacity for a family of four is still relatively high (US$1500 in 2006, as compared to US$10–50 for an electric shower). When replacing an electric shower, about US$1000–1500 are saved in hydropower installed capacity. The solar panels save electric power, but the period of investment return is still high – at least two years. Besides affecting the cash flow, it is necessary to raise awareness and improve building codes for the installation of solar heaters in new homes and buildings, since retrofitting in existing buildings is expensive. Some municipalities such as Porto Alegre, Campina Grande and Sao Paulo have already passed legislation to make solar collectors compulsory (Rodrigues and Mataja, 2004).

Solar thermoelectricity

In this case, sunlight is focused on a collector receiver to heat a fluid to a few hundred degrees Celsius, producing steam for electricity generation. The most popular technology is 'concentrated solar power – CSP', mainly those of parabolic design. The existing projects are still marginally competitive and research and development is still needed in this area. Large-scale power plants using parabolic mirrors operate in California (350MW) and others are being planned. Spain intends to start operating two units soon, totalling 100MW (Figure 8.24), and has more than 1000MW in final design phase (Stirzaker, 2006).

'Central tower plants' use a set of flat moving mirrors (heliostats) to concentrate the sunlight on a target, the collector tower. Liquid sodium (a metal with high thermal capacity) is heated to high temperatures and used to produce electricity. There are projects under development in the US for 10MW, 15MW and 64MW capacity. In South Africa, there is a project for a large plant, with 5000 mirrors, each with 140m².

Linear systems (Fresnel) use flat mirrors that focus sunlight on a linear absorber. Prototypes have been built in Australia and Belgium. These systems have lower costs as the heat absorbers are shared by a large number of small mirrors close to each other, not requiring rotating elements. The system efficiency is around 20 per cent; a maximum of 40 per cent was achieved by solar discs associated with Stirling turbine systems. Considering the total solar power conversion, efficiency is around 2.75 per cent (incidence of solar rays at 1kW/m²). The cost of the solar thermal units has been decreasing in the past few years (Figure 8.25).

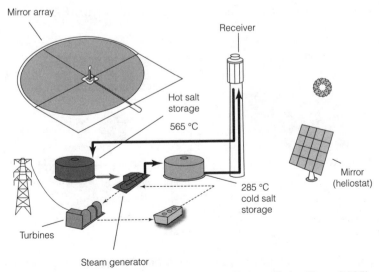

Figure 8.24 Typical solar thermal installation (Solar Tres, 2005)

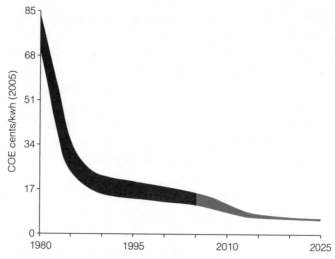

Figure 8.25 Historical and projected costs (US dollar cents per kWh, 2005 base) for solar thermopower (NREL, 2006a)

Photovoltaic (PV) panels

Photovoltaic cells, discovered in 1954 by Bell Laboratories researchers, convert solar energy directly into electricity: the photons absorbed displace free electrons from the semiconductor material. When the electrons leave their positions, the imbalance of the electric charges at the front and at the back of the cells generates a difference in potential, as is the case of conventional lead-acid batteries. A photovoltaic module is composed of cell panels, each having a width of 1 to 10cm producing 1 to 2W. The current generated is continuous, ideal for small applications, which can be converted into alternate current for larger equipment (Figure 8.26).

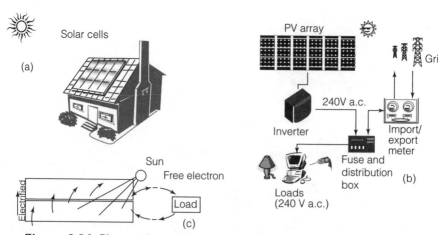

Figure 8.26 Photovoltaic system: (a) installation; (b) configuration; and (c) cell (ECO Centre, 2004)

Historically, photovoltaic power was applied in certain niches and special applications, such as isolated communities, electronic equipment (calculators, watches, communication), in satellites, remote sensing, cathodic protection of ducts and sign lighting along roads. The problem with niches is that they are usually small and, for large-scale production, cost reduction is required. In places with high insolation ($5kWh/m^2/day$), 5000kWh of power a day could be produced in a hectare covered with photocells with 10 per cent efficiency. The cell efficiency is about 15 per cent and may rise to 17.5 per cent in 2010 (Cameron and Jones, 2006). In laboratories, the efficiency reached 25 per cent (Quaschning, 2006). There are more than 6GW of photovoltaic panels installed in the world (and growing at a fast pace) and the power generation perspectives with photovoltaic panels are promising, including power produced by the consumers in solar roofs and feed-in into the grid (Figure 8.27). PVs may be one of the main technologies for future integration of decentralized energy systems.

The world production of panels in 2006 was of about 6GWp (Gigawatt peak power) and should increase to 14GWp in 2010. Germany is the present market leader (550MW in 2006), leaving Japan (330MW) and the US (130MW) behind. Previously, Japan was the group leader in PV modules technology, concentrating on the consumer market niche of electronic products (such as calculators and watches). The North-American industry traditionally concentrated on large-scale applications. Other important suppliers are China (50MW), Spain (50MW) and Italy (35MW) (Cameron and Jones, 2006). PV power generation varies according to the place and ranges from about 1000kWh/kWp in the south of Germany to 2400kWh/kWp in the Atacama Desert. The US has the largest number of offgrid panels-installed parks: 233MW. Germany has the largest PV production connected to the grid (1400MW) and the largest PV plant in the world (Gut Erlasse, with 12MW capacity generating 14GWh/year). The limiting factors of photovoltaic power are its cost, the little power produced and the lack of silicon in the market. Photovoltaic panels manufacturing requires large amounts of polycrystalline silicon and there is now a supply bottleneck, which constrains the technology expansion. Each Wp consumes 14g of silicon; the forecast for 2010 is that this value will fall to 8g/Wp. The present installed cost for photovoltaic systems connected to the grid is US$7000/kW (NREL, 2006b). A 2kW system costs US$17,000 and is able to generate 9.4kWh/day in Arizona, but only 6.2kWh/day in New York (Shephard, 2006). The initial cost of an offgrid module is also high – approximately US$600 per system. The module accounts for about 70 per cent of the system cost; installation accounts for 15 per cent and operation accounts for 15 per cent. Figure 8.28 shows the fall in PV systems costs, both observed and forecast.

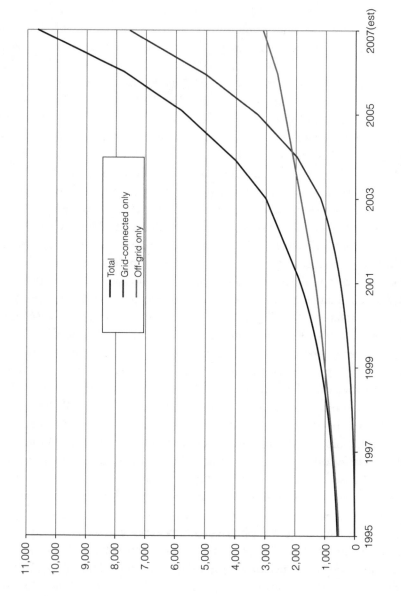

Figure 8.27 Solar PV, Existing World Capacity (MW), 1995–2007 (REN21, 2007)

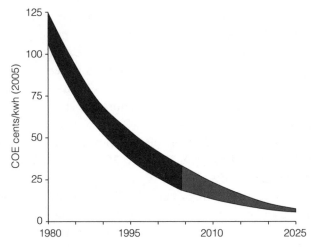

Figure 8.28 Past costs and future projections (dollar cents per kWh, 2005 base) for photovoltaic power (NREL, 2006a)

In remote rural areas, which cannot be connected to the grid, PV modules are used together with batteries, charge controllers and inverters. Despite being small, the power produced is enough to refrigerate vaccines and medicines and preserve food and fishing products, besides making small and micro companies viable, lighting houses, schools and medical centres, extracting and pumping water from wells, and for communication and entertainment. The batteries and panels discarded are a problem, as they contain lead and other dangerous heavy metals such as cadmium. Another severe problem is abandoning the modules for lack of maintenance; this frequently occurs in demonstration projects focused only on installing the system, with no adequate technical assistance or spare parts. In order to overcome this barrier, some programmes centralize the installation and maintenance of systems. Efficient financial arrangements allow the poorer population to repay the investment in the equipment by small value monthly payments, of about US$10 (Abavana, 2001; Ellegard et al, 2005).

Transportation

Sustainable transportation is always better than the vicious circle imposed by the construction of more roads in an attempt to accommodate more vehicles. It is not necessary to destroy a city's identity to reduce traffic jams and all the transportation solutions must be equitable, benefiting all its residents. The use of cars is inevitable, but its excessive use is a problem – and not a solution for urban mobility. As the space in the roads is – and will always be – limited, priority should be given for people and assets to move, not automobiles. For people, the best solution is public transportation. Developing a viable public transportation system cannot be an alternative that takes a generation a lifetime, or one that harms their health. Bus corridors and traffic management are relatively cheap and fast solutions. Non-motorized transportation can be encouraged within neighbourhoods and communities.

There are now around one billion vehicles circulating in the world, including motorcycles (Figures 8.29 and 8.30). The transportation sector represents 34 per cent of the total energy consumption of the industrialized countries, mainly in the form of cars. In 2004, the transportation sector accounted for 24 per cent of the CO_2 global emissions (26.6Gt), with a 2.25 per cent annual increase (or 2.44 per cent in the road sector) since 1990. The world average in the 2001–04 period was higher: 3.18 per cent a year. Whereas the increase in the carbon emission rates in the transportation sector of the Kyoto Protocol Annex I developed countries was 1.4 per cent a year, the rate in the developing countries was 5.65 per cent a year (IEA, 2006).

In developing countries, the number of cars is approximately 20 for every 1000 people, as compared to the 600 per 1000 in industrialized countries. If the use of cars in developing countries reaches the OECD levels, the problems related to the environment, infrastructure and land use will be insoluble.

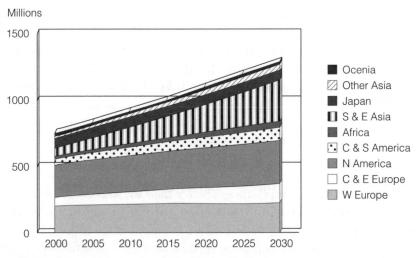

Figure 8.29 World trends: millions of vehicles, except motorcycles
(Walsh, 2005a)

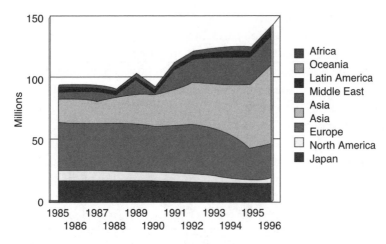

Figure 8.30 World motorcycle records (Walsh, 2005b)

The increase in population and its concentration in large urban centres increases the complexity of the issue, and the alternative adopted, as we are witnessing, is individual transportation. Although the need for adequate and efficient public transportation is practically a consensus, individual transportation still has a much higher acceptance, for reasons that go from personal mobility to safety and social status. Cargo transport by road also considerably burdens public infrastructure. Since the space on the roads does not grow at the same rate as that of vehicles, there is a progressive increase in travel time (Figure 8.31).

Externalities such as accidents and increased air pollution affect health systems and the economy as a whole. In metropolitan areas, light vehicles (automobiles) account for most of the carbon monoxide (CO) and hydrocarbon (HCs), plus a fraction of SO_2 emissions. Heavy vehicles (trucks and buses) account for most of the nitrogen oxide (NO_x) and, in many cases, particulate matter (PM) emissions, in addition to the fraction of SO_2. For constructive and thermodynamic reasons, Otto-cycle car engines work with less air excess and tend to form more CO and HC. On the other hand, the diesel-cycle heavy vehicle engines work with more excess air and tend to form more NO_x and PM.

Pollution reduction and increase in vehicle efficiency

Well-maintained vehicles are fundamental for tropospheric ozone (O_3) control formed from their predecessors. Vehicles emit large amounts of NO_x and one of the most important variables in the Otto-cycle engine emissions is the air/fuel ratio. The engine adjustment by manufacturers mitigates total emissions.[6] Figure 8.32 shows how HC and CO emissions

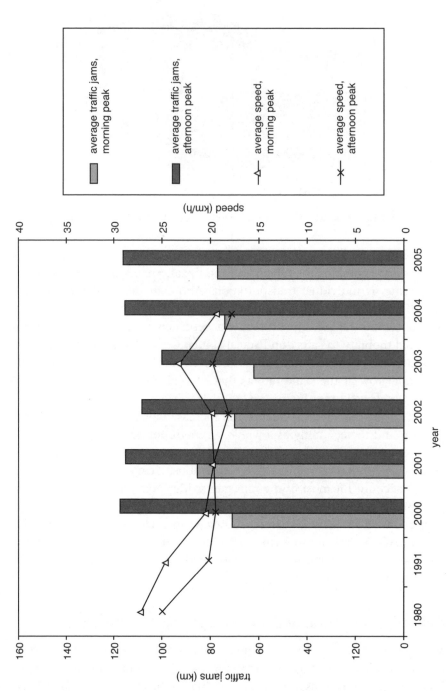

Figure 8.31 Traffic jams and average speed in Sao Paulo City (PMSP, 2007)

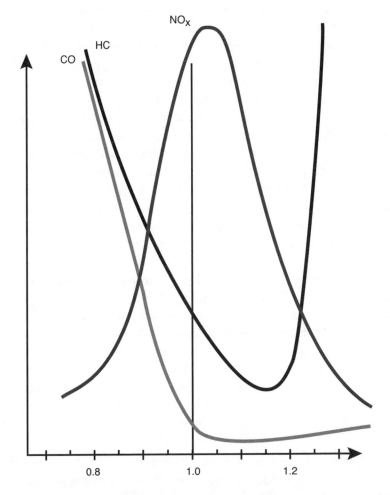

Figure 8.32 Variation in pollutant emissions by vehicles in function of the air:fuel ratio (KFZ-Tech, 2006)

decrease with the increase in air input in the engine combustion chamber, up to a point, and then increase again. On the other hand, NO_x increases and then decreases. The engine gases then go through exhaustion systems with catalysers which convert pollutants into CO_2, water, N_2 and N_2O.[7]

One of the major impurities in fuels currently used is sulphur (S). Besides being one of the main air pollutant components, the sulphur content in fuels (coal, natural gas and oil byproducts) is also a bottleneck for new technologies. Even in small concentrations, SO_2 and H_2S (sulphidric acid) corrodes the noble metals (platinum, palladium and rhenium) used in vehicle exhaust systems and in refinery catalytic reformers. Removal of contaminants is made by very expensive hydrodesulphurization chemical processes, which accounted for most of the 64 million tons of sulphur produced in the world in 2005 (USGS, 2006). Low-sulphur fuels are, therefore, a necessary condition for abating emissions from other pollutants. As desulphurization involves costs, fuel quality in developing countries is poor, which in turn constrains the introduction of new, more efficient and less pollutant vehicular technologies. The emissions from vehicles, *mobile sources of pollution*, are thus a fundamental factor for providing better air quality, reason for which industrialized countries have stricter emission standards for new models (European Commission, 2009a, b). Table 8.6 shows the average energy intensity of the means of transport by passenger and by freight. Rail is the most efficient means for transporting cargo and comparable to buses for transporting passengers. Public transportation requires a systemic approach, with comprehensive policies which take into account land use patterns, the road network, predicted expansions and the interference with the present infrastructure. The public sector formulates these policies, but does not usually have enough resources to implement them. Partnerships with the private sector are a solution, yet these require an adequate regulatory framework and remuneration of the capital invested, which frequently cannot be achieved.

Vehicular technology has improved over time, particularly in the reduction in emission of regulated pollutants, yet the gains in energy efficiency are frequently compensated by an increase in size and weight, mainly during periods of low-cost oil, as occurred in the 1990s (the so-called 'rebound effect'). With the lower oil prices in the 1990s, passenger car

Table 8.6 Average energy intensity of transportation modes in the OECD (Schipper and Meyers, 1992; updated with data from the European Environment Agency, 2000)

Passenger travel	
Travel mode	Intensity (MJ/passenger-km)
Automobile	2.3–2.6
Bus	0.6–0.8
Rail (excluding the US)	0.6–1.5
Air	2.7–3.0
Freight	
Mode	Intensity (MJ/ton-km)
Road	2.9–4.2
Railway	0.4
Maritime	0.7

consumers' interest in efficiency was reduced. Energy performance aspects became secondary as compared to aesthetics, comfort and power. Modern cars incorporated items with higher energy consumption, such as air-conditioning systems and hydraulic steering. As an example, over the years, the VW Gol (Figure 8.33) in Brazil had its weight increased from about 700kg to about a ton.

A modern vehicle and its accessories dissipate in the form of heat about seven-eighths of the energy contained in the fuel: half heats the tyres, pavement and the air around the vehicle. Only the remaining 6 per cent accelerate the car – and heats the brakes when one decelerates. Considering that about 95 per cent of the mass accelerated is the very car, not the driver, less than 1 per cent of the fuel energy moves its occupant. This is a negligible number, considering the automotive industry's 120 years of experience.

As of 2005, new increases in the price of fuels have forced the industry to seek alternatives. The technical solutions to reduce the transport problems involve:

- incentives to public transportation: fleet dimensioning, adoption of new vehicles, in sufficient number and with reasonable comfort level, accessible fares, route planning, bus corridors (BRT – bus rapid transit), subway and metropolitan trains;
- cargo transport by other modes (rail, river, maritime coastal) and by pipelines;

Figure 8.33 Advertisement for the VW Gol vehicle in Brazil, 1980, with a 50cv engine and fuel autonomy of 870km (Volkspage, 2009)

- urban and land use planning in general, foreseeing expansions and non-motorized transportation (cycleways);
- vehicle efficiency, both from engines and mechanics (work transmitted by the engine to the vehicle), as is the case of gasoline-electrical and diesel-electric hybrid technologies;
- stimulus to produce compact cars, utility trucks, motorcycles and three-wheelers (common in Asian countries);
- alternative fuels to gasoline (used in Otto-cycle cars) and in diesel oil (for heavy vehicles), as is the case of compressed natural gas (CNG) and of biofuels.

With electronic technology, the vehicles leave the factory adjusted to obtain maximum efficiency with minimum emissions. Further adjustments – such as inadequate conversions, tuning and exhaust pipe seal removal – and use of higher octane additives may cause an increase in power, but reduce the system service life and considerably increase pollutant emissions.

The efficiency of traditional engines varies between 20 and 25 per cent, but nowadays there are alternative technologies, such as the diesel-electric hybrid vehicles, which provide considerable gains. The internal combustion engine of the hybrid vehicle is smaller, but works non-stop, even when the vehicle is not moving. The surplus energy is accumulated in electrical batteries that release extra power to the engine when necessary, under higher load conditions (e.g. in ascending slopes).

The mechanical efficiency of the typical American car is about 35 per cent in the urban driving cycle and about 50 per cent on the highway driving cycle. The overall mechanical efficiency is 40 per cent on average and smaller for high-powered cars (for more details, see Lovins et al, 2005). However, for thermal efficiency – for which it is not practical to expect efficiencies higher than 50 per cent due to the thermodynamic cycle constraints – to increase the present average mechanical efficiency from 40 per cent to about 65 per cent is a reasonable goal. Increasing the mechanical efficiency for a given load requires that the necessary power to operate the engine is decreased – particularly the energy used to pump the fuel, to overcome friction and drive engine accessories. There are several ways to achieve improvements in mechanical efficiency: reducing friction in the parts; improving the vehicle aerodynamic configuration; reducing the power required from the engine; decreasing its size; or even adopting another configuration, such as diesel. As 75 per cent of the car driving force is caused by its weight, manufacturing lighter vehicles with alternative materials (such as polymers and aluminium) allows large fuel economy gains.

The Otto-cycle engine costs less than a diesel engine, but has a high power:weight ratio. Due to its high efficiency and lower fuel cost, light passenger diesel vehicles are popular in Europe, especially with the improvement in fuel quality (European diesel has low sulphur content). Gas turbines have been proposed for vehicles due to their low weight, low noise and lower exhaust pipe emissions (except for NO_x), besides being able to work with different fuels and high efficiency; however, at low power, they are still very expensive and not very efficient.

Certain advances in efficiency in vehicle and engine design are hindered by factors such as consumers' acceptance. These factors include capacity, performance, safety, comfort, visual appeal and even luxury. For these reasons, the maximum power in new cars has increased in recent years, from 70 to 90hp per ton. Although high power is only required in non-usual driving conditions, such as acceleration in high speed and in mountainous roads, the consumer is attracted by 'better performance', which invariably means higher consumption and more emissions.

Moreover, there is the efficiency in *pollutant removal* by the emission control systems. Vehicles leave the factory with catalysers in the exhaust pipe system, which convert NO_x and HC (primary pollutants which also form tropospheric O_3 secondary pollutant) into CO_2, N_2O (a greenhouse gas, although not toxic), N_2 and water. Catalysers contain noble metals (such as platinum and palladium) and have a relatively high cost; often replacement parts do not have these active elements, making the emission control system innocuous. Another problem affecting catalysers are poor quality fuels, especially those with high sulphur contents, which corrode the systems. For this reason, most developed countries require their fuels (diesel and gasoline) to have low sulphur contents, with 50 or less parts per million (ppm S). Since oil byproducts desulphurization implies costs for refiners, there is a certain resistance to promoting this improvement and laws with goals and deadlines are necessary, established early on to allow time for refineries to adjust (US EPA, 2007; European Commission, 2008a). Figure 8.34 shows a diesel and gasoline desulphurization scenario in different regions in the world.

High sulphur gasoline (Figure 8.35) and diesel represent a severe environmental problem in the large urban centres in the country, since the use of high sulphur content diesel in heavy vehicles emits larger amounts of fine particulate matter, a very toxic pollutant.

In order to decrease air pollution it is not only necessary to inspect industries, but also to act on the whole end-use energy chain, especially concerning the quality of fuel and automotive vehicles. Individual vehicle inspection is a complex and costly activity. Laws can dictate both pollutant

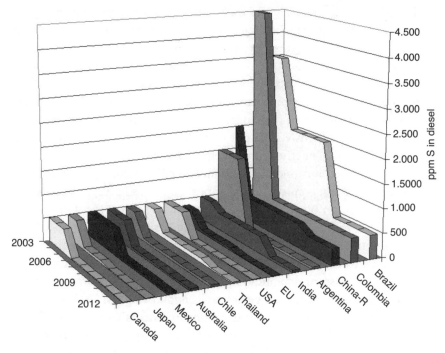

Figure 8.34 Sulphur contents (parts per million, or ppm S) in diesel, by country (Klein, 2003)

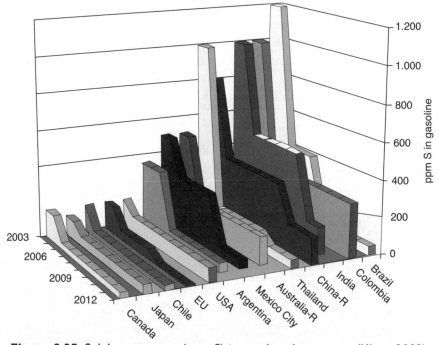

Figure 8.35 Sulphur contents (ppm S) in gasoline, by country (Klein, 2003)

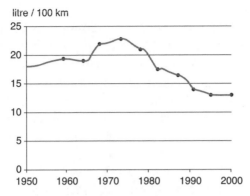

litre / 100 km

Figure 8.36 Evolution of US automobiles' average consumption (Smil, 2003)

emissions and energy efficiency for vehicles. Despite strong opposition from manufacturers, some governmental initiatives seek to overtax gasoline and luxury vehicles, or establish consumption efficiency standards. Once these pressures are overcome, vehicle efficiency programmes may be efficient instruments for reducing consumption (Figure 8.36 and Box 8.5).

Box 8.5 Vehicle fuel economy

Fuel economy is usually expressed as:

- the amount of fuel used per unit distance, for example, litres per 100 kilometres (L/100km, the European notation), where lower values are the more economic; and
- the distance travelled per unit volume of fuel used, for example, kilometres per litre (km/L, notation used in Japan, India and Latin America) or miles per gallon (mpg, US and UK notations), where the higher the value, the more economic the vehicle.

European diesel cars are more fuel-efficient, achieving 5 litres per 100km and CO_2 emissions (a proxy for fuel efficiency) of around 140g/km. However, the European diesel cars do not meet US local pollutant emission standards. Diesel engines have energy efficiency of 45 per cent, as compared to 30 per cent of gasoline engines. This is due to a higher compression ratio and a 10–20 per cent higher heating value (energy per unit volume) of diesel fuel. Fuel economy improves significantly with hybrid vehicle technology, reaching above 50km per litre – or 2 litres per 100km (Fujii, 2003). According to the new requirements on average fuel economy for car makers in Japan, by 2015 passenger cars need to have an average fuel economy of 16.8km/litre (or 6 litres/100km, or 39.5mpg) – a 23.5 per cent reduction as compared to 2004 levels (Hybrid Car Review, 2006). As a comparison, the US Corporate Average Fuel Economy (CAFE) standards required in 2006 that the fleets of passenger cars run at 27.5mpg (Hwang, 2004). In California, a vehicle efficiency programme has been implemented – distinct from other American states – with more advanced performance goals and conforming to environmental legislation, promoted by CARB (*California Air Resources Board*). The expressive goals provided for this programme valued electrical vehicles and very low emissions. At US Federal level, the 2007 Energy Bill provided efficiency standards (35mpg until 2020) and the use of biofuels limiting CO_2 emissions in vehicles (The White House, 2007). More recently, in 2009, the US President Barack Obama determined improvements in fuel efficiency to reach, by 2011, 35mpg or about 15km/litre (The White House, 2009). In the European Union, a recently agreed climate package set out average emission targets for the whole car industry of 120g of CO_2 per kilometre by 2012 for new cars, compared with current levels of 160g/km. The EU target for 2020 is 95g/km. But CO_2 emissions vary from car to car, and manufacturers have been given until 2015 to meet their specific targets for each model (BBC, 2009).

Figure 8.37 compares the efficiency targets in the US, California, Japan, Australia and China – three countries with very different realities – which indicate, however, similar goals for progressively incrementing their vehicles' energy performance.

Labelling is an important tool to inform the consumer. Figure 8.38 shows examples of labelling in different countries, some with an impressive level of detail. The full dissemination of energy efficiency rates and the establishment of performance goals may lead to significant results, with benefits not only in energy saving and reduction in air pollution, but also in income generation and increasing job opportunities.

Freight is another sector within transportation that should be mentioned. The share of road transport (by trucks) is above 50 per cent (Figure 8.39), with an increasing trend.

Emissions from trucks have been falling rapidly due to new vehicle technologies and cleaner fuels – especially the ultra-low sulphur diesel – which allows the adoption of more efficient pollutant control systems. New laws and programmes are under way to control emissions produced by bunkers, waterway, rail and air transportation. Limitations on emissions from train engines are few, but there are proposals under discussion to establish limits.

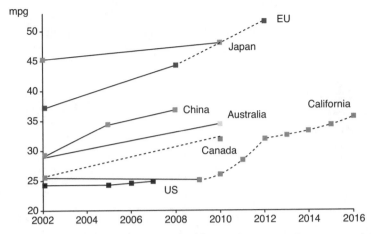

Figure 8.37 Vehicle efficiency targets (in miles per gallon, or mpg) in different regions of the world, concerning the values observed in 2002 (An and Sauer, 2004)

The air pollution generated by ships in harbour regions is quite worrying, which led the US to adopt oils with a maximum 500ppm sulphur content as from 2007 and 15ppm as from 2011 (US EPA, 2007). The European Union has also limited the sulphur content for ship fuels, according to the type (passenger or cargo), power, passages and mooring (European Commission, 2008a). In 2010 the ships circulating within Europe shall limit their fuel sulphur content to 100ppm. By an international convention (called Marpol), the Baltic Sea is a zone in which the SO_2 emissions are limited and a global limit is provided for the signatories (Brazil included) of 4500ppm sulphur for all ships (IMO, 2002).

Air transportation has become an integral part of 21st-century society, contributing to connecting continents. Unfortunately, it has also contributed to climate changes. However, international flights are not included in the goals established by the Kyoto Protocol and mitigation policies have not yet been imposed on the aviation sector. In the European Union, the GHG emissions of international aviation rose by 87 per cent between 1990 and 2004. As air traffic is foreseen to more than double between 2005 and 2020, if new policies are not implemented, the increase in emissions will jeopardize the efforts made in other sectors (European Commission, 2007).

Alternative fuels and new energy technologies

Correctly adjusted biofuel vehicles can provide a more economic and cleaner alternative for gasoline and diesel. Natural gas is one of the most used alternatives and, if compared to gasoline, its use may achieve up to a

(b)

Fuel Economy

CO₂ emission figure (g/km)

Ford Fiesta 1.4 TDCi
ZETEC

<100	A
101-120	B
121-150	C
151-165	D
166-185	E
186+	F

B   117 g/km

Fuel cost (estimated) for 12,000 miles
A fuel cost figure indicates to the consumer a guide fuel price for comparison purposes. This figure is calculated by using the combined drive cycle (lower urban and motorway) and average fuel price. It is calculated annually, the current cost per litre is as follows – petrol 78p, diesel 78p and LPG 39p (VCA May 2004).

£662

VED for 12 months
Vehicle excise duty (VED) or road tax varies according to the CO2 emissions and fuel type of the vehicle.

£85

Environmental Information

A guide on fuel economy and CO₂ emissions which contains data for all new passenger car models is available at any point of sale free of charge. In addition to the fuel efficiency of a car, driving behaviour as well as other non-technical factors play a role in determining a car's fuel consumption and CO₂ emissions. CO₂ is the main greenhouse gas responsible for global warming.

| Make/Model | Ford Fiesta 1.4 TDCi ZETEC | Engine capacity (cc): 1399 |
| Fuel type | Diesel | Transmission type: 5 speed manual |

Fuel Consumption:

Drive cycle	Litres/100km	Mpg
Urban	5.4	52.3
Extra-urban	3.8	74.3
Combined	4.4	64.2

Carbon dioxide emissions (g/km): 117g/km
Important note: Some specifications of this make/model may have lower CO₂ emissions than this. Check with your dealer.

LowC^{VP}

Department for
Transport

VCA

(a)

Fuel Economy
Passenger car petrol

1997
Year of application

Trade mark   **Opel**
Model   **Corsa X1.4 SZ**
3 doors SWING

Fuel   **Petrol**
Transmission   **Manual**
Vehicle size (length x width)   6,00 m²

Fuel Consumption
measured according to Directive 93/116/EC

7,3 litres/100 km

This is equivalent to   **13,6 km/litre**

Comparison of fuel consumption
with the average of all passenger cars with the same size

–25% and less	A
–15-25%	B
–5-15%	C
average	D
+5-15%	E
+15-25%	F
+25% and more	G

+8.3%   E

Fuel costs for 100,000km
determined on base of the fuel economy measured according to Directive 93/116/EC and a fuel price of

5.780 EURO

0,79 EURO/litre

The actual fuel economy will depend on how the car is used.

Fuel consumption is directly related to CO₂ emissions which contribute to global warming.

Further information is contained in brochures of the car

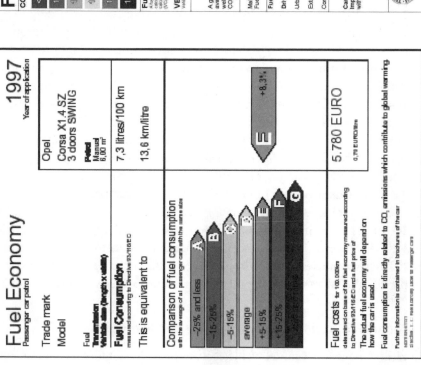

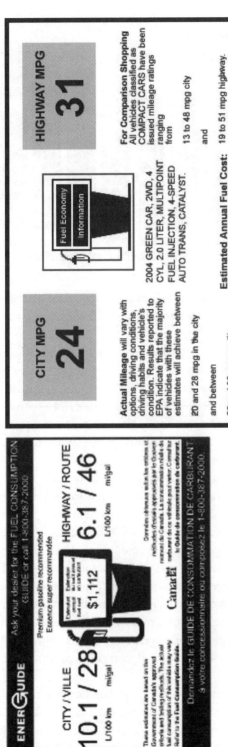

(c)

(d)

(e)

Figure 8.38 Examples of fuel economy labels: (a) European Community; (b) UK; (c) Canada; (d) US; and (e) Korea (Nogueira and Branco, 2005)

MTOE

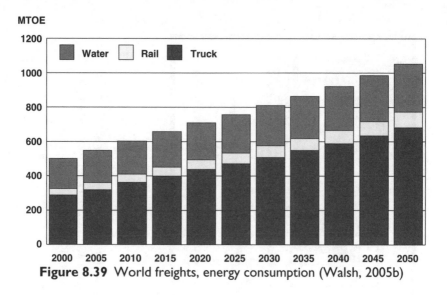

Figure 8.39 World freights, energy consumption (Walsh, 2005b)

70 per cent reduction in CO emission, and eliminate particulate matter and SO_x emissions. Both liquefied petroleum gas (LPG) and compressed natural gas (CNG) have a higher hydrogen:carbon ratio than gasoline and, therefore, emit less CO_2 per energy unit. Moreover, its higher octane rates allow their use under higher compression. Although significant changes in the engines are not necessary to allow the use of LPG or CNG, it is necessary to take precautions to prevent NO_x and HC emissions from increasing considerably due to inadequate conversions. Unfortunately, this is what happens in the great majority of cases, negatively contributing to tropospheric ozone and to urban pollution in general.

Hydrogen is an important energy carrier and can also be used for ultra-low emission vehicles, but its storage is a problem due to its low-energy density. The use of compressed hydrogen is the most viable form, although it is also possible to store liquid hydrogen or metallic hydrates. Hydrogen-based fuel cells are also under research and development. Even though its proponents state that hydrogen is not more dangerous than gasoline, safety problems have to be solved before it gains public acceptance. Hydrogen would need very significant changes to make it compatible with the existing infrastructure (production, storage and distribution). At present, the most likely hydrogen source is natural gas. Coal producers also have great interest in the hydrogen economy. In the future, it could be produced from biomass.[8]

Fuel batteries or fuel cells produce energy by electrochemical means, as opposed to the combustion processes in conventional engines. There are fuel cells of different types; the main candidate for use in automobiles is that based on the proton exchange membrane (also called solid polymer) due to

Table 8.7 Fuel cells under development

Alkalin	AFC
Phosphoric Acid	PAFC
Polymer Electrolyte Membrane	PEMFC
Molten Carbonate	MCFC
Solid Oxide	SOFC

its lower cost, adequate size, simple design and operation at low temperatures, under 120°C (Table 8.7). The technology was originally used in the US space programme.

Fuel cell batteries require hydrogen as fuel, which may be generated in the automobile itself from ethanol, methanol or natural gas (Figure 8.40).

Fuel cells are two to three times more efficient than internal combustion engines and, as the fuel is electrochemically converted, they do not emit pollutant gases. Widely used in the space programme in the US, their high cost and size until recently hindered their use in automobiles, but important innovations achieved in the last ten years make fuel cells one of the most promising technologies for the near future. It has yet to be established if hydrogen production will occur in the vehicle itself (e.g. from ethanol or methanol) or if it will be produced centrally and distributed in service stations.

Electrical vehicles using batteries prompt great interest nowadays, especially as urban vehicles. If the electricity moving them comes from a non-fossil source, they may represent a significant reduction in the emission of gases responsible for the 'greenhouse effect'. The main hindrance for

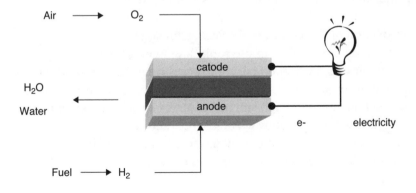

$$H_2 + \tfrac{1}{2} O_2 \longrightarrow H_2O + \text{electricity}$$

Figure 8.40 Fuel cell schematic diagrams

their implementation is the present state of chemical batteries technology, resulting in high cost, heavy vehicles and limited range. Furthermore, whereas a gasoline automobile can be fuelled in a few minutes, the battery recharge usually requires several hours. A large-scale introduction of electric vehicles would require great changes in infrastructure, not only in the power distribution system and in the automobiles, but also in the power generation industry.

Hybrid vehicles technology involves the use of two different engines responsible for driving the vehicle forward. The primary engine may be fuelled with diesel or natural gas, with a lower power than a conventional vehicle running at constant speed and charging batteries that feed the electric engine. The surplus energy generated can be used to charge the electric engine battery. With the configuration of hybrid vehicles, a fuel economy of up to 50 per cent is possible and about 70 per cent reduction in pollutant emissions. The great advantage of this technology is that the gasoline-fuelled engine works at a constant rotation and speed, saving fuel and reducing pollution and noise levels. Hybrid vehicles with gas turbine reach up to 40 per cent efficiency (30km – 18.64 miles/litre). In the US, hybrid vehicles are subsidized and attract privileges such as using preferential traffic lanes. Thus a hybrid electric vehicle combines a conventional propulsion system (gasoline, diesel, biofuels or other fuels, in an internal combustion engine, Otto or diesel cycles) with an electric motor supplied by a rechargeable energy storage system. This system recovers the energy not utilized, either by capturing kinetic energy via regenerative braking or using a small-size internal combustion engine to generate electricity by spinning an electrical generator. Energy is stored in batteries (lighter Lithium-ion batteries for cars are under development) and it is reused when necessary, in slopes or acceleration. Developing countries face problems concerning the efficiency in the transportation systems, among which are:

- production of vehicles with obsolete technology;
- deterioration of the fleet in use for lack of maintenance and poor roads;
- use of out-of-specification parts and accessories, such as false catalysers;
- alterations in the vehicle's original configuration (tuning);
- low fuel quality, with high sulphur contents and, in certain cases, lead;
- fuels altered with solvents, water or other substances;
- lack of vehicle safety and emissions technical inspections;
- fleet obsolescence, vehicles older than ten years.

Biodiesel

Biodiesel is a potentially important replacement for conventional diesel fuel. It can be obtained from many renewable raw materials, including soybean, rapeseed and palm oil, by a simple treatment process with methanol or ethanol, called *transesterification* (the byproduct is glycerin, which has to be separated). Other processes (such as acid catalysis) also produce biodiesel, which is still at an initial commercialization stage, but many types of the product are still at an initial development stage (Box 8.6).

Box 8.6 Biodiesel – past, present and future

Experiments with biodiesel started around 1850. In 1912, the compressor engine inventor, Rudolf Diesel, stated that 'the use of vegetable oils for engine fuels may seem insignificant today, but such oils may become, in the course of time, as important as petroleum and the coal-tar products of the present time'. Biodiesel's real 'revival' began in the 1990s in Europe, mainly from rapeseed. Biodiesel is a diesel replacement fuel for use in compression-ignition engines, manufactured from renewable, non-petroleum-based sources such as vegetable oils (soy, mustard, castor, canola, rapeseed and palm oils), animal fats (poultry offal, tallow, fish oils) and used cooking oils and trap grease (from restaurants and industry). Biodiesel growth from non-food feedstock is gaining special interest. In the US and the EU, algae-based biodiesel promises very high yields per area – 15 times more than palm oil, 60 times that of rapeseed and 200 times that of soybean (Emerging Markets Online, 2006; Bioenergy Site, 2008). Biodiesel production is based on trans-esterification of vegetable oils and fats through the addition of methanol (or other alcohols) and a catalyst, giving glycerol as a co-product. Different production technologies and feedstock make fuel characteristics vary significantly. Biodiesel production depends on feedstock and land availability even more than bioethanol production. Although biodiesel is considered a 'renewable' fuel, one of its feedstock is methanol, toxic and obtained from fossil fuels. Advanced processes include the replacement of methanol of fossil origin (Fischer-Tropsch technology and other advanced processes) by bioethanol (in Brazil by sugar cane ethanol). Biodiesel is also considered 'sulphur-free', which is the case unless the biofuel is produced by catalysis with sulphuric acid. The biofuel is hygroscopic (absorbs water) and easily biodegradable, which may be an environmental advantage, but also a quality problem, mainly when stored in hot and humid places. Overall, biodiesel combustion produces less pollutants than conventional fossil fuels, except for NO_x. In Indonesia and Malaysia, palm oil biodiesel production has been heavily criticized for the clearance of native rainforests, with consequent biodiversity losses and land-use change, besides greenhouse gas emissions. In order to expand the relatively small resource base of biodiesel, new processes have been developed to use recycled cooking oils and animal fats, although these are limited in volume. A new process entering the market is the hydrogenation of oils and fats, producing a biodiesel that can be blended with fossil diesel up to 50 per cent without any engine modifications. Synthetic biofuel production via biomass gasification and catalytic conversion to liquid using the Fischer-Tropsch process (biomass conversion to liquids BTL) offers a variety of potential biofuel production processes that may be suited to current and future engine technologies. Produced in pure form (100 per cent biodiesel, or B100), it is usually blended with mineral diesel at low levels, 2 per cent (B2)–20 per cent (B20). Blends higher than B5 require special handling and fuel management, as well as vehicle equipment modifications; the level of care needed depends on the engine and vehicle manufacturer. A European Union Directive (2003/30/EC) sets a voluntary target of 5.75 per cent biofuel (including biodiesel) consumption by energy content in 2010. The European Commission proposed a 10 per cent target by 2020. Some of its member states (Germany, France and Italy) are some of the largest biodiesel producers and users in the world. Other countries have also instituted public policy initiatives to encourage biodiesel production and use, and have done so generally through a combination of fiscal incentives and mandates or voluntary targets. This is the case of Argentina (biofuels' mandatory use of 5 per cent), Australia (production target), Brazil (B2 mandatory, moving to B5), Canada (proposed 5 per cent by 2010), France (10 per cent biofuels by 2015), India (policies to produce biodiesel from a plant called 'jatropha' in vast extensions of non-tillable land), Indonesia (biofuel consumption to reach 21 per cent by 2010 and 5 per cent by 2025), Malaysia (B5 programme), New Zealand (production target) and the US (grants, tax credits, mandatory volumes for fuel distributors). The potential market for biodiesel is estimated to be in the order of 20EJ by 2050, assuming development of synthetic biofuel production technologies (MI and IFQC, 2006; IEA, 2007).

Several types of biodiesel were successfully tested in long-duration tests in buses, trucks and tractors. Figure 8.41 lists the world's largest biodiesel producers.

Vegetable oils are also frequently considered for possible use as fuel in diesel engines including sunflower, soybean, peanut, cottonseed, rapeseed, palm and castor oils. Vegetable oils *in natura* were not very successful in replacing diesel, causing problems of carbon deposition in the engines, clogging of injection systems, high particulate matter emissions, reduced efficiency and frequent need of maintenance.

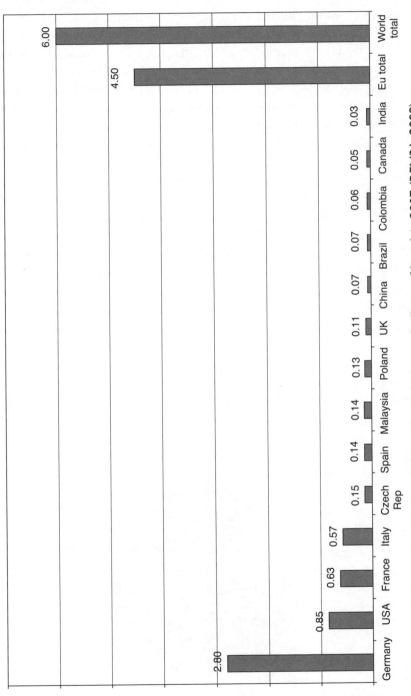

Figure 8.41 Top world biodiesel producers (millions of litres) in 2007 (REN21, 2008)

Bioethanol

Ethanol (C_2H_6O) is a fuel used mainly in Otto-cycle engines, efficiently replacing gasoline. Distinct from methanol, which is toxic and obtained from coal and other fossil sources, bioethanol is a very clean and renewable fuel. The traditional method of producing ethanol is by sugar fermentation processes and distillation. Ethanol can also be obtained from fossil sources by sophisticated processes (such as *Fischer-Tropsch*). The local benefits of using bioethanol as a fuel are evident in the city of Sao Paulo, Brazil, where the air quality improved with considerably reduced emissions of lead, sulphur, carbon monoxide and particulate matter. In addition, ethanol provides benefits globally by reducing CO_2 liquid emissions. Table 8.8 shows that the emission of 9.56×10^6 tons of carbon a year (about 15 per cent of the total emissions in Brazil due to the use of fossil fuels) is avoided by the use of ethanol as a replacement for gasoline.

Bioethanol is produced by the largest world supplier, currently the US, from corn and by Brazil from sugar cane. In Europe, ethanol is mainly produced from sugar beet and wheat. China, the third largest world producer in 2005 (Figure 8.42), produces ethanol from corn and wheat, but is intensifying the use of other cultures (sugar cane, sorghum and others) due to

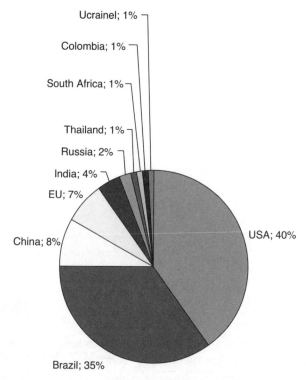

Figure 8.42 Top world ethanol producers (percentage from a total of 49.8 billion litres) in 2007 (REN21, 2008)

Table 8.8 Avoided carbon emissions by sugar cane in Brazil (Macedo, 1992)

	10⁶ tons of C/year
Ethanol substitution for gasoline	−7.41
Bagasse substitution for fuel oil (chemical and food industries)	−3.24
Fossil fuel use in the agroindustry (emission)	+1.20
Liquid contribution (absorption, mitigated carbon)	−9.45

Table 8.9 Production and prices of biofuels and gasoline, and economic transactions involved (data from FAO, 2007b; REN21, 2008; US DoE, 2007)

	Production 10⁹ l/year	*Costs (US$/GJ)*	*Total value of economic transactions (US$ billions)*
Ethanol (2007)	50	8–25	36
Biodiesel (2007)	7	15–25	4
Gasoline (2004)	1165	10	768

Note: US prices or gasoline and biodiesel; Brazilian prices for ethanol

the need to use grains as food (Worldwatch, 2006). Box 8.7 discusses this recent and controversial issue.

Global production scales of ethanol and biodiesel are now comparable, as shown in Figure 8.43.

Table 8.9 compares the ethanol and biodiesel production costs and gives an idea of the economic transactions involved, using market prices and volumes as proxies.

Box 8.7 Competition between bioenergy and food

The environmental sustainability of bioenergy has been seriously questioned after the recent ethanol boom in the world market, the main issues being the competition for the use of agriculture for fuel and food which was blamed for the unprecedented rise in the cost of grains in 2006, the only exception being sugar. Price fluctuations of grains occurred in the past, but the present rising trend is disseminated, generating inflation and debates on the future of agriculture and on how food will be supplied to the poor populations in developing countries. Together with rising prices there is great volatility, raising uncertainty in the markets. In this debate, there are several factors to consider:

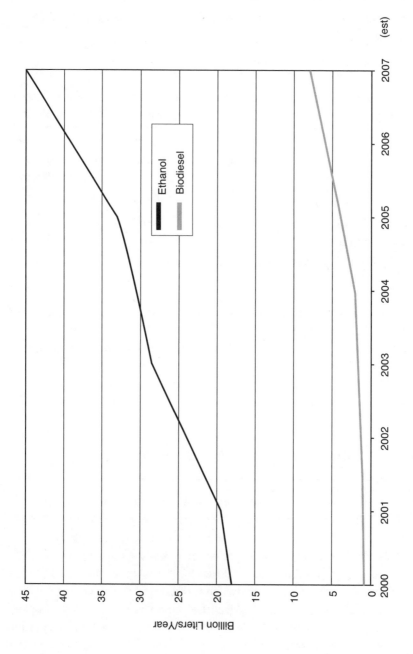

Figure 8.43 Ethanol and biodiesel production, 2000–07 (REN21, 2008)

- agricultural markets today are much more connected with other markets – such as that of bioenergy;
- markets are global: the grains produced in one country often cross the world to feed populations in another one;
- climate changes and fast urbanization have not yet changed the world standards for production and consumption (FAO, 2007a, b).

Figure 8.44 shows the growing trend in food consumption per capita in the world.

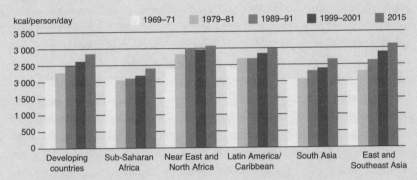

Figure 8.44 Food consumption trends (FAO, 2007c)

In 2006 there were about 850 million undernourished people in the world, mainly in Africa and Asia (Figure 8.45).

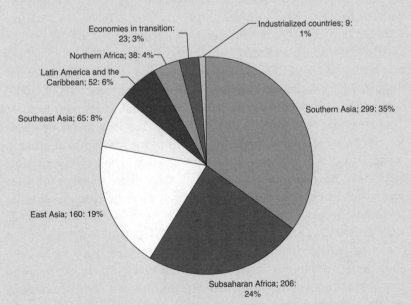

Figure 8.45 Undernourishment in the world: millions and percentages (FAO, 2007c)

Competition between energy and food can result in benefits, protecting small farmers and strategically controlling monoculture expansion. Considering this, the UN Food and Agriculture Organization proposed an initiative, the *International Bioenergy Platform (IBEP)*, to supply technical assistance and guidance for establishing policies and strategies in the agriculture and bioenergy sectors, quantifying resources and implications from country to country (FAO, 2006a). IBEP also acknowledges that one of the main reasons for the poor global food distribution are protectionist commercial policies practised by industrialized countries (FAO, 2007d). These policies cause other problems like the preference for local raw materials, mainly corn and other grains, leading to inefficient methods for biofuels production and generating high greenhouse gas emissions in their life cycles. Several initiatives seek to establish certification and sustainability standards for biofuels, some of them broadly overlap, but they are all generally consistent in their principles. So far, no one initiative has established itself as the leading forum for this activity, and none is backed by the force of law (WRI, 2008). There are publicly respected sustainability certification schemes, but these have not been developed to provide assurance for biofuels. Examples are the Forest Stewardship Council (FSC, 2009), the European Retailers' Produce Working Group (EUREPGAP, 2009), the UK Assured Combinable Crops Scheme (ACCS, 2009) and the LEAF Marque certification for farmers (LEAF, 2009). Nevertheless, there are schemes with stronger interfaces with bioenergy – the Round Table on Sustainable Palm Oil (RSPO, 2009), the Roundtable on Responsible Soy Oil (RRSO, 2009) and the Sao Paulo State Green Ethanol Program (SP, 2009). National policies in the UK (ECOFYS, 2006), Netherlands (Commission Cramer Report, 2009), Switzerland (EPFL, 2007) and Germany (UFOP, 2007) support assessment of sustainability and certification systems for biofuels. There is a clear need to harmonize criteria and activities, providing a basis for a single standard and methodology, or at least fewer than at present. An advantage of principles is that they are easier to understand, to apply from the outset, but they risk becoming just an abstract wishing list if not accompanied by concrete rules. Since no existing certification scheme has sufficient coverage for biofuel certification, meta-standard approaches were proposed as a basis for the current developments in the application of 'sustainability' assurance for biofuels. Providing answers on the effectiveness of biofuels in meeting each of these drivers has required careful and parallel development of policy, the meta-standard methodology and the meaningful interaction of the main stakeholders that are likely to be involved in delivering significant volumes of biofuels into the UK and the

Netherlands. The balance of representation in the stakeholder group is an important component of the validity, and therefore public acceptability, of the approach. There are several aspects to cover when brainstorming the sustainability of biofuels:

- investment in science and research, technological development and supply;
- production costs;
- sustained economic growth, macroeconomic impacts, local development and income distribution;
- public health, food security;
- social well-being and equity, community engagement, safety and amenity of the public environment, community services, cultural heritage, gender issues, social inclusion;
- job opportunities, labour rights, quality of jobs;
- land use, land tenure rights;
- effects on energy matrix (renewable and non-renewable energy consumption);
- total emission of greenhouse gases, application of fertilizer and pesticides, water and soil conservation, biodiversity issues, atmospheric emissions (both in agricultural and industrial phases), liquid emissions, solid residues;
- water consumption and resource competition; and
- infrastructure, investments (Lucon, 2008).

Desirable issues to have in an assessment include policy scenarios, land use models, impact indicators, spatial references for regional profiles and clusters, thresholds and targets, sensitivity analysis, data and indicator management, sustainability impact assessment tools and transferability. However, assessments can be endless and it is necessary to draw up guidelines. Practical experience shows that requiring such topics in a licensing process causes unnecessary delays and the Environmental Impact Assessment work looks more like an academic work. The Swedish company SEKAB has presented an interesting benchmark on the application of sustainability criteria in the real world. The company delivers about 90 per cent of all ethanol in Sweden for E85 and ED95 (ethanol for heavy vehicles). Sekab announced in June 2008 that it would buy certified sustainable ethanol from four Brazilian groups, through verifiable criteria. Such criteria would gradually be developed over the coming years and synchronized with international regulations when these are in place (Sustainable Business, 2008).

The successful – and replicable – Brazilian ethanol programme justifies promoting this fuel alternative in other countries that produce (or could produce) sugar cane (Box 8.8).

Box 8.8 The Brazilian ethanol programme (Proalcool)

The largest bioenergy programme in the world is the Brazilian sugar cane ethanol programme (Proalcool), established in 1976 as a reaction to the increasing costs of oil imports (which seriously threatened the national balance of payments) and to help to stabilize sugar production against cyclic variations in international prices. An important argument used in its favour is job generation, both specialized and non-specialized. The sector created over 700,000 jobs, 75 per cent of them direct (Goldemberg, 2004; World Bank, 2006). The programme was almost totally based on locally manufactured equipment, helping to create a strong agri-industrial system and more indirect jobs. The Brazilian government encouraged the production of ethanol from sugar cane and the adaptation of Otto-cycle engines to work with 'pure' ethanol (hydrated alcohol with 96 per cent ethanol and 4 per cent water) or *gasohol* (blend with 78 per cent gasoline and 22 per cent anhydrous ethanol). These two types of dedicated engines were called 'gasoline' and 'ethanol'-fuelled vehicles, respectively, both being replaced recently by flex-fuel vehicles (FFVs). The availability of pumps in the filling stations (leaded gasoline, phased out by E22) was one of the reasons for the success of the programme.

The added ethanol increased the octane fuel to 97 per cent and allowed the elimination of the very toxic lead tetraethyl additive; filling stations rapidly converted the pumps that formerly used the so-called 'blue gasoline' (with lead additive) into ethanol.

The other pumps, which contained unleaded gasoline (with less octane), supplied *gasohol*. In 1995, Brazil achieved a 12 billion-litre annual production (about 200,000 barrels a day), replacing half of the gasoline used in automobiles (Goldemberg et al, 2004). The engine technology evolved, the market gained confidence in the new fuel and, in 1995, half of all the automobiles in the country used *gasohol;* the rest ran on 'pure ethanol'. The programme led to technological developments, both in agricultural production and in sugar cane processing, causing the costs of ethanol to fall and the possibility of producing additional power based on biomass, from bagasse and agricultural wastes. However, in the 1990s, the fall in international oil prices reduced the relative price of gasoline and the ethanol producers opted for producing sugar to export, threatening the future of the programme. Consumers lost trust when the supply reduced and the sale of new automobiles using pure ethanol was radically reduced. This trend was only reversed after 2003, with the launching of the *FFVs* in the country. By means of electronic sensors this technology identifies which gasoline-ethanol blend goes through the vehicle injection system and adjusts the combustion conditions. With the *flex* vehicles, the consumer started to have full freedom of choice, mainly provided by the price at the pump. The recent advances made the *flex* technology relatively cheap (US$100 or less) and pollutant emissions regulated to close or smaller than those of gasoline. In 2006, the *flex* vehicle fleet in the country had reached two million, with more than 70 per cent of the sales of new vehicles, supplied by seven multinational companies. Subsidies to ethanol producers were removed with the growth in production and ethanol started to compete directly with gasoline in 2004 (Goldemberg et al, 2004).

About 15 per cent of the carbon emissions of fossil origin were saved with renewable ethanol: each thousand litres of sugar cane ethanol reduce the emission of 2.82 tons of CO_2 equivalent in gasoline (Macedo, 2004). Proalcool started with blending ethanol to gasoline and the mandatory adoption of E5 (5 per cent ethanol in gasoline) or higher seems to be a recommendable way for introducing ethanol in other countries, especially in developing ones that spend a great amount of their export earnings on imported liquid fuels. In addition, replacing gasoline with ethanol in these countries may result in benefits from the Clean Development Mechanism (CDM) of the Kyoto Protocol. Many countries produce sugar in old and obsolete plants and may derive great local benefits by modernizing their agri-industrial park. A standard ethanol plant with milling capacity of two million tons of sugar cane a year costs about US$150 million and a smaller plant costs roughly US$80 per tonne of cane crushed. To supply the plant, 33,000 hectares of land grown with sugar cane are necessary (the productivity is from 70 to 100 litres per ton of sugar cane). This plant produces two million litres of ethanol per day, which is enough to supply 100,000 vehicles a year with E100 (pure ethanol), or one million vehicles a year with a 10 per cent blend (E10). The ethanol production in a standard plant leads to a reduction of 564 tons a year of CO_2 equivalent. It is also possible to generate 34.7MW surplus power during the six-month harvest period, at a capital cost of US$24.3 million (or US$700/kW installed). Retrofitting existing plants is a cheaper alternative, yet with lower efficiency (Lucon and Goldemberg, 2006).

Another reason for the adoption of ethanol as a biofuel is the relatively small area of sugar cane needed to produce ethanol: about 29 million hectares of land suffice to supply all gasoline-fuelled cars in the world with

10 per cent ethanol (E10). In 2004 the sugar cane area harvested was 20.2Mha, of which 19.2 was in developing countries.[9] This is a small fraction of the primary crop areas on the planet, which in that same year was 1042Mha (FAO, 2006b). Sugar cane is a typical tropical country crop. Although the OECD accounts for two-thirds of world consumption of gasoline, the region has only 5 per cent of world sugar cane. Ethanol imports from developing countries are restricted by a series of mechanisms.[10]

Table 8.10 compares costs and efficiency of different biofuels.

The present cost of Brazilian ethanol varies between US$0.18 and 0.25 per litre, and has declined as production increased at a progress ratio of 30 per cent (Figure 8.46).

A comparison of the production costs of the Brazilian ethanol (price paid to producers) with those of gasoline at international prices (in the Rotterdam spot market) is shown in Figure 8.47, which also includes the average pump price for the two fuels. The lower heating value of ethanol is about 22MJ/litre, whereas that of gasoline is 33MJ/l. However, its higher octane and the adjustments in the injection system make the technical

Table 8.10 Comparison of different types of ethanol, gasoline and diesel (Pacheco, 2006; USDA, 2001 and 2006; Macedo, 2004; Woods and Bauen, 2003; IEA, 2005)

	Carbon emissions ($kgCO_2eq/GJ$)	Energy balance (GJ obtained/GJ from fossil fuels applied)	Costs (US$/GJ)
Gasoline	87	–	12.0
Diesel	95	–	13.6
Grain ethanol	58–79	0.7–2.7	17.0–18.0
Beet ethanol	26–92	1.36–2.06	16.6–18.6
Wheat ethanol	56–77	0.29–1.67	16.9–18.7
Corn ethanol	77–95	1.2	nd
Sugar cane ethanol	9–10	8.3–10.2	8.0–8.4
Pulp hydrolysis, wood and other inputs ethanol (pre-commercial technology	Variable	~10	~25

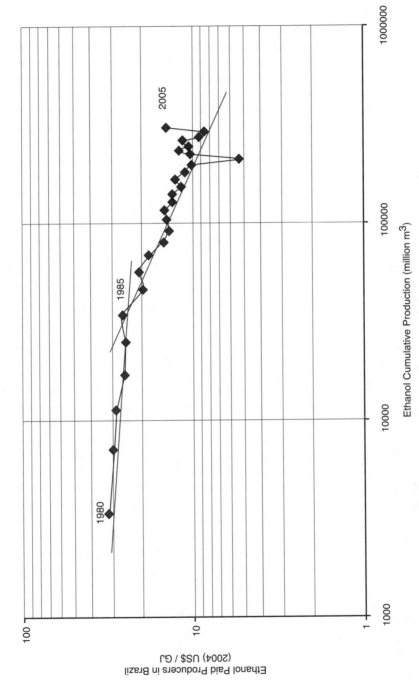

Figure 8.46 Ethanol learning curve in Brazil (Goldemberg et al, 2004; updated)

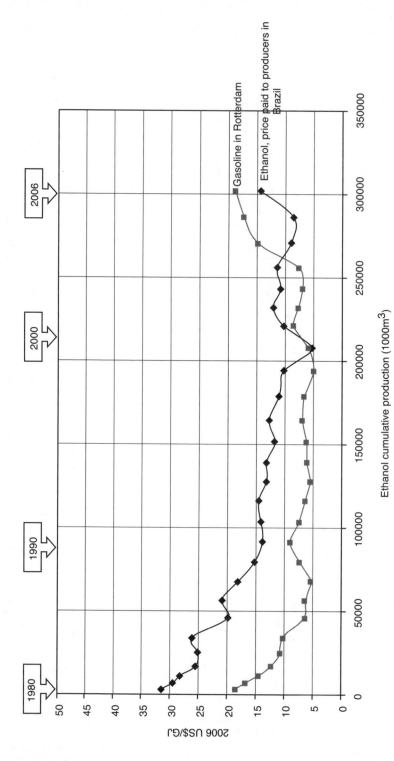

Figure 8.47 Learning curve for Brazilian ethanol and the price of gasoline in the Rotterdam spot market (Goldemberg et al, 2004; updated)

equivalence of ethanol to gasoline about 1.15 in terms of volume (CETESB, 2009).

Except for the case of Brazilian ethanol, the cost of this fuel is not yet competitive with the sale price of gasoline. Most of the countries, however, established heavy taxes on gasoline to discourage the excessive use of automobiles or as a way of strengthening the public treasury funds. Under the form of crossed subsidies, the difference between the price paid by the drivers for gasoline and the real cost is redistributed to lower the cost of alternatives, such as ethanol. So far this has guaranteed the survival of ethanol and biodiesel in developed countries. In fact, incentives have reduced the costs of ethanol in the US (Figure 8.48).

High expectations for second-generation biofuels mainly focus on the development of ethanol from cellulose, an abundant material all over the world, even in temperate climate countries. This type of alcohol may be produced from different types of biomass, including wood and garbage. Unlike conventional bioethanol produced by the fermentation of sugars, one has to break the molecules of cellulose in sugars before fermentation. This can be done in two ways:

1. *hydrolysis* (which may be either *acid* or *enzymatic*[11]), followed by fermentation; and
2. *gasification* (conversion into CO and H_2), followed by *syngas* fermentation or catalytic reform by the Fischer-Tropsch process (US DoE, 2006a).

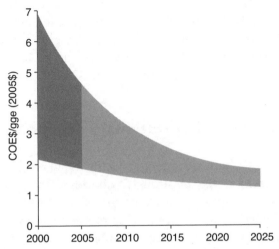

Figure 8.48 Costs (dollars per gasoline gallon equivalent – gge) of bioethanol in the US (NREL, 2006a)

Technology is still at development stage, with millions of dollars invested by the US government – whose goal is to reduce the cost to US$0.28 per litre by 2012 (US Senate, 2006). Production of ethanol from cellulose at competitive prices could promote a real energy revolution, expanding the potential of biomass for fuel production. Nowadays, the world biomass potentials are already very high and may be divided into three categories: present tillable lands, with com 200EJ (or 2×10^{20}J); production of biomass in marginal lands (100EJ); and wastes (100EJ) (Junginger et al, 2006). Biofuels may successfully replace oil by-products and their importance lies exactly in their wide availability, low costs, technology accessibility, easy transportation and storage, versatility of use in engines, along with socio-economic and environmental benefits. As seen before, there are different types of biofuels and distinct ways for obtaining them. Their environmental impacts vary according to the place and the way in which the biofuels have been produced and consumed, but these impacts can be mitigated by adequate land–use planning considering:

- preservation of sensitive ecosystems and of biodiversity (a problem with Indonesia palm biodiesel);
- competition for land with food and with settled populations (a severe problem in India);
- preservation and multiple uses of water resources (mainly in irrigated plantations); and
- fertilizer availability and impacts along with plague control (a very vulnerable point in monocultures).

Biofuel analysts also consider their socio-economic impacts, such as job generation, local jobs and income. European legislation is about to incorporate life-cycle analysis, particularly the concerns on emissions of greenhouse gases that include the indirect effects on land use and fossil fuels applied in the production cycle.

Industry and other stationary pollution sources

Industry is a very dynamic sector in which the use of energy and the resulting pollutant emission may be strongly reduced. In the *stationary pollution sources* (industries, thermopower plants and others), it is possible to obtain large pollution abatement by means of combustion controls modifying the configurations (scorching and staged combustion) and by adopting post-combustion controls (such as injection of reducing agents in the exhaust gases and post-combustion denitrification).

Technologies for prevention and control of pollution from stationary sources

Thermopower plants, refineries, metallurgies, incinerators and cement industries are sources with high NO_x emissions, cause for concern in the analysis of previous studies on the environmental impact of industries. Since nitrogen is present in the air, combustion produces NO_x, and it is mainly at this stage that plants' emissions can be minimized. Options are reduction of the burning temperature (when possible), the elimination of 'dead zones' in the combustion chamber and the use of *low-NO_x* burners, which may be combined with other control technologies (Table 8.11).

For SO_2 exhaust gases – mainly those from thermopower plants – chemical neutralization systems with burned lime (CaOH) or magnesium hydroxide $Mg(OH)_2$ are utilized, especially in wet scrubbers, with 95 per cent typical efficiency (US EPA, 2000). During coal combustion in fluidized bed, quicklime ($CaCO_3$) is added. Particulate matter emitted by stationary sources can be reduced in several ways and at various costs, to meet local needs and legal requirements for final emissions. Pollution management becomes more difficult when the loads are dispersed. Thus generally, environmental control focuses mainly on:

- concentrated loads, large industrial and power generation processes;
- fuel quality (such as the elimination of lead from gasoline);
- product technological standards (such as vehicle emissions);
- emission standards breaches (such as technical inspection and black fume control of the fleet of vehicles in use); and
- processes with potential emissions of dangerous and toxic substances (such as heavy metals and radiative materials).

Table 8.11 NO_x control technologies

Technology	NO_x reduction (%)
Overfire air (OFA)	20–30
Low NO_x burners (LNB)	35–55
LNB + OFA	40–60
Scorching, staged combustion	50–60
Selective non-catalytic reduction (SNCR)	30–60
Selective catalytic reduction (SCR)	75–85
LNB + SCR	50–80
LNB + OFA + SCR	85–95

Figures 8.49 and Table 8.12 summarize these technologies.

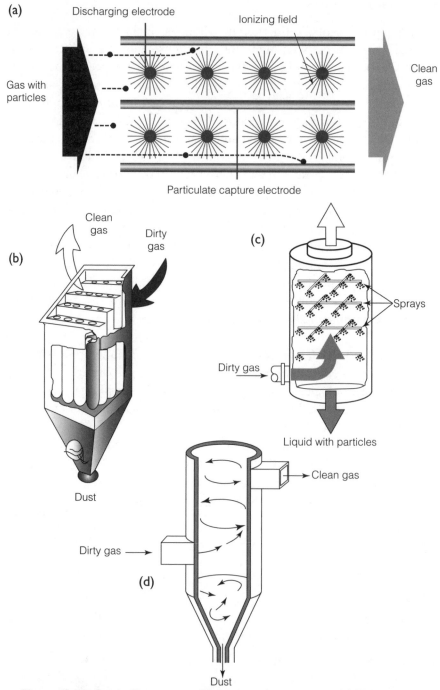

Figure 8.49 Particulate matter (PM) control equipment: (a) Electrostatic precipitator; (b) fabric or bag filter; (c) wet scrubber; (d) cyclone

Table 8.12 Main post-combustion methods for abating particulate matter (PM)

System	Description	Removal efficiency
Electrostatic precipitator, EPS	High-voltage charges in wires ionize gases and particles; plates of opposed charges attract particles; plate movements drop particles on the collectors. With high efficiency, they are able to deal with high discharges or take little space (even in restaurants).	99% (for 0.1 > d(m) > 10) < 99% (for 0.1 < d(mm) < 10)
Fabric or bag filter	Made of different materials, they follow the domestic vacuum cleaner principle, by positive or negative pressure. More expensive and complex, they require maintenance. They retain fine particles with high efficiency.	up to 99.9%
Wet scrubber	Gas enters into contact with liquid flow, which retains particles. There are two major types: tower and trays or cylinder filled with gas-liquid contact means. This may involve chemical reactions (e.g. lime with acid fumes).	95–99%
Cyclone	'Dirty' gas enters a lateral inlet and goes through a spiral in the cylinder; as speed is reduced, particles fall down the cone. There may be multi-cyclones with separate air flow, which capture fine particles (up to two microns).	90–95% (PM > 10mm) or 70–90% (fine particulate matter)

Industrial efficiency

In global terms, the industry accounts for about 35 per cent of power consumption and has a 25 per cent potential for efficiency gains, 30 per cent of which is possible in engine efficiency (Table 8.13).

There are several 'horizontal technologies' for energy conservation that are applied in many industries. They can be of two types, according to Table 8.14.

There are several advances in specialized technologies for the production of steel, chemical products, non-ferrous metals (such as aluminium and zinc), paper and pulp, food and beverages. Heat recovery, use of

Table 8.13 Energy intensity for industrial sectors (World Bank, 2006)

Sector	Indicator	China	OECD	Best practice available
Iron and steel		36	18–26	16
Cement	GJ/t	5.6	3.7–4.4	3.4
Oil refining		3.5–5.0	2.9–5.0	1.3–3.8
Ammonium		39–65	33–44	19.1
Aluminium	MWh/t	16.3	14.1–19.3	nd

Table 8.14 Horizontal technologies for industries

Type of horizontal technology	Application	Example
Components in the basic items of equipment in all industry areas	Engines/gears	Development of faster and more intelligent engine controllers (e.g. with new electronic power systems)
	Boiler for steam or hot water production	Low-emission burners
	Compressors	Overinsulation against noise for direct use in the workplace, with no losses with compressed air networks
	Energy management systems	Industrial and building processes
Technologies for individual applications, greatly varied	Process control	New sensors, microelectronics in general
	Separation of substances at low temperatures	Membranes
	Concentration by refrigeration	Replacement of evaporation, which requires more energy
	Laser processing	Hardening, cutting and perforation in steel
	Infrared heating	Drying
	Solar heating	Heat, refrigeration, airconditioning

biogas, power cogeneration and prevention of input physical losses are some options (Table 8.15).

Most industrial processes in use today were developed at a time of abundant and cheap energy, when there were no environmental concerns or they were not well understood. This is the reason for the existence of so many opportunities for improvements in energy saving, either to increase competitiveness or to improve the public image of industries which reduce pollution. In developing countries, industry was established much later. In the old colonies, most of the industrialized products were imported; over the years, as the local markets grew, production units were transferred to developing countries. The equipment transferred was usually second-hand or obsolete, but still served the purpose of producing low-quality consumer goods. More recently, with market globalization and the quest for lower costs, the improvements made in the industrialized countries started to reach the developing countries. Initially, these countries were exporters of primary goods (agricultural commodities and mineral products) and then moved on to the manufacturing industry, of higher added value. Later, in some of them, the production was directed to microelectronics, fine chemistry and services.

Electricity consumption in residential, commercial and public sectors

Approximately 26 per cent of all end-use of energy used in the world occurs in residences and this fraction is higher in developed countries (Table 8.16).

In industrialized countries, where the housing problem has been largely solved, the task is mainly to retrofit the existing buildings to conserve energy. Considerable energy savings can be obtained in this process. Besides stricter building codes for new buildings and maintenance requirements for the existing ones, energy certificates are required and financial incentives are granted (such as tax reduction and financing) to more efficient technologies. With these measures, Switzerland obtained 50 per cent energy savings in a 20-year period. In developing countries the problem is different, as are the opportunities for efficiency gains. Since there is a huge deficiency in housing, new buildings can incorporate improvements. This is a very promising area as experience shows that the cost of more efficient buildings is not much more than conventional ones. This process can be accelerated by adequate building codes and standards. Buildings in developing countries do not usually require ambient heating or hot water, thus saving significant amounts of energy and costs. In addition, using almost

Table 8.15 Economic potentials (percentage) of energy efficiency, 1997 (UNDP, UNDESA, WEC, 2002)

Sector	Western Europe		East Europe	US		Canada	Japan	South-eastern Asia	India	China	Latin America		Africa
	2010	2020	2010	2010	2020	2010	2010	2020	2010	2010	2010	2020	2020
Iron and steel	9–15	13–20	24–32	4–8		29	10–12		15–25	15–25		10–28	7
Metallurgy									5–10	8–14			
Aluminium			24	2–4					15–20	20			45
Building materials	5–10	8–15	48						15–40	32			
Cement			16	4–8			2–8		17–27	10–20		11–38	10–15
Glass	0–15	15–25		4–8									
Refineries	5–8	7–10		4–8					8–10	10–30			
Basic organic chemistry	5–10									10–30			6
Heavy chemistry			31	4–9			5–10			10–30			19
Paper and pulp		50		4–8			6–18		20–25				
Food	10–15		23								6–20		16–30
Industrial cogeneration	10–20				10–18								
Manufacturing	10–20	15–25	22										
Mining					9	7							
Mineral processing								20					
Electric engines											15–30	30	
Textiles									23	15–28			
Refrigeration											27–42	15–30	
Process heat											10–20	21–44	

Table 8.16 End-use energy consumption in 2004 (IEA, 2006)

	OECD	Non-OECD	World
Residential consumption (Mtoe)	723	1297	2020
Total consumption (Mtoe)	3828	3817	7644
Residential/total	19%	34%	26%
Population (million)	1164	5189	6352
Residential consumption per inhabitant (toe)	0.62	0.25	0.32

exclusively local materials, they can benefit from the production of low-cost bricks and lower energy use, as occurs in India. In industrialized countries, the energy used in a year in a household (including maintenance) is about 20 times smaller than the energy embedded in the construction of the house. In developing countries, use and maintenance are practically 50 times smaller than the energy 'buried' in the construction. Concerning specific technologies for energy savings, there are three main areas of action: domestic appliances, lighting and ambient heating (Table 8.17).

An example of the gains in energy efficiency in US refrigerators is given in Figure 8.50. Despite the increase in size of refrigerators (tripling in 50 years), they use much less power and cost less.

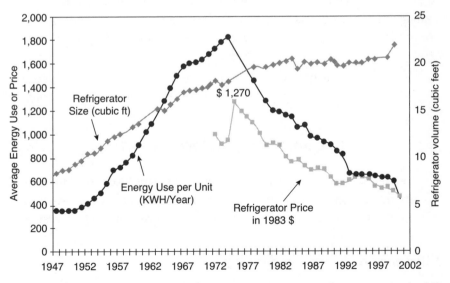

Figure 8.50 Energy consumption and size of domestic refrigerators in the US (Marmen, 2006)

Table 8.17 Good practices for energy conservation

Area of action	Equipment	Examples
House appliances	Refrigeration	Better insulation by vacuum plates; high-efficiency engines and compressors
	Stoves and ovens	Advanced microwaves, electromagnetic induction and improved insulation of ovens, replacement of electrothermy by resistances; replacement of primitive fuelwood stoves by efficient ones
	Washers	Equipment using less water, smaller washing and drying temperatures, higher rotation speeds that reduce thermal needs
	Television sets and computers	Flat screens and low-energy consumption in stand-by mode
Lighting	Lamp bulbs and controllers	High-efficiency lamp bulbs and reflectors; automatic control of artificial lighting in function of solar light; sensors controlling the lighting in an ambient, according to its occupation rate and advanced light control systems
	New building design	New 'passive solar' architecture
Ambient heating and hot water	Joint production	District heating; water heaters with condensers; advanced thermal pumps; heat recovery from equipment for local water heating
	Solar heaters	Water and swimming-pool heating, ambient heating, refrigeration and air conditioning

Combatting deforestation

Deforestation is one of the main causes for biodiversity loss and of an increase in carbon emissions all over the world. There are basically two alternatives to solve problems: increase the efficiency of fuelwood cooking and reforestation.

Efficiency of fuelwood cooking

The basic problem of employing fuelwood to cook is its low efficiency, usually below 10 per cent. This is the case of the three-stone cooking stove

(Figure 8.51a), widely used by low-income populations in developing countries. Although the energy produced is cheap, these stoves are very pollutant and prone to accidents. Basic improvements in primitive stoves cost little and increase their efficiency considerably. The first step to improve these stoves is a better design (*improved cookstoves*) to consume less fuelwood, charcoal, manure, agricultural wastes or kerosene. Metallic stoves (Figure 8.51b) or stoves with thermal insulation also provide better use efficiencies (10–20 per cent). More elaborate stoves cost little and allow considerable efficiency gains (25–40 per cent), particularly in the case of the *Jiko* ceramic stove, about a million of which are used in East Africa (Figure 8.51c).

Curiously, the Jiko stoves that were so successful in Kenya were not successful in Rwanda. Programmes for improving fuelwood stoves were successful in China, but not in India. It is difficult to understand the reason why programmes for disseminating better stoves were successful in some countries, but not in others; this seems to depend largely on the local culture, on community education and involvement, rather than on governmental action. Solar stoves are not very successful mainly because the cooking time is far too long.

After switching to efficient traditional biomass stoves, the next step is the adoption of propane (liquefied petroleum gas, or LPG), liquid petroleum products and electric stoves, climbing an 'energy ladder' for food cooking activities (Figure 8.52).

When going up this 'ladder' (Box 8.9), pollution reduction is dramatic: a gas stove emits 50 times less pollutants and is five times more efficient than a primitive stove. However, they are more expensive, and not always affordable for the poor. This is, however, the direction to take. Through subsidies and financing, several programmes in Africa, Asia and Central America have succeeded in disseminating more efficient stoves in rural areas and the periphery of cities (slum areas).

(a)   (b)   (c)

Figure 8.51 Stove evolution, from left to right: (a) traditional 'three-stone stove'; (b) metallic stove; and (c) Jiko stove (Kammen, 1995)

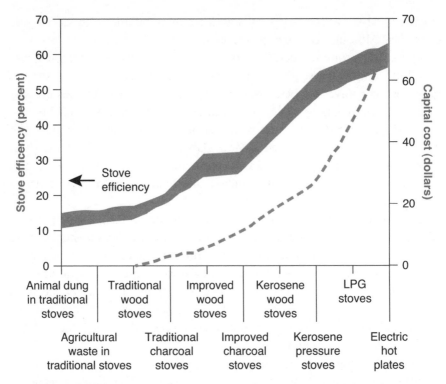

Figure 8.52 Efficiency of commercial and non-commercial cookstoves
(UNDP, UNDESA, WEC, 2002)

Box 8.9 The energy 'ladder'

Traditional fuels and stoves result in very high indoor emission levels,
which may be reduced with more efficient stoves (Figure 8.53).

Fuel switch depends on the availability of alternatives and on their cost.
This may be drawn by an 'energy ladder', which shows how the transition
to cleaner, more efficient and convenient energy sources has a direct
relationship with higher levels of development (Figure 8.54).

Reforestation

For degraded areas, *reforestation* offers an alternative to recapture the carbon in the air. Deforestation is responsible for the emission of about 1.6
billion tons of carbon every year, a huge amount comparable to the six billion tons a year emitted by fossil fuels. There are several practices to remove
carbon from the atmosphere:

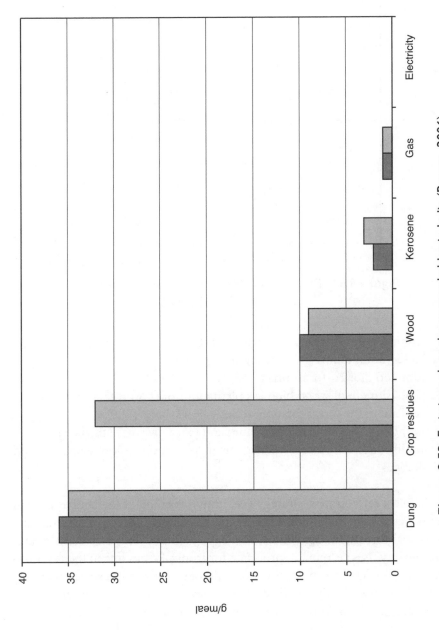

Figure 8.53 Emissions along the energy ladder in India (Barnes, 2006)

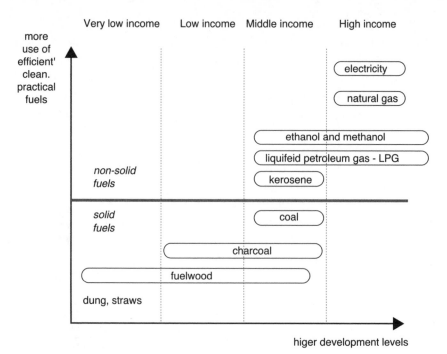

Figure 8.54 The 'energy ladder': ratio between home energy and income (WHO, 2006)

- reforestation of already cut or burnt forests;
- preservation of forests, allowing their growth;
- adoption of agro-forest practices;
- establishment of wood biomass plantations of short rotation;
- increase in the forest rotation cycle;
- adoption of low-impact harvesting and extractivism methods; and
- modification of forest management practices, emphasizing carbon storage.

While a reforestation strategy (i.e. immobilization of the land as a drain for the carbon in the atmosphere) seems to be more attractive in temperate or boreal forests, an agro-forest strategy (planting forests for energy and non-energy uses) is more appropriate for tropical areas due to the fast rotation of forest growth. Whereas about 20 tons of carbon per hectare a year can be captured in the tropical areas, in the temperate forests the typical capture rates are of approximately five tons of carbon per hectare a year.

One of the greatest benefits of reforestation is the reduction of the extractive pressure on virgin forests. The reforestation by agro-silviculture provides local income and a fuel source, so deforestation and degradation of neighbouring forests may be reduced.

However, the removal of carbon from the atmosphere in the form of biomass only occurs when plants are growing. Reforestation, therefore, only temporarily contributes to reducing the atmospheric carbon concentrations. After reaching maturity, the forest has to be kept untouched or replaced periodically, so that there is no new carbon released into the air. If the forest project is composed of a single species (such as eucalyptus or pinus), a perennial 'green desert' will be created. This may be justified in some cases (such as the production of charcoal for metallurgy to replace coal), but not in all cases. It is also necessary to prevent the phenomenon called 'leakage', that is, the induction of deforestation in another region due to the preservation of a reforested area.

There are possible solutions to these problems: several degraded areas, such as vegetation bordering rivers can be recovered with native species, forming biodiversity corridors considered permanent conservation areas. There is a wide range of estimations on the availability of land, growth rates and costs for reforestation. The Intergovernmental Panel on Climate Change (IPCC) established a group dedicated to methodologies on land use, land-use change and forestry – or LULUCF – conducting analyses which produced representative data:

- reforestation of 500 million hectares of degraded areas in the tropics and 100 million in Europe seems possible;
- if all this land was reforested, 50–150 billion tons (10Gt) of carbon equivalent (Ceq) could be removed from the atmosphere in a 100-year period (or 0.5–1.5Gt Ceq/year), significantly contributing to postponing global heating;
- while in North America the costs for absorbing carbon vary from 9–65/tCeq (or even more), US$7/tCeq costs may be obtained in tropical countries (IPCC, 2001).

On the basis of these numbers, it is reasonable to accept the possibility of capturing 1GtCeq/year (or about 20 per cent of the fossil fuel emissions today) by reforestation of 500 million hectares at a cost of US$10/tCeq. This would represent a total expenditure of US$10 billion a year, or less than 0.1 per cent of the world GDP. As will be seen in Chapter 9, the largest part of the other strategies to achieve the same goal requires costs that are at least ten times higher.

Notes

1 In the Rankine cycle, a working fluid is heated until it turns into a gas which moves a turbine connected to a power generator; the gas is then condensed, recycled and reheated. In the Brayton cycle, the working fluid (usually air) expands through a series of turbines, going through a second combustion chamber before expanding up to the ambient pressure (achieving high efficiency without exceeding metallurgic constraints).

2 In the reaction $[C + H_2O \rightarrow CO + H_2]$.

3 By the reaction $[CO + O_2 \rightarrow CO_2]$.

4 Typical emission factors are 0.086kgCeq/kWh for coal, 0.071kgCeq/kWh for oil and 0.049kgCeq/kWh for natural gas (IPCC, 2006).

5 As a comparison, the costs of the power produced with non-renewable technologies are approximately the following: coal 5.0¢/kWh; oil 6.0¢/kWh; combined cycle natural gas 4.5¢/kWh; nuclear 5.5¢/kWh.

6 In vehicles, a lambda probe device sends signals to the injection system which controls the air-fuel mix. The ideal mix is 14.8kg of air for each 1kg of fuel (lambda = 1), a case in which the pollutants CO, HC and NO_x undergo simultaneous oxidations and reductions, getting neutralized (NO_x contains excess oxygen, which is compensated by the oxygen demand from CO and HC). When the vehicle is under load conditions or accelerating, more fuel is necessary in the mix. Inadequate vehicle tuning, tampering and other misadaptations upset optimal fuel burning and considerably increase emissions.

7 N_2O is a greenhouse gas, which means that more efficient systems for reducing local pollutants eventually increase a parcel of the global pollutants. Conversely, a better HC burning reduces emissions of methane, CH_4, another greenhouse gas. See also IPCC (2006) and Environment Australia (2002).

8 Established in the US in the 1970s, the CAFE (Corporate Average Fuel Economy) programme defined goals for the fleet produced by each manufacturer and led to important progress, as evidenced in Figure 8.35. The CAFE-derived average economy estimated in the early 1980s was about 2.5 million oil barrels a day, about 25 per cent of gasoline demand (Hwang, 2004). In that legislation, the penalty for not complying with CAFE standards (U$5.50 per 0.1 mile per gallon below the standard for each vehicle of a given year-model) may be avoided by credits attributed when the average efficiency of a vehicle exceeds the standard established. As CAFE adopts different procedures for passenger vehicles and the so-called light commercial vehicles (more and more used as passenger vehicles and now accounting for a large share of sales), the efficiency in fuel use by these models has decreased steadily in recent years.

9 In Brazil, the State of Sao Paulo alone produces 62 per cent of the ethanol of the country, equivalent to nearly one-third of the world total. Even so, sugar cane occupies only 3.7Mha from a total 22Mha used for agriculture and pastures. Sugar cane expansion is possible by the intensification in cattle breeding and is being carefully followed up with social and environmental sustainability aspects in mind.

10 These mechanisms include customs overtaxing, quotas, local subsidies and non-tariff technical barriers to protect local industries where the cost of ethanol production is higher. Also worth mentioning is the fact that the bioenergy trade today also includes wood pellet exports from Canada to the US and Europe, as well as the palm

oil exports from Indonesia to Europe (Junginger et al, 2006). A technical objection that has been raised to 5–10 per cent ethanol blended in gasoline is the increase in evaporative emissions, which influence photochemical smog formation (ozone and other pollutants). The alternative proposed is to adopt an 85 per cent ethanol blend to gasoline (E85) which solves this problem. The problem of E85 lies in the lack of infrastructure of pumps and storage tanks of the filling stations in many countries (unlike Brazil) and in the resistance of local automobile manufacturers (Coelho et al, 2006). The adoption of the E10 blend does not require adaptations in the existing vehicles. In some years, the fleet is renewed with vehicles adapted to blends with a higher proportion of ethanol, as is the case of Brazil (E20–E25), or even flex vehicles. The smog problem may be solved by a comprehensive approach, involving a reduction of light hydrocarbons in gasoline and the available vehicle technology with better engines and emission control systems (Lucon et al, 2004).

11 The *cellulase* enzyme can be found in the stomach of ruminants; other enzymes obtained from fungi and genetic modification are also under development.

References

Abavana, C. (2001) 'The Ghana Renewable Energy Solar PV Portfolio: Emerging Experience and Lessons', Services Project. Experience with PV Systems in Africa. GEF Monitoring and evaluation working paper (2). N. Wamukonya, Roskilde, Denmark, UNEP Collaborating Centre on Energy and Environment, pp52–55

ACCS (2009) UK Assured Combinable Crops Scheme, www.assuredcrops.co.uk/ACCS2/

An, F. and Sauer, A. (2004) 'Comparison of Passenger Vehicle Fuel Economy and GHG Emissions Standards Around the World', Pew Center on Global Climate Change

Barnes, D. (2006) 'Clean Household Energy & Indoor Air Pollution', ESMAP, The World Bank. US Japan Bilateral Workshop on Climate Change, 22–23 March.

BBC (2009) Americas – Obama aims for oil independence. BBC News, http://news.bbc.co.uk/2/hi/americas/7851038.stm

Bioenergy Site (2008) Algae – a new source for Biodiesel for 2020, http://www.the-bioenergysite.com/articles/207/algae-a-new-source-for-biodiesel-for-2020

Cameron, A. and Jones, J. (2006) 'Photovoltaics – Raising Objectives', *Renewable Energy World*, vol. 9, no. 2, p89

Camp, V. (2006) Lake Nyos, Department of Geological Sciences, San Diego State University, www.geology.sdsu.edu/how_volcanoes_work/Nyos.html

Carpentieri, E. (2001) Sistema Integrado de Gaseificação de Madeira para Geração de Eletricidade, Brazilian Ministry of Science and Technology, http://200.130.9.7/clima/comunic_old/sigame02.htm

CETESB (2009) São Paulo State Air Quality Report (in Portuguese: *Relatório da Qualidade do Ar do Estado de São Paulo*). São Paulo State Environment Agency, http:www.cetesb.sp.gov.br

CLASP and APEC ESIS (2006) 'Energy Efficiency and Minimum Energy Performance Standards (MEPS)'. Collaborative Labeling and Standards Program and Asia Pacific Economic Cooperation Energy Standards Information System.

Apud The Engineering Curmudgeon (2006) Commentary on Product Development and Engineering Management, http://innovativethermal.com/engineeringcurmudgeon/

Coelho, S. T., Goldemberg, J., Lucon, O. and Guardabassi, P. (2006) 'Brazilian Sugarcane Ethanol: Lessons Learned', *Energy for Sustainable Development*, vol. X, no. 2, June 2006, pp26–39.

Commission Cramer Report (2009) Final report from the project group 'Sustainable production of biomass', www.mvo.nl/biobrandstoffen/download/070427-Cramer-FinalReport_EN.pdf

ECO Centre (2004) The ECO Centre's grid connected photovoltaic system, www.eco-centre.org.uk/the-eco-centre-solar-roof.html

ECOFYS (2006) Draft Technical Guidance for sustainability reporting under the Renewable Transport Fuel's Obligation. Low Carbon Vehicle Partnership, London, UK

Ellegård, A., Nordström, A. A. M., Kalumiana, O. S. and Mwanza, C. (2005) 'Rural People Pay for Solar: Experiences from the Zambia PV–ESCO Project, www.sei.se/energy/pvesco/download_reports/rural_people_pay_for_solar.pdf

Emerging Markets Online (2006) Algae 2020 Briefing, http://www.emerging-markets.com/algae/Algae2020StudyandCommercializationOutlook.pdf

Environment Australia (2002) A literature review based assessment on the impacts of a 20 per cent ethanol gasoline fuel blend on the Australian vehicle fleet, www.deh.gov.au/atmosphere/fuelquality

EPFL (2007) Second version of global principles for sustainable biofuels production, 23 October 2007. Roundtable on Sustainable Biofuels. École Politechnique Fédérale de Lausanne, Energy Center, http://cgse.epfl.ch/webdav/site/cgse/shared/Biofuels/Home%20Page/RSB-Second%20version%20of%20Principles.pdf

EUREPGAP (2009) European Retailers Produce Working Group, www.eurepgap.org/Languages/English/about.html

European Commission (2007) Aviation and Climate Change, http://ec.europa.eu/environment/climat/aviation_en.htm

European Commission (2008a) Environment – Air – Legislation, http://ec.europa.eu/environment/air/legis.htm#transport

European Commission (2008b) Environment – Air – Conference on Air Pollutant and Greenhouse Gas Emission Projections for 2020, http://ec.europa.eu/environment/air/transport/sulphur.htm

European Environment Agency (2000) 'Are We Moving in the Right Direction?' *Environmental Issue Report*, no. 12, http://reports.eea.europa.eu/ENVISSUENo12/en/page027.html

FAO (2006a) FAO Sees Major Shift to Bioenergy, www.fao.org/newsroom/en/news/2006/1000282/index.html

FAO (2006b) FAOSTAT Statistics. UN Food and Agriculture Organization, http://faostat.fao.org/default.aspx

FAO (2007a) Food Outlook – Global Market Analysis. UN Food and Agriculture Organization, www.fao.org/docrep/010/ah876e/ah876e06.htm

FAO (2007b) 'The State of Food and Agriculture 2007', FAO Conference, 34th Session, 17–24 November, ftp://ftp.fao.org/docrep/fao/meeting/012/sofaconf_c2007.pdf

FAO (2007c) The State of Food Insecurity in the World, www.fao.org/docrep/009/a0750e/a0750e00.htm

FAO (2007d) Committee on Commodities to Review Impact of Oil Prices and Biofuels. Newsroom, www.fao.org/newsroom/en/news/2007/1000543/index.html

FSC (2009) Forest Stewardship Council, www.fsc.org/

Goldemberg, J. (2004) 'The Case for Renewable Energies', Background paper for the Renewables 2004 Conference, Bonn, www.renewables2004.de/pdf/tbp/TBP01-rationale.pdf

Goldemberg, J., Coelho, S. T. and Lucon, O. (2004) 'How Adequate Policies Can Push Renewables', *Energy Policy*, vol. 32, issue 9, pp1141–1146

Goldemberg, J., Coelho, S. T., Lucon, O. and Nastari, P. M. (2004) 'Ethanol Learning Curve – the Brazilian Experience', *Biomass and Bioenergy*, vol. 26, issue 3, pp301–304

Grimm, H. P. (2004) 'Utilisation of Biomass – European Technologies and Expectations', LAMNET International Workshop on Bioenergy Policies, Technologies and Financing. Ribeirão Preto, September, www.bioenergy-lamnet.org/publications/source/chi2-int-forum/3-Session3-Grimm-LAMNET-WS-Guangzhou-0309.pdf

Hwang, R. J. (2004) 'US Experience with Fuel Economy Standards', Workshop for Fuel Efficiency and Low Sulfur Content, MMA, SMA-SP and Hewlett Foundation, Sao Paulo, December 2004

IEA (1994) 'Energy and Environment Technology to Respond to Global Climate Concerns – Scoping Study', International Energy Agency, OECD, Paris

IEA (2005) End-user Petroleum Prices. International Energy Agency, http://library.iea.org/Textbase/stats/surveys/mps.pdf

IEA (2006a) CO_2 *Emissions from Fuel Combustion*, International Energy Agency, Paris

IEA (2006b) Energy Balances of non-OECD Countries. International Energy Agency, Paris

IEA (2007) Biofuel Production. IEA Energy Technology Essentials (ETE02). International Energy Agency, OECD

IEA (2008) Worldwide Trends in Energy Use and Efficiency, *Key Insights from IEA Indicator Analysis*, www.iea.org/Textbase/publications/free_new_Desc.asp?PUBS_ID=2026

IMO (2002) International Convention for the Prevention of Pollution from Ships, 1973, as modified by the Protocol of 1978 relating thereto – MARPOL 73/78, www.imo.org/Conventions/mainframe.asp?topic_id=258&doc_id=678#30

IPCC (2001) Special Report on Land Use, Land-Use Change and Forestry, www.grida.no/climate/ipcc/land_use/index.htm

IPCC (2005) Special report on carbon dioxide capture and storage, Intergovernmental Panel on Climate Change, www.ipcc.ch/activity/srccs/index.htm

IPCC (2006) Guidelines for National Greenhouse Gases Inventories. Intergovernmental Panel on Climate Change, www.ipcc-nggip.iges.or.jp/public/2006gl/index.htm

Junginger, M., Faaij, A., Rossillo-Calle, F. and Woods, J. (2006) 'A Growing Role', *Renewable Energy World*, vol. 9, no. 5, p130.

Kammen, D. M. (1995) 'Cookstoves for the Developing World', University of California, Berkeley, http://socrates.berkeley.edu/~kammen/cookstoves.html

KFZ-TECH (2006) Exhaust Gas Treatment, www.kfz-tech.de/Engl/ Abgasentgiftung.htm

Klein, T. (2003) *Clean Air Initiative in Latin American Cities*, World Bank International Workshop, Lima-Callao, Peru, 12–13 May 2003

LEAF (2009) Marque certification for farmers, www.leafmarque.com/leafuk/producers/join.asp

Lovins, A. B., Datta, E. K., Bustnes, O. E., Koomey, J. G. and Glasgow, N. J. (2005) Winning the Oil Endgame, Earthscan, London, www.oilendgame.com

Lucon, O., (2008) Sustainability of biofuels production in Latin America. Working paper for the Biotop Project, under publication, www.top-biofuel.org/ index.php?option=com_frontpage&Itemid=1

Lucon, O. Coelho, S. T. and Alvares Jr, O. (2004) Bioethanol: the Way Forward. XV ISAF Conference, Sacramento, www.eri.ucr.edu/ISAFXVCD/ISAFXVAF/ BWF.pdf

Lucon, O. and Goldemberg. J. (2006) 'A 10% Ethanol in the Caribbean', CCAA Regional Trade and Investment Forum, Government of Trinidad & Tobago, US Department of Energy, Inter-American Development Bank, UN Development Program. Port-of-Spain,Trinidad, www.c-caa.org/conferences/energy06/presentations.html

Macedo, I. C. (1992) 'The Sugar Cane Agro-Industry: Its Contribution to Reducing CO_2 Emissions in Brazil', *Biogas and Energy*, 3(2)

Macedo, I. C. (2004) 'Greenhouse Gas Emissons and Energy Balances in Bio-ethanol Production and Use in Brazil, www.unica.com.br/i_pages/files/gee3.pdf

Marmen, L. (2006) Energy efficiency and Minimum Energy Performance Standards (MEPS). Collaborative Labeling and Standards Program (CLASP) e Asia Pacific Economic Cooperation Energy Standards Information System (APEC ESIS). *Apud* The Engineering Curmudgeon (2006) Commentary on Product Development and Engineering Management, http://innovativethermal.com/engineeringcurmudgeon/

MI and IFQC (2006), A biodiesel primer: market & public policy developments, quality, standards & handling. The Methanol Institute and International Fuel Quality Center, http://www.biodiesel.org/resources/reportsdatabase/reports/gen/20060401-gen369.pdf

MME (2006) National Energy Balance. Brazilian Ministry of Mines and Energy, www.mme.gov.br

Nakicenovic, N. (2004) *Long-Term Drivers of Climate Change*, International Energy Workshop, IEA, Paris, 21–25 June

Noer, M. and Kjaer, S. (2005) 'Development of Ultra Super Critical of Power Plants in Denmark', 17th Congress of the World Energy Council, www.worldenergy.org/ wecgeis/publications/default/tech_papers/17th_congress/2_2_02.asp

Nogueira, L. A. H. and Branco, G. M. (2005) *Promovendo a Eficiência Energética nos Automóveis Brasileiros* (Promoting Energy Efficiency in Brazilian Vehicles). CONPET Report, June, www.conpet.br

NREL (2006a) Cost Curves. US National Renewable Energy Laboratories, www.nrel.gov/analysis/slide_library.html

NREL (2006b) PV performance Calculator, http://rredc.nrel.gov/solar/calculators/ PVWATTS/

OESP (2006) 'O Custo da Vida Lenta nas Ruas' (The Cost of Slow Living on the Streets), *O Estado de S. Paulo*, 9.12.2006, p H3

Pacheco, M. (2006) 'US Senate Full Committee Hearing – Renewable Fuel Standards', Monday 19 June 2006. National Renewable Energy Laboratory, National Bioenergy Center, energy.senate.gov/public/index.cfm?IsPrint=true&FuseAction=Hearings. Testimony&Hearing_ID=1565&Witness_ID=4427

Planet Ark (2006) Energy-Hungry China Warms to Solar Water Heaters, www.planet-ark.org/dailynewsstory.cfm?newsid=36636

PMSP (2007) Município em Dados. Sao Paulo Municipal Government, www9.prefeitura.sp.gov.br/sempla/md/index.php?pageNum_sql=0&totalRows_sql =13&texto=Table&ordem_tema=4&ordem_subtema=10

Poole, A. D. and Geller, H. (1997) The Market of Energy Efficiency Services in Brazil (in Portuguese, 'O Mercado de Serviços de Eficiência Energética no Brasil'), www.inee.org.br/down_loads/escos/escomerc.pdf

Reeve, D. A. (2000) Global Change Strategies International Inc., The Capture and Storage of Carbon Dioxide Emissions – A significant opportunity to help Canada meet its Kyoto targets. Prepared under NRCan Contract File No. NRCan-00-0195. Office of Energy Research and Development, Natural Resources Canada, Ottawa, Ontario, http://www2.nrcan.gc.ca/ES/OERD/English/View.asp?pmiid=1505&x=1569

REN21 (2006) Renewable Energy Policy Network, Global Status Report 2006, www.ren21.net/pdf/REN21_GSR2007_Prepub_web.pdf

REN21 (2008) Renewable Energy Policy Network, Global Status Report 2007, www.ren21.net, www.ren21.net/globalstatusreport/default.asp

Rodrigues, D. and Mataja, R. (2004) 'Um Banho de Sol para o Brasil: o que os Aquecedores Solares Podem Fazer pelo Meio Ambiente e Sociedade', Vitae Civilis, www.cidadessolares.org.br

RRSO (2009a) Roundtable on Responsible Soy Oil, www.responsiblesoy.org/

RSPO (2009b) Round Table on Sustainable Palm Oil, www.rspo.org/

Shephard, S. (2006) Solar Energy for Everyone. Professional Builder, www.housing-zone.com/probuilder/article/CA6340267.html

Smil, V. (2003) *Energy at the Crossroads*, MIT Press, Cambridge, 2003

Solarpaces (2005) Spain Solar Tres, www.solarpaces.org

Solar Tres (2005) Spain Solar Tres, http://www.solarpaces.org/solartres.htm

Solar Wales Eco Centre (1996) Solar Electricity, www.ecocentre.org.uk/solar-electricity.html

SP (2009) Sao Paulo State Green Ethanol Program, www.ambiente.sp.gov.br/ etanolverde

Stirzaker, M. (2006) 'Solar Thermal Power, Mirrored Sunshine', *Renewable Energy World*, vol. 9, no. 2, p. 78

Sustainable Business (2008) Swedish Company Signs First Deal for Sustainable Brazilian Ethanol, SustainableBusiness.com News, 27 June , www.sustainablebusi-ness.com/index.cfm/go/news.printerfriendly/id/16298

The White House (2007) Energy for America's Future, www.whitehouse.gov/info-cus/energy

The White House (2009) Press Briefing Highlights, Monday 26 January 2009 at 6:30 pm, www.whitehouse.gov/blog_post/PressBriefingHighlights/

Tohoku Electric Power (2006) Environmental Action Report 2005. Improvement of Thermal Efficiency at Thermal Power Stations, www.tohoku-epco.co.jp/ enviro/tea2005e/03/03c.html

UFOP (2007) Commentary paper on the German Biomass Sustainability Ordinance. Union For the Promotion of Oilseeds and Protein Plants Registered Association, www.ufop.de/downloads/Commentary_paper_Feb2008(1).pdf

UNCTAD (2005) Biofuels: Advantages and Trade Barriers, www.unctad.org/en/docs/ditcted20051_en.pdf

UNDP, UNDESA, WEC (2004) World Energy Assessment 2004 Update. UN Development Program, UN Division for Economic and Social Affairs, World Energy Council, www.undp.org/energy/weaover2004.htm

UNDP, UNDESA, World Energy Council (2002) World Energy Assessment: Energy and the Challenge of Sustainability, www.energyandenvironment.undp.org/undp/index.cfm?module=Library&page=Document&DocumentID=5037

USDA (2001) Estimating the Net Energy Balance of Corn Ethanol. A report from Hosein Shapouri, James A. Duffield, and Michael S. Graboski to the US Department of Agriculture, Economic Research Service, Office of Energy. Agricultural Economic Report No. 721, http://www.ers.usda.gov/publications/ aer721/AER721.PDF

USDA (2006) The economic feasibility of ethanol production from sugar in the United States. United States Department of Agriculture

US DoE (2006a) Cellullosic Ethanol, Energy Information Administration, US Department of Energy, www.eere.energy.gov/biomass

US DoE (2006b) Solar Energy, www.eia.doe.gov/kids/energyfacts/sources/renewable/solar.html

US DoE (2006c) Wood waste, www.eia.doe.gov/cneaf/solar.renewables/page/wood/wood.html

US DoE (2007) Energy Prices, http://www.eia.doe.gov/emeu/mer/prices.html

US DoE (2008a) How Does a Wind Turbine Work? Energy Efficiency and Renewable Energy. Wind and Hydropower Technologies Program, http://www1.eere.energy.gov/windandhydro/wind_how.html

US DoE (2008b) Wind Energy. US Department of Energy, www.eia.doe.gov/kids/energyfacts/sources/renewable/wind.html

US EPA (2000) Air Pollution Control Fact Sheet. Flue Gas Desulfurization. EPA-452/F3-034, www.epa.gov/ttn/catc/dir1/ffdg.pdf

US EPA (2007) Clean Diesel Program for Locomotives and Marine Engines, www.epa.gov/otaq/regs/nonroad/420f04041.htm

US EPA (2009) National Clean Diesel Campaign, www.epa.gov/cleandiesel/

USGS (2006) Sulfur production report. US Geological Survey

US Senate (2006) Committee hearing statement from Dr Michael Pacheco, http://energy.senate.gov/public/index.cfm?IsPrint=true&FuseAction=Hearings.Testimony&Hearing_ID=1565&Witness_ID=4427

Volkspage (2008) Propaganda, www.volkspage.net/propaganda/gol80_01.jpg

Walsh, M. P. (2005a) 'Sustainable Transportation', *The Lessons of the Past 50 Years*, http://walshcarlines.com/mpwdocs.html

Walsh, M. P. (2005b) Worldwide emissions overview. Overview of International Goods Transport, Haagen Smit Symposium, http://walshcarlines.com/pdf/Haagen%20Smit%202005%20Worldwide%20Emissions%20Overview2.pdf

WHO (2006) *Fuel for Life: Household Energy and Health*. WHO, Geneva, ISBN978 92 4 156316 1, www.who.int/indoorair/publications/fuelforlife/en/index.html

Woods, J. and Bauen, A. (2003) 'Technology Status Review and Carbon Abatement Potential of Renewable Transport Fuels in the UK', UK Department of Transport and Industry Report B/U2/00785/REP URN 03/982, www.dti.gov.uk/files/file15003.pdf

World Bank (2006a) Clean Energy and Development: Towards an Investment Framework. Report DC2006-0002, http://siteresources.worldbank.org/DEVCOM-MINT/Documentation/20890696/DC2006-0002(E)-CleanEnergy.pdf

World Bank (2006b) 'World Bank's Energy Framework Sells the Climate and Poor People Short', September 2006, http://siteresources.worldbank.org/DEVCOM-MINT/ Documentation/20890696/DC2006-0002(E)-CleanEnergy.pdf

Worldwatch (2006) China Moving Away from Grain for Ethanol Production, www.worldwatch.org/node/3919

WRI (2008) Plants at the Pump: Biofuels, Climate Change, and Sustainability. World Resources Institute, http://pdf.wri.org/plants_at_the_pump.pdf

WTE (2006) Waste-to-energy, http://wte.cbj.net e http://cbll.net/articles/coal-question

YEROC (2007) The coal question, http://cbll.net/articles/coal-question

Chapter 9

Policies to Reduce Environmental Degradation

The main topics to be analysed in this chapter are the costs of environmental pollution, the policies proposed to reduce it, the barriers to the implementation of such policies and the measures needed to overcome them. To do so, it is useful to recognize that environmental problems occur at three levels: local, regional and global.

Geographical scale of impacts

Local pollution concerns the quality of air, water and soil, besides rendering services such as water supply, collection and disposal of wastes and sewage, street cleaning and others. Local government plan and manage land use, the economic practices of the private sector (industry, commerce services and agriculture), building codes and citizens' attitudes. Unfortunately, in many regions of the world a large proportion of the population live in inadequate conditions owing both to lack of resources or bad management of those available. Local pollution moves hand in hand with poverty, in both large and small towns, and is dealt with by municipalities.

Regional pollution is caused mainly by large sources (such as vehicles, thermopower plants and heavy industry), which are an integral part of life in more prosperous societies. Large metropolises and surrounding areas are most affected by this type of pollution. In some cases, regional pollution crosses borders, as in the case of tropospheric ozone, acid rain and ocean pollution. Regional pollution must be dealt with at the state, national and, eventually, international level.

Acidification is being considerably reduced in Europe (UNEP, 2006) and in the US (US EPA, 2006), as a result of emission reduction programmes in thermopower plants and industrial processes (Box 9.1).

Box 9.1 Prevention and control of acid rain in Europe and the US

The first evidence of extensive damage to the environment caused by acid deposition was the disappearance of fish from the lakes and rivers of Scandinavia and Mid-western Europe in the 1960s. The effect was so significant that it led to the establishment of the Convention of the UN on Long-Distance Transboundary Atmospheric Pollution. Later, in the 1980s, a protocol was signed to limit SO_2 emissions in Europe at least by 30 per cent. Several other protocols were signed later to limit SO_2, NO_x and O_3. In 1999, the Protocol to Abate Acidification, Eutrophication and Low Altitude Ozone brought an integrated approach. A few years later, restrictions on heavy metals and persistent organic pollutants (POPs) were added. In the US and in Europe, acid rain control is mainly applied to large-scale installations such as thermoelectric plants. Taking into account environmental quality data (acidity in river water, concentration of pollutants in the atmosphere), national and regional emission goals are defined, with the allotment of SO_2 and NO_x emission quotas for each enterprise (industries and thermoelectric plants). If emissions exceed the quotas, the enterprises will be fined or will acquire credits (Figure 9.1) from other enterprises that manage to surpass their goal (UNEP, 2002; US EPA, 2006).

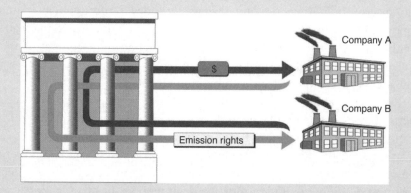

Figure 9.1 Local pollutant emissions market (UNEP, 2002)

As a result, most of the large European thermoelectric plants have opted for emission reduction solutions, such as:

- sulphur removal systems (desulphurization) for stack emissions;
- fuel switch (natural gas, renewable fuels, nuclear energy); and

- an increase in energy conversion efficiency.

Between 1980 and 2000, SO_2 emissions in Europe decreased by two-thirds. Projections for 2012 indicate that emissions will be halved, returning to the 1900 emission levels. As to the NO_x, emitted mostly by road transportation, the decrease was less significant: slightly over 25 per cent between 1990 and 2000. On the whole, acid rain gas emissions decreased by more than one-third between 1990 and 2000. Even so, acid rain deposition in Europe is still above critical levels, with irreversible environmental impacts (UNEP, 2006).

Global pollution is the third of the categories that can best be identified as global impacts or issues. The best known are the destruction of the stratospheric ozone layer, climate change, loss of biodiversity, desertification and persistent organic pollutants (Box 9.2). These problems cross national boundaries and may originate on one side of the planet and affect the other. Global issues can only be solved at the international level, usually under the auspices of the UN.

Box 9.2 Persistent organic pollutants (POPs) and their control

One of the aspects of modern industry that has had considerable impact on the waste management issue is the proliferation of chemical products. In 1990 there were about 100,000 synthetic substances on the market, an increase by a factor of 350 since 1940. Few of those substances were effectively tested, at high costs (UNEP, 1992). Among the recalcitrant substances (i.e. those that are difficult to destroy) made by man, some of the best known are chlorofluorocarbons (CFC), which destroy the stratospheric ozone layer and can be found in refrigeration systems, and in the production process of foam, fire control equipment, industrial solvents and in food preservation. The elimination of CFCs and other substances that destroy the ozone is the focus of the Montreal Protocol, 1987. CFCs, HFCs, PFCs and SF_6 are also gases that contribute towards global warming. Even if the production of those gases ceases completely, large quantities are present in equipment around the world which will liberate those gases for many years to come (e.g. when pieces are taken to a scrap-yard), contributing towards global warming and the destruction of the stratospheric ozone layer. Other recalcitrant substances that cause great concern are pesticides, mainly DDT, which is carcinogenic, and bio-cumulative, and was banned in most countries in the 1970s. DDT (dichloro-diphenyl-trichloroethane) was largely employed in the mid-20th century to combat mosquitoes carrying malaria and other diseases, and to this day there are controversies surrounding its use. In 1962, the American biologist Rachel Carson published the book *Silent Spring*, calling attention to DDT effects on humans and birds, which led to a widespread movement to ban the product. For many people, this event marks the beginning of the environmental movement. In 1976, an accident at a chemical industry at Seveso, 25km from Milan, Italy, resulted in over-exposition of a residential area to TCDD (2,3,7,8-tetrachloro-dibenzo-para-dioxin), causing several deaths and triggering a series of scientific studies and safety standards. In 1995, the UN Environment Programme (UNEP) proposed the adoption of the 'Stockholm Convention', an international agreement to ban POPs, defined as chemical substances that persist in the environment, bio-accumulate through the food web, and pose a considerable risk of causing adverse effects to human health and to the environment. Subsequently, a specialists' forum compiled a list of the 'Dirty 12', worst POPs, which includes eight organophos-phorate pesticides (aldrin, chlordane, DDT, dieldrin, endrin, heptachlor, mirex and toxaphene), two industrial compounds (hexachlorobenzene – HCB – and polychlorinated biphenyl – PCB) and two groups of industrial byproducts: dioxins (polychlorinated dibenzodioxins, or PCDDs) and furans (polychlorinated dibenzofurans, or PCDFs) (Figure 9.2). The Convention was implemented on 17 May 2004, with 151 signatory countries. POPs cross national boundaries and are considered a global threat: there are traces of DDT in Arctic seal fat, and species that bio-accumulate pesticides at the top of the trophic chain (such as the American eagle) are endangered. Large amounts of dioxins werereleased in the disaster at Seveso mentioned above and as a defoliator in the Vietnam war (the Orange Agent). Dioxins are present in food that contains animal fat (especially meat). Each day a North American ingests 119 picograms (10–12g) of dioxins (Schecter, 2001). Very small amounts, in the order of nano-grams (billionths of a gram), are sufficient to contaminate living beings. Because these amounts are so small, the usual means of detection cannot verify their presence and emission control becomes very difficult and expensive.

Combustion in general, especially thermal processes at high temperatures, emit POPs. The operating conditions are critical in these processes (combustion efficiency, pollution control mechanisms) to minimize the emission of these contaminants. Emissions from uncontrolled

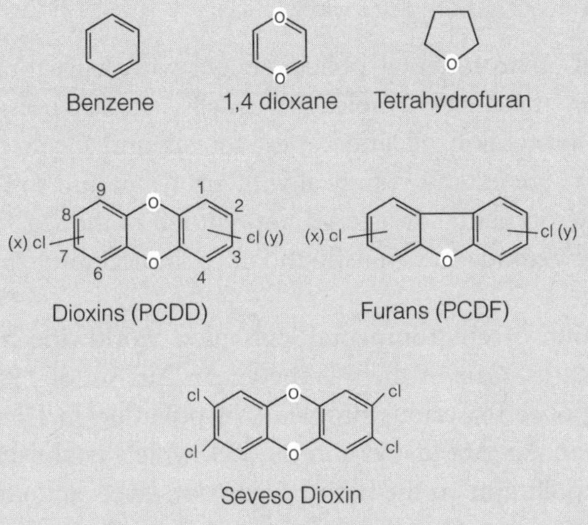

Figure 9.2 Examples of dioxins, furans and their aromatic cycles (Lusinchi, 2002)

waste combustion are higher. Various processes related to the production and consumption of energy are sources of POPs (Worldbank, 2006):

- production of organochlorinates (solvents, phenols, benzene);
- oil refining and catalyst regeneration;
- steel production and ash recirculation;
- primary copper casting;
- processing of metals for recycling (steel, aluminium, lead, zinc, copper and magnesium: burning electric cables and recovery of metals from ashes);
- coal coke production and carbochemical processes;
- cement furnaces (use of hazardous halogenated wastes as fuel);
- uncontrolled or poorly controlled incineration of urban wastes, industrial waste, wood waste treated with paint and varnish, hazardous waste, hospital waste, sewage treatment plant sludge, crematories and incineration of animal carcasses; uncontrolled gas burning in landfills;
- burning of biomass containing salt (HCl);
- uncontrolled and small-scale coal combustion;
- old, poorly maintained gasoline or diesel internal combustion engines (vehicles and generators);
- uncontrolled biomass burning (deforestation and agricultural waste);
- intentional or accidental fires in landfills and waste dumping grounds;
- burning of tyres, electric cables, electronic waste.

Environmental law and energy

Governmental environmental policies begin with legislation related with neighbourhood nuisances (unpleasant smells, smoke, noise and sewage) and with the protection of landscapes, forests and localized ecosystems. Over time, laws are extended to deal with air, water and soil pollution, and then cover environmental disasters and pollution of the sea. Then, at a later stage, they are extended to transboundary pollution and, finally, to global impacts.

The adoption of environmental legislation worldwide has some great historic landmarks. One of them is the Clean Air Act of 1956, adopted in Britain in response to serious problems of pollution in London. Another one is the Clean Air Act of 1970 in the US, which established procedures for managing pollution on the basis of emission levels and concentration of pollutants.

Coordinating all the activities requires policies and laws, harmonizing economic development, environmental protection and social inclusion, with eventual predominance of one of these concerns. To better understand the issue, it is worth describing (in Box 9.3) the 27 principles issued at the Rio-92 UN Conference on the Environment and Development – UNCED (UN, 1997) – four of which are highlighted in our analysis:

- the 'polluter-pays principle', which establishes that the cost of measures to be taken to reduce pollution should be reflected on the cost of goods and services that cause it, in the production process and/or in their consumption (this can be applied, for example, to the production of oil and coal);
- the 'precautionary principle' (mainly in high-risk activities, such as the generation of thermonuclear energy and in cases of irreparable damages to biodiversity);
- the concept of 'common but differentiated responsibilities' (often invoked by developing countries in discussions about climatic change and reduction of greenhouse gases); and
- the idea of 'public trusteeship' for environmental resources, by which it is considered government's responsibility to protect assets of common use such as air or water.

The Rio-92 Conference consolidated the concern with environmental problems worldwide, strengthening the rules to combat the planet degradation. Among its results stands out 'Agenda 21', a directive framework for sustainable development, and two of the most important MEAs in this area: the Climate Convention and the Bio-Diversity Convention.

Box 9.3 The Rio-92 UNCED principles

1 an anthropocentric view of sustainable development;
2 the sovereignty of states to exploit their own resources, taking responsibility for damages to the environment beyond the boundaries of their own jurisdiction;
3 the right to development that meets the needs of present and future generations;
4 environmental protection as an integral part – and not as an isolated one – of the development process;
5 cooperation among states and individuals to eradicate poverty, and reduce disparities in living standards as an indispensable requirement for sustainable development;
6 priority given to the situation and special needs of developing countries and of those most environmentally vulnerable;
7 common but differentiated responsibilities among developed countries (those with greater responsibility) and developing countries concerning environmental protection issues;
8 reduction and elimination of unsustainable patterns of production and promotion of appropriate demographic policies;
9 strengthening of endogenous capacity-building for sustainable development, through exchanges of knowledge, transfer of technologies, including new and innovative ones;
10 effective participation of the whole civil society in decision-making processes;
11 effective environmental legislation, reflecting the environmental and developmental contexts of each country;
12 establishment of a supportive and open international economic system, with favourable conditions for the economic growth and sustainable development of all countries, without arbitrary or unjustifiable discrimination, disguised barriers to international trade or unilateral actions to deal with environmental issues outside the jurisdiction;
13 the polluter-pays principle: liability and compensation for the victims of pollution and other environmental damages;
14 discouragement and prevention against relocation and transference of activities or substances that cause serious environmental degradation or are harmful to human health;
15 principle of precaution: when there are threats of serious or irreversible damage, lack of full scientific certainty shall not be used as a reason for postponing cost-effective measures to prevent environmental degradation;

16 internationalization of environmental costs (externalities), without distortions to international trade and investments;

17 assessment of environmental impacts as an instrument for planning and the emission of government permits/licences; environmental impact assessment, as a national instrument;

18 immediate notice of disasters and emergencies with transboundary effects and aid to the countries affected;

19 prior and timely notification and relevant information about potentially harmful activities;

20 full participation of women in environment management and development;

21 youth mobilization for a global partnership;

22 acknowledgement and support of indigenous populations;

23 the environment and natural resources of people under oppression, domination and occupation shall be protected;

24 protection to the environment in times of armed conflict;

25 peace, development and environmental protection;

26 peaceful resolution of environmental disputes by the appropriate jurisdictional means;

27 good faith cooperation for sustainable development.

At a country level, legal systems acknowledge the MEAs which were ratified and thus incorporated in environmental laws (Box 9.4).

Box 9.4 Multilateral Environmental Agreements (MEAs)

Multilateral Environmental Agreements (MEAs) aim to take measures to remedy, mitigate or otherwise deal with global and/or regional environmental concerns. Governed by international law, they can be embodied in one or more written instruments, with legal agreements between three or more countries (agreements between two countries are referred to as 'bilateral agreements'). Usually in an MEA there is a large number of states or international organizations (as Parties) to jointly address global issues and regional cross-border environmental problems, including pollution of rivers and seas that are part of several countries (e.g. the Mediterranean or the Great Lakes in US/Canada), and air pollution that is dispersed from one or several countries over several other countries (e.g. sulphur dioxide and dust from power plants in Europe). In the early MEAs from the mid-20th century, there were mainly sectoral agreements on how to exploit and share natural resources.

Environmental protection was a secondary objective, primarily focused on maintaining economic usefulness of natural resources. Modern MEAs started when the 1972 Stockholm Conference adopted the first global action plan for the environment, addressing its relationship with development and bringing other more comprehensive, system-oriented and trans-sectoral agreements. The 1992 Rio Conference (UN Conference on Environment and Development – UNCED) was an important landmark for a new generation of MEAs, with clearly established interdependence of social and economic development issues:

- the adopted Rio Declaration and Agenda 21 setting out principles and action plans;
- the Convention on Biological Diversity (CBD); and
- the UN Framework Convention on Climate Change (UNFCCC).

Framework conventions (such as the UNFCCC with the Kyoto Protocol) can develop protocols for addressing specific subjects requiring more detailed and specialized negotiations. More than 60 per cent of the present MEAs were established after 1992 and today there are over 500 MEAs, of which around 320 are regional agreements. Many MEAs have well over 50 per cent of the countries in the world as members. None of the main environmental agreements are exclusively oriented to protection and conservation; all of them share a common goal of sustainable development. Energy is a topic with strong interactions in many cross-cutting thematic issues of MEAs: pollution assessment and management, protection of biodiversity (Convention on Biodiversity, CBD), desertification and land protection from negative altering (UN Convention on Combating Desertification, UNCCD), protection of marine environment (the largest cluster of MEAs, including 17 Regional Seas conventions and action plans, and the Global Programme of Action for the Protection of the Marine Environment from Land-Based Activities – GPA), protection of wetlands ('Ramsar' Convention), protection of endangered species (CITES) and marine species (CMS), control of transboundary movement of hazardous wastes and their disposal (Basel Convention), prior informed consent for certain hazardous chemicals and pesticides in international trade (Rotterdam Convention), control and phase-out of persistent organic pollutants (Stockholm Convention on POPs) and protection of the atmosphere from substances that deplete the ozone layer (Montreal Protocol), and greenhouse gases (UNFCCC and the connected Kyoto Protocol, which is one of the most far-reaching MEAs, affecting all sectors of society). The development of MEAs is time consuming. They are often triggered by concerned scientists that highlight initial evidence of the scale of the problem and policy debates. The UN Environment Programme (UNEP, established in 1972) aids the process of bringing international consensus. MEAs come into force through an initial agreement (international legal instrument) signed between the (state) signatories, including provision of a minimum number of ratification from signatories needed to come into force. The country signs the convention, often by means of a government representative. This signals the intention of the country to become a member, but is not yet binding for the country. Then the parliament (or similarly elected body) of the country ratifies (approves the signing of) the convention, at which time the rules of the convention in principle becomes binding for the country. Once a country (or 'Party') ratifies, accepts, approves or accedes an MEA, it is subject to the provisions under the MEA, which will come into effect after a minimum number of countries have it ratified. The Kyoto Protocol, for example, was launched in 1997, signed and ratified by a majority of countries by 1999, but only came into effect in 2005 when Russia ratified it, bringing the amount of GHG emissions covered by the parties to the convention above a defined threshold (of 55 per cent) for the Convention to come into effect. Few MEAs are non-binding (the so-called 'soft law') instruments, which help to set priorities and sometimes lead to the development of consequent legally-binding, that is, with targets and timetables. MEAs are not self-executing, but implemented via national legislation and regulatory measures – and sometimes there may not be adequate resources to do so. There are cases in which achieving compliance to MEAs is hard or virtually impossible, more a matter of developing self-implementing rules and incentives. Some MEAs cover complex activities that make monitoring and measuring compliance extremely difficult. Besides substantial measures, compliance includes procedural ones, such as reporting. Some common components of MEA are:

- the Convention of the Parties (COP), membership and the body that ultimately takes all decisions about the agreement, adopting (a vote per member country) the text of the convention and any amendment to the text;
- the Secretariat to the Convention, managing day-to-day business and serving the COP with information about the implementation of the MEA;
- the executive and subsidiary bodies, usually assigned a specific task to work on (methodology development, fund managing, technology transfer);

- clearing houses, databases on specific issues under the convention, usually designed to assist signatories to honour their commitments;
- implementation actors at the national level, authorities and organizations with assigned responsibilities.

Financial mechanisms include:

- regime budgets, mandatory or voluntary (rarely materialized) trust funds administered by the Secretariats, proposed by Parties and approved by the COP;
- development assistance (including the official, ODA), funds provided via foundations (e.g. UN Foundation), bilateral arrangements, private sector donors and NGOs;
- the World Bank's Global Environment Facility (GEF), which funds only incremental costs of existing projects with the global benefits.

With focal areas on biodiversity, climate change, international waters, ozone depletion, POPs and land degradation, GEF is the main supporter for several MEAs such as the CBD or the Stockholm Convention. The Kyoto Protocol has specific 'Flexible mechanisms', including the Clean Development Mechanism, the Joint Implementation and Emission Trading. These mechanisms raise funds to assist other countries through cooperative project activities and through trading of emission reduction certificates (UNEP, 2008b). Limited enforcement is the most difficult point of MEAs, for which the international community can either ignore, assist (including financially) or put pressure on it. A positive case of MEA effectiveness (whether it resolves a problem that caused its creation) is the Montreal Protocol, with a very focused objective, clear alternatives available and excellent financial mechanism with strong multilateral support. Rarely, trade measures are taken against a country for not following the rules of the convention they have ratified. The linkage between the rules of the World Trade Organization (WTO) and those of MEAs is a subject largely discussed but with (very) few decisions agreed. The WTO 2001 Doha Round has brought about development and environmental issues, such as the definition and preference to the so-called 'environmental goods and services', or EGS (WTO, 2008).

Environmental support capacity: management by quality

An important issue in environmental protection is the so-called 'support (or carrying) capacity', based on the idea that there is a limit of environmental quality that must be protected through specific measures aimed at preserving the quality of a local environment (Box 9.5).

Box 9.5 Environmental support capacity

Support capacity is, basically, the natural capacity of the environment to cope with the impact caused by a polluter. It is a concept that is difficult to define (the capacity may be defined by the presence of a more fragile species, the concentration of one or more pollutants, or by another factor or set of factors). Complying with pollutant emission standards might not be sufficient enough when the pollutant level is near a saturation point. Environment management of the quality of the whole of the system (such as a river basin) is then necessary, which may adopt mechanisms such as reduction goals based on inventories and compensation of emissions (offsets) between new polluting projects and reduction measures (US EPA, 2008).

Environmental protection costs

The fact that there are technical solutions for environmental degradation problems does not imply that they will actually be adopted. There are many obstacles on the path to change and government intervention is frequently needed to overcome them. The first obstacle for the adoption of measures to decrease pollution is their cost. Installing pollution control systems (filters on the stacks of thermopower power plants, catalysers on automobile exhaust pipes, the collection and recovery of wastes and other materials) entails costs that may be considerable (Table 9.1). Preferably, pollution reduction should be preventive, that is, applied before it is generated. One of the ways of preventing pollution – and other environmental impacts – is the promotion of cleaner technologies, among which the ones that generate energy from renewable sources. The costs of those technologies have decreased over time and this tendency may be further accelerated by acting on learning curves (Box 9.6).

Box 9.6 Accelerated development of new technologies

Accelerating the development of new technologies is particularly relevant for the widespread adoption of renewable energies which are fundamental for environmental sustainability. The 'market penetration' is the result of a complex combination among the availability of competing energy sources, of the convenience of their use and their cost. Usually, prices decrease as sales increase owing to the economies of scale, according to the 'learning curves', of the type shown in Figure 9.3.

The 'progression ratio' (PR) measures the decrease in cost of a given technology as production increases. For example, a PR of 80 per cent means that the cost decreases by 20 per cent every time production doubles. The smaller the PR, the faster the decrease in cost. The justification to promote growth with accelerated development is to reduce the cost of the technology through large-scale sales and through efforts on research and development (R&D). Current proposals in this area are:

- large-scale purchases with government subsidies covering part of the costs;
- supplies contracts with feed-in tariffs; and
- mandatory legislation (Renewable Portfolio Standards – RPS), such as building codes.

In the case of subsidies, the financial cost is met by those who pay taxes. In the case of tariffs, it is met by the consumer base. While subsidies are easier to apply, favourable tariffs stimulate quality in energy services. Both systems may generate distortions in the market in the long run and, therefore, they must be progressively eliminated, as fostered technology reaches its maturation stage.

Pollution control effects are more effective in large-scale processes (thermopower power plants, heavy chemistry industries, steel plants, cement plants, paper and pulp industries and incinerators) because of the magnitude of the emissions, the investment capacity of the owners and their managerial capacity. Since a considerable portion of air pollution is caused by energy generation and use, the costs for its reduction have been frequently compared with fuel costs. The 1970s energy crisis significantly contributed to accelerating the adoption of several corrective measures, since the industry quickly realized that the most significant part of the

Table 9.1 Costs of environmental protection in OECD member states (OECD, 2007)

| Member State | Costs of pollution abatement and control (% GDP) | | | | | | | | | | | | | |
| | Public sector | | | | | | | Private sector | | | | | | |
	1990	1995	2000	2001	2002	2003	2004	1990	1995	2000	2001	2002	2003	2004
Canada	0.7	0.7	0.6	0.6	0.6	–	–	–	0.5	0.5	–	0.6	0.6	–
Mexico	0.3	0.3	0.5	0.5	0.5	0.5	0.5	–	–	–	–	–	–	–
US	0.6	–	–	–	–	–	–	0.8	–	–	–	–	–	–
Japan	0.3	0.5	0.5	0.5	0.5	0.5	0.4	–	0.8	–	–	–	–	–
Korea	–	0.7	0.8	0.8	0.8	0.8	–	–	0.7	0.6	0.6	0.6	0.6	–
Australia	–	0.5	0.2	0.2	–	0.2	–	–	0.3	–	0.2	–	–	–
N. Zealand	–	–	–	0.8	0.8	0.7	–	–	–	–	–	–	0.2	–
Austria	1.1	1.4	0.9	1.1	–	–	–	1.0	0.6	0.4	0.3	–	–	–
Belgium	–	–	–	–	0.5	–	–	–	–	–	–	0.6	–	–
Czech Republic	–	0.7	0.5	0.5	0.3	–	–	–	1.4	0.5	0.3	0.3	–	–
Denmark	–	1.3	1.4	1.4	1.4	1.4	1.3	–	–	–	–	–	–	–
Finland	–	0.5	0.5	–	–	–	–	–	0.5	0.5	–	–	–	–
France	0.5	0.6	0.6	0.6	0.6	–	–	0.3	0.3	0.2	0.2	0.2	–	–
Germany	–	1.5	1.3	1.2	1.3	1.3	–	–	0.5	0.3	0.4	0.3	0.3	–

Greece	–	0.3	–	–	–	–	–	–	0.3	–	–	–	–	–
Hungary	0.5	0.3	–	0.5	0.6	–	–	0.4	0.2	–	0.6	0.4	–	–
Iceland	0.3	0.3	0.3	0.3	0.3	0.3	–	–	–	–	–	–	–	–
Ireland	–	–	–	–	–	–	–	–	–	–	–	–	–	–
Italy	0.7	0.7	0.8	0.8	0.8	–	–	–	–	–	0.6	–	–	–
Luxembourg	–	–	–	–	–	–	–	–	–	–	–	–	–	–
Netherlands	0.9	1.3	1.1	1.2	–	1.1	–	0.7	0.5	0.5	0.5	–	0.5	–
Norway	–	–	–	0.5	0.6	–	–	–	–	–	–	–	–	–
Poland	–	–	0.7	0.7	0.6	0.7	0.8	–	–	1.2	1.1	0.7	0.7	0.6
Portugal	0.7	–	0.5	0.5	0.5	0.4	0.4	–	0.2	0.3	0.2	0.2	0.1	0.2
Slovakia	4.0	–	0.1	0.1	0.2	0.1	–	–	–	0.6	0.9	1.0	0.7	–
Spain	0.6	0.6	–	–	–	–	–	–	–	–	–	–	–	0.3
Sweden	–	0.2	0.2	0.2	0.3	–	–	–	–	–	0.3	0.3	0.3	–
Switzerland	0.7	0.8	0.8	0.8	0.7	0.7	–	–	–	–	–	–	0.4	–
Turkey	–	–	–	–	–	0.9	0.9	–	–	–	–	–	–	–
UK	0.4	–	0.4	0.4	0.4	0.4	–	0.3	–	0.4	0.2	0.1	0.2	–

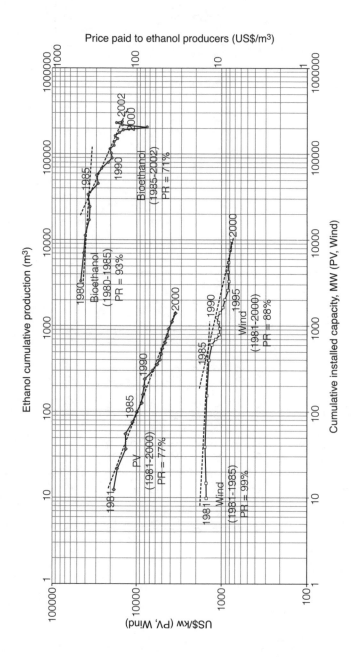

Figure 9.3 Learning curves for photovoltaics (PV), wind turbines and sugar cane ethanol (UNDP, UNDESA, WEC, 2004)

production system in use at the time – which had been built over the previous hundred years – was clearly inefficient and could easily be improved. A limiting factor for those initiatives is the fact that energy prices do not often reflect the real cost of energy, because there are various subsidies embedded and they do not consider externalities; in both cases, the costs are met by society as a whole (Box 9.7).

Box 9.7 The real cost of energy

Energy costs society billions of dollars in excess of what its users pay directly for it. The hidden costs include subsidies, environmental degradation, rising health costs and compensation for loss of jobs. It is hard to accurately gauge the damage caused by the various sources of energy to human health, agriculture, historical monuments and, above all, to the environment. Figure 9.4 illustrates the wide range of uncertainty existing in the attempts to quantify those externalities.

Some of the subsidies are relatively easy to identify. For example, in the case of coal, fiscal incentives and job maintenance in non-competitive mines are very common. There are, however, other costs that are controversial but which are very difficult to eliminate, such has mounting health expenses, crop loss and even military costs. In the US, for example, direct government subsidies reach approximately US$50 billion in the form of fiscal incentives and research funds, with US$26 billion allocated to fossil fuels, US$19 billion to nuclear energy and only US$5 billion to renewable energy sources. In Germany, in 1995, coal production was subsidized to the cost of US$6 billion per year; in Britain, US$8 billion; the OECD countries subsidized coal production with approximately US$16 billion per year. In countries that do not belong to OECD, subsidies are even higher, as shown in Table 9.2. The total amount of subsidies in the non-OECD countries is approximately US$250 billion per year (one-quarter of the energy market), equivalent to a subsidy of US$50 per ton of carbon. The former Soviet Union alone accounts for over 60 per cent of that amount.

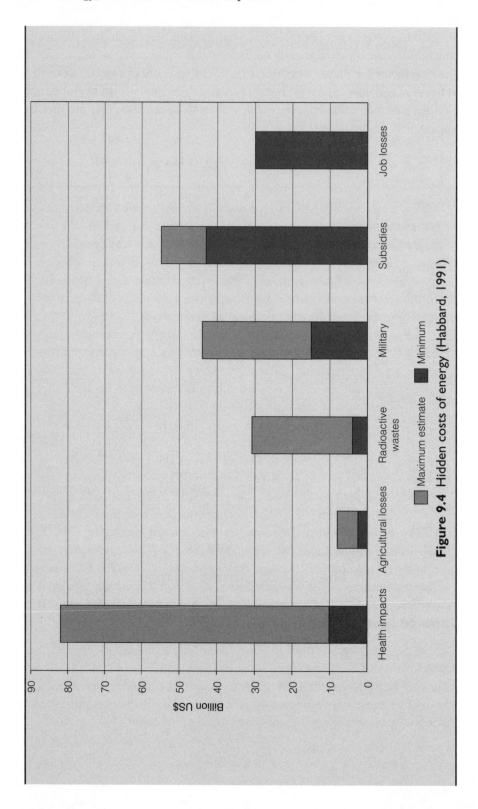

Figure 9.4 Hidden costs of energy (Habbard, 1991)

Table 9.2 Subsidies to energy (Burniaux and Martins, 1992)

Country, region or energy source	US$ billions (1995)
Energy exporters	35.5
China	14.2
Former USSR	163.2
India	6.0
Eastern Europe	21.7
Brazil	3.3
Rest of the world	7.4
Total non-OECD	254.2
Coal total	37.4
Oil total	142.6
Gas total	74.2

In order to identify the policies needed to avoid environmental degradation, an assessment can be made on the cost of repairing the damage caused or the cost of avoiding the problem. A comparison between them may help to decide what type of action is more convenient or more effective in terms of cost. In practice, mitigation costs are usually lower, but polluters frequently decide to run the risk of causing damage anticipating that they will not be fully charged for it. That approach may be adopted for any environmental problem, but is applicable with particularly interesting results for the problem of global climate changes.

The cost of climate change

Damage costs

The costs of damages caused by global warming as a consequence of the doubling of the CO_2 concentration in the atmosphere – which is likely to occur half way through the 21st century – has been studied by several economists. The most impressive analysis is that of the British economist Sir Nicholas Stern, whose conclusions are summarized in Box 9.8.

Box 9.8 Synthesis of the Stern Report (2006)

There is still time to avoid the worst impacts of climate change, a serious threat to the planet that demands urgent global answers. All the different costs and risks analyses used indicate that prompt intensive action is, by far, better than inaction. Climate change will affect the basic elements of human life: water, food, health and the environment; hundreds of millions of people will be affected by starvation, drought and floods. The costs and risks of climate change will be equivalent to 5 per cent of GDP permanently; taking into account greater impacts and risks, the estimates rise to 20 per cent. In contrast, the costs of actions to mitigate emissions may be limited to around 1 per cent of the global GDP per year. In the next 10–20 years, the investment will have a profound effect on the climate of the planet from 2050 onwards. The economic impacts will be similar to those of the world wars and the 1929 crisis, but it will be impossible to reverse the consequences of these impacts. Therefore, immediate action is necessary, with mutually reinforcing approaches at regional, national and international levels. If no action is taken, the concentration of greenhouse gases in the atmosphere may double to above pre-industrial levels in 2035, leading to an increase in average temperatures of over 2°C. In the long run, there would be more than a 50 per cent chance for the temperature to exceed 5°C, something that is extremely dangerous and is equivalent to the change in average temperatures from the last ice age to today. The radical change in the world's physical geography will lead to changes in human geography – where and how people live. Even moderate levels of global warming will have serious impacts on the world output, on human life and on the environment; all countries will be affected, and the most vulnerable will be the poorest. Adaptation to climate changes is essential and should be accelerated, so as to create resilience and reduce costs for the changes that will occur in the next 20 years and which cannot be reversed; in developing countries alone it will cost billions of dollars every year and will put more pressure on scarce resources. Stabilization costs are significant, but manageable; delayed action is dangerous and much more expensive. Stabilization at between 450 and 550ppm CO_2 eq (in relation to the present levels 430ppm CO_2 eq, increasing by more than 2ppm per year) requires emission reductions of at least 25 per cent from present levels until 2050; maybe much more, perhaps about 80 per cent. It is hard enough to stabilize concentrations at 450ppm. The estimates of costs to stabilize concentrations at between 500 and 550ppm are around 1 per cent of the global GDP, if we act immediately. The costs may be lower if there are gains in efficiency or if co-benefits, such as air-pollution reduction, are taken into account. Costs will be higher if it takes too long for technologies to be incorporated and if policy-makers fail to adopt them. The cost of actions is unevenly distributed around the world. Even if rich countries reduce their emissions by 60–80 per cent until 2050, developing countries need to take significant measures, too – which does not mean bearing all the costs, since carbon markets are evolving. Acting may create jobs and business opportunities of hundreds of billions of dollars each year. Climate changes are the most serious market failure the world has ever seen – and interact with other market imperfections. The electricity sector will have to de-carbonize by at least 60 per cent until 2050 (to 500ppm) and deep emission cuts will be necessary in the transportation sector. Even with renewable sources and other low-carbon technologies, fossil sources will provide at least half of all the primary energy needed in 2050. Coal will remain important and CO_2 capture at the source is fundamental. Also essential are cuts in industrial, agricultural and deforestation emissions. Three elements are necessary for an effective response:

1 setting a price on carbon through taxes, trade or regulations;
2 supporting innovation and the development of new technologies; and
3 removing barriers to energy efficiency, information access and education on climate change.

Several countries and regions have already adopted some sound policies: the European Union, California and China are the most ambitious in terms of reducing emissions. The Climate Convention and the Kyoto Protocol provide the basis for cooperation, but stronger actions are needed in the whole world. Different approaches, in accordance with the circumstances, provide a contribution, but individual actions are not enough and it is paramount to create an international vision on long-term goals. Key elements of that framework include: emission trading; coordinated international technological cooperation; action to reduce deforestation; and adaptation and development assistance, mostly for the poorest and international financing mechanisms.

For the US, the estimated cost of damages results are 1.0–1.3 per cent of the GDP, as shown in Table 9.3. These estimates are compatible with the order of US$100 billion in damages caused by Hurricane Katrina in 2005, in New Orleans (Insurance Journal, 2005a, b).

Table 9.3 Costs of climate change in the US (billions of dollars),
according to three authors

Strongly affected sectors	Nordhaus (1993)	Cline (1992)	Fankhauser (1992, 1993)
Agriculture	1.0	15.2	7.4
Coastal areas	10.7	2.5	2.3
Energy	0.5	9.0	0.0
Other sectors			
Wetland areas and loss of species		7.1	14.8
Health and amenities		8.4	30.3
Others		11.2	12.1
Subtotal	38.1		
Total	50.3	53.4	66.9
Total as a GDP percentile	1.0	1.1	1.3

Impacts could be expected to be more significant in developing countries for the following reasons:

- the agricultural sector represents a much larger fraction of GDP than in developed countries (around 30 per cent, as compared with less than 3 per cent);
- rising sea levels will flood large areas, since a great portion of those countries is located just above sea level (e.g. Bangladesh and small islands in the Pacific);
- countries do not have resources to adapt to temperatures higher than the present ones. This is the special case of Africa, South and South-East Asia, where higher losses related to the GDP are expected (IPCC, 2007).

It is important to highlight that adaptation to climate change is a complementary measure to mitigation efforts, never an alternative to it.

Mitigation costs

There are many benefits in avoiding climate changes through conservation of energy, fuel change and CO_2 capture by means of reforestation or other methods. There are also various cost estimations for these options. In order to calculate mitigation costs, two approaches may be adopted:

1 top-down aggregate models based on the historic ratio between energy consumption, prices and income, which analyse how changes in one sector of the economy affect other sectors and regions. Traditionally, top-down models tend to have few details about energy consumption, and cannot accurately simulate the feedback involving economic incentives (such as prices, interest rates and other factors) and technical changes;

2 bottom-up models, based on the sum of detailed costs of the various technologies available, with the resulting energy consumption and the way this may be affected by new technologies. The problem with this approach is one of 'closure', that is, how much of the total universe was represented in the sample of technologies chosen. Certain effects cannot be incorporated in this model, such as the fact that the increase in energy efficiency in automobiles has the perverse effect of encouraging more trips ('rebound effect').

It is possible to have an idea of the results of top-down econometric models for the US from Table 9.4, which essentially establishes a carbon tax on fossil fuels that is necessary to reduce their use, according to their relative contributions to CO_2 emissions.

Cost estimates for CO_2 emission stabilization at 1990 levels in OECD countries vary greatly. Many bottom-up studies suggest that the costs to reach that goal in the next two decades may be negligible; most of the top-down studies suggest that they may eventually exceed 1–2 per cent of the GDP. Among the top-down models that indicate lower long-term costs are those that are optimistic in relation to the potential of the use of taxes that

Table 9.4 Cost of alternative policies to attenuate climate change
(Nordhaus, 1993)

Political options	Reduction Tax 1995 (%)[a]	Carbon Tax 1995 (1990 US$)[b]	Annualized global annual impact (1990 US$ billion/year)[c]
Optimum policy	8.80	5.24	16.39
20% reduction in emissions from the 1990 levels	30.80	55.55	−762.50
Climate stabilization	47.40	125.80	−1962.00

Notes:
[a] Reduction in greenhouse gas emissions below the baseline.
[b] Tax on greenhouse gas emissions in American dollars for CO_2 equivalent emissions in carbon weight.
[c] Present value of the difference between base value and cases without control, with a real interest rate of 6 per cent a year.

are recycled in the economy through the reduction of other taxes. There are great discrepancies between the results of different studies of this type for the OECD, as well as for developing countries. The IPCC (2007) compared the results of numerous studies in different countries.

Energy policies

In order to overcome barriers to energy efficiency and to promote the growth of energy from renewable sources, a set of financial and regulatory instruments are used by the governments. The most important *financial instruments* used are the following:

- new taxes or changes in existing taxes reflecting externalities in some cases;
- incentives and normal commercial loans, or loans that include some form of subsidies ('soft loans');
- price policies: incorporating externalities (Box 9.9) so as to more accurately reflect the real social cost of supply and final use. By doing so, energy use could be discouraged, and users could respond by replacing one source with others or changing their consumption patterns.

The most important *regulatory instruments* adopted are:

- environmental regulations in general;
- equipment performance standards;
- government purchase policies (procurement) which favours certain types of equipment or energy sources;
- the imposition of a minimum percentage of renewable sources of energy in the portfolio of energy companies;
- integrated resource planning;
- informative programmes; and
- minimum performance standards (as in the CAFE case in the US in 1975, already mentioned).

Regulation and standardization are a highly efficient means to force a given technology to improve more quickly, yet there is the risk of simply leading to its acceptance and of discouraging the search for better technologies. In order to avoid this situation it is advisable for governments to specify the desired result by means of strategic goals within a certain time limit, rather than specify the technology to be adopted. This way, industries are allowed to do what they do best, that is, deciding on the best technology to reach a desired goal.

Box 9.9 Environmental accounting: the 'green' GNP

Conventional national revenue accounting does not fully take into consideration some categories of expenses:

- 'defensive expenses', be it for prevention of pollution or for its total cleaning (although this expense is not accounted for separately, it is considered as growth in GNP);
- 'the consumption of non-renewable resources', since a country that quickly uses up its natural resources may show a high growth rate in conventional revenue accounting, but a much lower growth rate when depletion of resources is taken into account, because that will be reflected in future balances;
- 'conflicting use of environmental services', which is the case of the atmosphere, used by producers as an input (waste deposit) and by users as a consumption good.

Many analysts have pointed out the deficiencies in the usual accounting of national revenues. In the first place, they do not generally provide an adequate measure of well-being; in addition, they fail to provide correct information that may lead to the adoption of relevant policies for a sustainable development that is concerned with society's resources: economic growth when its resource base – capital reserves combined with natural resources – is growing. Similarly to GDP, GNP has not been devised as a measure of resources availability. In terms of accounting, instead of a balance sheet (which lists all the assets, including resources available), GNP is a demonstration of the results of the period. The usual accounting procedures require that companies take into consideration capital stock depreciation, amortization and the depletion of resources. As the GDP measures production growth, it does not take into account the depreciation of physical or natural capital; particularly, it does not take into account environmental items and natural resources, the depletion of which are difficult to gauge. In order to correct these flaws, proposals were made to include the effect of changes in environmental quality in the GDP. The need for those corrections is dramatically demonstrated by the fact that, in many countries, the constant increases in GDP have masked the effects of decades of environmental degradation. In the same period, the GDP, environmentally adjusted, declined. In the past, that was the case of the former Soviet Union and today is the case of China. The four approaches that follow are commonly adopted to calculate changes in the environment and reflected in a connected GDP measure:

- 'the environmental expenditure focus', used in the US, subtracts expenses with pollution reduction from the GDP;
- 'the physical accounting focus', used in Norway and in France, establishes auxiliary (satellite) accounting to take into consideration resource flows and reserves;
- 'the depreciation focus' adjusts the net gross product by subtracting the value of natural resources reduction; and
- 'the comprehensive focus' makes use of physical measures, as well as their value.

Integrated resource planning

The current world energy system has developed over the years without serious concerns about optimization, since fossil fuel costs were very low until the 1970 oil crisis. This is no longer the case and thus any expansion in the energy system should meet demand at the lowest possible cost. In some cases, energy conservation and the retrofit of industrial installations may be more advantageous than building new plants or choosing natural gas instead of coal for generation plants. To illustrate this, Table 9.5 presents a

Table 9.5 Costs of meeting the electricity demand, in dollar cents/kWh, by energy-saving and generation measures (Boneville Power Administration, 1990)

	Saved	*Generated*
Conservation		
Refrigerators	1.3	
Water heating	1.9	
Retrofitting existing single-family residences	3.3	
New single-family households	3.3	
Hydropower		
Improvements in existing plants efficiency	3.4	
New small hydro plants		2.0
Cogeneration		4.0
Improvements in the transmission lines	3.6	
Gas turbines		2.5
Coal-fired generators		4.0

comparison of the cost to supply electricity demand from a variety of sources or through conservation measures. As an example, a supply curve can be built with the accumulated electricity services (new supplies or the result of energy efficiency) on the horizontal axis and the incremental cost of each supply addition on the vertical axis. In terms of supply, the vertical axis is the cost of the energy produced by generation plants; for demand, it is the cost of electricity conserved, calculated on a life-cycle with a given discount rate. Figure 9.5 shows a typical supply curve for Sweden.

Supply curves were calculated for various countries, using different hypotheses and discount rates. For the US, an estimate of potential electricity savings is illustrated as a percentage of the system demand when using more efficient technologies in order of increasing costs per unit saved (Figure 9.6).

Once an energy supply curve is obtained, it is possible to produce a curve for CO_2 emission reduction costs. In order to do that, the cost per ton of carbon is avoided as a result of the adoption of different options for new energy supply (or energy efficiency) in relation to a baseline, which is usually the electricity system in operation before the effects of technological improvements were introduced. Although management on the demand

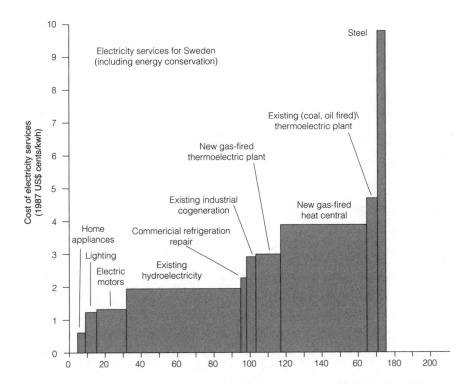

Figure 9.5 Energy supply curve for Sweden, including energy conservation, in US$ cents/kWh, at 6 per cent real discount rate (Schipper et al, 1989)

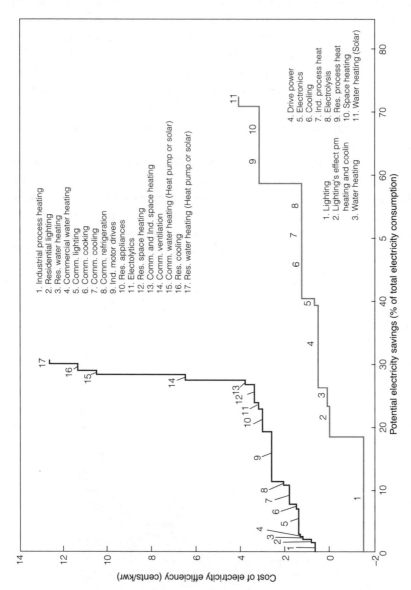

Figure 9.6 Energy supply curves for the US according to two sources: left, Electric Power Research Institute (EPRI); and right, Rocky Mountain Institute (RMI) (Fickett et al, 1990)

side is essential for the sustainability of energy systems, most energy supply companies are not interested in the subject because they believe that these measures would affect their revenue. Global abatement costs for CO_2 emissions for a number of options, including reforestation, have been calculated recently (Figure 9.7) and indicate that 27Gt CO_2 eq may be mitigated at a cost of less than €40 per CO_2 ton.

Barriers for emission reduction and overcoming policies

Historical evidence shows that there is a gap between the best pollution-reduction technology available and technologies used in practice. There is also a substantial difference between what industrial plants and existing equipment are capable of attaining in terms of efficiency and what is actually reached. These differences arise from a combination of two major factors:

- 'Hidden costs' of the technology used (such as less reliability, common in new systems) and the fact that the different technologies available do not exactly provide the same service (such as the comfort and freedom offered by privately-owned automobiles in comparison with urban public transport systems).
- 'Uncertainties' about future prices, lack of information, deficient decision-making processes, imperfect market structure and institutional weaknesses, including restrictive governmental regulations and property rights.

Besides that is the problem of delays and low adoption rates of new, more efficient technologies, which conceal the fact that low-income users have implicit discount rates that are much higher than nominal market discount rates. For example, it is estimated that consumers use implicit discount rates of 20 per cent on average to buy air conditioners, with a substantial variation according to income class. Discount rates varying from 45 per cent to 300 per cent for refrigerators are common. These factors help to understand why the global cost of energy efficiency policies (and consequently of climate change) is not simply the sum of the costs of technologies to reduce the emissions that cause them. It depends critically on the nature and on the type of new incentives that may result in additional costs. When taken into consideration, these incentives may generate double economic dividends that partially compensate for the additional costs of the technical measures adopted. The incentives used to overcome barriers and facilitate the adoption of technologies that result in emission reduction include:

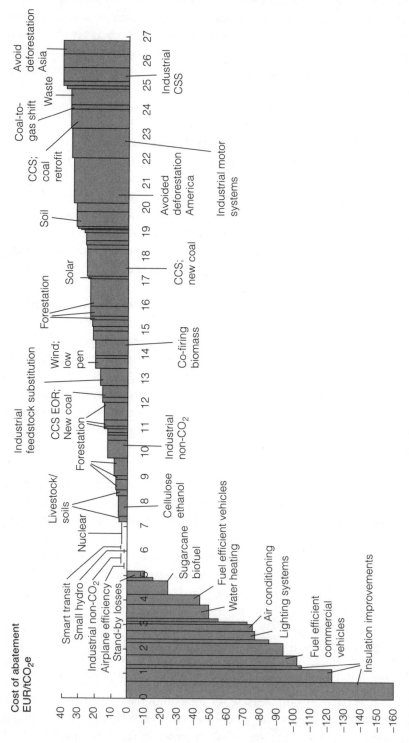

Figure 9.7 Global costs of additional measures for the abatement of greenhouse gases, in euros per ton of CO_2 equivalent and billions of CO_2 eq per year, 2030 horizon (Vattenfall, 2007)

- 'Exchanging emission rights', which constitute a decentralized method to convert a goal for global emissions of a pollutant into plans to reduce individual sources. In a typical example, a regulatory body specifies a maximum global limit for total emissions of a given pollutant. The regulatory body distributes a certain amount of licences for each allotted quota. Emitters are allowed, however, to negotiate licences among themselves. Emissions with low marginal reduction costs have an incentive to reduce their emissions so that they can sell their licences to companies with higher marginal reduction costs. The global goal is then accomplished at a reduced cost.
- 'Agreements negotiated with the industry' are highly favoured in the EU.
- 'Standards and labelling', largely used in industrialized countries, but not yet in developing countries.
- 'Research and development programmes', subsidized by the government or by the industry, which are very common in the US.
- 'Other incentives', such as accelerated depreciation provisions and reduced consumer bills to reflect energy conservation and economy.

The optimum combination of action programmes ultimately depends on the institutional context of the countries and the political acceptance of those measures. This combination varies among economic sectors and along time. An important priority in the early stages of implementation is the removal of existing barriers for the best technologies available. However, it is improbable that any significant change in technical and consumption standards will take place in the absence of price controls, be it by means of taxes, incentives or negotiable permissions to emit. This change will ultimately depend on the continuity of the policies, including trust in their long-term stability, in the elimination of profiteers, in the progressive character of their implementation and in the way the revenues generated by price controls is recycled in the economy.

Box 9.10 Vehicular standards

Vehicle efficiency and emission standards are important tools in policies for the environment, energy and public health. Since there are often conflicting interests that postpone decisions, international experience indicates that adopting the following principles is recommended (Energy Foundation, 2001):

Overeaching principles

1   Clean vehicle strategies should promote air quality (including air toxics) and greenhouse gas goals in parallel. Noise pollution should be considered as well.
2   Vehicles and fuels should be treated as a system.
3   New vehicle standards for greenhouse gas emissions and conventional pollutants should be fuel-neutral.
4   Policies should be based on full life-cycle emissions, including vehicle and fuel production, distribution and disposal.
5   Cost-effectiveness should be considered in achieving the goals.
6   Economic instruments should be used to promote clean, efficient vehicles and fuels.
7   Policies for clean vehicles should be mutually re-enforcing, not conflicting. For example, economic policy should support mandatory standards.
8   Clean transportation strategies should promote inherently clean vehicles.
9   New vehicle industries in developing countries should be based on new technology, and not be a dumping ground for old technology.
10 The recommendations in this paper also include vehicles and fuels that are especially important for developing countries (mopeds, tuk-tuks, buses, etc).
11 A truly effective programme will require the active involvement of government at the national, regional and municipal level.

Principles for fuels

1   Lead should be immediately banned in all fuels.
2   Near-zero sulphur (10ppm or less) should be introduced in all fuels except residual bunker fuel:
    a. Use longer time horizon, but stricter targets.
    b. Do in one step, not more.
3   Sulphur content in residual bunker fuel and heavy fuel oil should be significantly reduced worldwide, particularly in sensitive areas.
4   Benzene levels in gasoline should be capped at no more than 1 per cent worldwide. In addition, gasoline aromatic content should be controlled.
5   Compressed Natural Gas (CNG), Liquefied Petroleum Gas (LPG) and other alternative fuels need clear content standards for environmental performance; these standards should be set at the onset of a fuel's introduction.

Principles for conventional pollutants and yoxics – standards

1 Emissions standards worldwide should be based on the best available technology.
2 Future new vehicle standards should be fuel-neutral.
3 Vehicles that perform the same function should be required to meet the same standards, based on the capability of the leader, not the laggard.
4 Vehicle standards and fuel standards should be linked.
5 Particulate emissions standards should be designed to reduce the number of particles as well as the mass.

Principles for conventional pollutants and toxics – controlling emissions over the lifetime of the vehicles

6 Test procedures should reflect real-world operating conditions for all vehicles and engines.
7 Inspection and maintenance programmes should be used to control life-time in-use vehicle emissions. Programmes should separate inspection from repair, and post-inspection diagnostics should precede repair.
8 On-board diagnostic systems that identify failure modes and store failure data should be required for all new vehicles.
9 On-board measurement with real-time logs should be required for all new vehicles.
10 Manufacturers should be responsible for in-use (real-world) emissions in normal use.
11 Regulators should focus on in-use testing of heavy-duty vehicles. Upgrading the in-use fleet beyond what new vehicle standards and normal turnover can accomplish.
12 Cost-effective retrofit programmes should be established for all vehicles. Retrofit standards must be matched by appropriate fuel standards (e.g. low-sulphur, no-lead gasoline). Testing must be done to verify efficacy of retrofit programmes.
13 Scrappage and other policies should be used to speed fleet turnover.

Principles for greenhouse gases

1 Measures to reduce greenhouse gas emissions from all vehicles (including at least 25 per cent average reduction for new personal

passenger vehicles over the next decade) should be adopted. Mechanisms could include:

- voluntary agreements with manufacturer;
- fuel efficiency standards;
- tailpipe greenhouse gas standards; and
- financial incentives.

2 Reduction measures should be designed to avoid promoting increases in size, weight or power.
3 Effective strategies should be undertaken to reduce the climate impact of emissions from aviation and freight transportation.
4 Other greenhouse gases should be reduced in concert with CO_2 reductions.

Principles for advanced technology

1 Governments should have strong advanced technology programmes that reflect clear sustainable development goals.
2 Programmes should be designed to reduce conventional pollutants, greenhouse gases, toxics and noise together, not one at the expense of the other.
3 These programmes must have clear performance targets.
4 Such programmes should not be a substitute for taking action in the short-term, but a complement.
5 Evaluation of technologies should consider:

- life-cycle analysis – including fuel and vehicle production and disposal;
- real-world performance over the full vehicle lifetime;
- whether the technology is inherently clean;
- potential for market saturation.

6 As technologies progress from research to development, their potential for commercialization should be emphasized. Safety, quality and public acceptance are key factors.
7 Both standards and market incentives should be used to commercialize advanced technologies.
8 Government policies should encourage the introduction of incremental technologies as they are developed.
9 Programmes to develop new technologies should be coordinated across jurisdictions to help develop economies of scale.

Control of deforestation

Deforestation is a recurring subject in international multilateral negotiations. In general, developed countries are reluctant to offer economic incentives to revert the deforestation process and prefer to make use of commercial instruments or establish sanctions (Box 9.11). Reacting to this, developing countries, especially Brazil, claim that primary forests in Europe have been destroyed long ago (Figures 9.8a, b) and that CO_2 historical emissions predominantly derive from industrialized countries (Figure 9.9). In fact, Brazil still has 69.4 per cent of its primary forests (4.4M km^2), whereas in Europe the percentage is 0.3 per cent and in North America it is 34.4 per cent (Embrapa/CNPM, 2006).

The principles involved in this dispute are those of the '*polluter-pays principle*' (those who have caused damage should repair it) and of *common but differentiated responsibilities* (all should repair the damage, but according to their contribution to the total impact). Developed countries state that climate change issues have only recently been acknowledged, which would exempt them from their historic responsibility and would determine that all should act in the same way from now on. This impasse in negotiations may be interesting from a commercial point of view, but not in terms of global sustainability. In the same way as greenhouse gas emissions from burning fuels must be reduced, some effective measures must be taken to reduce deforestation. Almost a third of the remaining primary forests of the world are in Brazil (Figure 9.10) and deforestation is one of the major sources of greenhouse gases.

As mentioned, there is very close interlinking between topics of environment, development and trade. Trade and the environment are closely related topics, since they refer to 'individual' production (exports) and to 'common' (natural) resources. Behind all those principles, however, there are frequently market protectionist instruments, mainly in agriculture but also in industry, for the fear of causing the loss of jobs to countries with cheap labour. On the other extreme, there is the socio-environmental dumping, that is, exportation of products and services that use child labour or cause the destruction of sensitive ecosystems (Box 9.11).

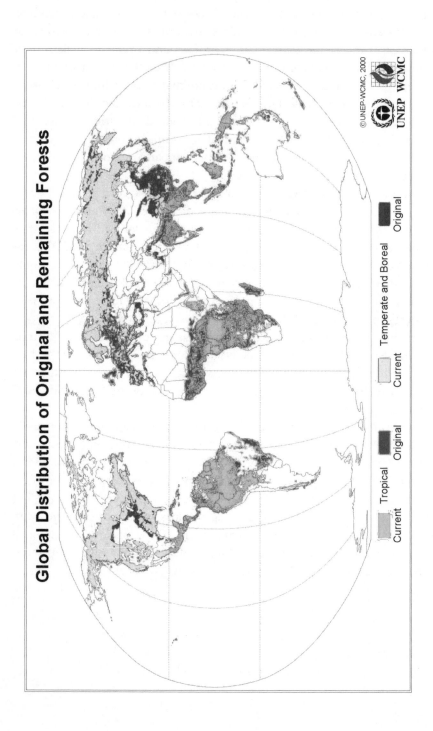

Global Distribution of Original and Remaining Forests

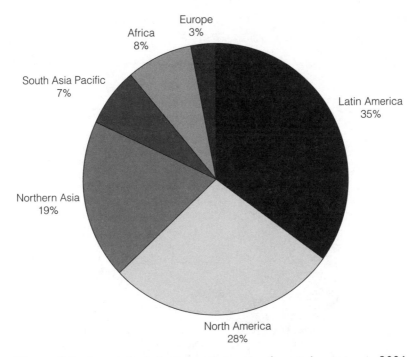

Figure 9.8a (opposite), b. Remaining native forests by region in 2006 (Embrapa/CNPM, 2006; UNEP, 2008a)

Box 9.11 Trade and the environment

In negotiations at the WTO, OECD countries, especially the EU, are adopting social and environmental clauses in their regional commercial agreements (OECD, 2006 and 2007). There is a vast array of possible actions, from 'dialogues' to commercial sanctions, such as technical barriers to exports that disregard social and environmental rules. Developing countries have opposed the US attempt to incorporate working practices into commercial agreements. The same happened in relation to the EU, in 2003, concerning the introduction of social and environmental rules in the global agenda. A WTO landmark was the 2001 Ministerial Declaration, signed in Doha, Qatar. This document acknowledges the importance of considering sustainability aspects and access to markets in commercial negotiations, so as to provide more favourable conditions for developing countries. Paragraph 31 of the Declaration deals with the relationship between international trade and multilateral environmental agreements (MEAs, such as the Kyoto Protocol

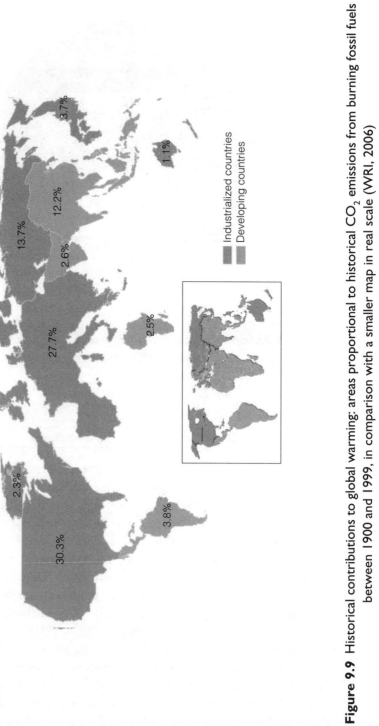

Figure 9.9 Historical contributions to global warming: areas proportional to historical CO_2 emissions from burning fossil fuels between 1900 and 1999, in comparison with a smaller map in real scale (WRI, 2006)

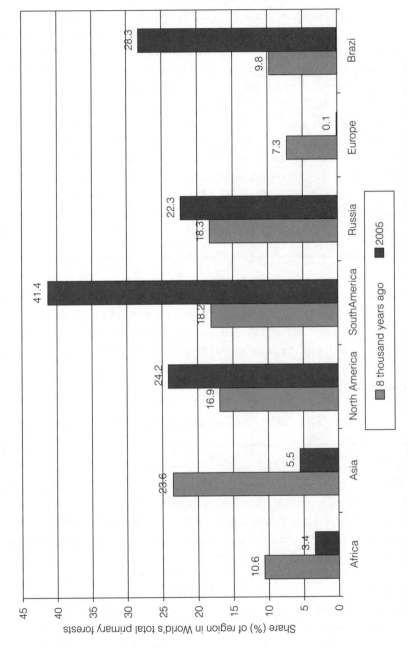

Figure 9.10 Regional shares in total original primary forest cover (EMBRAPA/CNPM, 2006)

and the Biodiversity Convention), and the so-called environmental goods and services, which should be given preferential treatment. The list of those goods and services is the subject of discussions among the different groups of countries: whereas the OECD proposes a list including pollution control technologies and services, developing countries try to expand it to include topics such as eco-tourism and biofuels (Lucon and Rei, 2006). According to environmentalists, the negotiations of paragraph 31 of the WTO Doha Declaration should, in theory, have a more comprehensive and unified focus, based on mutual concessions, but in practice discussions are fragmented, carried out on the basis of economic bargains (Pfahl, 2004). Besides agriculture and environmental assets and services, there are other important issues in the WTO agenda, such as intellectual rights (e.g. technology royalties for wind turbines). Among developing countries, several meetings are taking place with the aim of promoting (South–South) cooperation for the dissemination of ethanol as a biofuel (Coelho et al, 2006).

The Kyoto Protocol Clean Development Mechanism (CDM) may be one of the solutions, but the operationalization of its rules for changing soil and forest is not clearly defined yet. Moreover, CDM involvement represents a minute part so far of the necessary abatements (Box 9.12). Therefore, additional measures are urgently needed, including an international agreement on deforestation.

Box 9.12 Stabilization wedges and assimilation inertia

The ultimate objective of the UN Framework Convention on Climate Change is to achieve stabilization of greenhouse gas concentrations in the atmosphere at a level that would prevent dangerous anthropogenic interference with the climate system. Such a level should be achieved within a time frame sufficient to allow ecosystems to adapt naturally to climate change, to ensure that food production is not threatened and to enable economic development to proceed in a sustainable manner. This is graphically represented in Figure 9.11, where CO_2 concentration in the atmosphere (in 500ppm) is associated with greenhouse gas emissions. Between 1954 and 2004, the annual emissions of greenhouse gases have increased from little less than two to seven billion tons of carbon equivalent (Gt Ceq). In order to keep CO_2 concentrations in the atmosphere around 500ppm, it is necessary that by 2050 a total 175Gt Ceq be abated (mitigated) by all possible means, such as the recovery of forests, widespread use of renewable energy and an increase in energy efficiency, among others. If nothing is done and present emission tendencies continue (business-as-usual), CO_2 concentrations will reach around 850ppm in 2054, seriously affecting the Earth's climate balance.

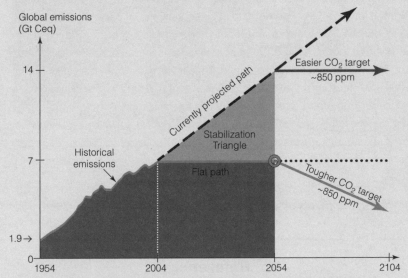

Figure 9.11 Schematic representation of the relationship between global emissions of greenhouse gases and CO_2 concentrations in the atmosphere (Pacala and Socolow, 2004)

By 2012, 28Gt Ceq should be abated, a figure that represents nearly 70 times the overall result expected by the Climate Convention Executive Board for the Clean Development Mechanism for that date, which was about 0.71Gt Ceq (2.6Gt CO_2 eq) distributed in 2800 projects, according to the CDM Executive Board (as of 19 December 2007, UNFCCC, 2006). At an estimated cost of US$100 per ton of carbon equivalent, mitigating 175Gt eq in 50 years would demand US$17.5 trillion. As a comparison, the global GDP was US$65 trillion in the year 2006 alone (CIA, 2007). A consensus for urgent and efficient solutions is undoubtedly necessary. The sooner they are adopted, the less significant the impacts and the lower the costs to avoid them. Inertia should always be taken into account: a new technology takes time to be put into practice and it takes even more time for natural systems to assimilate their beneficial impacts (Figure 9.12).

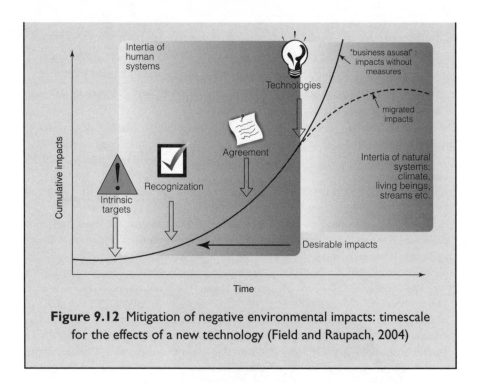

Figure 9.12 Mitigation of negative environmental impacts: timescale for the effects of a new technology (Field and Raupach, 2004)

References

Bonneville Power Administration (1990) '1990 Resource Plan', Portland, Oregon

Burniaux, J. M. and Martins, J. O. (1992) 'The Effect of Existing Distortions in Energy Markets on the Cost of Policies to Reduce CO_2 Emissions', OECD Economic Studies, vol. 19, Paris

CIA (2007) Factbook, www.cia.gov

Cline, W. (1992) The Economics of Global Warming, The Institute of International Economics, Washington DC

Coelho, S. T., Lucon, O. and Guardabassi, P. (2006) 'Biofuels: Advantages and Trade Barriers'. UNCTAD, Geneva, www.unctad.org/en/docs/ditcted20051_en.pdf

Embrapa/CNPM (2006) 'Embargo Ambiental Ameaça Exportações do Agronegócio', Folha de S. Paulo, 10.12.2006, pB8

Energy Foundation (2001) Bellagio Memorandum on Motor Vehicle Policy. Principles for Vehicles and Fuels in Response to Global Environmental and Health Imperatives. Consensus Document: 19–21 June, Bellagio, Italy, http://www.theicct.org/documents/bellagio_english.pdf

Fankhauser, S. (1992) 'Global Warming Damage Costs: Some Monetary Estimates', Centre for Social and Economic Research on the Global Environment (CSERGE), University College, London Global Environment Change Working Papers – GEC-92-2a

Fankhauser, S. (1993) 'Global Warming Damage Costs: Some Monetary Estimates', Centre for Social and Economic Research on the Global Environment (CSERGE), University College, London Global Environment Change Working Papers – GEC 93

Fickett, A. P., Gellings, C. W. and Lovins, A. B. (1990) 'Efficient Use of Electricity', Scientific American, September, pp65–74. *Apud* Leonardo Energy, www.leonardo-energy.org/drupal/monthly_archive/2007/01

Field, C. B. and Raupach, M. R. (2004) *The Global Carbon Cycle: Integrating Humans, Climate, and the Natural World*. SCOPE 62. Scientific Committee on Problems of the Environment, www.icsu-scope.org

Habbard, H. M. (1991) 'The Real Cost of Energy', /Scientific American/264(9), pp36–42

Insurance Journal (2005a) Munich Re Analyzes Katrina/Rita Impact; Insured Loss Around $40 Billion, www.insurancejournal.com/news/international/2005/09/28/60241.htm

Insurance Journal (2005b) RMS Total Economic Loss for Katrina at $100 Billion+ www.insurancejournal.com/news/national/2005/09/02/59111.htm

IPCC (2007) Adaptation. Summary for policymakers, Contribution of Working Group II to the Fourth Assessment Report of the Intergovernmental Panel on Climate Change, www.ipcc.ch/pdf/assessment-report/ar4/wg2/ar4-wg2-spm.pdf

Lucon, O. and Rei, F. C. F. (2006) 'Identifying Complementary Measures to Ensure the Maximum Realisation of Benefits from the Liberalisation of Trade in Environmental Goods and Services, Case Study: Brazil'. OECD Trade an Environment Working Paper no. 2004-04, OECD, Paris, www.oecd.org/dataoecd/18/53/37325499.pdf

Lusinchi, M. (2002) 'Dérivés chlorés dans l'environnement'. Planetecologie, www.planetecologie.org/ENCYCLOPEDIE/RubriqueMois/ChloreEnvt/Dioxineset Furanes.htm

MDIC (2006) Ministério do Desenvolvimento, Indústria e Comércio Exterior, www.mdic.gov.br

Nordhaus, W. D. (1993) 'Climate and Economic Development – Climates Past and Climate Change Future', in *Proceedings of the World Bank Annual Conference and Development Economics*, Washington DC, pp355–376.

OECD (2006) Environment and Trade, www.oecd.org/department/0,2688,en_2649_34183_1_1_1_1_1,00.html

OECD (2007) OECD in 2007 Figures, Environmental data compendium, www.oecd.org/document/19/0,3343,en_2825_495628_39503891_1_1_1_1,00.html

Pacala, S. and Socolow, R. (2004) 'Stabilization Wedges: Solving the Climate Problem for the Next 50 Years with Current Technologies', Science 305, pp968-971

Pfahl, S. (2004) 'The new EU approach to the WTO negotiations related to MEAs – Para 31(i) DDA, global governance and the need to address the MEA – trade linkage in the UN-System'. Friends of the Earth Europe, Greenpeace & German NGO Forum on Environment & Development Working Group on Trade

Schecter, A. (2001) 'Levels of Dioxin in US Food Supply (1995)', *Journal of Toxicology and Environmental Health*, Part A, 63: pp1–18

Schipper, L., Barlett, S., Dianne, H. and Vince, E. (1989) 'Linking Life-Styles and Energy Use: A Matter of Time?', Annual Review of Energy and Environment, 14, pp273–320

Stern, N. (2006) Review on the Economics of Climate Change, www.hm-treasury.gov.uk/independent_reviews/stern_review_economics_climate_change/ster nreview_index.cfm

UN (1997) Earth Summit – UN Conference on Environment and Development, www.un.org/geninfo/bp/enviro.html

UN (2008) UN Conference on Environment and Development – UNCED, www.oecd.org/document/19/0,3343,en_2825_495628_39503891_1_1_1_1,00.html

UNDP, UNDESA, WEC (2004) World Energy Assessment 2004 Update

UNEP (1992) The World Environment 1972–1992, M. K. Tolba (ed.), UNEP, Chapman and Hall, London

UNEP (2002) '*A Guide to Emissions Trading*' ISBN: 87-550-3150-1, www.unep.org

UNEP (2006) Geo Yearbook 2006, http://www.unep.org/geo/yearbook/yb2006/

UNEP (2008a) Geo Yearbook 2008, UN Environmental Programme, www.unep.org/geo/yearbook/yb2008/

UNEP (2008b) Multilateral Environmental Agreements (MEAs), www.unep.fr/shared/publications/cdrom/DTIx0899xPA/session03_%20Introduction_to_MEAs.ppt#256,1

UNFCCC (2006) CDM Executive Board Statistics, http://cdm.unfccc.int/Statistics

US EPA (2006) Acid Rain Program, US Environmental, www.epa.gov/airmarkets/arp

US EPA (2008) Cap and Trade, Clean Air Markets, Office of Air and Radiation, US Environmental Protection Agency, http://epa.gov/airmarkets/cap-trade/index.html

Vattenfall (2007) 'Global Mapping of Greenhouse Gas, Abatement Opportunities up to 2030'. Executive summary. Vattenfall's Global Climate Impact Abatement Map, 18 January 2007

World Bank (2006) Persistent Organic Pollutants, http://web.worldbank.org/WBSITE/EXTERNAL/TOPICS/ENVIRONMENT/EXTPOPS/0,,contentMDK:20487906menuPK:1165805pagePK:148956piPK:216618~theSitePK:408121,00.html

WRI (2006) Contributions to Global Warming, images.wri.org/map_cartogram_global_warming_large.gif

WTO (2008) An introduction to trade and environment in the WTO. World Trade Organization, www.wto.org/english/tratop_e/envir_e/envt_intro_e.htm

Chapter 10

World Energy Trends

The world energy consumption grew by an average 2.2 per cent annually between 1971 and 2006; in developed countries by 1.4 per cent and in developing countries by 3.2 per cent. These differences were more marked in 2006, when consumption grew by 2.7 per cent globally; 8.5 per cent in developing countries and −0.2 per cent in the OECD region. As shown in Figure 10.1, the energy consumption in the OECD countries stabilized from 2000 onwards and was recently surpassed by non-OECD members.

If the present composition of sources remains unaltered, significant environmental problems will occur, particularly climate change caused mainly by CO_2 emissions from fossil fuels. In developing countries, energy consumption has increased rapidly and will continue to grow in future due to population growth and economic factors – political independence, integration to the world economy and access to information. For some developing countries, especially sub-Saharan Africa, population growth (Box 10.1) will be the dominant factor. The combination of population increase and economic factors has increased commercial energy consumption by about 4 per cent a year in developing countries during the last two decades, that is, a duplication in consumption every 17 years.

Box 10.1 Populational growth

Population growth is one of the major determinant factors of the increase in energy consumption. Between 1850 and 1990 the average annual population growth was 1.1 per cent and the total energy consumption was 2.2 per cent (Figure 10.2).

The IEA projects a world population of about 8.2 billion people in 2030. World population is assumed to grow at an annual average rate of 1 per cent, from an estimated 6.5 billion in 2006 to 8.2 billion in 2030. Population growth slows progressively over the projection period in line with past trends: population expanded by 1.4 per cent per year from 1990 to 2006. The population from non-OECD countries as a group continues to grow more rapidly.

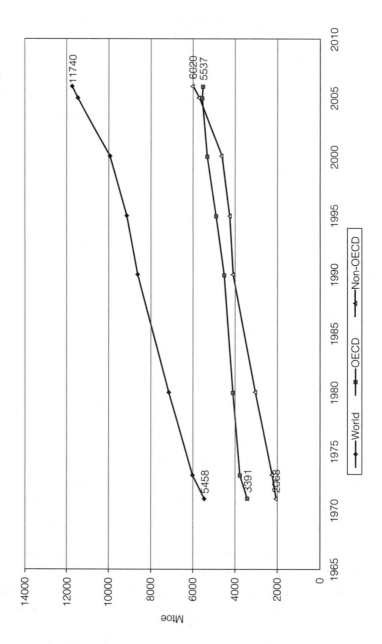

Figure 10.1 Primary energy in OECD, in developing countries and in the world, from IEA (2008) data

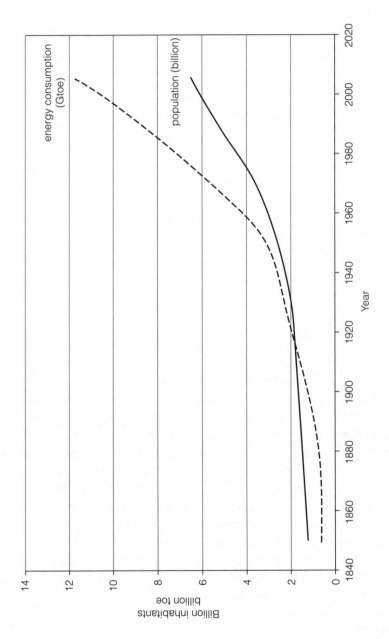

Figure 10.2 Population and energy use; data from Holdren (1991), updated with IEA (2008)

According to Figure 10.3, the main causes of population growth are:

- unwanted pregnancy;
- demand for a large family to work; and
- population momentum, a consequence of a young population age structure.

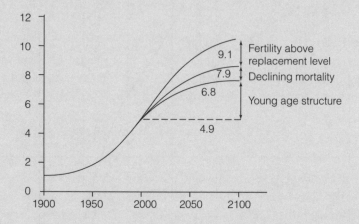

Figure 10.3 Causes of population growth (Bongaarts, 1999)

It is possible to lower the population in the year 2100 from 10.2 to 8.3 billion by strengthening family planning programmes to reduce unwanted pregnancies. Reducing the demand for large families by investments in human development may lead to a further reduction from 8.3 to 7.3 billion in 2100. The population momentum may slow if the pregnancy average age is increased. An additional reduction of 7.3 to 6.1 billion in 2100 could be achieved by increasing the timing of the next pregnancy by five years. All these reductions are theoretical limits above what can be attained and indicate possible action for achieving a real reduction in population growth in the next century. As is well known, developed countries have undergone 'demographic transitions' leading to the current situation in which the total fertility rate (TFR) is approximately two – the population replacement rate. These predicted levels of a decrease in the TFR are very complex and synergistic in nature. Developing countries are expected to follow a similar trend.

Projections

Two of the leading references in energy projections, issued annually, are:

1 the World Energy Outlook (WEO) from the International Energy Agency (IEA, 2008d) of the OECD; and
2 the International Energy Outlook (IEO), from the Energy Information Administration of the US Department of Energy (EIA-DoE, 2008).

The IEA scenarios are reasonably reliable and, in a way, coherent with those of the IPCC and the Stern Report on the impacts of climate changes. It is important to stress that long-term projections are subjected to huge variations as a result of a small change in premises (Box 10.2).

Box 10.2 Trend analysis methodologies

Energy projections are important tools for policymaking and market analysis. They work with the possibilities of what might happen (tendencies, rather than specific real-world outcomes), given the specific assumptions and methodologies used. Model premises should as much as possible be policy-neutral, unbiased and provide reliability in the final results. Such models are abstractions of energy production and consumption activities, regulatory activities, and producer and consumer behaviour.

Statistical trends based on past data pose risks of becoming too simplistic. Projections are highly dependent on the data, analytical methodologies, model structures and specific assumptions used in their development. Among other input data, two of the most important are population and gross domestic product. Also, indicators are used that relate these inputs to energy use and carbon emissions.

Even with good quality data and well understood trends, there will always be uncertainties, especially long term. Examples are removal or introduction of subsidies and technology improvements. Many events that shape energy markets are random and cannot be anticipated, and assumptions concerning future technology characteristics, demographics and resource availability are necessarily uncertain. For this reason, outlooks should not have a long timeframe (ideally less than 30 years), but enough for model-oriented actions to take place. Usually, they are built scenarios, considering high or low economic growth, consumption, emissions or environmental and resource constraints.

Table 10.1 Assumptions: average populational and GDP growth rates (% per year) according to the IEA World Energy Outlook (2008) and the EIA-DoE International Energy Outlook (2008)

Region	Population		GDP			
	IEA 2006–30 All scenarios	EIA-DoE 2005–30 All scenarios	IEA 2006–30 Reference scenario	Reference scenario	EIA-DoE 2005–30 High economic growth scenario	Low economic growth scenario
OECD	0.4	0.4	2.0	2.3	2.8	1.8
North America	0.8	0.8	2.2	2.6	3.0	2.0
US	0.8	0.8	2.1	2.5	3.0	1.9
Europe	0.2	0.2	1.9	2.3	2.7	1.8
Pacific	-0.1	-0.1	1.6	1.8	2.3	1.4
Japan	-0.3	-0.3	1.2	1.1	1.5	0.6
Non-OECD	1.1	1.1	4.8	5.2	5.7	4.8
Eastern Europe-Eurasia	-0.2	-0.2	3.7	4.4	4.8	3.9
Russia	-0.6	-0.6	3.6	4.0	4.5	3.5
Asia	0.9	0.9	5.7	5.8	6.2	5.3
China	0.4	0.4	6.1	6.4	6.8	5.9
India	1.1	1.1	6.4	5.8	6.2	5.3
Middle East	1.7	1.7	4.3	4.0	4.5	3.6
Africa	2.0	2.0	4.1	4.5	5.0	4.0
Latin America	1.0	1.0	3.1	3.9	4.7	3.5
Brazil	0.9	0.9	3.0	3.6	4.0	3.1
World	1.0	1.0	3.3	3.0	4.4	3.5

The WEO2008's historical data are from 2006; the IEO2008's are from 2005. With projections extended to 2030, both focus on commercial energy, although non-commercial energy sources play an important role in some developing countries. Countries are grouped according to the OECD and non-OECD members.[1]

Several scenarios were constructed to foresee the combination of several sources of energy that will be needed in the next decades. The *Reference Scenario* gives the populational trends of current incomes and energy prices, as well as the present energy policies assumed. Tables 10.1 and 10.2 give an idea of such assumptions.

The growth rate in world GDP – the main driver of energy demand in all regions – averaged 3.2 per cent from 1990 to 2006 and was assumed by the IEA to average 3.3 per cent per year over the period 2006–30, reflecting the rising weight in the world's fast-growing economies of non-OECD countries. The average growth rate nonetheless falls progressively over the projection period, from 4.2 per cent in 2006–15 to 2.8 per cent in 2015–30, remaining high in China, India and the Middle East.

The effects of the late-2008 financial crisis are not reflected in these assumptions and their long-term repercussions are impossible to predict. Fuel prices may be affected, changing the assumptions made for the WEO2008 and the IEO2008.

The IEA Reference Scenario embodies the effects of policies and measures that were enacted or adopted by mid-2008, even though many of them have not yet been fully implemented. Table 10.3 presents results by region and Table 10.4 the results by fuel and global sector.

Table 10.2 Fossil energy (real term, 2007 US$ per unit) prices, scenario assumptions

Fuel	Region	Scenario	2007		2030	
			IEA	EIA-DoE	IEA	EIA-DoE
Oil						
(barrel)	World	Reference	69.3	72.3	122.0	113.1
		Low price				68.9
		High price				185.7
Natural Gas (MBtu)	US	Reference	6.8		16.1	
	Europe		7.0		14.2	
	Japan (LNG)		7.8		16.1	
Steam coal (ton)	OECD		72.8		110.0	

Table 10.3 Total energy demand and final electricity consumption; IEA reference scenario in selected regions

Region	Energy consumption (Mtoe)		Growth (% per year)	Electricity consumption (TWh)		Growth (% per year)
	2006	2030		2006	2030	
OECD	5536	6180	0.5	9035	11,843	1.1
North America	2768	3180	0.6	4413	5774	1.1
US	2319	2566	0.4	3723	4723	1.0
Europe	1884	2005	0.3	3022	3980	1.2
Pacific	884	995	0.5	1601	2089	1.1
Non-OECD	6011	10,604	2.4	6630	16,298	3.8
Eastern Europe-Eurasia	1118	1454	1.1	1165	1860	2.0
Russia	668	859	1.1	682	1081	1.9
Asia	3227	6325	2.8	3669	10,589	4.5
China	1898	3885	3.0	2358	6958	4.6
India	566	1280	3.5	506	1935	5.7
Middle East	522	1106	3.2	539	1353	3.9
Africa	614	857	1.4	479	997	3.1
Latin America	530	862	2.0	777	1498	2.8
World	11,730	17,014	1.6	15,665	28,141	2.5

Alternative scenarios are also presented in these reports:

- the IEA WEO2008 (database year 2006) presents energy scenarios for the case of actions aimed at stabilizing carbon concentrations in the atmosphere at levels considered safe (550 and 450 parts per million of CO_2; the latter is more ambitious and therefore requires more effort than the previous one);
- the US EIA-DoE IEO2008 (database year 2005) presents energy trends for high and low economic growth cases, and paths for different perspectives of future regional gross domestic products (GDP). The IEO2008 also considers a high energy price case and, alternatively, a low price case, not included in this book. This report also shows analyses by fuel (oil, gas, coal, nuclear, renewables) and sector (industry, transport and other).

Scenario outcomes are summarized in Table 10.5.

Table 10.4 IEA reference scenario results by fuel and main sectors, World

World, IEA ref	Total energy demand			Power generation			Industry			Transport*			Other sectors (residential, commerce, services)		
	2006	2030	Growth (% year)	2006	2030	Growth (% year)	2006	2030	Growth (% year)	2006	2030	Growth (% year)	2006	2030	Growth (% year)
Shares (%)															
Coal	26	29	2.0	47	47	2.0	25	25	1.8				4	3	-0.5
Oil	34	30	1.0	6	3	-1.3	15	12	0.7	94	92	1.4	16	14	0.7
Gas	21	22	1.8	21	23	2.4	20	18	1.4				20	20	1.2
Nuclear	6	5	0.9	16	13	0.9	26	32	2.7				26	34	2.3
Hydro	2	2	1.9	6	6	1.9	5	4	0.7				5	5	1.1
Biomass and wastes	10	10	1.4	2	4	5.4	9	9	1.9	1	4	6.8	28	22	0.3
Other renewables	1	2	7.2	1	4	7.1	0	0	7.8				0	2	7.4
Total (Mtoe)	11,730	17,014	1.6	4424	7130	2.0	2181	3322	1.8	98	137		2937	3918	1.2

* Remaining shares in transport correspond to non-specified 'other fuels'

Table 10.5 IEA WEO2008 and EIA-DoE IEO2008 results for total energy demand, electricity and energy-related CO_2 emissions, by region

Region	Source and type of data		Year	Energy demand Mtoe	Electricity consumption 1000 TWh	Energy-related CO_2 emissions		
						Gt	Tons per capita	Tons per million, 2000 US$ (PPP)
OECD	IEA	B	2006	5536	9.0	12.8	10.8	–
	EIA-DoE	B	2005	6071	9.9	13.6	11.6	461
	IEA	R	2030	6180	11.8	13.2	10.1	–
	EIA-DoE	R		7205	13.5	15.5	12.0	296
	EIA-DoE	L		6619	na	14.2	11.0	–
	EIA-DoE	H		7842	na	16.9	13.1	–
Non-OECD	IEA	B	2006	6011	6.6	14.1	2.6	–
	EIA-DoE	B	2005	5577	7.5	14.5	2.7	529
	IEA	R	2030	10,604	16.3	26.0	3.8	–
	EIA-DoE	R		10,302	19.7	26.8	3.8	274
	EIA-DoE	L		9291	na	24.2	3.4	–
	EIA-DoE	H		11,433	na	29.7	4.2	–

World							
IEA	B	2006	11,730	15.7	27.9	4.3	–
EIA-DoE	B	2005	11,647	17.3	28.1	4.3	494
IEA	R	2030	17,014	28.1	40.6	4.9	–
IEA	X		15,483	30.2	31.6	3.8	–
IEA	Y		14,361	29.0	24.5	3.0	–
EIA-DoE	R		17,506	33.3	42.3	5.1	282
EIA-DoE	L		15,909	na	38.4	4.6	–
EIA-DoE	H		19,275	na	46.6	5.6	–

Note: (B) baseline; (R) reference scenario; (L) low-economic growth alternative scenario; (H) high-economic growth alternative scenario; (X) carbon stabilization 550ppm CO_2 policy alternative scenario; and (Y) 450ppm CO_2 policy alternative scenario

Conclusions from the outlooks

Several conclusions can be drawn from the IEA WEO2008 and EIA-DoE IEO2008. Both reports have very similar baseline data, which facilitates comparison.

For the year 2030, the IEA reference scenario leads to lower levels of energy consumption than the EIA-DoE reference case. This may be attributed to the fact that the WEO considers the effect of ongoing policies, while the IEO is based more on economic forecasts.

The alternative scenarios have high levels of energy consumption and carbon emissions. Reference and high economic growth paths are not environmentally sustainable, and therefore urgent and ambitious energy savings and greenhouse gas mitigation actions are necessary. In both cases, the major threats related to energy are adequate prices, secure supply and environmental damage caused by excessive consumption.

The development pathway of non-OECD countries still follows the Kuznet's curve, instead of leapfrogging gains already achieved by OECD nations. Non-OECD energy consumption overtook that of the OECD in 2005 and the share will be 62 per cent by 2030. Non-OECD countries account for 87 per cent of the increase in the world primary energy demand between 2006 and 2030. China and India account for just over half of this increase.

Globally, fossil fuels will remain the predominant source of energy for a long time. In particular, oil is the world's vital source of energy and will remain so for many years to come, despite the most optimistic assumptions about the pace of development and deployment of alternative technology. Oil prices, an important factor for global economic health, will grow systematically. The inelasticity of oil demand in terms of prices will also grow. Rising oil prices will be followed by those of natural gas and, in a smaller proportion, by coal. These factors increase the potential impacts of a disruption in supply.

Global primary demand for oil (excluding biofuels) rises by 1 per cent per year on average; demand for natural gas (mostly for power generation) grows more quickly, by 1.8 per cent per year; coal advances by 2 per cent a year on average, and nuclear power in primary energy demand edges down (to 5 per cent by 2030). Modern renewable technologies grow more rapidly, overtaking gas to become the second-largest source of electricity, behind coal, soon after 2010. Wind, solar, geothermal, tide and wave energy together grow faster than any other source worldwide, at an average rate of 7.2 per cent per year over the projection period. The share of non-hydro renewables in total power generation grows from 1 per cent in 2006 to 4 per cent in 2030 (hydropower output increases, though its share of electricity drops to 14 per cent). However, to achieve these results, massive investments in energy infrastructure will be needed (over 2007, US$26 trillion in 2007–30).

In the reference scenarios, CO_2 emissions will increase 1.6 per cent per year (IEA) to 1.7 per cent per year (EIA-DoE); developing countries will account for the bulk of this increase, although their per capita emissions will be less than those of the OECD.

According to the EIa-DoE report, under a low economic growth alternative scenario, the energy consumption is 9 per cent below the reference scenario baseline. Reduction is of 1.6Gtoe, a figure equivalent to 87 per cent of the consumption of the European Union in 2006.

Environmentally sustainable IEA alternative scenarios (500ppm and 450ppm) foresee that the demand for energy by 2030 is up to 16 per cent less than that of the reference scenario. Savings of 4.9Gtoe are approximately the consumption of the US, China, India and Brazil together in 2006. The 450ppm Policy Scenario (IEA) assumes much stronger and broader policy action from 2020 onwards, inducing quicker development and deployment of low-carbon technologies; the scale of the challenge is immense and profound shifts in energy demand and supply in the two climate-policy scenarios call for huge increases in spending on new capital stock, especially in power plants and in more energy-efficient equipment and appliances.

For all the uncertainties highlighted in the predictions, the energy world will be much changed in 2030 compared with today.

Technological change

Technological changes altering the penetration of the energy sources (Box 10.3) are key factors to achieve long-term sustainability.

Box 10.3 Rise and fall of the different primary energy sources

The use of primary energy sources has evolved since 1860, according to Figure 10.4, which shows that wood – the main source of energy until then – was replaced by coal, dominant until 1920, then gradually replaced by oil and gas. The extrapolation after 2000 is simply indicative: the priority is to establish the rate at which new sources of energy and associated technologies will replace the old ones and what can be done to accelerate the change.

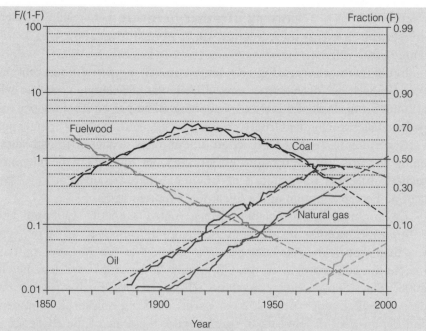

Figure 10.4 Historic curves of market penetration for different sources of energy (Nakicenovic, 1997)

The International Institute for Applied Systems Analysis (IIASA) and the World Energy Council collaborated on a study of social, economic and technological development scenarios (WEC, 1993). The 'ecological' scenario incorporates simultaneous policies for economic growth and for environmental protection, presenting the conditions for achieving a high degree of sustainability and equity in the world, with a new global energy matrix, and with a higher share of renewable sources growing significantly after 2050 due to the contribution of solar technologies (Figure 10.5).

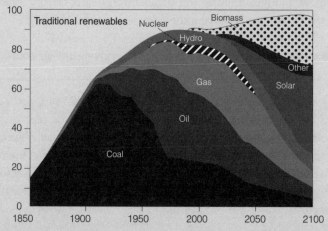

Figure 10.5 'Ecological' scenario (UNDP, UNDESA, WEC, 2004)

Energy intensity trends

The evolution in energy intensity (energy per income, I = E/GDP) along time reflects the combined effect of structural changes in the economy, in the composition of energy sources and in the efficiency in energy use. Despite being acknowledged as a very rough indicator, energy intensity has some attractive characteristics: whereas energy and the GDP per capita vary by more than one order of magnitude among the developed and developing countries, energy intensity does not change by more than a factor of two (Figure 10.6).

The factors determining the evolution of energy intensity are:

- dematerialization;
- fuel use intensity; and
- recycling.

Dematerialization of economy

Dematerialization of economy means using less material for the same end. An example of this is the use of glass fibre to replace copper in telephone transmission lines. Other examples are the replacement of steel by polymers in automobiles, or thinner sheets with higher resistance alloys to replace thicker sheets of conventional steel. In the US, the participation of basic materials in the GNP decreased by nearly 30 per cent since 1970 (Figure 10.7).

Fuel use intensity

Fuel use intensity measures the amount of energy necessary to manufacture a given product (as, for example, the fuel used per ton of steel or the power used per kilogram of polyethylene). Table 10.6 provides typical values of energy intensity for some basic materials, foreseen and achieved. In most cases, forecasts were exceeded.

Table 10.6 Improvement in fuel use intensity (Hollander, 1992)

Industry sector	Expected (%/year)	Achieved (%/year)
Steel	0.9–2.4	2.1
Chemical products	0.6–1.7	3.4
Paper	1.3–2.2	4.7
Oil	0.5–0.9	2.5

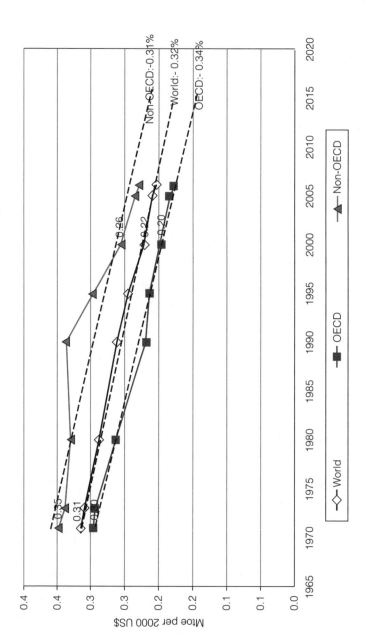

Figure 10.6 Energy intensity: primary energy over the GDP by the purchase parity power, linear trends and their slopes (data from IEA, 2008a, b)

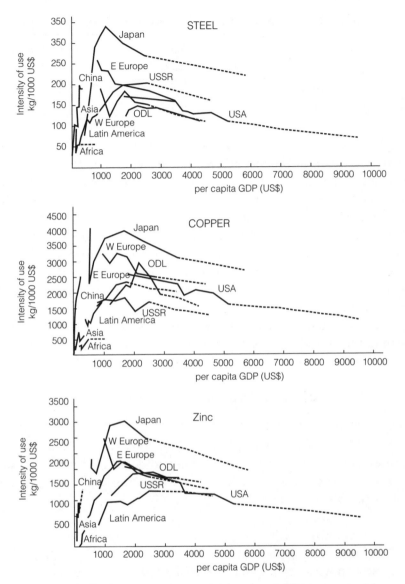

Figure 10.7 Evolution in intensity in the use of different materials

Recycling

The decarbonization of economy (Box 10.4) is a consequence of its dematerialization. *Recycling* expands the concept of dematerialization and, if taken to its limits, will effectively contribute to a decrease in pollution. Table 10.7 shows that the energy necessary for recycling a few basic materials is usually smaller than that necessary to produce them from the raw material. However, in some cases, recycling is not technically or economically viable.

Table 10.7 Energy spent in material recycling (Hollander, 1992)

	Glass toe/kg	Steel toe/kg	Plastic toe/kg	Aluminium toe/kg
From the raw material	6.5	35.0	35.0	100.0
Recycled material	4.5	15.0	15.0	25.0

Aluminium leads in recycling as its conversion uses only a quarter of the energy necessary to produce it from raw material. For glass and plastics, recycling is much less attractive owing to the difficulties of separation, decontamination and transportation. The challenge lies in creating other systems that use recycled materials in high-value applications, such as recycling used plastic bottles into new ones. The reduction in volume and disposal at the source are also strategies of interest for recyclers. Recycling may be stimulated by laws that make it compulsory, as in Brazil with cell phone batteries and old tyres. In Switzerland the law also includes automobiles and electronic equipment.

Legislation tends to increase the scope of *take-back* systems, by which manufacturers have to collect, occasionally recycle and adequately dispose of the products they generate.

Box 10.4 Global economy decarbonization

The concepts of economy dematerialization and reduction in the fuel use intensity can also be used to analyse the carbon emission reduction, and that of other pollutants associated with burning fossil fuels. Consider the four variables as follows:

1 carbon emissions (C);
2 energy consumption (E);
3 economic activity assessed by the GDP; and
4 population (P), one can write:

$$C = (C/E) \times (E/GDP) \times (GDP) = (C/E) \times (E/GDP) \times (GDP/P) \times (P)$$

where (i) E/GDP = I, energy intensity or the energy necessary to produce one GDP unit; (ii) C/E is the economy carbonization rate (usually assessed in tons of carbon per TEP); (iii) GDP/P is the per capita income; and (iv) P is the population.

The carbon emission rate of increase ($\Delta C/C$) is, therefore, given as the sum of four factors:

$$\Delta C/C = \Delta(C/E)/(C/E) + \Delta(E/GDP)/(E/GDP) + \Delta P/P + \Delta GDP/P/GDP/P$$

Similar equations can be established for other pollutants. An analysis of past trends indicate that:

- the world economy decarbonization has been decreasing by 0.3 per cent per year ($\Delta(C/E)/(C/E) = -0.3$ per cent per year);
- the world economy energy intensity has been decreasing by approximately 2 per cent per year ($\Delta(E/GDP)/(E/GDP) = -2$ per cent per year);
- the GDP has been increasing by 3.2 per cent per year ($\Delta(GDP/GDP) = +3.2$ per cent a year);
- this is due to a populational increase by 2 per cent per year ($\Delta P/P = +2\%$ a year) and a per capita increase in the GDP ($\Delta(GDP/P)/(P/GDP)$) of 1.2 per cent per year.

Thus, $\Delta C/C = -0.3 - 2.0 + 1.2 = 0.9$ per cent.

The carbon emissions have been increasing by 0.9 per cent a year. To stabilize the present emissions, that is, to have $\Delta C/C = 0$, the following would be necessary:

- reduction in the populational growth from 2.0 per cent to 1.1 per cent per year; or
- reduction in the per capita income from 1.2 per cent to 0.3 per cent per year; or
- increase in the decarbonization rate from −0.3 per cent to −1.2 per cent per year; or
- reduction in the energy intensity decrease rate from −2.0 per cent to −2.9 per cent per year.

In the last 30 years, developed countries have effectively been decarbonizing. As a whole, in the period 1970–94, the global carbonization rate has been kept approximately constant, as shown in Figure 10.8.

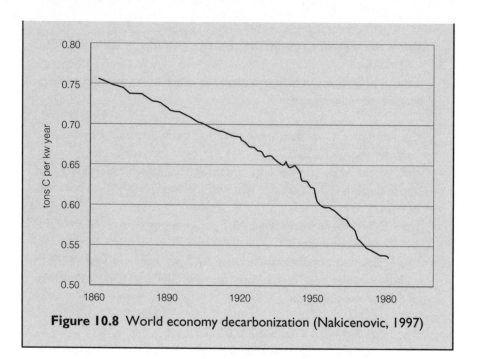

Figure 10.8 World economy decarbonization (Nakicenovic, 1997)

Note

1   There are three basic country groupings in the Organization for Economic Cooperation and Development, OECD: North America (US, Canada and Mexico); OECD Europe; and OECD Asia (Japan, South Korea and Australia/New Zealand). The non-OECD grouping is divided into five separate regional subgroups: non-OECD Europe and Eurasia, non-OECD Asia, Africa, Middle East, and Central and South America. Russia is represented in non-OECD Europe and Eurasia; China and India are represented in non-OECD Asia; and Brazil is represented in Central and South America.

References

Bongaart, J. (1999) 'Population Policy Questions in the Developing World', Science 263, pp771–776

EIA-DoE (2008) International Energy Outlook 2008. September 2008. Energy Information Administration. Office of Integrated Analysis and Forecasting. US Department of Energy, Washington, DC 20585, www.eia.doe.gov/oiaf/ieo/index.html

Holdren, J. P. (1991) 'Population and Energy Problem'. Population and Environment: a Journal of Interdisciplinary Studies, vol. 12, no. 3, pp231–255

Hollander, J. M. (1992) *The Energy-Environment Connection*, Island Press, Washington DC

IEA (2008a) Energy Balances of OECD Countries, International Energy Agency, Paris

IEA (2008b) Energy Balances of non-OECD Countries, International Energy Agency, Paris

IEA (2008c) World Energy Outlook 2008. International Energy Agency, Paris

Nakicenovic, N. (1997) Decarbonization as a long-term energy strategy. In Environment, energy, and economy: Strategies for sustainability, Yoichi Kaya and Keiichi Yokobori (eds), UN University Press, Tokyo, www.unu.edu/unupress/unupbooks/uu17ee/uu17ee0h.htm

UNDP, UNDESA, WEC (2004) World Energy Assessment 2004 Update. UN Development Program, UN Department of Economic and Social Affairs, World Energy Council, www.undp.org/energy/weaover2004.htm

WEC (1993) Energy for Tomorrow's World. World Energy Council, Kogan Page, London

Chapter 11

Energy and Lifestyles

Most of the strategies adopted so far to induce countries to move towards an energetically-sustainable future have been based on technical solutions, such as *energy efficiency* (which can be seen as an 'amplifier' of the existing fossil fuel reserves, which are limited) and a transition to the *use of renewable energy sources* that may, in time, replace fossil fuels. However, a strategy that has been less studied is the *change in consumption patterns and lifestyles*, which could be a lot less energy-intensive than those now predominant.

Strategies and creative ideas can do much for urban planning and public transport. For example, in the area of public transport, adequate management can restructure living and working patterns, reduce distances covered or simply discourage the use of automobiles in cities. That can be done through taxation, tolls, zoning or parking regulations. In addition, it may be important to replace transport services with communication services via the internet.

Lifestyle and consumption patterns

In general, lifestyle and consumption patterns are considered synonymous. The term *lifestyle*, as used by social scientists, refers to values, that is, social preferences, and there is a difference in grade between them, as pointed out by Nader and Beckerman (1978):

> *The sum of a large number of changes in consumption patterns may even lead to changes in values along time, but many behavioral changes are necessary to change the scope of lifestyle or to lead to the adoption of new styles. The use of the automobile, for example, changed Americans' living standards in just a few decades.*

The vision of these authors may be extended even further, comparing the evolution in lifestyles with the evolution of life itself: species evolve by adapting to a changing environment to such an extent that they may become, in some cases, very different from the species they originated from. The driving force of changing lifestyles may often be technological development. The speed in the adoption of electricity, air transport and radio and television, as basic ingredients of present lifestyles all over the world, point in that direction, despite cultural and social differences between countries and within them. In this sense, the introduction of the automobile in human society should be compared to the great changes in the evolution of life. The US has a 'true automobile culture' (Box 11.1). There, mass transport is responsible for only 6 per cent of all passenger journeys, while in Germany that percentage is above 15 per cent and in Japan it is 47 per cent.

Box 11.1 The 'rebound-effect'

Some economists claim that as efficiency in energy use increases, people are encouraged to spend more of it. Because of this 'rebound-effect', the effort to increase efficiency would be wasted. A case in point lies in the US residential sector, the increase in consumption of which is presented in Table 11.1.

Table 11.1 The 'rebound-effect' in the US (Loma et al, 2000)

Final use	Efficiency loss
Heating	10–30%
Air conditioning	0–50%
Water heating	<10–40%
Lighting	5–12%
Automobile transport	10–30%

The introduction of minimum performance standards (CAFE standards) in automobiles has decreased gasoline consumption per kilometre, but not the number of kilometres driven. With lower fuel costs, many users have replaced their small cars with larger cars. The fact that increased energy efficiency has resulted in an increase in the consumption of energy is significant, but it has not entirely offset the benefits that energy efficiency brings to society. Depending on the initial conditions, users' per capita income and variations in the price of energy, the negative consequences of increased efficiency may lead to a consumption of 10 to 40 per cent of the expected gains. Cost is important in this respect and the increase in efficiency must come together with price rises that make the additional use of energy less attractive (Schipper, 2001).

The consumer market demands comfort that often neutralizes gains in efficiency. For example, Table 11.2 presents data for the Volkswagen Golf, which was one of the best-selling models in the world (23 million units between 1975 and 2002). The vehicle reduced its fuel consumption by less than 6 per cent over 28 years, or 15 per cent over 18 years (with the same power). Its weight, on the other hand, has increased by 50 per cent over 28 years, despite the use of lighter materials.

Table 11.2 Comparison of Golf models between 1975 and 2003 (Throne-Holst, 2003)

Model, year, engine (litres)	Power (hp)	Consumption (litre/10km)	Weight (kg)
Golf LS 1975 1.6	70	0.70	780
Golf CL 1985 1.6	75	0.78	870
Golf GL 1995 1.6	75	0.72	1060
Golf Edition 2003 1.4	75	0.66	1174

One example of a simple change in behaviour is to take turns with neighbours when driving to work. Such change does not represent a transformation in lifestyle or in the way we value cars, but it could eventually lead to such changes. In order to test those hypotheses a study was carried out in Sweden, where the use of electricity for water heating, lighting, cooking and home appliances was measured in a large number of virtually identical households. As the end use systems were basically the same in all the houses, so the variations in use of energy may be attributed to differences in behaviour. The results are shown in Figure 11.1 and indicate variations around an average value. It is probable that if the cost of electricity increased, or if income decreased, the average consumption would decrease, and people would slowly adapt to the new conditions. If new technologies for lighting were introduced, electricity consumption would decrease as well, thus confirming the evolutionary character of consumption patterns that might eventually lead to new lifestyles. A clear example of effective action is the replacement of conventional incandescent bulbs with fluorescent ones (Table 11.3).

Another example of voluntary actions is the recent 'carbon offsetting' movement (Box 11.2).

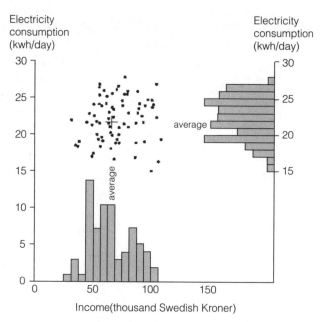

Figure 11.1 Use of electricity in Sweden (Schipper et al, 1989)

Table 11.3 Efficiency in the replacement of lighting sources

Source	Light flux in lumen[1] (lm)	Light flux per power (lm/W)	Service life (h)
Candle	12	0.2	–
Kerosene lamp	10	0.1	–
Gas lamp (LPG)	1000	1	–
Incandescent lamp (60W)	730	12	1000
Halogenous lamp (75W)	1500	20	2000
Tubular fluorescent lamp (20W)	1250	63	8000

Box 11.2 Carbon offsetting

Offsetting is a way of compensating for the emissions produced with an equivalent carbon dioxide saving. Carbon offsetting involves calculating emissions from everyday actions (often related to energy use, such as driving a car, heating a home or travelling by air) and then purchasing (or otherwise obtaining) 'credits' from emission reduction projects (e.g. in renewable energy and energy efficiency). These projects have prevented or removed an equivalent amount of CO_2 elsewhere, leading to a 'zero' overall effect. The place where the greenhouse gases are emitted or compensated is not relevant, since such gases have a long life-span and tend to mix evenly in the atmosphere (DEFRA, 2008b). The first task is to calculate GHG emissions. Figures can vary due to the different sources of data used and different methodologies employed for calculating emissions. Emissions are considerably region-specific (e.g. electricity produced by hydro or coal-fired power plants, use of biofuel blends in fossil fuels) and therefore emission factors vary. To illustrate, Table 11.4 presents some emission factors from the UK Code of Practice.

Among other emission calculation tools available are:

- the 2006 IPCC Guidelines for National Greenhouse Gas Inventories (IPCC, 2006);
- the GHG Protocol (with customized figures for countries like Mexico and India) and the Corporate Standard (GHG Protocol, 2008);
- the ICLEI's CO_2 Calculator (ICLEI, 2008);
- the US Emissions Calculator (US EPA, 2008);
- France's Bilan Carbone (ADEME, 2008).

Once calculated the 'environmental burden', it is necessary to identify and implement the offset project (or to contract a provider to do so). There are variations in the project costs and therefore in the price of offset credits, due to different types and scales of project supported. Guaranteeing that the emissions reductions actually take place depends upon a rigorous assessment (according or not to the Kyoto Protocol CDM rules[2]) of the emissions reductions generated by a given project in comparison with a baseline scenario which assumes that the project does not take place otherwise (thus following the 'additionality principle', which states that the carbon savings must be in addition to reductions that would be made anyway – a marked departure from 'business-as-usual'). To clearly determine how much carbon is actually emitted and sequestered is sometimes a difficult task. This includes verification systems for emissions reductions, transparency on the methodologies and procedures used; and avoiding double counting, ensuring that emissions counted in an offset product are not counted elsewhere, for example, as savings through an emissions trading scheme. 'Leakages' or emissions avoided on one site simply being moved somewhere else (such as deforestation) must be avoided. The permanent creation of new woodland removes carbon from the atmosphere and can be considered as carbon offsetting, provided such plants remain over time.[3] Thus, permanence (or ensuring that emissions reductions were not simply put off until later) is another principle that

Table 11.4 Emission factors indicative for carbon offsetting in the UK (DEFRA, 2008a)

Fuel type or mode	Unit	$kgCO_2$ per unit
Average UK electricity	kWh	0.5266
Diesel oil	litres	2.360
Petrol (gasoline)	litres	2.315
Natural gas	kWh	0.206
Car (petrol, average)	vehicle.km	0.2095
Car (diesel, average)	vehicle.km	0.1987
Motorcycle (average)	vehicle.km	0.1067
Bus (diesel, average local)	passenger.km	0.0943
Underground	passenger.km	0.0526
Rail (national)	passenger.km	0.0602
Flight (long haul, average)	passenger.km	0.1009

will need to be addressed. This may include land ownership (tenure) rights. There is a wide range of organizations offering offsets but not all are reliable, and working in a robust and responsible manner. The UK government has endeavoured to establish a voluntary Code of Best Practice for the provision of carbon offsetting to consumers. The purpose of establishing a Code was to raise standards, ensuring consumer confidence in an emerging market. The Code sets standards for:

*   robust and verifiable emission reduction credits;
*   accurate calculation of emissions to be offset, using statistics and factors published for this purpose by the government;
*   clear information for consumers regarding the mechanism and/or projects supported;
*   transparent pricing; and
*   timescales for cancelling credits.

Carbon offsetting is not the solution to the problems of climate change, but it has a positive effect, both environmentally (carbon mitigated and local co-benefits, especially those in project host developing countries), in terms of raising awareness and identifying sources of impacts, and in providing mechanisms for investment in low-carbon technologies. Moreover, carbon offsetting does not actually reduce the emissions contributing to climate change and should not be an excuse for maintaining unsustainable consumption patterns. These tools encourage consumers to use the *personal choices* available to them in the best possible way, first trying to avoid the occurrence of emissions, then minimizing them, and, finally, when unavoidable, mitigating remaining carbon dioxide emissions through carbon offsetting.

The mechanistic view on changes in lifestyles veils cultural, religious and educational differences, but seems to be quite convincing when explaining the homogeneity of consumption patterns in many parts of the world.

Consumer profiles

In order to further explore this point of view, consumers could be divided into the following groups:

- the comfort-seeking ones;
- the 'diligent' ones;
- the indifferent ones;
- the domineering ones; and
- the non-conformists.

These groups were used in a study (Baranzini and Giovannini, 1995), in which each group is part of a grouping ('cloud') characterized by the consumption of individuals belonging to that group. An alternative division is used by Baranzini and Giovannini, who chose the following consumer groups:

- 'squanderers', who do not care about saving energy;
- 'moderates';
- those with an 'ecological bias', who fight for regulations; and
- 'technology enthusiasts', attracted to any kind of novelty.

In principle, all the consumers would be divided into four 'clouds', as indicated in Figure 11.2. In the evolutionary view of those consumption patterns, 'clouds' would change in shape (consumers may move from one 'cloud' to another over time) and therefore future energy consumption might be predicted, provided that the number of consumers in each 'cloud' and their trajectories were known. Up to this moment, this approach has not been very promising, owing to the arbitrary nature of the choices we can make concerning trajectories.

Per capita energy consumption

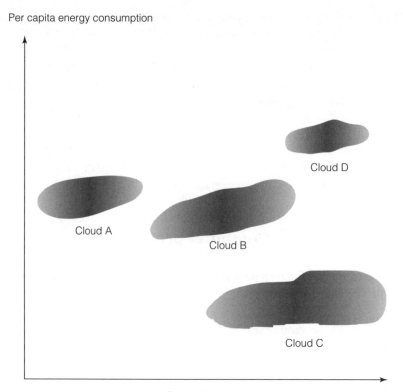

Figure 11.2 Consumer 'clouds'

In conclusion, three approaches were tried to predict the future consumption of energy and the resulting environmental consequences, proposed by economists, technologists and social scientists. Their main characteristics are presented in Table 11.5.

Although much successful effort has been made to integrate those approaches, the fact remains that as soon as one tries to predict the future, uncertainties increase and their number increases even more as the time span is extended. Therefore, research in the energy area seems to confirm the old saying that 'the only way to predict the future is to build it', leaving as little as possible to chance.

Notes

1   One lumen (lm) is equivalent to 1/680W emitted with a wavelength of 555nm, which equates to the maximum sensitivity of the human eye.
2   For Certified Emission Reduction credits (CERs, emission reductions of unit equal to one metric ton of carbon dioxide equivalent), this assessment is ultimately made by the Kyoto Protocol Clean Development Mechanism (CDM) Executive Board. CERs

Table 11.5 Different approaches to the problem of energy consumption reduction

	Economists (econometric 'top-down' models)	*Technologists ('bottom-up' models)*	*Sociologists*
Basic pattern approach	Sophisticated extrapolation of the past	Feasible alternative technologies	Alternative consumption and lifestyle
Main driving force	Markets	Governments and subsidies	Values
Timescale	Medium- and long-term (5–10 years)	Medium- and long-term (10–30 years)	Long-term (50 years)
Main limitations	Cannot account well for the feedback between economic factors, such as prices and technological changes	Cannot account well for costs and the feedback between technical process and consumption	Choices are too many and difficult to quantify

may be used by Annex I countries towards meeting their binding emission reduction and limitation commitments. For Voluntary or Verified Emission Reduction Credits (VERs, emission reduction projects that are developed by small-scale projects outside the CDM), this assessment is made by a third-party organization chosen by the project developer, that is, not at this stage through an internationally agreed body. CDM is the highest internationally agreed standard for emission reductions.

3   For the CDM, forestry projects are awarded temporary credits to take into account the nature of carbon sequestration in trees, expiring after a set period of time and requiring the credits to be renewed or replaced. Very roughly, a grown tree in the South American Atlantic Rainforest 'stores' around 200kg CO_2 and a hectare of native trees reforested captures 2667kg CO_2 per year over 30 years. Reforestation cost estimates are around US\$5000 per hectare, a value four to six times higher if permanent maintenance is included.

References

ADEME (2008) Bilan Carbone. Agence de l'Environnement et de la Maîtrise de l'Energie, http://www2.ademe.fr/servlet/KBaseShow?sort=-1&cid=96&m=3&catid=15730 and www.ademe.fr

Baranzini, A. and Giovannini, B. (1995) Institutional and Cultural Aspects of Energy Consumption Modelling, International Academy of the Environment Working Paper 28, Geneva

DEFRA (2008a) Draft code of best practice for carbon offset providers accreditation requirements and procedures, February, www.defra.gov.uk/environment/climate-change/uk/carbonoffset/pdf/carbon-offset-codepractice.pdf

DEFRA (2008b) UK – Environmental Protection – Climate change and energy – Cost of carbon – Carbon offsetting, www.defra.gov.uk/environment/climatechange/uk/carbonoffset/index.htm

GHG Protocol (2008) Calculation tools. World Business Council for Sustainable Development and World Resources Institute, www.ghgprotocol.org/calculation-tools/all-tools, www.ghgprotocol.org/standards/corporate-standard

ICLEI (2008) Personal CO_2 calculator. ICLEI – Local Governments for Sustainability, http://www3.iclei.org/co2/co2calc.htm and www.iclei.org

IPCC (2006) Guidelines for National Greenhouse Gas Inventories. Intergovernmental Panel on Climate Change, www.ipcc-nggip.iges.or.jp/public/2006gl/index.html

Loma, G., Greene, D. and Difiglio, C. (2000) 'Energy Efficiency and Consumption – the Rebound Effect – a Survey'. Energy Policy 28, 396

Nader, L. and Beckerman, S. (1978) 'Energy as it Relates to the Quality and Style of Life', Annual Review of Energy 3, 1

Schipper, L. (2001) 'On the Rebound: the Interaction of Energy Efficiency, Energy Use and Economic Activity', Energy Policy vol. 28, pp6–7

Schipper, L., Barlett, S., Dianne, H. and Vince, E. (1989) 'Linking Life-Styles and Energy Use: A Matter of Time?', Annual Review of Energy and Environment, 14, pp273–320

Throne-Holst, H. (2003) 'The fallacies of energy efficiency: the rebound effect?', National Institute for Consumer Research (SIFO), Oslo, www.sifo.no/files/file54378_trondheim_paper_nov2003.pdf

US EPA (2008) Emissions Calculator. United States Environmental Protection Agency, www.epa.gov/climatechange/emissions/ind_calculator.html and www.epa.gov/cleanenergy/energy-resources/calculator.html

Chapter 12

Energy and the Science Academies

There is a general belief that technological and scientific developments in the last 200 years have solved many of humanity's problems – the elimination of diseases and the increase in average life time, and have extended comfort and prosperity to one-third of mankind (about two billion people), an unprecedented fact in history. Ancient Rome, in its splendour, gave its citizens an excellent standard of living, but at the cost of the labour of approximately 100 million enslaved human beings. Only 1 per cent of the world population, at the time, benefited from the prosperity of the Imperial City.

Essential for these advancements are appropriate sources of energy; 80 per cent of which are derived today from fossil fuels: coal, oil and gas. These fuels were the springboard for the extraordinary technical progress of the 20th century. The problem is that the progress based on them cannot last: fossil fuel reserves are finite and present oil reserves will not last more than 40 or 50 years; geopolitical problems are making access to these resources more and more difficult because of the growing dependence of the US on imported oil, and the increase in consumption by China and other developing countries.

The Middle East Wars have a lot to do with that, as recently pointed out by none other than Alan Greenspan, former president of the Federal Reserve, the US central bank, from 1988 to 2006. Two-thirds of humanity lack access to the comforts of modern civilization – based, in fact, on the use of fossil fuels – which is unacceptable from a moral point of view and is a source of permanent sociopolitical instability, generating, among other things, illegal immigration to Europe and North America. Moreover, fossil fuels are 'poisoning' the atmosphere with the emission of gases responsible for local pollution and for global warming (and the resulting climate changes), the most evident manifestations of that problem. In other words, the technical progress achieved in the 20th century is not sustainable in the medium-term, but the problem has to be solved in the next decades, that is, by the present generation, in order to avoid an unprecedented crisis in modern history.

In order to analyse this situation and propose solutions, the world's science academies (including those from the US, England, France and Russia) have set up a group of 15 scientists who prepared a report after two years' work entitled 'Lighting the Way – Toward a Sustainable Energy Future'. The initiative for the study came from the Chinese and Brazilian Academies of Science. The report presents the views of highly-qualified scientists, describes the problem objectively and analyses possible solutions, without any political considerations. It does not tell governments (or other sectors of society) what they should do and how, but what needs to be done.

The recommendations in that report therefore represent the best that scientists can suggest to authorities. They are, basically, the following:

- For industrialized countries, the best solution, and the cheapest one, is the increase in energy efficiency, that is, energy saving, for which there are technologies already available. Those countries are using energy very inefficiently. Improving that efficiency will by no means harm the quality of life of their population, as has been shown in California, where the per capita consumption of electricity is the same as it was 20 years ago.
- For developing countries the strategy is to adopt – early in their development process – the best and most efficient technologies available (so as not to repeat the path followed in the past by industrialized countries, when they industrialized). In other words, developing countries may 'leapfrog', adopting the best technologies available.
- Increasing the use of renewable energies, in their various forms, including biomass, which offer great opportunities for technological progress and innovation, besides simultaneously solving climate change and energy security problems. Examples of success are the sugar-cane ethanol programme in Brazil, the widespread use of wind energy in Germany and Spain, and photovoltaic energy in Japan.
- Promoting the development of technologies for energy storage, which could substantially reduce costs and expand the contribution from a variety of new energy supply options.
- Introducing technologies for fossil fuels – particularly for coal – carbon capture and sequestration (CCS), which could play an important role in the reduction of global emissions of carbon dioxide, provided such technologies are proved viable from the technical, economic and environmental point of view, something that has yet to happen.
- Nuclear energy, which has been recognized as capable of providing a significant contribution if problems such as cost, safety, disposal of radioactive waste and proliferation of nuclear weapons are adequately solved.

This is a broad 'menu' of solutions that represents the best that scientists from all over the world can suggest to the authorities, but of course it is up to the governments to choose the most appropriate ones, considering the particular characteristics of each country (Goldemberg, 2007; InterAcademy Council Report, 2007).

References

Goldemberg (2007) Energia e as Academias de Ciências, O Estado de São Paulo, 19 November, page A2, http://txt.estado.com.br/editorias/2007/11/19/opi-1.93.29.20071119.2.1.xml

InterAcademy Council Report (2007) Lighting the Way: Toward a Sustainable Energy Future, www.interacademycouncil.net/?id=9481

Energy, Environment and Development Timeline

15 billion BC – Origin of the Universe.

5 billion BC – Beginning of solar fusion.

4.6 billion BC – Winds on Earth, ocean currents.

4.3 billion BC – Life on Earth: photosynthesis and breathing. First coal, natural gas and oil deposits.

5000BC – Discovery of fire: humans control their environment.

4500BC – Plough moved by animal traction in Mesopotamia.

3500BC – Use of wind and water in rudimentary machinery and transport.

2600BC – Glass in Mesopotamia; ceramic bricks in India.

1500BC – Thermal water used by Romans, Chinese and other peoples.

1000BC – Coal use in China.

550BC – Chinese invent mass production method of steel instruments.

AD60 – Heron from Alexandria describes an experiment with steam propulsion.

1013 – Chinese transport natural gas from superficial wells with bamboo (first ducts) to produce porcelain.

1100 – Windmills used in Europe.

1180 – Coal systematically mined in England.

1415 – First regular public lighting in London.

1442 – Royal Charter, first known governmental provision for tree protection in the Portuguese Law, norms for cutting wood, which was necessary for the fleet.

1472 – Leonardo da Vinci, Italy, designs a centrifugal pump, bicycle, belts, pulleys, levers, gears, universal joints, flying machine, helicopter, parachute and other inventions in his notes.

1600 – Firewood crisis in England.

1662 – Robert Boyle, Ireland, formulates laws of gas expansion.

1668 – John Wallis discovers the conservation of momentum principle.

1680 – Christian Huygens, France, and Denis Papin, the Netherlands, conduct experiments with pistons, precursors of the internal combustion engines.

1687 – Isaac Newton publishes *Principia Mathematica*, describing physics' natural laws. He develops calculus, the concept of force, laws of movement, gravity and optics.

1698 – Thomas Savery patents the first steam machine to pump water from mines.

1712 – Thomas Newcomen's steam machine, more efficient and potent (2500hp).

1740 – Beginning of commercial coal mining.

1747 – Benjamin Franklin conducts experiments with electricity and deduces the existence of positive and negative charges.

1765 – James Watt, Scotland, enhances the steam machine with a separate condenser and allows uses other than pumping water.

1774 – Antoine Lavoisier, France, demonstrates mass conservation in chemical reactions.

1783 – Glaude de Jouffroy d'Abbans, France, builds the first steam boat.

1799 – Alessandro Volta, Italy, invents the voltaic battery, the first electric battery.

1802 – High-pressure steam machine invented by the Englishman Richard Trevithick.

1803 – Coal gas lights factory in Scotland and kerosene lights Parma and Genoa, Italy.

1803 – Richard Trevithick invents the steam train engine.

1807 – Robert Fulton takes the first commercial trip on a steam boat, covering 150 miles in 32 hours.

1809 – Gas lighting in London.

1816 – Robert Stirling, Scotland, invents the internal combustion engine.

1821 – The Englishman Michael Faraday discovers the electric engine principles.

1822 – The Frenchman Jean-Baptiste Fourier publishes his heat conduction theory. Seven years later he conceptualizes the greenhouse effect.

1824 – Sadi Carnot, France, establishes the foundations of thermodynamics.

1827 – Georg Ohm, Germany, publishes the law of electricity.

1831 – Michael Faraday discovers the principles of the electric generator; Joseph Henry publishes the description of an electric engine.

1839 – The Englishman William R. Grove invents the fuel cell. The Frenchman Edmund Becquerel discovers the photovoltaic effect.

1843 – James Joule experimentally demonstrates energy conservation (First Law of Thermodynamics).

1848 – First oil wells drilled in Baku, Asia.

1850 – Modern energy: use of coal in steam machines (trains).

1850 – Rudolf Clausius, Germany, publishes the first enunciate of the Second Law of Thermodynamics.

1855 – Abraham Gesner extracts kerosene from coal. Benjamin Silliman, US, distills oil-obtaining solvents, lubricants, kerosene, gasoline and tar, giving the start to a rush for its exploitation, reducing the demand for whale oil.

1857 – The Frenchman Alexandre Becquerel conducts experiments with fluorescent light.

1859 – Edwin Drake drills the first commercially productive oil well in Pennsylvania, US; beginning of the oil industry.

1860 – Etienne Lenoir invents the gasoline engine.

1862 – John D. Rockefeller builds an oil refinery in Cleveland, Ohio, US.

1864 – Siegfried Marcus, Austria, builds a one-cylinder vehicle, a precursor of the modern automobile.

1867 – John D. Rockefeller founds Standard Oil Company, the first oil monopoly which would later result in Exxon, Mobil, Amoco, Chevron, Arco, Conoco and Texaco.

1873 – James Clerk Maxwell, Scotland, describes the nature of electromagnetic radiation; J. S. Newberry, US, the theory of oil origin.

1875 – Power generation by oil and coal; air pollution is intensified.

1876 – Nicholas Otto, Germany, builds the four-cycle internal combustion engine, incorporating the principles of ignition, combustion and cooling. German Carl von Linde patents the por ammonia compressor refrigerator.

1877 – Ludwig Boltzmann, Austria, publishes formulae relating energy and temperature.

1878 – First hydropower plant built at Niagara Falls, US.

1878 – Thomas Edison invents the electric incandescent lightbulb, replacing kerosene, and the oil industry plunges into recession.

1880 – Coal thermal power generation.

1881 – First commercial electric vehicle in Europe. Edison Machine Works, New York, builds the first commercial generator.

1884 – Charles Parsons patents a steam turbine in England.

1885 – Gottlieb Daimler and Karl Benz, working separately in Germany, invent the modern gasoline engines for a three-wheel carriage and a motorcycle. The following year they introduce the automobile in Europe, establishing a market for the American oil; gasoline was a cheap byproduct of kerosene distillation, used as a solvent. First gasoline pump.

1886 – George Westinghouse and William Stanley build an electric current transformer, allowing long-distance transmission. First alternate current generation in Barrington, Massachusetts. Charles Hall, US, obtains aluminium from bauxite electrolysis.

1889 – Heinrich Rudolf Hertz, Germany, develops the electromagnetic theory.

1890 – Royal Dutch Petroleum Co. later Shell, is founded.

1892 – German Rudolf Diesel patents the diesel engine. Charles and Frank Duryea introduce the automobile in the US. Automobiles produced in Paris for the European market.

1893 – Julius Elster and Hans Geitel invent the photoelectric cell in Germany.

1894 – In Germany, the Russian Wilhelm Ostwald formulates the fuel cell principle.

1895 – Henry Ford introduces his first automobile.

1895 – Frenchman Antoine Henri Becquerel announces the radioactive properties of uranium.

1896 – Chemist Svante Arrhenius relates the greenhouse effect to CO_2.

1898 – In France, Marie and Pierre Curie isolate radium and polonium; the first radioactive elements are discovered.

1899 – Ernest Rutherford, England, reveals the nature of radioactivity.

1903 – First plane, by the Wright brothers, in North Carolina (three years later, Santos Dumont conducts the first flight with take-off in the presence of experts, officially witnessed in Paris).

1903 – First great thermopower plant in Chicago.

1904 – Einstein's theory of relativity demonstrates the relationship among mass, energy and the speed of light ($E = mc^2$).

1904 – New York subway opened – the first underground railway.

1905 – Hermann Nernst, Germany, enunciates the Third Law of Thermodynamics.

1908 – Henry Ford introduces the T Model, mass produced.

1930 – First oil tanker spills, in Point Reyes, US.

1933 – Oil discovered in Saudi Arabia.

1935 – Fluorescent lightbulbs independently developed in Germany and in the US.

1935 – Beginning of PCBs (polychlorinated biphenyls) production, toxic products present in oil for power transformers banned in 1979.

1936 – First great hydropower plant over 1000MW: Hoover Dam, near Las Vegas.

1942 – First controlled nuclear fission: Enrico Fermi, Chicago.

1944 – First nuclear reactor operates in Richland, Washington, US.

1947 – California starts a forest management system, having sustainable production as a goal.

1950 – Smog damage to vegetation first reported (Berkeley, California).

1951 – First thermonuclear power generation: Idaho Falls, US, by the Atomic Energy Commission.

1952 – A four-day smog, caused by coal burning, mainly with SO_2 and irritating particulate matter, kills 4700 in London.

1954 – M. King Hubbert, Shell geologist, predicts the peak of the US oil production in 1965 (it actually occurred in 1970).

1957 – The first nuclear thermopower plant in the US (Shippingport); establishment of the International Atomic Energy Agency (IAEA) to promote pacific uses and ensure international guarantees.

1957 – Fire in the nuclear weapons factory in Colorado Rocky Flats emits plutonium into the atmosphere; kept secret until 1969, when a second fire emits more plutonium. Fire in the plutonium production reactor in Windscale (later Sellafield), in the north of England, spreads radioactive iodine and polonium.

1960 – Iraq, Iran, Kuwait, Saudi Arabia and Venezuela form the OPEC.

1960 – First law for controlling vehicular emissions, California.

1962 – Rachel Carson publishes *Silent Spring*, on the effects of pesticides in the environment; the work is a landmark in environmental awareness.

1966 – First superconductor engine.

1966 – Oil found in Alaska (US), but works on the oil duct are halted for environmental reasons until 1973.

1967 – Oil tanker *Torrey Canyon* spills; countries do not count on international laws to punish tanker owners.

1968 – In Europe, a movement concerned with the environmental problems in the participants' countries and globally is started, designated the Rome Club. The participants – experts in different areas of human knowledge – gathers in Rome to discuss current and future crises for humanity.

1968 – Nuclear Non-Proliferation Treaty – NPT.

1968 – International Conference promoted by UNESCO on the Rational Use and Conservation of Biosphere Resources.

1969 – Brussels Convention imposes objective responsibility for accidents and spillage on the signing countries. The owner of the oil tanker is made responsible, which leads to the establishment of a fund for compensations with indemnity caps destined to the victim state.

1969 – President Nixon, US, signs the National Environment Policy, which forces the government to assess its projects. In 2002, the Bush administration states that the law does not go beyond its territorial waters.

1969 – Patrick Moore founds the NGO Greenpeace, which coordinates actions against nuclear tests in the Aleutian Islands.

1970 – Aswan Hydropower Plant, Egypt, starts operating after the transference of archaeological monuments.

1970 – Commercial solar photocells generate power.

1970 – Oil found in the North Sea by British Petroleum (BP); the area became one of the world's major producers.

1970 – Clean Air Act, US, to control air pollution, makes the adoption of catalytic converters in automobiles compulsory.

1970 – The US Environmental Protection Agency (EPA) is established. The California Environmental Quality Act makes it compulsory for entrepreneurs to produce an Environmental Impact Report for new projects.

1971 – Denmark establishes the first Ministry for the Environment.

1971 – Ramsar International Convention on Wetlands, Iran.

1972 – Club of Rome publishes the report 'The Limits to Growth', calling attention to the fact that humanity would compulsorily have a limit of growth with the economic model then used, based on exacerbated consumption and highly concentrated on a few nations.

1972 – The United Nations Conference on the Human Environment is held in Stockholm, Sweden. Delegates from developing countries advocate their right to economic growth opportunities at any cost. At the end, the ideal form of environmental planning is proclaimed to be that which associated ecological prudence with pro-development actions. These countries also manage to approve the declaration that under-development is one of the most frequent causes of pollution in the world currently; therefore, environmental pollution control should be considered a development subprogramme and the joint action of all governments and supranational organizations should converge to eradicate poverty from the world. Twenty-five fundamental principles guiding international actions in the environmental area are approved, such as: the valorization of man within the environment as one that transforms it, but as one that depends on it to survive, and that the human being is the most important being in the world, as he promotes social progress, creates wealth and develops science and technology. By the Stockholm Declaration, a country should guarantee that its actions do not harm other countries. UNEP – United Nations Environment Programme – is established.

1973 – First oil crisis caused by OPEC, which quadrupled its price in a year; until 1974 the Arab countries ban exports to the US in retaliation for their support of Israel, starting a world economic crisis.

1974 – First remediation programme for areas where nuclear tests had been conducted (Los Alamos, US).

1974 – International Energy Agency is established in Paris to coordinate oil distribution.

1976 – The largest oil field in the world is discovered in Mexico.

1976 – International community bans the use of environmental modification techniques such as cloud seeding and defoliating (agent orange).

1976 – Liberian oil tanker *Argo Merchant* spills in the North Atlantic.

1977 – Law enacted in the US for remediating abandoned mines.

1978 – Iran revolution starts the second oil crisis; prices double.

1978 – 223,000 tons of oil spill from oil tanker *Amoco Cadiz* on the French coast.

1979 – Nuclear accident in the Three Mile Island Plant (Pennsylvania, US) leads to halting new projects.

1979 – Accident between the *Atlantic Empress* and another supertanker on the Tobago coast, the largest disaster ever recorded; 278,000 tons of oil spilled into the sea.

1980 – Iraq invades Iran in a dispute for the strategic outflow in the Shatt al-Arab area.

1980 – Oil exploitation forbidden in ecological reserves in Alaska (withdrawn in 2002).

1981 – Amendment to the Law of Endangered Species allows the destruction of certain habitats, while others are preserved.

1981 – Shell, Exxon and Texaco employees inform on the spillage of MTBE (methyl tri butyl ether) in filling stations, contaminating the underground water in the US.

1982 – Montego Bay UN Convention on the Law of the Sea consolidates uses and proposes resolution of disputes on spillages by an international court, with headquarters in Germany; agreement establishes civil responsibilities, extracontractual and personal.

1982 – First decommissioning of an operating nuclear plant (Shippingport, US).

1983 – The third largest accident involving ships: *Castillo de Bellver*, South Africa coast; 252,000 tons of oil.

1984 – In Brazil, the large Itaipu and Tucuruí hydropower plants start operating.

1984 – Ninety-three deaths and 2500 homeless due to the burst of a Petrobrás pipeline in the Vila Socó favela, Cubatão, Brazil.

1984 – US seeks a permanent deposit for nuclear wastes.

1986 – Nuclear accident in the Chernobyl nuclear plant, USSR; reactor burns for ten days and emits 200 times more radiation than the atomic bombs of Hiroshima and Nagasaki; radioactive clouds reach Europe; US$130 billion estimated damages.

1986 – In Brazil, Angra 1 nuclear power plant starts operating. At the same time, a deep well revested with concrete, supposedly for testing explosions, is found at an aeronautics base at the Cachimbo Range, in the south of Pará.

1986 – EPA announces that 35 per cent of the US underground gasoline tanks leak.

1987 – The first permanent deposit of radioactive wastes (Yucca Mountain, US) is designated.

1987 – Lebanese militia 'Free Forces' allow storage of toxic waste from Italy, Germany, Canada and Belgium, contaminating 70 per cent of the water sources in the country.

1987 – Earthquake in Ecuador destroys the major oil pipeline in the country.

1987 – Montreal Protocol for protecting the ozone layer gradually eliminates chlorofluorocarbons (CFCs) production and use, as well as other substances. Acceptance by governments (156 ratifications in the first year) and industries (which found markets for replacements) contributes to the success of the international treaty.

1987 – European 'zebra' mollusc proliferates in North America, clogging ducts in hydropower plants.

1987 – Climatologist James Hansen reports on the greenhouse effect to the US Congress; increase in global temperature as a sign of human alterations in the atmosphere.

1987 – Bruntland Commission Report, 'Our common future', conceptualizes sustained development for the rational use of resources and transgenerational rights.

1989 – Accident with the Exxon Valdez oil tanker in Alaska; 37,000 tons (40 million litres) spill, contaminating 1600km of coastal area; insurance company has to pay US$250 million; Exxon pay a US$100 million fine in a US$1.1 billion court litigation.

1990 – Iraq invades Kuwait; US starts the Gulf War, which costs US$8 billion and causes several environmental aggressions.

1990 – The Intergovernmental Panel on Climate Change (IPCC) publishes its first assessment report on global warming.

1991 – *ABT Summer* sinks in Angola, the second largest accident (260,000 tons).

1991 – Energy experimentally produced by controlled nuclear fusion in England by the Joint European Torus.

1991 – In the Gulf War, Iraq sabotages Kuwait oil terminal, with great spillages in the Persian Gulf.

1992 – (3rd) Earth Summit in Rio de Janeiro. UN Conference results in Agenda 21 and the Climate and Biodiversity Conventions. The UN Conference on Environment and Development was held in Rio de Janeiro, on 3–14 June 1992, better known as Rio-92, with the participation of 170 nations. Rio-92 had as main goals to identify regional and global strategies for actions concerning the major environmental issues, to examine the world environmental situation and the changes occurring after the Stockholm Conference and to examine strategies for promoting sustained development and poverty eradication in developing countries.

1992 – Greek oil tanker *Aegean Sea* spills in La Coruña, Spain.

1992 – MTBE blended in gasoline (10–15 per cent) in the US to reduce carbon monoxide in the air.

1993 – Liberian ship *Braer* sinks and oil spills in the Shetland Islands, Scotland.

1996 – Cargo vessel *Sea Empress* sinks on the Welsh coast, United Kingdom.

1997 – Kyoto Protocol proposed in the Conference of the Parties on the Climate Convention: 38 industrialized countries have to cut greenhouse gas emissions by 5 per cent from 1990 levels by 2012; 160 countries sign the Protocol.

1998 – Oil pipeline spillage in the Niger River mouth, in Nigeria.

1998 – US Government announces a $1 billion penalty to diesel engine manufacturers for violating environmental laws.

1998 – During CoP-5, Argentina and Kazakhstan voluntarily pledges to reduce greenhouse gas emissions, splitting the front of developing countries that are opposed to cuts before 2012.

1998 – President Clinton signs the Kyoto Protocol, but the US Congress fails to ratify.

1999 – 162-year-old Edwards Dam, in Maine, US, is breached by government order to allow fish migration.

1999 – Hong Kong directs $3.75 billion to reduce nitrogen oxide levels by 80 per cent by 2005.

2000 – Rupture of a Petrobras pipeline linking the Duque de Caxias Refinery to the Ilha d'Água terminal causes the spillage of 1.3 million tons of fuel oil into the Guanabara Bay; oil stain spreads over 40 square kilometres.

2000 – OPEC decides to increase production and oil prices fall.

2000 – UNESCO declares Mata Atlantica a natural patrimony of humanity; only 3 per cent of the original cover remains.

2000 – Millennium Declaration is signed at UN Summit by 147 government leaders and is adopted by 189 countries; its central core are the 8 Millennium Development Goals for excluding extreme poverty and for eradicating social exclusion by 2015.

2000 – North Pole icecap melts for the first time in recorded history, opening a mile-wide patch of open ocean.

2000 – The Royal Sweden Academy acknowledges that the Earth has never been so hot in recorded history.

2000 – EPA, US, determines a 97 per cent reduction in diesel sulphur by 2006.

2001 – Oil tanker *Jessica* spills in Galapagos, Ecuador.

2001 – World Treaty for eliminating 12 persistent organic pollutants (POPs) is signed by 127 countries.

2001 – Europeans decide to implement the Kyoto Protocol without the US.

2001 – About 12.5 per cent of the Amazon forest has been destroyed.

2001 – Marrakesh agreement, Morocco; 160 countries approve rules for implementing the Kyoto Protocol.

2001 – Terrorist attack on the World Trade Center in New York. Months later, the US invades Iraq and the energy safety issue gains momentum.

2002 – Scientists report that 22–47 per cent of the plant species on the planet are endangered. Ocean levels will rise 3–5cm in the century (Mark Meier, expert in glaciations).

2002 – Denmark generates 13 per cent of its electricity with wind; the goal is 50 per cent by 2030.

2002 – Japan and the European Union ratify the Kyoto Protocol.

2002 – WWF International emits report stating that humanity uses 20 per cent more resources than the planet can regenerate.

2002 – US Senate approves permanent nuclear deposit in Yucca Mountain, Nevada.

2002 – The 4th UN World Summit on Sustainable Development (WSSD) is held in Johannesburg, South Africa, aiming to reduce extreme poverty and to eradicate social exclusion. The central topic of the meeting is compulsory goals of 10 per cent of renewable energies by 2010, above the 4.5 per cent of 2002. Other themes are sanitation and potable water, protecting sea life and the oceans, equity and access to technology.

2002 – The ship *Prestige* spills twice the *Exxon Valdez* amount of oil on the Spanish coast.

2002 – Federal US Government loosens anti-pollution laws.

2002 – Europe bans single-compartment oil tankers as from 2010.

2003 – Civil war in Nigeria, the greatest oil producer in Africa; US attacks Iraq.

2003 – Deforestation in Brazil, caused by livestock breeding, lumber merchants and soybean, beats record: 26 million hectares.

2003 – Sulphur stocks beat record due to excessive production by the energy industry: 64 million tons/year.

2003 – Since 1880, the hottest years on Earth were 1998, 2002 and 2003.

2003 – In the US, coal and oil thermopower plants have to reduce mercury emissions by 70 per cent in the next 15 years.

2003 – US Court declares the federal law illegal that excuses thermopower plants from using anti-pollution equipment.

2004 – Royal Dutch Shell executives make it public that they underestimated their proved oil reserves.

2004 – OPEC cuts production and barrel price rises to US$55; in Jordan, the World Economic Forum acknowledges oil as 'the most significant factor of global instability'; Russian giant Yukos is sold in an operation suspected of corruption.

2004 – World Bank estimates that China loses 8–12 per cent of its GDP due to pollution.

2004 – British scientists report that the Earth should be halfway towards its sixth extinction process, started 50,000 years ago.

2004 – Scientists report on the absorption of carbon dioxide by the oceans, increasing their acidity and affecting shells, animal shells and corals.

2004 – Antarctic icecap melts twice as fast as in 1990.

2004 – Russia ratifies the Kyoto Protocol, which comes into force early in 2005.

2004 – In Brazil, 47 per cent of the Amazon is occupied or exploited.

2004 – (3rd) IUCN World Congress in Bangkok includes motion to reduce noise in the oceans; sonars used for military ends and oil prospection cause large numbers of deaths among whales.

2004 – Intense use of dirty energy in China causes world concern as to the accumulation of mercury in water and in the food chain.

2005 – Development of the LNG market in Qatar.

2005 – IEA revises its scenarios for more oil consumption; oil reaches US$60 per barrel and knocks down stocks in the stock market; members of the peak-oil movement believe that half of the underground oil has already been exploited.

2005 – Russia and Ukraine start a dispute for natural gas, affecting the supply to Europe. In the following year, Bolivia nationalizes its gas industry, increasing prices and reducing the supply to Brazil and Argentina.

2005 – The Kyoto Protocol comes into force (16 February), seven years after its negotiation.

2006 – Stern Report relates measures for mitigating greenhouse gas emissions to the world GDP: 1–5 per cent if immediate actions are taken or 20 per cent + if they are postponed. The US starts to change positions due to internal pressures (Al Gore's film, pro-ethanol agricultural lobby, need for technological development to keep competitivity) and external pressures (dependence on oil, geopolitical instability).

2007 – (4th) IPCC report, strong impact on public opinion about vulnerabilities and impacts. Mitigation strategies aim mainly at energy efficiency, renewable energy sources, cleaner use of coal and deforestation reduction. Agenda to adapt to impacts is still very incipient. In Heilingendamm, Germany, G-8 + 5 Meeting stresses the conflict of positions concerning reduction goals for developing countries post-2012 (US, Germany, France, UK, Japan, Italy, Russia) versus advances in the WTO, plus reduction of poverty, plus historical responsibility of the developed ones (China, India, Brazil, South Africa and Mexico).

2007 – In the 13th Conference of the Parties to the UN Convention on Climate Change in Bali, Indonesia, discussions are started for the second period of the Kyoto Protocol. Among the themes addressed are the financial compensation for prevented deforestation, the establishment of more ambitious goals for the Annex I countries, actions for reducing quantifiable and verifiable emissions for the developing countries, technology transfer, adaptation to climate change affects and sanctions for the non-abidance to the agreements. An ad-hoc working group (AWG) should conduct the plans of action. Australia announces the ratification of the Protocol, isolating the US.

2008 – A political crisis between Russia and Ukraine puts at risk the supply of natural gas to Europe.

2009 – As a consequence of the late 2008-financial crisis, Barack Obama, elected US President, calls for urgent energy efficiency measures, especially from car manufacturers.

2009 – The 15th UNFCCC CoP in Copenhagen discusses the future of the global climate multilateral regime.

Conversion Units

Fractions and Multiples

Fraction		Prefix	Symbol
10^{-1}	0.1	deci	d
10^{-2}	0.01	centi	c
10^{-3}	0.001	mili	m
10^{-6}	0.000006	micro	μ
10^{-9}	0.000000001	nano	n
10^{-12}	0.000000000001	pico	p
10^{-15}	0.000000000000001	femto	f

Multiple		Prefix	Symbol
10		deca	da
10^2	100	hecto	h
10^3	1000	kilo	k
10^6	1,000,000	mega	M
10^9	1,000,000,000	giga	G
10^{12}	1,000,000,000,000	tera	T
10^{15}	1,000,000,000,000,000	peta	P
10^{18}	1,000,000,000,000,000,000	hexa	E
10^{21}	1,000,000,000,000,000,000,000	zeta	Z

International System

IS (International System)

Magnitude	Unit name	Symbol
length	metre	m
mass	kilogramme	kg
time	second	s
temperature	kelvin	K
amount of substance	mole	mol

Amount	Name	Symbol	Definition
force	newton	N	$kg\ m\ s^{-2}$
pressure	pascal	Pa	$kg\ m^{-1}\ s^{-2}\ (= N\ m^{-2})$
energy	joule	J	$kg\ m^2\ s^{-2}$
power	watt	W	$kg\ m^2\ s^{-3}\ (= J\ s^{-1})$
frequency	hertz	Hz	s^{-1} (cycles per second)

IS decimal fractions and multiples of units with special names

Physical amount	Unit name	Symbol	Definition
length	ångstrom	Å	$10^{-10}\ m = 10^{-8}\ cm$
length	micron	µm	$10^{-6}\ m$
area	hectare	ha	$10^4\ m^2$
pressure	bar	bar	$10^5\ N\ m^{-2} = 10^5\ Pa$
mass	ton	t	$10^3\ kg$
mass	gram	g	$10^{-3}\ kg$

Conversion factors

Energy

Into:	TJ	Gcal	Mtoe	MBtu	GWh
from:			*multiply by*		
TJ	1	238.8	2.388×10^{-5}	947.8	0.2778
Gcal	4.1868×10^{-3}	1	10^{-7}	3.968	1.163×10^{-3}
Mtoe	4.1868×10^{4}	10^{7}	1	3.968×10^{7}	11,630
MBtu	1.0551×10^{-3}	0.252	2.52×10^{-8}	1	2.391×10^{-4}
GWh	3.6	860	8.6×10^{-5}	3412	1

Units for energy balances and analyses of greenhouse gas emissions

1 metric ton (*ton*)	= 1000kg
	= 2204.6lb (pounds)
	= 0.984lt (long tons)
	= 1.1023st (short ton)
1 cubic metre (m³)	= 1000 l (litres)
	= 264.2 gal US (gallon, US)
	= 220.0 gal UK (gallon, UK)
	= 6.28981bbl (barrel)
	= 35.3147ft³ (cubic foot)
1 km²	= 1,000,000m²
	= 100ha
	= 0.3861sq mi (square miles)
1 Mha (million of hectares)	= 10 thousand km²
	= 2.471 million acres
Equivalence of mass between carbon (C) and carbon dioxide (CO_2)	$C/CO_2 = 1/3.67 = 12/44$
degrees Celsius, degrees Fahrenheit, Kelvin	$tc = (tF - 32)/1.8$ (in which tC is the temperature in degrees Celsius and tF the temperature in degrees Fahrenheit)
	$tc = tk - 273.15$ (in which tC is the temperature in degrees Celsius and tk the temperature in Kelvin)

	0°C = 273K approx.; the differences in temperature given in °C (= K)
ppmv	parts per million (10^6) in volume
ppbv	parts per billion (10^9) in volume
pptv	parts per trillion (10^{12}) in volume
/y	a year

kilowatt-hour (kwh)	= 3600 joules (J)
calorie (cal)	= 4.1868 joules (J)
Btu	*British Themal Unit* = 252cal = 1055J
Btu per hour (Btu/hr)	= 0.293071l watt (W)
1 ton (refrigeration)	3.517kW
kilowatt,	1kW = 1.341hp = 1.360cv
hp (*horsepower*),	1hp = 0.7457kW = 1.0138cv
cv (cavalo-vapor)	1cv = 0.7355kW = 0.9863hp
MWe	megawatts of electricity
1 mpg (mile per gallon)	0.425km/litre (1 mile = 1.6093km) (1 gallon = 3.785 l)
tce	tons of coal equivalent
toe	tons of oil equivalent = 7.2 boe = 10Gcal = 41.87GJ = 11.63MWh = 39.68Mbtu
boe	barrels of oil equivalent = 0.14 toe ~ 0.158987m^3 of oil
Kt	kilotons, 10^{3}t
GtC	gigatons of carbon 1 GtC = 10^{9}tC = 3.67Gt CO_2
Tg C	teragrams of carbon, 1 TgC = 1 MtC
1 m^3 of oil	~ 0.872t oil

1 m³ of fuel oil	~ 1t fuel oil
	~ 9.59Gcal
	~ 0.959 toe (10,000kcal/kg)
	~ 40.15GJ
	~ 11.15MWh (860kcal/MWh)
	~ 1090m³ dry natural gas
	~ 1.94t coal (type 5200)
	~ 1.56m³ LPG
	~ 3.06t fuelwood
	~ 1.48t charcoal
1 m³ of diesel oil	~ 0.84t diesel
	~ 7.70Gcal
	~ 0.770 toe
	~ 35.52GJ
1 m³ of automotive gasoline	~ 0.74t automotive gasoline
	~ 8.48Gcal
	~ 0.848 toe
	~ 32.22GJ
1 m³ aviation gasoline	~0.72t aviation gasoline
	~0.763 toe
	~31.95GJ
1 m³ of anhydrous ethylic alcohol (ethanol)	~ 0.791t anhydrous ethanol
	~ 0.534 toe
	~ 22.35GJ
1 m³ of hydrated ethylic alcohol (ethanol) (denaturated)	~ 0.809t hydrated ethanol
	~ 0.510 toe
	~ 21.34GJ
1 m³ of naphtha	~ 0.720t naphtha
	~ 0.765 toe
	~ 32.05GJ
1 m³ of 'other oil energy products'	~ 0.872t 'other oil energy products'
	~ 0.890toe
	~ 37.25GJ
1000 m³ of dry natural gas	~ 8.80Gcal
	~ 36.84GJ
	~ 0.880 toe (10,000kcal/kg)
	~ 0.92m³ fuel oil
	~ 1.78t coal (type 5200)
	~ 1.43m³ LPG
	~ 2.80t fuelwood
	~ 1.36t charcoal

1000 m³ of wet natural gas	~ 9.93Gcal
	~ 41.58GJ
	~ 0.993 toe (10,000kcal/kg)
1000 m³ of coke gas	~ 0.430 toe
	~ 18.00GJ
1000 m³ refinery gas	~ 0.650 toe
	~ 27.43GJ
1 t coal	~ 0.480 toe (range 0.285–0.570 toe/t)
(vapour, type 5200kcal/kg)	~ 20.52GJ (range 12.35–23.86GJ/t)
	~ 0.52m³ fuel oil
	~ 560m³ of dry natural gas
	~ 0.80m³ LPG
	~ 1.58t fuelwood
	~ 0.76t charcoal
1 t coal	~ 0.642 toe / 0.740 toe
(metallurgical)	~ 26.88GJ / 30.98 GJ
1 m³ liquefied petroleum	~ 0.55t LPG
gas, LPG	~ 0.661 toe
	~ 25.56GJ
	~ 0.64m³ fuel oil
	~ 700m³ of dry natural gas
	~ 1.25t coal (type 5200)
	~ 1.97t fuelwood
	~ 0.95t charcoal
1 t fuelwood	~ 3.33m³ ('collected' fuelwood) or
	~ 2.55m³ (commercial fuelwood)
	~ 0.310 toe
	~ 12.98GJ
	~ 0.33m³ fuel oil
	~ 360m³ of dry natural gas
	~ 0.63t coal (type 5200)
	~ 0.51m³ LPG
	~ 0.40t charcoal
1 t charcoal	~ 4m³ charcoal
	~ 0.646 toe
	~ 27.06GJ
	~ 0.67m³ fuel oil
	~ 730m³ of dry natural gas
	~ 1.31t coal (type 5200)
	~ 1.05m³ LPG
	~ 2.06t fuelwood

I t sugar cane juice	~ 0.062 toe
I t sugar cane molasses	~ 0.185 toe
I t sugar cane bagasse	~ 0.213 toe
	~ 8.92GJ
	~ 2.48MWh (a 860kcal/kWh)
I t black liquor (paper industries)	~ 0.296 toe
I t tar	~ 0.855 toe

Emission factors (reference values, from IPCC, 2006) for combustion processes (kg of greenhouse gas per TJ on net calorific basis)

Fuel	CO_2			CH_4			N_2O		
	default	minimum	maximum	default	minimum	maximum	default	minimum	maximum
Crude oil	73,300	71,000	75,500	3	1	10	0.6	0.2	2
Orimulsion (bitumen 30% in water)	77,000	69,300	85,400	3	1	10	0.6	0.2	2
Liquid Natural Gas (LNG)	64,200	58,300	70,400	3	1	10	0.6	0.2	2
Gasoline									
Automotive (with 22% ethanol)	54,054	52,650	56,940	3	1	10	0.6	0.2	2
Aviation	69,300	67,500	73,000	3	1	10	0.6	0.2	2
Jets	69,300	67,500	73,000	3	1	10	0.6	0.2	2
Aviation Kerosene	71,600	69,800	74,400	3	1	10	0.6	0.2	2
Kerosene	71,900	70,800	73,600	3	1	10	0.6	0.2	2
Shale Oil	73,300	67,800	79,200	3	1	10	0.6	0.2	2
Diesel	74,100	72,600	74,800	3	1	10	0.6	0.2	2
Residual Fuel Oil	77,400	75,500	78,800	3	1	10	0.6	0.2	2
Liquefied Petroleum Gas	63,100	61,600	65,600	1	0.3	3	0.1	0.03	0.3
Ethanol	61,600	56,500	68,600	1	0.3	3	0.1	0.03	0.3

Naphtha	73,300	69,300	76,300	3	1	10	0.6	0.2	2
Bitumen	80,700	73,000	89,900	3	1	10	0.6	0.2	2
Lubricants	73,300	71,900	75,200	3	1	10	0.6	0.2	2
Petroleum Coke	97,500	82,900	115,000	3	1	10	0.6	0.2	2
Refinery Inputs	73,300	68,900	76,600	3	1	10	0.6	0.2	2
Other oils									
Refinery gas	51,300	45,800	76,600	1	0.3	3	0.1	0.03	0.3
Paraffin Waxes	73,300	72,200	74,400	3	1	10	0.6	0.2	2
White Spirit (Petroleum Ether) and Special Boiling Point Spirit (SBP)	73,300	72,200	74,400	3	1	10	0.6	0.2	3
Other Petroleum Products	73,300	72,200	74,400	3	1	10	0.6	0.2	2
Anthracite Coal (high-quality coal, with 10% less volatiles)	98,300	94,600	101,000	1	0.3	3	1.5	0.5	5
Coke Coal	94,600	87,300	101,000	1	0.3	3	1.5	0.5	5
Other Bituminous Coal	94,600	89,500	99,700	1	0.3	3	1.5	0.5	5
Sub-Bituminous Coal	96,100	72,800	100,000	1	0.3	3	1.5	0.5	5
Lignite	101,000	90,900	115,000	1	0.3	3	1.5	0.5	5

Fuel	CO$_2$			CH$_4$			N$_2$O		
	default	minimum	maximum	default	minimum	maximum	default	minimum	maximum
Shale Oil and Tar Sand	107,000	90,200	125,000	1	0.3	3	1.5	0.5	5
Coal Bricks	97,500	87,300	109,000	1	0.3	3	1.5	0.5	5
Patent fuel	97,500	87,300	109,000	1	0.3	3	1.5	0.5	5
Coke									
Blast-Furnace and Lignite Coke	107,000	95,700	11,9000	1	0.3	3	1.5	0.5	5
Coke Gas	107,000	95,700	11,9000	1	0.3	3	0.1	0.03	0.3
Coal Tar	80,700	68,200	95,300	1	0.3	3	1.5	0.5	5
Bygases									
Industrialized Gas	44,700	37,800	55,000	1	0.3	3	0.1	0.03	0.3
Coke Oven Gas	44,700	37,800	55,000	1	0.3	3	0.1	0.03	0.3
Blast Furnace Gas, air flow	260,000	219,000	308,000	1	0.3	3	0.1	0.03	0.3
Blast Furnace Gas, oxygen flow	172,000	145,000	202,000	1	0.3	3	0.1	0.03	0.3
Natural Gas	56,100	543,00	58,300	1	0.3	3	0.1	0.03	0.3
Municipal Solid	91,700	73,300	121,000	30	10	100	4	1.5	15
Waste (non-biomass fraction)									
Industrial Waste	143,000	110,000	183,000	30	10	100	4	1.5	15

Residual Oil	73,300	72,200	74,400	30	10	100	4	1.5	15
Peat	106,000	104,000	108,000	1	0.3	3	1.5	0.5	5
Solid biofuels									
Fuelwood and its wastes	112,000	95,000	132,000	30	10	100	4	1.5	15
Black liquor	95,300	80,700	110,000	3	1	18	2	1	21
Other Solid Primary Biomass (ex. bagasse)	100,000	84,700	117,000	30	10	100	4	1.5	15
Charcoal	112,000	95,000	132,000	30	10	100	4	1.5	15
Liquid Biofuels									
Biogasoline	70,800	59,800	84,300	3	1	10	0.6	0.2	2
Biodiesel	70,800	59,800	84,300	3	1	10	0.6	0.2	2
Other Liquid Biofuels	79,600	67,100	93,300	3	1	10	0.6	0.2	2
Gaseous Biomass									
Landfill Gas	54,600	46,200	66,000	1	0.3	3	0.1	0.03	0.3
Sludge Gas	54,600	46,200	66,000	1	0.3	3	0.1	0.03	0.3
Other Biogases	54,600	46,200	66,000	1	0.3	3	0.1	0.03	0.3
Other non-fossil biofuels									
Municipal Wastes (biomass fraction)	100,000	84,700	117,000	30	10	100	4	1.5	15

Source: IPCC (2006) Guidelines for National Greenhouse Gas Inventories. Volume 2 – Energy, www.ipcc-nggip.iges.or.jp/public/2006gl/vol2.htm

Index